Tests of global governance

"Cooper makes a compelling case for his own version of a new diplomacy, one that involves many different actors in non-traditional settings such as UN conferences. Although Cooper is unsparing in his analysis of the limits of these new trends, he also gives us reason to hope that the new diplomacy can be a bridge between a territorially defined, state-centred Westphalian world and the varied, plural, multi-layered world of global governance."

Anne-Marie Slaughter, *Dean, Woodrow Wilson School of Public and International Affairs, Princeton University*

"This is an important book for anyone interested in international public policy. It gives a very clear picture of the workings of the 'actually-existing' legislative process of global governance (problem-specific, global conferences) and the central, perhaps essential, role of 'middle powers' and Canada in particular."

Craig N. Murphy, *M. Margaret Ball Professor of International Relations, Wellesley College, USA*

"Cooper is one of the first scholars to utilize systematically UN conferences as a laboratory for testing as yet unexamined hypotheses concerning the interface between contemporary multilateral diplomacy and what can be considered as new forms of global governance. As a result, this book is path-breaking in its rethinking of the boundaries of global governance and of the intersection where top-down and bottom-up multilateralism meet. The Canadian state-society complex is implicated all the way through this excellent book."

W. Andy Knight, *McCalla Research Professor, University of Alberta Co-Editor of Global Governance Journal*

Tests of global governance: Canadian diplomacy and United Nations world conferences

Andrew F. Cooper

United Nations
University Press

TOKYO · NEW YORK · PARIS

© United Nations University, 2004

The views expressed in this publication are those of the authors and do not necessarily reflect the views of the United Nations University.

United Nations University Press
United Nations University, 53-70, Jingumae 5-chome,
Shibuya-ku, Tokyo, 150-8925, Japan
Tel: +81-3-3499-2811   Fax: +81-3-3406-7345
E-mail: sales@hq.unu.edu general enquiries: press@hq.unu.edu
http://www.unu.edu

United Nations University Office at the United Nations, New York
2 United Nations Plaza, Room DC2-2062, New York, NY 10017, USA
Tel: +1-212-963-6387   Fax: +1-212-371-9454
E-mail: unuona@ony.unu.edu

United Nations University Press is the publishing division of the United Nations University.

Cover design Joyce C. Weston

Printed in Hong Kong

UNUP-1096
ISBN 92-808-1096-0

Library of Congress Cataloging-in-Publication Data

Cooper, Andrew Fenton, 1950–
Tests of global governance : Canadian diplomacy and United Nations world conferences / Andrew F. Cooper.
   p. cm.
Includes bibliographical references and index.
ISBN 9280810960 (pbk.)
1. United Nations—Congresses. 2. United Nations—Canada. 3. Diplomacy—Case studies. 4. Canada—Foreign relations–1945– 5. World politics—1989—Case studies. 6. Non-governmental organizations. 7. International relations. I. Title.
JZ4984.C67   2004
341.23′71—dc22   2004007655

Contents

Acronyms vii

Preface ix

1 United Nations world conferences as tests of global governance: an overview 1

2 Emerging tests of diplomacy: transition from earlier UN world conferences 12

3 Tests of partnership: between statecraft and society-craft 40

4 Tests of leadership: the prime ministerial role 69

5 Tests of discipline: imposition or negotiation of the system of governance? 94

6 Tests of sovereignty: an evasive and estranged diplomacy? 122

7 Tests of the civilisational divide? The Cairo International Conference on Population and Development 152

8 Tests of difference: women's ownership of the Beijing
   conference 184
9 Tests of value with respect to Durban and beyond: anomaly or
   end of the life cycle? 223

Notes 254

References 261

Index 286

Acronyms

AFN	Assembly of First Nations
APEC	Asia Pacific Economic Cooperation
ASEAN	Association of South-East Asian Nations
BCNI	Business Council on National Issues (Canada)
CANZ	Canada-Australia-New Zealand group
CCIC	Canadian Council for International Cooperation
CCO	Conservation Council of Ontario
CEN	Canadian Environmental Network
CIDA	Canadian International Development Agency
CIIA	Canadian Institute of International Affairs
CPCU	Canadian Participatory Committee for UNCED
CPPA	Canadian Pulp and Paper Association
CSW	United Nations Commission on the Status of Women
DEA	Canadian Department of External Affairs (prior to 1989); External Affairs and International Trade Canada (between 1989 and 1993)
DFAIT	Canadian Department of Foreign Affairs and International Trade (after 1993)
ECLAC	Economic Commission for Latin America and the Caribbean
ECOSOC	United Nations Economic and Social Council
EU	European Union
FOE	Friends of the Earth
FLS	Forward-looking Strategies for the Advancement of Women to the Year 2000
FSC	Forest Stewardship Council
FTA	Canada-US Free Trade Agreement

G-7	Group of seven industrialised countries
G-77	Group of 77 developing countries
GFC	Global Forestry Convention
GNP	Gross national product
GST	Goods and Services Tax (Canada)
ICHRDD	International Centre for Human Rights and Democratic Development
ICPD	International Conference on Population and Development
ILO	International Labour Organization
INGOs	International NGOs
IPPF	International Planned Parenthood Federation
IRB	Immigration and Refugee Board
JUSCANZ	Informal group made up of Japan, the United States, Canada, Australia and New Zealand and a number of other states including the Netherlands and Norway
LIFT	Low Income Families Together
NAC	National Action Committee on the Status of Women (Canada)
NAFTA	North American Free Trade Agreement
NATO	North Atlantic Treaty Organization
NGOs	Non-governmental organisations
NIEO	New international economic order
NIHR	Norwegian Institute of Human Rights
OECD	Organisation for Economic Co-operation and Development
ODA	Official Development Assistance
OSCE	Organization on Security and Cooperation in Europe
PCO	Privy Council Office
PFA	Beijing Platform for Action
PMO	Prime Minister's Office
PPF	Planned Parenthood Federation of Canada
PRC	People's Republic of China
Prep	Com Preparatory Committee
SWC	Status of Women Canada
UNCED	United Nations Conference on Environment and Development
UNCHR	United Nations Commission on Human Rights
UNCTAD	United Nations Conference on Trade and Development
UNDP	United Nations Development Programme
UNEP	United Nations Environment Programme
UNESCO	United Nations Educational, Scientific and Cultural Organization
UNFPA	United Nations Fund for Population Activities
UNHCR	United Nations High Commissioner for Refugees
UNICEF	United Nations Children's Fund
UNIFEM	United Nations Development Fund for Women
WCAR	World Conference against Racism
WEDO	Women's Environment and Development Organization
WEOG	Western European and Others Group
WSC	World Summit for Children or Children's Summit
WSSD	World Summit for Social Development or Social Summit

Preface

At the heart of this book is an extended examination of the interface between diplomatic method and new forms of global governance. Because of the complex dynamics involved in the series of United Nations world conferences, a focus on this set of activity allows an extended examination of a number of important theoretical debates central to the study of international relations. On a case study basis the work demonstrates that global governance is a differentiated multi-spectral site of activity within which states and non-state actors alike, particularly NGOs, play varied but vital roles.

The role of Canada and Canadians with respect to the UN world conferences is given special attention as both a unique and representative sample of how this dualistic interplay between diplomacy and global governance and evolving forms of state and society-craft has played out over time in a policy rich setting. The sweep of the study extends from the 1992 Rio UNCED conference, through the 1993 Vienna Conference on Human Rights, the 1994 Cairo Conference on Population and Development, the 1995 World Summit for Social Development, and the 1995 Beijing Conference on Women, to the Durban World Conference on Racism held amidst great controversy just prior to 11 September 2001. Apart from its focus on the machinery and impact of the UN conferences in general terms, a set of narratives is provided that sets out the expanding cast of people and governing institutions within Canada that were involved with these forums. Though a relatively small entity – commonly labelled a middle power – Canada has had arguably a disproportionate amount of influence over the proceedings of some of the more important conferences. It has also been a state that has been flexible and creative with regard to partnerships with key NGOs and advancing new concepts such as in the area of sovereignty, though not without some measure of difficulty on certain issues (most notably on Indigenous issues).

The picture that emerges, although it does not translate into a complete recipe for a shift towards democratic governance, at least suggests a deepening network of institutions, actors, and organisations. The appearance of complex regimes governing the major arenas of world politics points to a very different framework than that located in the old Westphalian state-centric world. At a country-specific level, the analysis supports the view that a deep residue of multilateralism still exists in Canada but argues that this tradition faces on-going challenges from a variety of sources.

My concern in researching and writing this work was not so much to connect with and make evaluations about the entire array of technical detail attendant to these large international conferences, rather it was to use these diverse sites as a means to better understand the themes that I consider to be central to the contemporary analysis of comparative foreign policy and the global policy agenda.

In helping me develop and refine my interpretation of these patterns of activity and architecture I have benefited from the conversations and debates I have had with a wide variety of academics and policy-makers. Canadian-based scholars and practitioners from whom I have gained numerous insights include David Black, Louis Bélanger, Alan Cairns, Daniel Drache, Michael Hawes, George Haynal, John Kirton, Tom Keating, Andy Knight, Gordon Mace, Maureen Molot, Kim Nossal, Les Pal, Evan Potter, Donald Savoie, Claire Turenne Sjolander, Heather Smith, Denis Stairs, Janice Stein, Jean-Philippe Thérien, Bob Wolfe, and Bob Young. Globally, I have tapped into the expertise and intellectual curiosity of Ann Capling, Charles Doran, Jacques Fomerand, Richard Higgott, Brian Hocking, Bill Maley, Iver Neumann, Laura Neack, Philip Nel, Chris Sands, Ian Taylor, Janis van der Westhuizen, Geoff Wiseman, and Duncan Wood.

The straddling nature of my institutional affiliation meshes with the hybrid character of this project. I remain appreciative of the support that the University of Waterloo has given me over the years, but I am also extremely indebted to John English who provided me with the opportunity to take part in the creation and operation of the Centre for International Governance Innovation (CIGI). Through this transition I have had the pleasure of working with Lena Yost and others at CIGI, and Alistair Edgar, who has taken over the position of Executive Director of the

Academic Council on the United System (ACUNS). Jane McWhinney, Nigmendra Narain, Rick Theis, and Andrew Thompson helped at key stages throughout the research and editing process. The endeavours of Andrew and Jane – who along with Jean-Philippe Thérien carefully read the manuscript – were especially valuable for the completion of this project.

I am very pleased that the United Nations University Press accepted this manuscript for publication. Through the concerted efforts of the Rector of the United Nations University, Hans van Ginkel, and the Senior Vice-Rector and Head of the Peace and Governance Program, Ramesh Thakur, UNUP has continued to enhance its already stellar reputation at the forefront of the nexus between ideas and institutional development. Scott McQuade, the Publications Officer, and Gareth Johnston provided a model of both efficiency and stylistic appreciation at the UNUP itself.

Funding and other forms of support were provided by the Social Sciences and Humanities Research Council of Canada, the Canadian Department of Foreign Affairs and International Trade, the library at the Canadian Institute of International Affairs, the Canada-U.S. Fulbright Program, and the Nitze School of Advanced International Studies, Johns Hopkins University, Washington, DC where I was a visiting scholar in 2000.

As with my previous manuscripts Sarah Maddocks contributed to a congenial ambience that allowed a balance between work and a wide variety of other pursuits, an environment for which I am extremely grateful and wish to continue for as long as possible. For my dedication, however, I look not forward but back to the memory of John Holmes, the much-missed doyen of Canadian foreign policy and eminent internationalist. Although I was never formally under his tutelage a student, I was privileged to be mentored by him and to gain from his vast store of knowledge and first-hand experience how much diplomacy, institutional design, and multilateral leadership matter in the process of international change

1

United Nations world conferences as tests of global governance: an overview

The series of world conferences sponsored by the United Nations (UN) over the past decade form the context for an extended debate about the relationship between global governance and diplomacy and the role of the state and societal forces in the post–Cold War era. These conferences shifted the focus of UN attention away from attempts to accommodate globalisation through integrated economic interaction towards the promotion (if far from complete acceptance) of universal social values and a demand for transparency and greater inclusion in international power structures and decision-making processes. The extent to which this alternative agenda was novel in form, intense in application, or far-reaching in scope remains moot. What stands out, however, as a point of entry for this book is the question of the degree of latitude – or set of permissive conditions – that has become available for the institution and the machinery of this type of reform to make a difference in the international arena.

UN-sponsored conferences as test sites of change in international relations cannot be separated from the overall fortunes of the UN. Building on the momentum of what has been termed the "return to the UN" (Berridge, 1991; Weiss, Forsythe and Coate, 1994), the world conferences rose to the top of the intellectual and policy agenda at a time of transition. Once released from the older constraints of bipolarity and East/West rivalry, the UN gained recognition as an essential ingredient in the building of an authentic new world order based on collective action with a commitment both to inspire and to solve problems on a planetary level (the literature on the debate about this order has become vast; see, for example, Clark, 2001a; Hall, 1996; Williams, 1998). The UN benefited from the willingness of at least some actors in the international system to think beyond the narrow parameters imposed by the structure of the Cold War. In keeping with the development of "an ethos of its own" (Roberts and Kingsbury, 1994: 24), the UN concomitantly gained stature as a promoter and populariser of progressive remedies for a variety of the world's ills.

Despite these enhanced credentials, the limitations on such an ultra-ambitious range of goals must also be acknowledged. The UN's moment of opportunity – and certainly, any taste of triumphalism – did not last long. Any hope of a widely shared agreement concerning the legitimacy or the capacity of the UN to champion an ambitious cluster of reform-oriented initiatives eroded with attempts to move forward either on a basis of a cluster of principled ideas or with a changed architecture. Many of the traditional flaws of the UN, instead of being corrected, persisted and were even exacerbated under the weight of its new responsibilities. The leadership made available by the UN for the world conferences had an uneven quality. Sometimes it was innovative and even inspiring; at other times it was muted or proffered in an extremely cautious manner. The UN could only be as robust an institution as its member states allowed it to be. Even the loose consensus among members who were willing to state that the UN should embrace some tenets of change through the medium of the world conferences broke down with respect to administrative functions and the allocation of material resources and expertise. The management of the world conference remained an unwieldy and highly differentiated enterprise.

Disputed perspectives on UN world conferences

Given these impediments, it is not surprising that UN conferences have fallen far short of the claims – either negative or positive – often attributed to them. Their characterisation through a range of critical lenses gives very different emphases, and draws widely diverse conclusions. A populist neo-liberal line of argument condemns the UN conferences for their excessive reach, seeing them as part of a plan (or even a conspiracy) by a narrow élite to impose a radically altered way of doing things in the international arena. In its most extreme form, this attack conjures up an image of "world government". More commonly, the conferences are stigmatised not only for being a waste of money but for providing another channel and excuse for regulation (see, for example, Rabkin,

1998).¹ From the point of view of the Anglo-American realist school, during the time between the end of the Cold War and the Durban Conference on Racism immediately preceding the events of 11 September 2001 the UN conferences are seen as an irrelevant form of diplomatic activity. In this view, what is needed to maintain an efficient international order (and national interest) has been sacrificed to an ideal of what should be, or is, right. Compared to the "real business" of diplomacy, through bilateral dialogue and bargaining, therefore, realists say, this strand of multilateralism (akin to its many predecessors) should be dismissed as "a babel of voices, a confusion of tongues" that serves "no very useful purpose" (Watson, 1982: 151).² Or, as Alan James has put it with respect to a different time and context, these conferences have become "little more than contemporary froth" in world politics (James, 1980: 932).

Alternatively, for the proponents of global transformation the world conferences are often damned with faint praise. Although they are seen to be moving in the right direction, as tests of global governance they are graded as "could do better" because they do not go far enough in embracing a genuine form of bottom-up multilateralism. The conferences may help nudge the process along the correct path of change, but they do not represent the goal. Indeed, they may even delay this goal by introducing alternative means of closure and control in a top-down fashion (representative samples from this school include work by Lipschutz, 1992 and Palan, 1999).

Critics have made little attempt to trace the trajectory of the UN world conferences in terms of their original motives and the way they were reconfigured or refined when confronted either by opportunities or by obstacles. All of these lines of criticism, therefore, miss out on the rich detail that makes these conferences such a valuable laboratory for the study of international politics during the interregnum decade after the Cold War. While long in conjecture about the conferences constituting an attempt on the part of a UN-centred cohort to impose a formula of top-down "global government", the neo-liberal view is quite divorced from the reality (with all the nuance of negotiated compromise) of what took place on the ground. Lacking interest in questions about ideas, values, and identity, realists have for the most part simply ignored the phenomenon.

World society advocates across the spectrum set an extremely high and demanding bar for these forums. From their perspectives, the only standard by which to judge the impact of the UN conferences must be their ability to animate a normative revolution in global governance, that is to say, to motivate a leap ahead towards the emergence of a cosmopolitan citizenship and an ethos of transparency and accountability. They contrast this anticipated mode of "humane" governance, embedded in democratic civil society with the "inhumane" governance of market forces, corporate power, and state coercion (see, for example, Falk, 1995; Falk, Kim and Mendlovitz, 1991). By these criteria, the UN conferences are at best a very incomplete accomplishment. As Richard Falk has made the point:

> The UN conferences on global issues held during the first half of the 1990s illustrated [a] new political energy as focused on environment, women, human rights, and development. But what was lacking was a cross-issue orientation that would be necessary to sustain coherent politics from below that could in some ways balance the coherence of neo-liberalism in its different, but mutually reinforcing, forms. (Falk, 2000: 379)

The argument of this book is that the UN world conferences did both less and more than their critics suggest. Far from raising the spectre of "world government", their institutional format is not taken to represent a dramatic break with the intergovernmental model of the conduct of international relations. States still remain the principal agents within the UN-centred process of communication and negotiation. Yet, contrary to the view that the UN conferences amount to theatre and little else, the contention in this book is that they have acted as a vehicle for bending the rules in terms of where, how, and with whom the pattern of diplomatic interaction is played out.

Equally, notwithstanding the disappointment of world society advocates about their level of delivery, the UN conferences have advanced an agenda based on more open forms of representation and discourse. Although not yet at the cusp of a new structure of global governance, these events nevertheless operate along the front lines of the intellectual debate and adaptive delivery processes that are compatible with this goal.

Furthermore, the argument is made that these manifestations of global change go well beyond mere machinery. To be taken seriously in any test of impact, global governance must contain a substantive core of concern for the betterment of the human condition. However, the significance of the way this element emerged through the mechanism of UN world conferences should not be exaggerated. In declaratory terms, there was no single blueprint for a progressive strategy. The Commission on Global Governance in *Our Global Neighbourhood* exhorted the world to respond to the demands of global change by offering "freshness and innovation in global governance" (Commission on Global Governance, 1995: XVI). Nevertheless, the design for change remained the sum of all the parts encompassing the entire life of these UN conferences.

In operational terms, the repertoire for implementation remained highly truncated. Commitments made by states often proved empty or at most shallow, particularly regarding efforts to redistribute costs and resources. The UN conferences were able to produce some advances in the context of rules, norms, and institutional development. However, they were less successful in turning resolutions and plans of action into concrete forms of delivery, either in mobilising public goods or in responding to problems on an issue-specific basis.

Still, despite such reservations, the impact of the UN world conferences should not be minimised. In their overall focus, they have sketched an extension of what Inis Claude had earlier termed "a kind of international New Dealism, an adaptation of the welfare state philosophy to the realm of world affairs" (Claude, 1984: 66). More specifically, each of the major conferences at the core of this book targeted a particular cluster of issues at the heart of the agenda of global welfarism (on this theme, see particularly Ryan, 2000). These conferences, in sequence, were: the June 1992 Rio de Janeiro UN Conference on Environment and Development (UNCED), or Earth Summit; the June 1993 Vienna World Conference on Human Rights; the September 1994 Cairo International Conference on Population and Development (ICPD); the March 1995 Copenhagen World Summit for Social Development (WSSD) or Social Summit; the September 1995 Beijing Fourth World Conference on Women: Action for Equality, Development and Peace; and in August and September 2001, the Durban World Conference against Racism, Racial Discrimination, Xenophobia and Related Intolerance (for an official review of these conferences, see UN Briefing Papers, 1997).

Nor can these conferences be taken exclusively as one-off, self-contained, and discrete events. An enormous amount of thematic continuity may be traced throughout the entire series. As underscored by the chapter structure of this book, a number of key, more focused tests ran through the life of these conferences.

A good deal of learning and cross-fertilisation also took place on both procedural and substantive levels. Patterns of institutional procedure built up in one conference seeped into the others. So did patterns of trust (and suspicion) between the various actors. The spillover of ideas and issues became marked features of the negotiations. Principles and concepts entertained during one conference cut deeply through others. Issue linkage extended throughout the process, at times on an ad hoc basis and other times in a more systemic manner.

World conferences on the front lines of "new" diplomacy

This more comprehensive understanding of governance gives solid justification for diplomacy to be brought into the centre of the analysis. To be sure, any such privileging exercise may be highly contested. The role of diplomacy and diplomats, no less than the institution and machinery of the UN, has been at the receiving end of charges of perceived failure of diplomacy. In realist terms, this failure stems from the abdication of diplomats to discard their prime responsibility – the promotion of the national interest (for a clear exposition of this view, see Berridge, 1995; James, 1993). Immersed in the culture and the socialisation process of the UN system and the attractions of the world conferences, diplomats have lost their way. Being part of the process has become a substitute for keeping their eyes on what they are there for in the first place. Through the world society lens, on the other hand, diplomacy (as defined by the activities of professional representatives of the state) is not only of decreasing relevance but may indeed be detrimental in that it restricts and holds back other modes of communication and negotiation sanctioned by the Westphalian international system. This sense of, and distaste for, an inherent deficiency in orthodox diplomacy is captured most vividly in attacks on intergovernmental diplomacy as being "unauthentic" (Constantinou, 1996: 4).

There are signs, however, that this polarisation is dissolving with the emergence of a "new" diplomacy. Rather than being confirmed in rigid either/or terms as part of the problem, diplomacy is increasingly being seen as having at least the potential to be the means of working to a creative (if still incomplete) architecture in international affairs. The most enthusiastic supporters of the world conferences not surprisingly see this mode of diplomacy as integral with respect to this goal. When Kofi Annan refers to a "new diplomacy", for example, he perceives it as providing a vehicle and a route for movement in the direction of global governance (Annan, 1998).[3]

What is more striking are signs of a trend towards accommodation among critics of traditional diplomacy from the world society (albeit not the realist) viewpoint. These critics acknowledge that even the limited availability of a bottom-up form of diplomacy has meant that "such conferences can have meaningful outcomes" (Schechter, 2001: 221).

In reviewing what is new about the new diplomacy, one has to be careful to avoid an ahistorical analysis. New diplomacy, to Harold Nicolson and others of his generation, meant "open" as opposed to "closed" or secretive diplomacy (Nicolson, 1939). In the late 1960s "new" diplomacy meant diplomacy that emphasised multilateral relations (Review Committee on Overseas Representation 1968–69, 1969). Many of the features at the heart of contemporary diplomacy reflect these same attributes.[4] Yet, this continuity should not overshadow the enormous amount of change generated in the post–Cold War decade. States (and especially the traditionally dominant states) may well remain the lead agents in working towards negotiated agreements through forums such as the UN conferences. Diplomatic openness, however, is no longer simply a question of allowing a wider audience to watch the proceedings. Other states than the United States and the other permanent members of the Security Council within the UN have carved out space for themselves within the international system. The logic of an activist and fully engaged wave of societal forces (in an array of manifestations) must be taken into account as well.

Through one lens, then, an extended analysis of new diplomacy is contingent on assessing the reconfiguration of "actorness". From one angle this lens reveals a hyper-extension of the influence of the United States even at the expense of the other agenda-setting large powers, not to mention the middle powers, smaller countries, and non-governmental networks. The values of the post–Cold War decade, and the structure of power and wealth within the international economy, have been largely defined by the United States – the one remaining superpower or hegemon. The pull of these cumulative forces of integration binds all other world actors to an imposing (but often unreliable) Gulliver.

From another angle, however, the ties are not to but around Gulliver. Instead of conceding all the advantages that the giant claims by virtue of its great strength, the emergence of a new diplomacy allows a greater balance of authority to take shape, a balance that is further reinforced by the multilateral bias in equilibrating activity. Whereas bilateral and/or summit diplomacy by its very nature allows a tilt toward a closed ambit for diplomacy, multilateralism is far more porous, giving greater accessibility to actors, who in addition to status possess imagination, agility, and persistence (on the larger theme of agility in diplomacy, see Strange, 1992: 10). States with the determination and skill to grind away at the process and the ability to provide touches of creativity can (to use the oft-cited cliché) punch above their weight. The determining factor is not so much the structural asymmetry between the state actors but the talents they apply. Considerable room is similarly available for non-state groups that are ready and able to raise their game to take advantage of the opportunities (see, for example, Higgott, Underhill and Bieler, 1999).

Showcasing Canada as a representative and unique case

Canada provides both a representative and unique case that can serve to illustrate the connection between the UN world conferences, the promotion of global governance, and the rise of new diplomacy. In many ways Canada may be regarded as the quintessential beneficiary of global change in the post–Cold War decade. The opportunity lay open for

Canada to reap dividends from its long-standing championing of the United Nations and of multilateralism. In accordance with accepted discourse, these features were part of the Canadian psychology or DNA (Keating, 2002: 1–16). Any extension of the institutional fabric to accommodate the realities of the post–Cold War world seemed, therefore, to play right into Canada's diplomatic strengths. Canada also appeared to possess the mode of operation – and toolkit of skills – most appropriate to take advantage of the breaking of the log-jam that had been imposed by the dictates of bipolarity (on this theme, see Cooper, 1997a). Coalition building on an issue-specific basis was Canada's forte. Persuasion rather than power continued to be its tactic of choice – and necessity.

The areas in which space opened up were areas where Canada's ingrained traits and practices in international affairs could be useful. Among the accepted notions underpinning the international system that went through a re-evaluation was the primacy of an older conception of security. As long as the global agenda was divided up on a hierarchical basis between "high" and "low" issues, the constraints on non-hegemonic – but not inconsequential – actors overwhelmed the attendant opportunities. The flattening of the issue arena had a contrary effect. This was especially true for Canada, whose international personality had long been detached from the application of a military profile or culture to foreign relations. In style, the image (or, more accurately, the self-image) of Canada was one in which the role of a demander was subordinated to that of a negotiator. Canada did not present itself as a challenger to the United States or other leading states in the international system. What it sought and expected was a role of responsibility that would affect the way the system worked in practice.

Given its material and psychological limitations, Canada had been increasingly ill-suited to make this sort of difference on security maintenance. The pursuit of global governance and some aspects of welfare creation held far more promise. Canada's abundant (if arguably, contracting) bureaucratic resources enhance its effectiveness to perform such a role. Not only do they allow Canada to be present at the multiple sites of international negotiation, such as the UN world conferences, but they make it possible for Canadian representatives to play a comfortable insider role, blending routine activity with attention to particular issues. Factoring in the societal component, the activity of non-governmental organisations (NGOs) in particular, to this global governance/welfare agenda makes it even clearer how quickly Canadian diplomacy – for all its limitations – has adjusted to system-change. Medium-sized powers such as Canada tend to focus only on issues that offer a solid rationale for their participation. Compared to the need to maintain security, an explicit link between the global governance/welfare agenda and the national interest is difficult to ascertain. The rationale for diplomatic engagement in these areas is therefore to be found in Canada's double identity – or dual personality – as a good international citizen and a status-seeker.

Just as crucially, international diplomacy has become thoroughly immersed in domestic politics and policy making. As Gil Winham has pointed out, the newly technical nature of the agenda – and the process of bureaucratisation, in particular – has contributed to this evolution (Winham, 1993), as have societal forces, by their nature and through their demands. These added elements of complexity have strained the application of Canadian diplomacy. On one side of the ledger, they add vitality (and credibility) to Canada's reputation as a cosmopolitan good international citizen while increasing the channels for diplomatic interaction. On the other side, they contribute to the managerial problems associated with fragmentation and possible overstretch. They also raise the political, policy, and image stakes attendant on Canada's performance in the international arena.

A strong image of Canadian diplomacy extending back to the post–World War era has been that of a go-between or helpful fixer, mediating either on an inter- or intra-bloc basis. Another has been that of a loyal (albeit not totally subservient) follower. The imperative has traditionally been to support, manage, and reproduce the rules of the game within the international system (Cooper, Higgott and Nossal, 1993: 22–32). One need here was to rein the United States in when it became either too isolationist or too zealous in its unilateralism. Another was to try to bring in (or socialise) the traditional outsiders in the international system, whether in terms of the East/West or the North/South dimension. A final priority for Canada was to maintain its position and level of representation in the upper echelons of the international system. The repertoire in all three components was similar: a quick and responsive form of diplomacy, a reliance on the selective mobilisation of like-minded groupings, avoidance of being isolated and cut out of the loop, and an emphasis on problem-solving. While opening up windows of opportunity for the diplomatically astute, the 1990s revealed a number of unforeseen challenges and vulnerabilities along a wide spectrum.

Previewing the specific set of tests

Having rehearsed the centrality of the nexus between the ends of global governance and the means of diplomacy, it is necessary to locate this dynamic in a series of specific tests that serve as the backbone for this book. The first test relates to the degree of departure found in the UN conferences profiled throughout. The notion of UN conferences as an expression of global organisation took hold in the 1990s with the end of the Cold War and accentuated globalisation. But the conferences highlighted in this work represent a transition not a complete break with past practices. The recognition that international problems concern everybody and could only be dealt with on a global basis had appeared much earlier and needs to be appreciated when teasing out the tests of diplomacy. The second test questions whether or not the different worlds between state and societal forces have been merged through the operation of the UN conferences. Bringing NGOs into such a partnership lies at the heart of any definition of global governance. Built into any authentic partnership, however, is not just a sustained form of dialogue but tangible delivery thus raising the bar of this test. The third test hangs on the issue of leadership. At one level this test personalises the state, in that it puts an enormous onus on elected politicians at the apex of government to showcase themselves through events such as UN conferences. Yet, as illustrated in the case of Canada, this test is a complex one. Any impetus towards advancing the agenda of global governance is constrained by domestic limitations both in terms of fragmentation of decision making and a struggle for resources. The fourth test brings to the fore the contestation between very different organising guidelines for the international system. The perspective that individual UN conferences embody a new type of post–Cold War multilateral settlement or global accord (with a compensatory component in terms of distribution and regulation) (Deacon, Hulse and Stubbs, 1997: 87) is countered by the view that these events lie under the "disciplinary" cloak intended to deflect and offset the momentum towards a neo-liberal market order. Instead of being sites of emancipation these conferences become arenas simply for introducing a different recipe "to institutionalise the supremacy of prevailing elements" (Gill, 1997: 6–7). The fifth test cuts into the overarching debate about sovereignty. When sovereignty is constructed as autonomy, room for cooperative problem solving both inside and outside the national space is opened up. When the concept of sovereignty as territory is paramount, though, a harder shell forms. Even in a country such as Canada, often assumed to be post-modern in its orientation, state officials adopt a tough posture in defending its prerogatives as the final authority within a given territory. The sixth test, concerning the putative clash of civilisations at the UN conferences, relates both to an architecture of global governance that transcends cultural boundaries in principle and a diplomatic repertoire that allows mediation to take place on the ground. The rigid definition of "us and them" offered by Samuel Huntington (Huntington, 1996) is juxtaposed with scenarios that purport that there is a willingness to think and act outside the "civilisational" box in order to deal with "issues of common concern" and search for "common ground" (Evans, 1997). The seventh and final test hinges on the question of ownership within the UN conferences. The role of women and women's rights illuminates such a test. If the claims concerning the fundamental alteration of the rules of the game of the structure of governance – and the ability of diplomacy to act as a conduit rather than an obstacle in the pursuit of that goal – contain any validity both the room for participation by women and the boundaries of women-centred agenda must be reordered in a decisive fashion.

All of these tests reinforce the potential of diplomacy to act as what has been termed a "boundary-spanner" on the front lines of global governance (Hocking, 2000).[5] One side of diplomacy remains rooted in the traditional fabric of the Westphalian world. Another side has moved towards innovation in both style and substance. Control through a narrow state-centric model vies with a more diffuse and transparent structure on a global scale. The international arena becomes thoroughly penetrated and integrated by the domestic context and constituencies. Rigid hierarchy gives way to a variegated pluralism in the global agenda, in which a variety of issues struggle for institutional attention and priority in terms of problem-solving techniques.

Navigating these tests requires two interrelated approaches. On a case-by-case basis, the need is for a combined inside/outside examination of diplomatic machinery and techniques vis-à-vis the UN world conferences. Through this narrative process the creative tensions between the traditional mode of statecraft and the pressures from an emergent society-craft will be detailed. How are these two types of diplomacy shaped and re-shaped? What are the stages (and impact) of the entanglement between them? Do they meet and access their formerly divergent worlds in a comprehensive or narrowly constructed fashion? Or alternatively do they, despite the notion of some set division of labour, persist as parallel and separate entities?

Conceptually the need is for a focus that recognises the value of diplomats – in all of their guises and their various forms of behaviour – but situates this role as an integral part of the larger system of interaction within the global system. The renewed interest in diplomacy emerges not because of its special condition, but rather because diplomacy acts both as a prism and a refractor for what is happening in both the larger policy environment and the international landscape. Whatever the debate about its exact meaning, and the degree to which diplomacy is actually new, selective questions about diplomacy act as both a vector and filter for a number of the bigger questions about global governance. More than anything else it is this function that redefines diplomacy and makes it matter.

2
Emerging tests of diplomacy: transition from earlier UN world conferences

A starting point for any comprehensive examination of Canadian diplomacy in the context of the United Nations conferences must be recognition of the major challenges that they posed for diplomacy. What room for manoeuvre did Canada possess in international politics, as played out in the changing context of post–Cold War UN world conferences? The position of the United States as the one remaining superpower exacerbated its tendency towards extreme positions – with rapid shifts between withdrawal and over-reaction to crises (see, for example, Jervis, 1993). While most pronounced in security matters, this volatility came to the fore on the social multilateral agenda as well. The sources and manifestations of tension in international politics became more jagged and dispersed, rather than giving way to a uniform pattern of convergence in which the parameters of consensus widened (and became more inclusive). Instead of modifying the United States' behaviour in the responsible and consistent manner Canada had hoped for, the end of the Cold War simply reconfigured fundamental divisions in alternative guises.

Opposition to the expansion of the social agenda, to the assertive engagement and empowerment of non-governmental groups, and to the end of insulation between the international and the domestic remained as intense (if not more so) in the post–Cold War environment. Far from simply moving to an elevated position in the international system on the wave of global change (and the momentum of its long-standing reputation), Canada found the diplomatic environment to be an increasingly competitive one in which it could not take its status for granted. With the end of the discipline of the Cold War came not only a flattened agenda but a flattened constellation of state actors. If established middle-power countries such as Canada could seek and find room to think and act differently from the "bigs", so too could other countries – even those without solid traditions of this style of diplomacy – try to overcome their legacy of subservience to big brother.

Nor could the direction and speed of change be taken for granted. Predictions of Canada's increasing potential to influence the contemporary agenda – with a new golden age of Canadian diplomacy – came face to face with the stresses released by these developments. For all its initial desire to make a bold statement through the UN conferences, Canada soon tempered its stance. Ambition to push ahead was replaced by caution and the displacement of resources. Pressure for results became blurred with concern about avoiding risks and embarrassment. Keenness for the credibility and effectiveness of the institutional structure as the motor for the UN conferences was marred by a heightened recognition of the numerous flaws inherent in this structure.

The theme of transition allows for a sweeping discussion, along both an episodic and a substantive axis, about the elements of change and continuity in UN world conferences. Do these conferences represent something distinctive about the way in which the post–Cold War order developed? If so, what characteristics set them apart from UN conferences in the post-1945 period?

One dimension that merits attention along these lines concerns the intensity of the process of change. The boldest way of looking at UN world conferences is as one aspect of a decisive break from the status quo associated with the older order, a component of a unique seismic event. If seen as what John Lewis Gaddis has termed a defining or landmark moment, these conferences may be one of those rare points of punctuation in history at which old patterns of stability have broken up and new ones have not yet emerged to take their place (Gaddis, 1992; Knutsen, 1999; Reynolds, 1992).

The era-clearing paradigm, however, is not the only interpretation. The type of international summitry these conferences represent can also be perceived as a more subtle departure from previous patterns, as a continuation of a longer historical trajectory that dates back a number of decades into the post-war era. Despite their expanded agendas and higher profile, the UN world conferences could be treated as part of a long and gradual pattern of change in ideas and institutional development. To the extent that they do signify that elements of "fundamental rules and institutions underlying international relations have indeed gone through some motions of change" (Holsti, 1998: 289; 1993), this process of departure is, at the most, one that "combine[s] old institutions with new realities" (Hall, 1996: 164).

A second dimension that needs scrutiny is the scope of the normative consequences of the UN conferences. If we take the dramatic interpretation of transition, we may see the UN world conferences as manifestations of the dominant post–Cold War consensus bound up with the inevitability (and beneficial effects) of universal principles such as free trade, liberalism, and human rights on a universal basis. This unidimensional portrayal is expressed most forcefully by Francis Fukuyama, who highlighted the triumph of liberal ideology, the economic market, and political democracy (Fukuyama, 1992, 1993). Yet a closer view of the UN conferences reveals them as sites of fundamental dispute over procedures and values, with a more complex and fragmented architectural texture. They are characterised by unevenness, contradictions, and fractures (see, for example, Hoffmann, 1990, 1998) rather than by an advancing worldwide convergence. The results of a detailed study also support the view of the UN conferences not as hegemonic enterprises but as sources of compensation if not outright opposition to such a monolithic world order.

A third dimension that invites examination relates to the more operational forms of change manifested through these international conferences. This dimension of enquiry focuses on the evolving balance between structure and agency. The collapse of bipolarity constituted a decisive rupture, with the static quality of that older order giving way to a more fluid environment allowing greater flexibility and agility. By interjecting more of a bottom-up or diffuse quality, this departure would allow in the UN system not only more manoeuvring room for secondary countries but higher credibility and profile for non-state actors. Marie-Claude Smouts makes this argument for a new inclusiveness:

> The UN remains the forum where broad debate ... can be organised, provided that not only states are drawn in but also social actors. From this standpoint, the Rio Environmental Conference, despite its 'fairground' atmosphere, and the Vienna Conference on Human Rights, despite its slim results, have been important events. Those are the kinds of 'happenings' where minority groups could eventually get to participate in the process of global governance. (Smouts, 1999: 40)

Nonetheless, despite the vigour of this line of argument, scenarios of wider participation are not uniformly accepted. Indeed, the very notion of opening up the international system (or, for that matter, diplomacy) has been fiercely contested. While many of the dominant Cold War assumptions have quite clearly disappeared, any sense of release from that period may be exaggerated.

What has changed, according to the proponents of this view (such as Richard Falk) is simply that there is a much better appreciation of what constitutes structural power. Although they acknowledge some elements of a loosening process, most notably in the declining relevance of geopolitics and military muscle, the tightened grip of the new international consensus over the economic-social agenda is in the forefront of their vision.

It is by tackling these important sets of distinctive but intersecting questions that we can best enter an analysis of the UN world conferences as they have taken shape over the past decade. Whatever the differences of overall interpretation, a close look at these dimensions offers a more complete understanding of the causes and effects of transformation. To ascertain whether these conferences constitute a series of small steps already in train or an unexpected giant leap forward, the dynamic of the UN world conferences prior to the end of the Cold War must be examined in some detail. Such an extended analysis will also help us to highlight the changing perception of benefits and costs to the major actors, together with the mutation in the nature of the actors themselves. While providing a multi-layered conceptual framework, therefore, this treatment is not premised on the study of transition in the abstract. What is crucial is to ascertain which aspects of the international system are changing, with special reference to the emerging tests of diplomacy contained in this transition stage (on this point, see Vincent, 1983).

A sudden transformation or an incremental process?

The image of the UN world conferences as a dramatic departure from the old order is best captured by framing them in the context of the East/West conflict. What stands out here in bold relief is the degree of constriction imposed by and through the Cold War era. Few international conferences in the social domain were held during the 1950s and 1960s. Even the small number of conferences that went ahead were downplayed and undervalued. The 1968 Teheran Conference on Human Rights, most notably, was accorded only interim status. A number of conferences held under the auspices of the UN Economic Commission for Europe (Rome 1954, Belgrade 1965, Prague 1971) were reduced to symposia or technical and scientific assemblies.

Beyond these quantitative limitations, qualitative barriers to progress were quite steep. Both sides of the Cold War divide attempted to directly control the agenda and the access provided to individual actors. Most significantly, the 1972 Stockholm Conference on the Human Environment was marked by problematic gaps in participation with the United

States and the United Kingdom denying the German Democratic Republic (East Germany) an invitation because it was not yet a member of any of the UN specialised organisations. Although this behaviour conformed to the guidelines of the so-called Vienna formula that laid down the informal rules of diplomatic representation, it smacked of the politics of exclusion waged against East Germany since its formation. To compound the sense of imbalance, the Federal Republic of Germany (West Germany) was given the right of representation at the conference only because of its entry into UNESCO within the UN system. Refusing the option of having East Germany attend Stockholm merely as an observer, the Eastern bloc retaliated against what it considered unfair treatment by boycotting the forum.

The other major conferences during this early era were hampered by variations of such ritualistic performances. All featured a high degree of ideologically based rhetoric. To give just one illustration of the flavour of this discourse from the side of the Eastern bloc, the Soviet Union vehemently denounced the West's concern about excessive world population growth at the 1974 Bucharest Conference on Population as an "imperialist" myth aimed at keeping the developing countries in a position of subjugation. As the Soviet deputy minister of health accused: "It is clear that such an approach has nothing to do with the real reason for backwardness and [constituted an attempt] to direct attention from carrying out needed social reforms" (quoted in Gladwin Hill, "China and Soviet Spar at Meeting", *New York Times*, 22 August 1974, p. 6).

In one view, as diplomatic tests, these conferences were passive and rigidly synchronised talking shops; in another, they were considered sites for the activation of linkage politics. All hope of producing a final document that constituted anything more than a synthesis of opinions – never mind a blueprint for action – at the 1984 Mexico City Conference on Population, was bogged down under the weight of a host of supplementary resolutions brought forward by both the Western and Eastern blocs. Some of these resolutions attested to the heating up of the ideological struggle in the early 1980s. Several of the draft amendments pushed forward by the United States reflected the Reagan administration's bid to make the connection between issues such as population growth and economic development more explicit so as to reflect the dynamism of a free market economic philosophy. The Soviet Union, for its part, introduced a tough statement on nuclear disarmament, hoping to link the escalation of the arms race with the ongoing problems associated with hunger, disease, and overpopulation.

The intrusion of a number of more specific geopolitical concerns added a further tone of rigidity to the tests. Approximately 90 recommendations were put forward for consideration at the Mexico City conference, specifically condemning the Israeli occupation of Palestine and Arab land and the establishment of settlements in particular. Verbal bickering over the use (or abuse) of the terms "Palestinian women" and "Zionism", as well as the targeting of apartheid and imperialism dominated the proceedings of the 1985 Nairobi Women's Conference to such an extent that Canadian activist Doris Anderson in frustration complained: "Countries used their time on the platform to wage political war on their enemies instead of talking about women" (Doris Anderson, "Big miracle in Nairobi was too much to expect", *Toronto Star*, 10 August 1985; see also Michael Valpy, "Earlier divisions haunt UN women's meeting", *Globe and Mail*, 26 July 1985).

It needs to be mentioned, though, that the structure imposed by bipolarity and the Cold War did retain elements of flexibility within it. The discipline imposed by the system allowed these conferences to be mobilised as agenda-setting and problem-solving mechanisms. The breakthrough of the Stockholm Conference on the Human Environment stands out in this regard. Despite the non-participation of the Eastern European bloc at the Stockholm conference, it was not relegated to a downgraded status or functional irrelevance. Not only were 113 nations officially represented, but the conference was swept up in a wave of positive attention.

The success of this conference was due to a combination of good luck and timing. As the boycott by the Eastern bloc was announced only five months before the Stockholm meeting was to take place, the conference was able to retain the momentum that had already built up. Until the end of 1971, the Soviet Union with Czechoslovakia had participated as members of the preparatory committee. Even with the boycott, the Soviet bloc countries were able to provide additional input into the proceedings through the ongoing activities of their nationals who continued to act as scientific advisors to the conference and through the submission of the conference resolutions to the General Assembly at the 1972 session. Nor did any other detrimental spill-over effects accompany the boycott, in that neither Cuba nor the non-aligned movement pulled out of the conference. On the contrary, some offset for the absence of the Soviet bloc was provided by the attendance of the People's Republic of China (PRC) after its admission to the UN. Unwilling to sit and watch on the sidelines, the PRC quickly made its presence felt both on policy (re-opening the draft declaration on the human environment for discussion) and procedural questions (proposing various ad hoc committees and working groups).

The problem-solving orientation of the Stockholm conference was encouraged by a combination of intellectual, episodic, and political shifts. There seems little doubt that the willingness of some (Western) governments to address policy issues on matters relating to resource depletion and pollution was stimulated by the impact of books such as Rachel Carson's *Silent Spring* (Carson, 1962). The major oils spills caused by the sinking of the *Torrey Canyon* in the English Channel and the blow-out of an off-shore drilling platform near Santa Barbara, California intensified this catalytic effect (see, for example, McCormick, 1989). Finally, thought and action to deal with the environment were enlivened not only by the rise of an increasingly vital (if highly segmented) green movement but by the emergence of a transnational and epistemic community centred on the expansion and promotion of scientific knowledge. At the forefront of this trend were commentators such as Barbara Ward who (together with René Dubos) produced the report for the conference. With this wealth of supportive conditions, the Stockholm conference was able to make good headway. It produced an action plan with over 100 recommendations covering issues ranging from the curtailment of ocean dumping to wildlife preservation. Institutionally, it moved forward to establish a new unit to coordinate and stimulate national and international environmental efforts. The overall result included a heightened awareness and legitimacy for environmentalism on the policy agenda and some confirmation of the mode of solutions. Tests of autonomy and sovereignty began to be made conditional on performance, and self-help began, at least on a case-by-case basis, to lean towards cooperation across borders.

The other pre-1990s conferences faced difficulty in meeting this standard of performance. Unable to weld together a coherent view about what constituted a population problem, the final document from the 1974 World Population Conference in Bucharest produced no clear plan of action (United Nations, 1974). A deeply ingrained set of geopolitical questions militated against any relaxation away from rigidity to a more flexible problem-solving mode. Unable to build a majority vote for its own agenda, the United States flirted with the role of spoiler as opposed to that of leader. As Maureen Reagan, the US president's daughter, who headed the US delegation at the 1985 World Conference on Women in Nairobi, protested: "If we don't think we can have a meaningful conference why should we participate?" (quoted in "Women's issues take back seat as UN meeting ends", *Montreal Gazette*, 29 July 1985).

Yet, despite these constrained circumstances, these conferences were productive. Worst-case scenarios threatening a complete paralysis of the conferences did not transpire. Although delayed, the Mexico City conference was ultimately able to finesse an awkward agreement on the outrider issues besetting the conference. The United States, finding itself almost completely isolated on the Israel/Palestine question, kept up a protracted resistance through a series of amendments. But once it had passed the deadline for the scheduled closure of the conference, the

American delegation backed away from this stance and allowed the conference's 88-point final declaration to be approved by consensus. A similar pattern ultimately emerged at the Nairobi conference. Notwithstanding procedural wrangling, floor fights, and a few separate votes on specific paragraphs that could not be agreed to informally, no single question was allowed to be a deal-breaker. A workable – if awkward – compromise was reached to substitute "racism and all forms of racial discrimination" for the controversial "Zionism". The final document, titled "Forward-Looking Strategies", papered over controversy through a consensus agreement.

In the realm of action, incremental progress was detectable through the cycle of early UN conferences under review. Moving beyond the results achieved in the Bucharest document, the World Population Plan of Action agreed to at Mexico City contained a number of tangible proposals, which included the collection of basic data and communication and education with respect to family planning. Despite progress, however, serious obstacles continued. The implacable opposition by the Vatican/Holy See to making family planning services more accessible had to be circumvented. Commitment in principle to do more in the area of population policy was impeded by the practical constraints imposed by the lack of capabilities. Although the UN had established a unit with a budget of US$50 million in 1967 to help nations develop population management programmes, little coordination or further institutional development had come about. Complicating both of these problems was the Reagan administration's pledge to stop financing multilateral population control programmes that sanctioned abortion (Finkle and Crane, 1975).

The 1968 Teheran Conference on Human Rights falls into the same ambivalent category. Any quick review of this conference reinforces the impression of intractable division on geographic/ideological lines. The prevalent theme of the three-week meeting was the condemnation of racism and racial intolerance. The core resolution condemned South Africa's apartheid policy as a crime against humanity and a "threat to international peace and security". Against Western opposition, the latter resolution also condemned the "major trading partners" of South Africa for their defiance of UN resolutions ("UN meeting urges ban on racism", *The Times* (London), 6 May 1968). One variation on this theme came with the effort by the Soviet Union and its allies to pass a resolution banning Nazi and neo-Nazi parties (in the context of the temporary electoral strength of the National Democratic Party in West Germany). African and Asian countries targeted the legacy of slavery and colonialism, emphasising the struggle against racial discrimination and the right to self-determination (Lyons, 1989). The constructive side of the Teheran conference came out in a number of other resolutions that were harbingers of a widening agenda. A nascent women's caucus among the delegates put forward a "charter" of female equality, urging all states to eliminate discrimination. While such a resolution may be dismissed as a meaningless gesture, it still belies the notion that the international system through the entire post-1945 era was completely immutable. As in other areas of agenda change – most notably the bias away from civil and political rights towards economic, social, and cultural rights – calls for political action as a means for preparing for a new regime for human rights overtook the traditional concern of the UN, as featured in the proclamation of the Universal Declaration. As Jack Donnelly acknowledged, the Teheran International Conference on Human Rights "mark[ed] the beginning of the authoritative re-conceptualisation of the UN's role and priorities" (Donnelly, 1981: 634).[6]

The prospect of convergence at the end of the Cold War

The end of bipolarity and geopolitical struggle between the United States and the Soviet Union offers an opportunity to look beyond the accepted notions of transition in international relations generally and tests of diplomacy more specifically. Just as there was some room available in the older order for innovation, so the constraints of that order were released only incrementally and in unexpected ways. For many commentators, one of the main assumptions with respect to the process of change was that the process of change was associated with a high degree of convergence. While Fukuyama's notion of the end of history has prompted a bevy of rebuttals (for a measured response, see Halliday, 1994, 1997), a sense of convergence at the "end of history" was nevertheless anticipated in a number of other ways. The most important expression of this expected new consensus – through the eyes of these believers – was the globalisation of certain principles including multilateralism, liberalism, and human rights. "Herald[ing] a move beyond the ideological History in which humankind had been entrapped during most of the preceding two centuries" (Clark, 2001a: 38), the extension of this belief system was thought to hold out the potential for promoting a more transparent, open, and integrated system.

The strength of this assumption of convergence crested on a number of intellectual and empirical developments. The internationalisation of human rights has been at the forefront of the post–Cold War agenda. Just as the fall of Communism precipitated the spread of democracy in central and eastern Europe, the end of apartheid and the transition from the military regimes and dictatorships in Latin America and certain parts of Africa contributed to a similar trend in other areas of the world.

Rights-based discourse became a pre-eminent form of policy debate, extending beyond questions of traditional security to questions of economic well-being and environmental health. The impetus towards multilateralism was helped by an analogous dynamic, as part of an extension of the learning process tied not only to problem solving but to risk aversion. As illustrated by the "arrival" of what John Ruggie terms "the domain of global ecopolitics" at the 1972 Stockholm conference (Ruggie, 1988: 159, 169),[7] functional issues were increasingly seen to lie beyond the existing capabilities of states to manage on an interstate basis. The drive to deal with these sorts of issues through collective action at a supranational level accelerated accordingly.

Not unexpectedly, momentum in this direction was complicated when the North/South dimension was brought into the analysis. Despite the image (or, more accurately, the myth) of solidarity among the countries of the third world, as evidenced by their behaviour in the UN world conferences of the 1960s and 1970s, states in the South became uncomfortable and largely unsuccessful at trying to act as a monolithic bloc. In tandem with the Communist bloc, the South could mobilise on select symbolic issues relating to racism. The long-standing targets of this activity were the white minority regimes in Southern Africa. In addition to voicing attacks against South Africa's apartheid policies, an African-sponsored resolution at the Teheran conference called on Britain to take all necessary measures, including the use of force, to end Rhodesia's Unilateral Declaration of Independence. The conference also appealed to South Africa and Rhodesia to treat their imprisoned opponents in accordance with the standards of the Geneva Convention.

Another face of this diplomacy of solidarity was turned towards Middle East politics. Between the 1975 Mexico City and the 1985 Nairobi Women's Conference, the Arab countries were instrumental in redirecting the anti-racist campaign towards "Zionism". Through the sheer weight of resolutions, this activity had an impact that sparked major controversy which cut deeply into the operational process through the earlier series of conferences. When viewed retrospectively, however, the impact was felt more as an irritant than as an effective mechanism of departure. At the Nairobi conference, for example, the host country felt obliged to propose alternative language on Zionism and racism in order to move the Forward Strategies document forward. The result was an uncomfortable compromise, with a number of African and Arab countries continuing to vent their frustration with speechmaking and at least one country (Iran) refusing to accept the consensus at all.

After these twin "lowest common denominator" cases, the approach of the South became less cohesive. Initiative-oriented performance at the earlier UN-sponsored conferences either had a personalistic or country-specific flavour. In the first category fell the high-profile presence of Indira Gandhi at the Stockholm conference. Indeed the Indian Prime Minister (apart from Olof Palme from the host country) proved to be the dominant leader in attendance. In the latter category fell those countries – above all China and the Philippines – that treated the agenda at the UN population conferences as means to advance and legitimate their national policies.

The material issue that provided additional glue to hold the South together before the end of the Cold War was the demand for a form of new international economic order (NIEO). This message received strong diplomatic backing – a month before the Stockholm conference – at the 1972 United Nations Conference on Trade and Development (UNCTAD) held in Santiago, Chile (for background, see UN Institute for Training and Research, 1976). By setting out a formal institutional design for the promotion of an NIEO, this meeting signalled its determination to close the gap between the living standards of the North and the South (Herter and Binder, 1973: 11; Murphy, 2001). At the forefront of the Stockholm conference was the concern expressed by Prime Minister Gandhi (as the voice of the South) that environmentalism should not be subordinated to the developing countries' push to increase their standard of living. As she asked: "How can we speak to those who live in villages and in slums about keeping the oceans, rivers and air clean when their own lives are contaminated at the source?" (quoted in Ramakrishna, 1992: 195).

Questions about the nature of this economic divide permeated the population conferences as well. The overarching theme emphasised by Mexican president Miguel de la Madrid Hurtado was the promotion of development as the means of coming to terms with population pressures. For the South the answer was not simply to decrease population growth rates but to provide "better living conditions" for the existing population. Accordingly, development strategies pursued by the South became inextricably linked with the exigencies of the international political economy. One suggested route forward favoured a cluster of measures aimed at alleviating restrictive practices in the North and cutting back the debt burden (Oakland Ross, "'Man is the priority,' global population conference told", *Globe and Mail*, 7 August 1984). Another was to link population and migration on the international policy agenda. As de la Madrid proclaimed, strategies of the future must contain either "an internal policy of comprehensive and balanced development, or understanding between governments concerned in the case of external migration" ("Plea made for migrants' rights", *Associated Press*, 16 August 1984).

Fast-forwarding to the 1990s, we can hear echoes of these sentiments at all the major conferences held during that decade. As perceived by the developing countries at the 1993 Rio conference, the main source of danger in imposing higher environmental standards was a potential break with the post-1945 settlement regarding development assistance. The only way these countries would buy into a new environmental regime was to be granted an extensive compensatory package (see, for example, Victor Mallet, "South prepares common stance for Rio Summit", *Financial Times* (London), 30 April 1992). A similar approach was taken at the 1993 Vienna Conference on Human Rights. Faced with pressure to conform to a universal code of principles, many developing countries continued to fight for the right to development as a quid pro quo. In its most robust formulation, this set of rights was defined as the right of the people in developing countries to achieve a decent standard of living free from the obstruction of outside forces.

It may be argued, of course, that these material interests in themselves were not enough to hold the South together as a single operational unit. Even in the heyday of the Group of 77 (G-77), and the rising demand for the NIEO in the 1970s and early 1980s, the sense of collective interest and alignment among developing countries could be overestimated. Amid calls for solidarity there was great divergence on economic strategy, marked with competition and antagonistic claims on economic matters. While some countries continued to resist the pull to liberal orthodoxy, others were engaged in frantic processes of adaptation by embarking on impressive new strategies or undergoing dramatic reversals of approach (on this theme of fragmentation, see Harris, 1986).

This pull to the mainstream was accelerated by the "triumph of the market" and liberal capitalism that purportedly took place in the immediate post–Cold War era. The new order, however, was not without its own brand of disorder. Although subjected to a greater weight of disciplines, the hierarchical division among countries was no longer as clearly defined as in the older categorisation between North and South. The rigid fault lines of the Cold War years were replaced by a flatter and less constrained system. As James Mittelman has described it: "Globalisation acts to render obsolete invented divisions of the world into developed and developing countries, industrialized and industrializing nations and core and periphery" (Mittelman, 1995: 273).

Opposition to the new order was inspired by normative perceptions as much as by substance relating to the distribution of material benefits. As illustrated most vividly at the 1993 Vienna Conference on Human Rights, one major source of emergent tension was the uneven way in which the export model of liberal values was pursued. The end of the structural conditioning that had been imposed by bipolarity made the problem of selectivity – and double standards – more acute. For instance, the intervention by the "coalition of the willing" in the Gulf War was contrasted by several delegations from non-Western countries – particularly those from Islamic countries – with non-interference in Bosnia. As with the South Africa/apartheid issue in the Cold War years, a draft declaration on Bosnia was presented not as a response to a country-specific situation but as a cause. With this reconfiguration of the South, the issue of Bosnia extended beyond the human rights issues dominating the agenda of the Vienna conference into issues relating to genocide, and peace and security issues.

In no way, however, could this resistance be interpreted as a straightforward replica of the North/South issue. If Vienna brought out new forms of solidarity, it also demonstrated the extent of unevenness in the diplomatic approach of what had been deemed the South. The African countries in particular were reluctant to privilege the Bosnia issue at the expense of other agenda items. To do so, they argued, would merely reinforce the notion of a hierarchy of cases. Violations in any part of the world should not be treated differently – or left out of action plans. Going back to the lowest common denominator approach, this sense of fragmentation was masked by an upgrading of symbolic issues. Item 9 at the Vienna conference returned to familiar themes focusing on apartheid, the rights of the Palestinians in the Israeli-occupied territories, the persistence of racism, and the treatment of migrant workers. The only significant – and controversial – variation on this set of themes was the call for an international definition of terrorism in order to distinguish the legitimate struggles of peoples under colonial or alien determination and foreign occupation from the activities of terrorists or internal secessionists (see, for example, Linda Hossie, "North–South split over turf", *Globe and Mail*, 23 October 1992).

Another major source of tension was found at a point where material capabilities and non-material claims intersected: the growing resistance on the part of many non-Western countries to the West's attempts to establish the primacy of its views on human rights, on the grounds of cultural relativism. As shall be discussed in greater detail in a later chapter, this was an argument of convenience as well as commitment. Politically, the argument of cultural relativism served as a useful tactic behind which "problem countries" could hide their domestic records of human rights deficiencies. Many of the most vocal cultural relativists were, not surprisingly, countries in violation of (or non-party to) international conventions on torture, summary or arbitrary execution, and disappearances. If an argument can be made that "the doctrine of human rights can be misused to disguise Western imperialism", it is equally true that "the doctrine of cultural relativism can be misused to conceal or justify oppression by Asian states" (Freeman, 1995: 15).

Economically, the willingness of non-Western countries to advocate cultural relativism was linked to their ascendant economic or political profile. This was the case with self-confident countries such as Malaysia, which in the context of the early 1990s were deemed to be among the winners within the changing international economic environment. Bolstered by the sparkling success of the Asian development model in the early 1990s, Malaysian leaders could talk and play a tough diplomatic game in terms of their participation (or non-participation) at the Rio and Vienna conferences. The Malaysian environmental minister did not attend any of the meetings up to the final Prep Com IV during the UNCED process. Prime Minister Mahathir Mohamad put the onus on the West to budge on the environmental agenda, waiting until May 1992 to indicate his decision to attend the Rio conference (see, for example, Nossal and Stubbs, 1997; Vatikiotis, 1992). Such tactics on the part of non-Western countries were not only premised on a rejection of the merits of Western individualism on moral or social grounds but were a means "to reflect their new and elevated status within the global political economy and to free themselves from the last vestiges of colonial influence and control" (Evans, 2001: 95).

The cluster of non-Western countries that included Malaysia and other rapid developers thus had some luxury of coherence in their expressions of diplomacy. They could reject the disciplines linked to new conditions placed on their behaviour and the assumption that one agenda fits all. However, their sensitivity to diversity was complemented by an independence regarding their need to adjust to the "disciplines" imposed by the global economic structure. This luxury was unavailable to most other non-Western countries. Needing additional financial assistance, most countries in Africa and Latin America simply could not stand aloof and sharply differentiate themselves as resisters within the negotiating process. Whatever their own commitment to universality, these countries had to direct their activities towards winning compensation for extended international governance in one area through financial and technical transfers – or some other form of quid pro quo.

The end of the Cold War – bluntly put – meant a welter of contradictions as much as it meant homogeneity. Freedom from the confines of bipolarity coincided with the ushering in of a tightened system of global economic integration. But the disintegration of the same system, in which multiple issues had been seen through a single prism, brought with it a mosaic of multi-dimensional values and interests. The contemporary world order – even (or, perhaps more accurately, especially) when viewed through a narrow state-centric lens – may indeed contain some relatively "cohesive" qualities (Shaw, 2000: 95). Yet, the "messy" (Held et al., 1999: 85) or even "ramshackle" (Strange, 1996a: 199) quality of this structure cannot be left out of this portrait.

Structural constraints to the power of agency?

From the discussion in the two preceding sections, it may be concluded that the importance of structure should not be over-exaggerated in any discussion of the evolution of UN conferences. Even before the forces of globalisation and interdependence accelerated in the 1990s, there were already signs that the hold imposed by structural constraints was loosening. Under conditions that allow greater room for diplomatic expression, as witnessed during the post–Cold War years, therefore, the openings would be expected to widen, at least on an issue-specific basis. This release from constraint is supported when the power of agency in the nexus between global governance and diplomatic method is taken into consideration. This shift in emphasis redirects attention from systemic constraints to "purposeful actors" whose actions contribute to the reproduction or transformation of international society (for the most authoritative analysis on this relationship, see Wendt, 1987).

The starting point for this rearticulation in the tests of diplomacy is that the sources of agency have become more diverse. Throughout the Cold War era, alternative policy responses or initiatives came mainly from individual change agents or through the talents of qualified secondary state powers. Indeed, recent changes in the international system have increased the potential of these actors to exercise influence via entrepreneurial and technically oriented activity. To these traditional sources of agency, however, may be added the growing influence of non-traditional actors. As space has opened up for the agency of individuals and secondary or middle powers, so has operational room opened up for non-state actors through non-governmental organisations (NGOs), or civil society.

A select group of individual change agents, whether described as social engineers or policy entrepreneurs (Rosenau, 1990: 333–387) who have transcended the confines of national interest and gate-keeping, managed to place their stamp on the intellectual discourse and policy agenda of the world conferences since the 1970s (Kaufman, 1988; Riddell-Dixon, 1997). The prototype of this sort of change agent in the context of UN conferences is Maurice Strong. In his capacity as secretary-general of both the 1972 Stockholm conference[8] and the 1992 Rio conference, Strong provided both selective diplomatic entrepreneurship and a sense of institutional memory on a grand scale. As the first secretary-general of the United Nations Environment Programme (UNEP), Strong used his position, as both bully pulpit and organisational lever, more to shape the institutional framework for implementing the agendas of these two conferences than to set their agendas. As one colleague portrayed the energetic Strong during the Stockholm conference: "He is a man who cultivates his own vision, who wanted to see into the future and save the world. His instrument was to be neither pen nor sword, but diplomacy, notes verbales, bureaucrats, reports, working groups, agreed procedures" (Stone, 1973: 2; Strong, 2001: 115–133).

Strong's personal style of diplomatic agency intersected with (and transcended) the structures of the international system. In the East/West context, Strong had to circumvent the Soviet boycott imposed during the Stockholm conference. In the North/South context, he had to work hard to allay the suspicions of the developing countries that a conference on "pollution" was a device to divert attention from the South's demands for an NIEO. Even though his charm offensive was instrumental in convincing Indira Gandhi to attend the conference, the Indian Prime Minister's performance at Stockholm magnified rather than tempered this North/South rift. Nor did Strong's successful campaign to locate the UNEP in Nairobi overshadow completely the original opposition by the West to this move (see, for example, Cox, 1969).

Strong's diplomatic agency also proved a hard act to follow. With the impressive series of world conferences in train over the next decade, considerable opportunity became available for individuals to perform as change agents. But few of these opportunities were grasped in the bold manner Strong had personified in his activities. The only recent performance of this brand of institutional entrepreneurship appears to have been that of James Grant at UNICEF, who led the campaign to designate 1979 as the International Year of the Child as well as triggering the push for the 1990 World Summit for Children (WSC), or Children's Summit (Deacon, 1999; Emmerij et al., 2001: 113). Grant seized the moment of the end of the Cold War to grasp a peace dividend. His call for the summit echoed Strong's urgency during the Stockholm and Rio process: "The potential advance is so important for future prosperity and peace in the world as to merit a special meeting of political leaders to consider how the major opportunities for protecting children might be seized over the next decade" (quoted in David Crane, "Canada's help urged to organise summit on world's children", *Toronto Star*, 9 January 1989).

Most of the diplomatic activity of individual leaders at the UN conferences, nevertheless, was carried out in more routine fashion. At the 1993 Conference on Human Rights in Vienna, Ibrahima Fall, the UN Assistant Secretary General, Human Rights (and former foreign minister of Senegal), provided an effective but low-key form of leadership in his capacity as the secretary-general. So did the Chilean Ambassador Juan Somavia, in his role as Chair of the Preparatory Committee at the World Summit for Social Development. The leader whose style most closely approximated the heroic style adopted by Strong and Grant proved to be Dr. Nafis Sadik, Executive Director of the UN Fund for Population Activities (UNFPA). At the opposite end of the spectrum, the leadership of Gertrude Mongella, Assistant Secretary General, Division for the Advancement of Women, was widely criticised in her role as secretary-general of the Beijing Women's Conference, on the grounds that it was not sufficiently robust.

The second category of change agents is the cluster of secondary countries with the potential to exercise non-structural forms of leadership. The significance of "middle power" leadership over a range of issue areas – with particular reference to the social agenda – has taken on enhanced resonance in the post–Cold War era. This analysis has been driven in large part by the recognition that the powers at the apex of the international hierarchy have not taken on this role themselves. This inability – or unwillingness – is especially evident on the part of the United States. Although it capitalised unequivocally on the collapse of bipolarity, most notably in the security domain, the expression of US leadership is more ambiguous when traced across the expanded international agenda. Certainly the United States did not evolve into an instinctive multilateralist. Its attitude to cooperative solutions – especially those directed through the UN – remained ambivalent at best. Obsessed by interstate competitiveness, the United States (and to a lesser extent Japan and the major EU countries) found it difficult to adjust either to an issue-specific or to a sustained cooperative mode of behaviour. As Martin Shaw notes: "The relationship of the West to the global layer exacerbates the problem of Western power" (Shaw, 2000: 255). Although the West is relatively united on the principle of developing global economic institutions, their practical development often brings out the contradictory interests of the main Western entities. When it comes to political and legal institutions, the West is even more divided. American institutions project extremely ambivalent attitudes: "Although US administrations recognise in a general way the need for legitimisation which the United Nations provides, they adopt highly instrumental stances towards it, habitually withholding financial contributions and bypassing its Security Council whenever it seems unlikely to deliver the desired results" (Shaw, 2000: 256).[9]

By way of contrast, many middle powers have a highly developed multilateralist diplomatic identity. They have had considerable experience in taking initiatives and building coalitions in the absence of (or sometimes lukewarm support from) the great powers. They take the UN more seriously and they concentrate their skills on issues that require collaborative solutions but lack attention from the major players. Their behaviour has manifested through a range of shapes and styles. Working within the boundaries imposed by bipolarity and the Cold War conflict, middle powers used different approaches in an effort to increase their room for manoeuvre. Sweden stands out as the classic illustration of a "heroic" middle power (Cooper, 1997b; Cooper, Higgott and Nossal, 1993). Swedish initiatives in the international social domain tended to be ambitious exercises involving a great deal of organisational effort and risk-taking. They were also highly politicised, in the sense that they required a high degree of commitment and political will.

Sweden's actions with respect to the 1972 Stockholm conference meshed closely with this heroic model. Sweden boldly moved out in front with respect to agenda setting, its willingness to host the conference, and the mobilisation of political support. The original idea for the conference is attributed to Sverker Astrom, Sweden's ambassador to the UN, who brought the proposal to the meeting of the economic and social council in July 1968 (Stone, 1973: 18). At the Stockholm conference itself, Prime Minister Palme proved to be a combative host. Certainly, by publicly levelling the charge of "ecocide" against the United States for their practices in Vietnam, Palme risked a walk-out by the United States, as the head of the American delegation accused him of a "gratuitous politicising of our environmental discussions" (quoted in Gladwin Hill, "Draft calls for ecological responsibility, 'Deeply Disturbed' U.S. Says", *New York Times*, 7 June 1972; Fredriksson, 1986).

Canada engaged with the social international agenda in a characteristically low-key, routine style that conformed to its traditional preference for acting as a quiet "bridge" or "linchpin". Examples of this mediatory impulse abound in the earlier series of UN conferences. To give one illustration: from the lead-up to the Stockholm conference, Canadian officials enthusiastically took on the task of trying to convince the PRC to attend. Along the same lines, Canadian technical experts were sent to a variety of developing countries to help them draw up their national environmental reports (Rowland, 1973: 47). If self-congratulatory language belied the modesty of Canada's efforts, the effectiveness of these activities framed self-accounts by others about Canadian quiet diplomacy. In the words of one observer/participant, the success attributed to the conference was helped enormously by the "important role played by the faceless [Canadian] civil servants who helped draft the conference document [as well as] the effectiveness of the Canadian delegation, both in formal sessions and behind the scenes in achieving agreement" (Chant, 1972: 12).

An almost identical account may be offered of Canadian diplomacy at the 1974 Bucharest population conference. Interpreting its pattern of interaction as another application of the same helpful fixer qualities, credit was given to Canada for facilitating the cross-linkages that enabled the expanded agenda to move forward. Although overshadowed by the more controversial debates dominating proceedings, this sophisticated coupling

– "namely, the incorporation into the World Population Plan of Action of a principle concerning resource-environment considerations in population planning" – drew appreciation from two credible insiders (Brooks and Douglas, 1975: 6).

Driven by the problem-solving/risk-aversion dynamic surrounding the environmental arena, the Canadian government showed a degree of financial generosity in funding the Stockholm secretariat and eventually the UNEP as a permanent institution (Dobell, 1985: 249). However, Canada was initially far less prepared to move out in front to support the work of the UNFPA under the auspices of the United Nations Development Programme (UNDP). Until Canada established its own birth control policy at the domestic level, for example, it was explicitly reluctant to externalise these activities. As Mitchell Sharp made clear: "We cannot go leaping into an area without determining first where the priorities are and what are the domestic implications" ("Canada's role in population group affected by domestic policy", *Globe and Mail*, 3 March 1970). What seemed reasonable caution to the government was thus described as foot dragging by advocates of birth control on the international stage. As a Canadian representative of the International Planned Parenthood Federation (IPPF), Rev. Robert B. MacRae, stated: "I am embarrassed to be a Canadian when I go abroad on Planned Parenthood business and I am embarrassed at the UN on this matter" ("Canada's role in population group affected by domestic policy", *Globe and Mail*, 3 March 1970).

In changing course on this issue, domestic attitudes had to catch up with the evolution of widely accepted international practices, as well as the ideas and actions of some transnational societal forces. By the time of the 1974 Bucharest conference, it merits notice, Canada had discarded its cautious financial stance and had become, on a per capita basis, the fifth largest supporter of the UNFPA (CIDA, 1987, 1989).

A self-help quality also permeated Canada's diplomacy on international social conferences. Canada's interest in the Stockholm conference was triggered as much by a pragmatic desire to "do something" to curtail environmental shocks as by a sense of good international citizenship. Its attention was directed not only to ecological crises occurring over the horizon but to averting crises of the type already precipitated by the oil spill of the US tanker *Arrow* off the Nova Scotia coast in 1970. It sought collective solutions that would also add legitimacy to its domestic self-help legislation in the form of the Canada Water Act of 1970 and the Clean Air Act of 1971 (for background, see Griffiths, 1987).

An additional ingredient of Canadian diplomatic behaviour was its sometimes uncaring – even hypocritical – quality. Canada clung tenaciously to some points of principle beyond the point where it could be said to represent good international citizenship. This was particularly true of Canada's unwillingness to bend at Stockholm on the "polluter pays" rule to allow compensation to developing countries. As Senator Alan McNaughton declared, in announcing that Canada was only reluctantly budging because of the wider implications of the conference to North/South relations: "Our position has been that the polluter must pay. If we receive a shipment of food from a [developing] country and refuse entry to it because it doesn't meet our environmental standards, why should we have to pay compensation to the country that shipped it?" (quoted in Rowland, 1973: 58).

Juxtaposed with this hard-line stance was an air of distraction vis-à-vis the participation of Canadian ministers at some of the UN conferences. Notable in this respect was the behaviour of Jeanne Sauvé, then minister of the environment, who headed the Canadian delegation to the Bucharest population conference. Her opening statement that "Canada is here to listen and to learn" went over well with the assembled representatives (Sauvé, 1974). Soon after giving this message, however, Sauvé departed for the Black Sea on vacation. In the absence of the minister and a concerted form of political engagement, leadership of the Canadian delegation was left with the team of officials.

A strong dose of diplomatic status seeking may also be detected in other aspects of Canada's approach. The go-between work with the PRC on the Stockholm conference reinforced the impression that Canada had moved out in front of other countries through its recognition of the PRC, and the "mentoring" of developing countries in their preparations for Stockholm also had meaningful ramifications. In other (often declaratory) expressions, however, status seeking just reinforced an impression of self-congratulation and smugness. This attitude was especially prevalent in the aftermath of the Stockholm conference, promoted to a large extent by the interface between the work of Maurice Strong as an individual change agent and Canadian sponsorship of initiatives at the national level. This face of status seeking is captured in the statement by Jack Davis, Canada's then minister of the environment, who claimed that the "success of the first UN Conference on the Environment was due in large measure to the leadership shown by Canada and by Canadians" (Dobell, 1985: 246).

Care not to overestimate the influence of Canada should not downplay the steadfastness of Canadian diplomacy in reining in the overzealousness of others through these earlier UN conferences. Although much of this activity was directed towards the Communist countries and the South, efforts were equally applied to restraining bursts of US unilateralism as featured in the Reagan years. At the Mexico City Population Conference, the head of the Canadian delegation, Senator Lorna Marsden, showed a fierce determination to take on the Reagan administration. Marsden clearly distanced Canadian policy from the unidimensional bias of the US approach. Downplaying the market as the deus ex machina to population pressure, she attempted to nuance the debate: "We do not believe that economic policy in and of itself can resolve population problems" (quoted in Oakland Ross, "U.S., Soviets ride hobbyhorses at population control talks", *Globe and Mail*, 8 August 1984). The Canadian delegation also joined a variety of other countries in criticising the Reagan administration for externalising its anti-abortion stance, that is, for denying any family-planning money to international organisations that promoted abortion. Rejecting any such linkage, Marsden noted: Canada "leaves decisions on [family] planning to recipient countries" (quoted in Oakland Ross, "U.S., Soviets ride hobbyhorses at population control talks", *Globe and Mail*, 8 August 1984).

At the 1985 Nairobi Women's Conference, the Canadian delegation adopted more subtle tactics in order to help end the deadlock between the United States and the combination of the Soviet bloc and the developing countries. Although this activity remained totally consistent with Canada's quiet diplomacy/helpful fixer code, this form of brokerage mechanism strengthened Canada's claim to flexibility and speed in responding to new conditions and circumstances. In the congratulatory words of Tom Axworthy, Prime Minister Pierre Trudeau's former principal secretary, this use of statecraft represented "a singular contribution to the success" of the conference (Tom Axworthy, "Canada can be proud of its role in Nairobi", *Toronto Star*, 25 August 1985). The North-South Institute also praised this activity as a model of "effective middle-power diplomacy in the multilateral arena" (North-South Institute, 1989: 4).

The third category of agents that merit extended consideration are NGOs with an interest in the international social agenda. Historically, this form of agency was visible but subordinated to the state-centric structure. Openings in that structure had appeared at the international level in the immediate post-war period, especially with the San Francisco conference of 1945 that led to the establishment of the UN. The US delegation in San Francisco was accompanied by over 40 NGOs (Consultation between The United Nations and Non-Governmental Organizations, 1949) and 1,200 NGOs attended the conference (Willetts, 1982: 11). This presence helped ensure some standing for civil society within the UN machinery, as legitimised by Article 71 of the Charter. The role of these groups in this early period, however, was only distinctly related to the "new more complex form of multilateral global governance" that became visible in the 1990s (Held et al., 1999). As laid out in the provisions for consultations through the UN Economic and Social Council (ECOSOC), national delegations set – and implemented – the rules for "consultative standing". The essential criteria for this status were that the organisation's activities "should fall within the Council's competence ... namely economic and social life", that it should have "an established headquarters, an administration, authorized representatives and a policy-making body, and that it be international in scope" (Willetts, 1982: 12).

The traditional hallmark of Canadian foreign policy has been its closed approach to policy making. A small tightly knit group of politicians and officials acted with a great deal of autonomy from social influences to shape Canada's approach to international affairs. An extensive pattern of consultation with the representatives of the Canadian public was thought to be neither valuable nor necessary. The domestic structural circumstances of the NGOs played into this pattern; up to the late 1960s and early 1970s NGOs concerned with foreign policy issues were relatively few in number. Significantly, only 18 NGOs appeared before the Standing Committee on External Affairs and National Defence in 1970–1971, which discussed Prime Minister Trudeau's Foreign Policy for Canadians. Although this foreign policy review acted as a catalyst for activity, most NGOs were then small, immature, and financially weak, with limited research capacity and lobbying repertoire (Cooper and Pal, 1996).

This combination of factors set the limits for the presence and impact of NGOs during the earlier series of international social conferences. Few NGOs attended the 1968 International Conference on Human Rights, and those that did participate were limited to observer status. The main openings for participation by non-state actors were in a technical capacity. Despite the best efforts of Maurice Strong to engender greater diplomatic inclusiveness, the official component of the Stockholm conference moved very little beyond this traditional format. The Friends of the Earth and the World Wildlife Fund were invited to address the plenary,[10] but any extension of the role of NGOs with respect to the negotiations met with strenuous resistance from diverse countries. The inclusion of non-state actors into the diplomatic process retained a narrow technical bias. Room opened up for technical experts, as witnessed by the establishment of a committee of consultants led by René Dubos and Barbara Ward convened at Founex, Switzerland as part of the Stockholm process. But apart from this narrow form of integration state and non-state actors inhabited parallel worlds (UN Conference on the Human Environment, 1972).

The technical bias corresponded with the Canadian approach through all of these conferences, as Canadian representation relied on the selective use of technical experts. When John Humphrey (who had served in such a distinguished fashion at the San Francisco conference)[11] was unable to attend the Teheran International Conference on Human Rights, for instance, Ronald St. John Macdonald, Dean of Law of the University of Toronto, was invited to attend as a member of the Canadian delegation.[12] To supplement this knowledge base, a meeting was held in Montreal with a small number of academics prior to the conference. The onus that Canada put on sending technical experts to facilitate the participation of developing countries stands out similarly in the Stockholm conference process. NGOs were not ignored totally, as pre-conference hearings were held in several cities. However, these consultations had an ad hoc and a pro forma quality to them. In the opinion of Donald Chant, the meetings were held "at the last minute [and] notice was short, background information from Ottawa was scarce, and few [citizen groups] were able to prepare presentations of real substance" (Chant, 1972: 11).[13] In confirmation of this impression of bias, no citizen groups or NGOs were included in the official Canadian delegation for Stockholm.

The transformational aspect of the Stockholm conference, in terms of NGO participation, had more to do with the accentuated intensity of their unofficial activity than a change in their official status. This period saw an increase in what came to be termed a "counter-consensus", a substantial clusters of individuals and groupings (with some 400 NGOs attending) with ethical concerns relating to disarmament, human rights, population issues, international equity, and solidarity with oppressed people (Detter de Lupis, 1989).[14] From the perspective of the Stockholm conference, however, the privileging of consensus is misleading. Very little sense of agreement radiated from this conference beyond a sense of opposition to the status quo. Each of the individuals and NGOs had a very distinctive agenda. Even the tone fluctuated between an earnestness on issues such as "the limits to growth" and a desire to just have fun, as expressed through street theatre and rock concerts. The result was a high degree of fragmentation as well as intellectual and policy exuberance.

The unofficial component of the Stockholm conference congregated around a number of separate events: a formal but parallel environmental forum held at an abandoned airport, which was open to international, national, and local groups; the Folkets or people's forum under the auspices of Scandinavian political and environmental groups; informal meeting of scientists; and demonstrations by NGOs such as Greenpeace, Friends of the Earth, Alternative City, the Oi Group, and the Hog Farm (Tussie and Riggirozzi, 2001: 171). These outside events attracted leading figures of the transnational counterculture, including Margaret Mead, Gunnar Myrdal, and Barry Commoner.

These activities not surprisingly attracted a lot of criticism. The style of the unofficial events was ridiculed by the defenders of orthodox statecraft for contributing to an environmental Woodstock or "circus" (Knelman, 1972–1973: 28). The emphasis on protest rather than solving problems or averting crises was seen (somewhat naïvely, given the constraints imposed on NGOs) as a missed opportunity. An article in *Science* magazine objected in open despair at the backlash against technical expertise: "Never before in UN history have non-governmental groups had the opportunity to interact and possibly influence the representatives of nations, and it is feared that the forum might become a 'sideshow' distracting attention from the Conference itself" (Bazell, 1971).[15]

One of the most tangible signs of Maurice Strong's willingness to act as a diplomatic agent of change came in his response to these activities. Rather than bridling at the unofficial components of the Stockholm conference as an intrusion on his planning, he chose to try to accommodate and run in tandem with them. Given the amorphous nature of these activities, such tactics were difficult to pursue let alone accomplish. Amidst the fragmentation and volatility of these events only a tactical or symbolic reconciliation could be achieved. In public relations terms, however, Strong's approach was valuable in supporting the impression that the conference was something different in international relations (Herter and Binder, 1973: 34–35).

Against this background the 1974 Bucharest conference may be cast as a partial transition in the process of departure. As at Stockholm, the element of NGO mobilisation that attracted most attention displayed the politics of protest. Standing apart and aloof from the official conference, the parallel forum centred on consciousness-raising activities and alternative methods of discourse and action. At a cursory level, therefore, it was tempting to interpret these activities as simply a distraction from the core proceedings – "more messy, more lively and in many ways a lot more fun than the goings-on in the center ring" (Nan Robertson, "Parley Gives Bucharest a Taste of Over-population", *New York Times*, 24 August 1974). And yet, signs of consolidation among NGOs and civil society may be identified. Key figures in the ascendant women's movement were present, including Germaine Greer and Betty Friedan. Evidence of a greater (and a hardening) mobilisation among abortion activists, family planners, right-to-lifers, and lobby groups campaigning against the systematic use of birth control in developing countries was also abundant among the 1,200 attending the forum, or population tribunal. The established nature of the forum was indicated by the choice of the University Law School as its venue.

In the Canadian domestic context, the pattern of interaction between government and NGOs contained elements of both continuity and change from Stockholm. The consultative mechanisms used by the Canadian government retained their cursory quality. Early in 1974, the Canadian Institute of International Affairs (CIIA) was commissioned to accept briefs from individuals and groups with concerns about population issues; the results of this *sondage* of public opinion were to be sent to the government as it prepared for the Bucharest conference (Canadian Institute of International Affairs, 1974). A similar type of off-loading was used in sponsoring NGO representatives to attend the conference, with the Canadian Council for International Cooperation (CCIC) being charged with coordinating a meeting of 200 representatives from 40 NGOs as a prelude to the conference and for purposes of the selection process. As incomplete as these preparations were, they did allow a far more inclusive process, with representation from a diverse constellation of groups, among which were the Catholic Women's League, the National Farmers' Union, the Calgary YMCA, CARE Canada, Oxfam, SERENA, the Toronto Alliance for Life, the Roman Catholic Diocese of Charlottetown, and Dr. Thomas Roulston of Winnipeg, the past president of the Family Planning Federation of Canada (Kathleen Rex, "Planner says Canada exploits third world", *Globe and Mail*, 13 May 1974). The procedure also allowed for a high degree of competition (and potentially some indirect control by government), as there were several applicants per available space.

The sense of departure from state-centric structures was compounded in the mid-1980s by developments in the intergovernmental dimension of Canadian policy formation. To try to ease the problems of coordination (and competition), an interdepartmental committee was established for the International Conference on Population in Mexico City. In addition to having representatives from the Canadian International Development Agency (CIDA), Status of Women, National Health and Welfare, and External Affairs (the forerunner of DFAIT, the Department of Foreign Affairs and International Trade), this committee was opened up to non-governmental representation with the inclusion of Dr. Roulston, the then chair of the Canadian population task force, and a representative of the ad hoc inter-church committee in Toronto. In a reversal of previous experience, NGOs shaped some aspects of bureaucratic representation on this committee. Most notably, the suggestion by Planned Parenthood that it be included in the planning process helped ease the way for Status of Women's participation on the committee. The presence of NGO representatives also facilitated the deepening and widening of the consultative process between the committee and NGOs. Groups that had had little contact with government up to that time, such as Match International, were participants. Other groups, including the CCIC, the ad hoc inter-church committee, and the YMCA, could build on previous links.

At the 1984 Mexico City conference itself, the NGO–government connection grew closer in a variety of ways. Practices that encouraged easier forms of interaction became more common. The whole Canadian delegation stayed at the same hotel, for example, meeting every morning to review tactics and allocate responsibility. They also hosted two informal sessions to brief NGO representatives and members of the Canadian press corps.

This interaction between selected governmental officials and NGO representatives became even closer during the 1985 Nairobi Women's Conference. As in the environmental and population arena, much of the momentum towards securing this relationship was derived from the nature of the issue area itself. The pursuit of what Jack Donnelly has termed "promotional regimes" (Donnelly, 1993), and the need for action on control of reproductive functions, equal pay for equal work, and elimination of gender stereotypes helped create a sense of purpose across the state/societal divide. Running with this opportunity, effective agency was exerted through a "change team" of "femocrats". The deputy head of the Canadian delegation at Nairobi was Maureen O'Neil, the coordinator of Status of Women Canada. NGO advisers included Sylvia Gold, president of the Canadian Advisory Council on the Status of Women; Chaviva Hosek, president of the National Action Committee; and Denyse Bélanger-Rochon, president of the Fédération des femmes du Québec. Lindsay Niemann operated from her position as Special Coordinator for the Nairobi Conference, within the department of External Affairs.

To point out these developments is not to suggest that that they led towards a fully integrative process; the activities of NGOs remained severely restricted by the established rules of procedure. The organisers of the Mexico City conference laid out strict rules of protocol: four accredited delegates were allowed to be in attendance at the plenary assembly; and one representative per country could serve on the drafting committee. Squeezed by these rules, the Canadian delegation was limited to 15, with only one representative from the NGO sector. Informally, sanctions were applied to groups that criticised not only their own but other governments by name. Distribution of the magazine of the Canadian Population Task Force was stopped at the Mexico City conference, for instance, because of an article condemning the "appallingly" high rate of female infanticide in China due to the PRC government's imposed family planning programme. What was deemed by the UN to be maintenance of the accepted rules of procedure was interpreted by the representatives of the Canadian Population Task Force as constituting "an unwarranted censorship of NGOs" (Marilyn Wilson, Coordinator of the Canadian Task Force, quoted in "Censors rile Canadian group", *Globe and Mail*, 9 August 1984).

Both domestically and internationally, there remained serious problems with respect to follow-up. While intense scrutiny was directed towards select social issues at the conferences, focus within Canada was dissipated at the post-conference stage through a combination of NGO and bureaucratic fragmentation, and the intrusion of situational factors such as the 1984 election and the subsequent change of government. The greatest dilemma at the international level was the lack of enforcement power. If Nairobi constituted a success at the declaratory level, through the adoption of universal forward-looking strategies to the year 2000 and the framing of implementation targets, many obstacles stood in the way of meeting these governmental and societal challenges. The integration of women's concerns in the policy formulation and decision making of governments, as well as the on-going work of international bodies, remained out of reach.

At the edge of transition

It has been suggested that some space had developed for a new stage of diplomatic transition prior to what have been considered the seismic events of the end of the bipolar era (Fukuyama, 1992: 25–38). If not yet fully released, many of the components that became the template of the post–Cold War era were already on tap. Concepts that blossomed in the 1990s – on the environment, population, and human rights – had germinated slowly from the late 1960s until the late 1980s. While the established institutional infrastructure was not entirely open and amenable to this process of transformation, neither did it remain entirely closed. Cracks in the status quo widened through necessity due to a greater appreciation of the need for new mechanisms to deal with unfamiliar problems. But the vagaries of domestic politics contributed a great deal to the process, especially in Canada, whose internal compass was undergoing a major resetting during this period. As attested by the extension of the UN world conferences, the result was a stimulating (albeit awkward and intermittent) pattern of incremental adaptation in which the ad hoc, "complex", and "messy" aspects mentioned above became more prominent.

States and governments remained central to undertaking this changing agenda. Nonetheless, the agenda would not (and could not) be met exclusively by states and governments. On the frontier of new tests of diplomacy with the advent of new roles for actors in a very different context, the evolution of the international conferences indicated the extent of the transition already in train by the mid-1980s towards a more catalytic relationship between state and non-state actors. While few were ready to talk of the emergence of a robust global system of global governance with the full participation of civil society before the end of the Cold War, the complexity of this interactive dynamic had become apparent. With the politics of protest, and the circulation of radical ideas, the distance between states and NGOs appeared to widen. However, with new signs of transparency and accountability, some of the boundaries were becoming less clearly demarcated.

Amidst all these currents the forces of transition remained uneven in their cause and consequence. Steady innovations in communication and technology were autonomous from the big bang of the end of the Cold War. Fears (or hopes) of the demise of sovereignty had predated the burst of enthusiasm over the extension of responsibilities beyond borders in the 1990s. The difference between the two eras was in the stakes involved in the tests of global governance and diplomacy. With the end of the Cold War security questions could no longer easily be posited as a comprehensive rationale for not moving forward on the type of issues central to the agenda of the UN conferences. A universalistic drive remained highly contested and deflected, to be sure, but it could not be stopped without negotiation. Issues that had to be addressed as problem-solving or crisis-averting in the 1960s to the 1980s could now be debated more critically, as the path to a very different ethical or moral construct. Nor could the state be defined as the only legitimate actor in world affairs.

There is a need, then, to look beyond this formative stage and see how the various tests embodied in the UN world conferences evolved further to incorporate these changes into the actual working of global affairs, helping to decide what issues and interests were given voice and standing in the move towards what some have termed "multiple, overlapping political processes at work at the present historical conjecture" (Held et al., 1999: 85).

3

Tests of partnership: between statecraft and society-craft

Tracking the trajectory of diplomacy in the post–Cold War period conflates inevitably into sensitive tests about the nature of the diplomatic machinery surrounding the UN world conferences. Who has control over who may participate? What are the mechanisms for deciding an agenda, choosing a site, and setting the fundamental rules of the game? Such tests are at the heart of the entire debate about authority and legitimacy in international relations.

The fundamental test of the new diplomacy (and diplomats) from a classical realist position rests on how effectively it can carry out its traditional interstate function in the context of new patterns of state–societal interaction. Any tilt towards a diplomacy that places a high premium on "social work" is disputed and denigrated by traditionalists (Mandelbaum, 1996).[16] To them, the mainstay of traditional diplomacy or statecraft remains bilateralism, as exercised through techniques such as crisis and coercive diplomacy and the practice of resident diplomacy. They emphasise the retention of order (as opposed to social justice and equity) in the international system. The attraction of the new, whether on the agenda, in the forums, or in the parameters for negotiation, is subordinated to the security of the status quo.

To members of the "world society" and "international civil society" schools of thought, such orthodoxy distorts the complexities of world politics. At the very least, these thinkers reject the rigid state-centred framework for not being inclusive enough on the basis of a need for a less static and enclosed approach. Thomas Princen, a representative of scholars who urge a more flexible (and putatively accurate) take on diplomacy, raises the bar for diplomatic behaviour: "Although the work of foreign ministries remains essential for conducting the affairs of state, a much more complex picture of diplomacy emerges when one considers the expansion and complexity of issues, global communications, and the involvement of non-state and intergovernmental organizations" (Princen, 1994: 31).[17]

Taken at its most extreme, this argument is that the state is in a condition of terminal decline – or to use Jan Aart Scholte's dismissive phrase, "past history" (Scholte, 1997: 21). Held back by their inability to adequately respond to the forces of globalisation and transnationalisation, governments are cast into a limbo of irrelevance. Moreover, on normative grounds, this erosion of diplomacy (defined as the activities of professional representatives of the state rather than as the settlement of international disputes by negotiation) is held to be a good thing. In this critical view, diplomacy is considered to be dysfunctional; it holds back the more benign non-state forces underpinning world society – with a move from statecraft to society-craft – from generating a more peaceful environment than that which has characterised the centuries dominated by the Westphalian international system (for a fuller discussion of these debates, see Cooper and Hocking, 2000).

The UN world conferences offer an impressive (and intriguing) canvas for taking up the challenge of this test. Through the most robust interpretations, the UN conferences constitute a shake-up not only in what was discussed in international negotiations, but in the locus of this activity, how it was done, and by whom. By any quantitative and qualitative standard, the UN conferences signify a fundamental change in "actorness" as expressed through the heightened participation of civil society generally and NGOs more specifically. Chronologically, a massive leap can be traced from the important – albeit still quite restricted – presence of NGOs in the 1960s and 1970s to the high-water mark of participation at the Rio conference and beyond. Substantively, this trend opened up the possibility of a fuller and deeper integration of the "two worlds" among state and societal forces (Rosenau, 1990). Whereas the trend in the 1960s and 1970s had been towards parallel and separate activity, the UN conferences highlighted in this book took the process of co-existence, or even partnership, between these manifestations of statecraft and society-craft, to a much higher level.

Beyond the "two-worlds" of statecraft and society-craft?

A fuller exploration of the pattern of relationship between government and non-governmental organisations (NGOs) in the evolution of diplomacy reveals a consensus that NGOs have become more closely entangled in the practice of diplomacy. Differences in opinion among academics and practitioners have centred, however, on how the forces behind this process of interaction – and the attendant consequences – should be interpreted. As suggested earlier by the theme of transition, the end of the Cold War severely reduced, if it did not end completely, the disciplines imposed by the system of bipolarity. Yet, while this break from the Cold War stand-off was the crucial catalyst in opening up this "unique and quite extraordinary brew" (Hall, 1996: 169), a host of other factors also come into play as both triggers and receptacles for change in the relationship between governments and NGOs.

At the structural level, the emerging pattern of interaction within the dynamics of diplomacy can be looked at through the lens of the globalisation debate generally and, more specifically, as a challenge of communication, technology, and information sharing. A need became apparent not only to re-evaluate the means of addressing issues but to rebalance the roles of a wide range of players – whether traditionally associated with diplomacy or not. At the situational level, the loosening grip of orthodox statecraft to accommodate a mix of statecraft and society-craft was reinforced by the need for governments to negotiate with their domestic publics in different ways. While the thesis of the "hollowing out" of state capacity should not be over-drawn (Weiss, 1998), governments do face a sustained dilemma concerning both legitimacy and resources. This dilemma, manifested in a severe commitment/capability gap, is particularly acute in the Canadian case.

The perceived meaning behind these changes in the pattern of relationship between governments and NGOs has become highly contested. For those adhering to state-centred assumptions, the role of NGOs in diplomatic practice remains subordinated to the activities of national governments and their agents among the ranks of professional diplomats. Some choose to ignore the phenomenon altogether. Others, while acknowledging with Hedley Bull that "other entities" besides nation states have long possessed "standing in world politics" (Bull, 1977: 162), still downplay their influence. NGOs may be "in" the diplomatic game, with a heightened profile in terms of agenda setting, but this change has not elevated them to a status equal to states and the pattern of intergovernmental relations. As Denis Stairs makes this argument with some eloquence, the impetus towards change associated with NGOs should not override a sense of continuity: "These reflections lead to an alternative, if somewhat old-fashioned, interpretation of what the NGO phenomenon really represents – an interpretation that accords rather better than the radical view with the recent behaviour of the Canadian foreign policy community, among a handful of others. For when all is said and done, the

NGOs ultimately amount to public service interest groups. The NGOs do what interest groups have always done, and governments respond to them accordingly" (Stairs, 1998: 42).

Operating on the basis that state and societal actors continue to live in separate – and unequal – worlds, adherents to this point of view make the argument that little has changed in world politics. NGO representatives may have extended their ability to pressure or even advise state officials, but a boundary still exists between these functions and NGOs' participation in decision-making processes. Domestically, these thinkers accord no equality between the roles of state and societal actors. The presence of NGOs, whether in various mechanisms for consultation or as part of Canadian or other delegations, is not a right but a privilege that can be granted or taken away by government. Internationally, the attribution to NGOs of a legal personality is minimised. While NGOs may have gained greater access to world conferences, they say, any move to elevate their position in the process – beyond the ability to speak, propose, and respond – is inappropriate. Presence does not translate into the power to decide. As Stairs rests his case: NGOs may "pressure the state system to act" but they cannot "actually take its place" (Stairs, 1998: 40).

To those who reject these state-centred assumptions, on the other hand, this perspective distorts the complexities and the contours of world politics. In its most ambitious expression, the ascendancy of societal actors is seen not only as inevitable but as desirable. Far from disguising their desire for a diplomatic disappearance act, these critics have long considered the "deliquescence" or "melting into nothingness" of state diplomacy as a moral imperative due to what were considered the ethical and operational shortcomings of diplomats (ranging from a lack of moral sensitivity to crass opportunism) (Eayrs, 1971: 69). Indeed, Stairs has characterised this glee as more representative of normative judgement than detailed analysis: "The system is changing, thank Heaven! Or, the system is changing, we hope!" (Stairs, 1998: 40).

At the very least, the attitude of this camp is to dismiss the ingrained state-centred framework for not being sufficiently inclusive. They identify a need for a more flexible, multi-dimensional approach that coincides with the flatter, seamless, asymmetrical, network-oriented, and unbounded conditions of the post–Cold War era. As Thomas Princen has contended, there is a sound logic as well as an ethical concern for redefining diplomacy away from a purely state-centric perspective to a shape that reflects the complexity of new components of multilateral global governance: "Diplomacy is not just the traditional conduct of the affairs of states, but a range of relationships conducted by states and non-state actors that involve negotiations and institution building" (Princen, 1994: 42; see also Wapner, 1995).

Raising the question of partnership allows the discussion of the nexus of statecraft and society-craft to move beyond the constrictions of this either/or dichotomy. At a declaratory level it takes seriously the call for such forms of partnership within the UN system. In the words of the current secretary-general, Kofi Annan: "Non-governmental organisations are now seen as essential partners of the United Nations, not only in mobilising public opinion, but also in the process of deliberation and policy formulation and – even more important – in the execution of policies, in work on the ground" (UN Press Release, 1997).

At an operational level, the test of partnership between statecraft and society-craft takes seriously the complexity concerning "multilayered governance" and a "diffusion of political authority". This architecture does not necessarily signify a transformation towards a "post-statist" world, never mind a world state. Yet, says Martin Shaw, it challenges the traditional notion that the state is the "uncomplicated" centre of authority (Shaw, 2000: 95). In this emerging configuration, a holistic pre-eminence of the state is not taken for granted, but it is not assumed that NGOs or civil society are equal to states. What it allows are sites for diverse patterns, each with very different channels, methods, and layers for interaction. On many issues, state and societal actors will be alienated from each other. On other issues, however, the interaction will be ratcheted up from lobbying to working together in a fashion that belies the "two worlds" image. Communication, negotiation, cooperation in drafting and other matters – and delegation on these issues – will form the crux of this new partnership (for one take of this image, see Morss, 1991).

It needs to be reiterated that this developing pattern of partnership is far from consistent or comprehensive, on the contrary, it is highly ad hoc, awkward, differentiated, and case-specific. What is clear, though, is that if UN world conferences do indeed provide a rich laboratory as a site of "multi-layered governance", one of the crucial tests will be in the appearance of an integration (albeit not a complete merger) of statecraft and society-craft.

Tests of partnership at the Rio and Vienna conferences

The Stockholm and the Rio conferences are commonly viewed as twin landmarks in the evolution of international environmental policy. The United Nations Conference on the Human Environment of 1972 in Stockholm is associated with the first generation of international activities in the 1960s and 1970s, while the United Nations Conference on Environment and Development of 1992 (UNCED) symbolises the ascendancy of environmental issues on the global agenda in the 1980s and

1990s. In style and substance, there is a strong sense of progression between the two events. Both attracted considerable attention from the public and the media and acted as impressive stimuli for thought and action. The presence of Maurice Strong as secretary-general of both conferences added to this continuity. At the same time, however, important differences in the decision-making processes of the two conferences become apparent when they are examined through a traditional statist prism. While the only prominent heads of government at Stockholm were Olof Palme from the host country and Indira Gandhi, the Prime Minister of India, 105 heads of state or government attended the Earth Summit in Rio. The end of the Cold War reinforced this new direction. With the Soviet bloc boycotting the 1972 conference because of the exclusion of East Germany, the scale of representation at Stockholm had been substantially reduced. The spectrum of countries in Rio was appreciably broader, with over 150 countries participating.

As significant as this change in representation was, the fundamental difference between the negotiations at Stockholm and at Rio was a change in the nature of participation of non-governmental actors. At a conference-wide level, this shift was highlighted by the sheer number of activists from NGOs in attendance: over 1,200 environmental organisations were accredited observers to the final meetings of the Preparatory Committee (Prep Com) of UNCED in contrast to the approximately 250 groups in attendance at Stockholm. More significantly, the roles played by the NGOs became more diverse. In the "parallel" conference at Stockholm in 1972, many NGOs were no more than critical observers at the margins of the conference. In Rio's parallel conference, the Global Forum, approximately 20,000 environmentalists participated, and representatives from a large number of NGOs also took part in the official proceedings. Even though the decision was made only after considerable internal wrangling by the national delegations, an NGO "inside" presence was agreed to by the Preparatory Committee for the Rio conference and endorsed by the General Assembly. Moreover, this participation rose well above the role of passive observers with little or no status. NGOs were allowed to intervene in the plenary and main committees, taking into account only time considerations; and their representatives could make oral presentations to the drafting committee in its formal sessions and in further meetings as necessary.

At the national level, the Canadian experience serves as a typical, yet rather unique, test for the changing dynamic between statecraft and society-craft. The main feature of this test was the nature of partnership forged between state officials and NGO representatives. To facilitate and coordinate the role of the NGOs in the preparations for the Rio conference, the Canadian Participatory Committee for UNCED (CPCU) was formed in the autumn of 1990. This structure allowed an institutionalised form of access for participating NGOs throughout the two-year life of the Rio conference. Internally, this partnership featured a high integration of key functional activities, such as the writing of the national report. At the first Prep Com, Canada not only had more NGOs on its delegation than any other country but was the country that opened up the process by including a statement by an NGO in its plenary statement. And with each successive Prep Com, this format was consolidated. Eventually, the official Canadian delegation at Rio included five representatives from NGOs covered by the CPCU umbrella (see, for example, Bernstein and McGraw, 1992: 7; for some more detail, see Cooper and Fritz, 1992).

The inclusion of NGOs in the policy-making process helped to extend the parameters of Canadian diplomacy at Rio, particularly in the symbolic arena. Prompted by the work of the NGOs in the CPCU, Canadian diplomacy paid special attention to the multitude of legal and institutional questions involved in the drafting of the Earth Charter (later renamed the Rio Declaration) as a non-binding declaration of principles. The comprehensive action plan of the NGOs was to make a concerted push (in dialogue with their constituent communities) to strengthen the Canadian commitment to Agenda 21 as a "visionary document". In this way these activist societal groups succeeded in keeping highly sensitive issues such as gender concerns and the rights of Indigenous peoples visible on the negotiating agenda. Even opposition members of parliament, who had previously been almost entirely left out of the preparatory process, conceded that NGOs "actually may have changed the minds of the government delegation" (Hunter, 1992: 10339).

The NGOs also supplemented Canadian technical and entrepreneurial diplomacy at the Rio conference in a variety of ways. To some extent, the NGOs bolstered the technical skills of the Canadian delegation. Throughout the UNCED negotiations the groups within the CPCU provided alternative sources of information and, more tangibly, expertise in the language of texts. As the national coordinator of the CPCU told the Parliament Standing Committee on the Environment in May, 1992: "I think the point has been made over and over again to NGOs, both formally and informally, that there are various lacunae, various gaps, within the technical dialogue, and it is felt that the technical expertise within the NGO community can be extremely productive" (Canada, House of Commons, Standing Committee on the Environment, 1992: 74:71).

Entrepreneurially as well, then, Canadian diplomacy could be reconfigured through this form of NGO participation in negotiations. Most significantly, the exercise of coalition building moved beyond being an intergovernmental process to a being dynamic encompassing state and non-state actors. In the Canadian push for a convention on high sea fishing, for example, the development of more extensive cooperation between Canada and a group of like-minded countries including New Zealand and Australia (through the so-called CANZ group) was aided by links forged between Canadian NGOs and NGOs in those countries. The New York Declaration on High Seas Overfishing (1992), which was released in the run-up to the actual Rio conference, was written by a combination of state officials and NGOs.

The state–NGO partnerships at Rio were characterised by their diffuseness, in terms of issue set and actors involved. Their extensive agenda not only covered the Earth Charter and the fisheries but also global warming, the depletion of the ozone layer, and forestry. Although far from comprehensive, the range of NGO activists brought into the nexus was quite broad. Elizabeth May represented the Canadian Environmental Network (CEN) at the first Prep Com, Mark Wareing from the Western Canadian Wilderness Committee attended Prep Com II, and Probe International's Janine Ferretti, whose special interest was climate change and toxic and hazardous wastes, participated in Prep Com III.

The relationship between statecraft and society-craft at the Vienna Human Rights Conference, by contrast, featured a more discrete style (on the wider framework and possibilities, see Steiner, 1991; see also NGO-Newsletter, 1994). The organisational links forged to allow a working relationship were less ambitious than at Rio. Instead of being developed in the context of a CPCU equivalent, the relationship was built through the Human Rights Centre at the University of Ottawa. In contrast to the formalised procedures of the Rio process, therefore, the nexus at Vienna had a more ad hoc and disjointed quality. At the same time, the network on international human rights operating through the University of Ottawa had a privileged role, as the Canadian delegation included Jan Bauer, the network coordinator. That being said, however, in the components of the human rights dossier in which the constructive relationship had taken hold, the bonds appear to have surpassed the level of engagement found in the Rio model. This bonding process was especially noticeable in the relationship between women's groups and a cohort of Canadian state officials. In this domain, more than any other, the term "symbiotic", as suggested by Brian Hocking in his portrayal of "catalytic" diplomacy, is justified (Hocking, 1995; Pal, 1995). Again, to showcase this nexus is not to minimise the tensions that continued to emerge in a number of other areas of public policy (including some controversial issues that spilled over into the Vienna negotiations). Nonetheless, at the core of the women's rights dossier, it was the pull towards firmer integration that stood out[18] (for one personal commentary on the good working relationship between state officials and NGOs, see Rosemary Brown, "Canada speaks out", *Vancouver Sun*, 19 February 1992).

This partnership rested in good part on the pillar of process. As at Rio, the Canadian government strongly supported diplomatic initiatives to open up the rules of procedure to maximum NGO participation. To reinforce this move towards transparency, NGOs were given frequent and flexible access through a series of round table meetings, seminars, and workshops leading up to the Vienna conference. At the conference itself, the Canadian delegation made considerable effort to engage the NGO community. For instance, Canadian state officials held one "set-piece" meeting with Canadian NGOs in which delegates and NGOs exchanged views on developments to date and work to come. As a confidence-building measure, the Canadian delegation assured the NGOs of their willingness to engage in ongoing close consultations during the conference. At the transnational level, Canadian officials took the stand throughout the proceedings that NGOs with conference status should have the same right to speak during the Vienna negotiations as at the UN Commission on Human Rights (CHR) and other thematic UN conferences. In principle, they championed giving greater access to NGOs both at the plenary sessions and on the key drafting committees. Canadian officials promoted a series of consultations between NGOs and like-minded countries that shared Canada's views on procedure and access; they also worked to secure and broaden NGO participation from the North and the South throughout the Prep Com process.

Substantively, there was a symbiosis between Canadian state officials and NGO representatives in terms of issue definition. This aspect of catalytic diplomacy was most pronounced on the need to mainstream women's rights into the human rights agenda. However, a similar dynamic appeared on a number of more specific topics. For one thing, there was a coincidence of interest on the need to help women who had been victims of systematic sexual assault in the former Yugoslavia; both Canadian state officials and representatives of NGOs vigorously condemned violence against women in Bosnia as a violation of international human law. Although rape was not explicitly included in the "grave breach" provisions of the Geneva convention, both state and society representatives considered acts of sexual violence to fall within the definition of "inhumane treatment" and "general suffering", or acts causing serious injury to body or health. Both Canadian state officials and NGO representatives pushed for more robust mechanisms for investigating and bringing to trial the perpetrators of such acts. They also joined forces to institute within the UN mechanisms the role of a special rapporteur on violence against women with a comprehensive investigative and reporting mandate, an international criminal court for women, and the use of gender-specific data (for an excellent analysis, see Pal, 1994).

The motivations behind the partnership

These snapshots together provide a valuable overview of the ways in which the integration of statecraft and society-craft has unfolded. To explore the complexity of this pattern of interaction more thoroughly, however, we must delve more deeply into the matter. One avenue of entry is through the motivational dimension. The "different worlds" perspective has traditionally accentuated the solid reasons that keep state and NGO actors apart. Indeed, as will be discussed below, many of these differences continue to be highly pertinent. Still, they should not overshadow the fact that there are many important reasons why the state and NGOs have moved closer together in the application of diplomacy.

One key reason for this changing relationship has to do with legitimacy. A fundamental tenet of this concept from the point of view of NGOs is that representatives of civil society have a right to be engaged in a "real partnership" with state officials. This right, they claim, goes hand in hand with the rebalancing of the perceptions of credibility. Canadian NGOs credit themselves (and have been given considerable credit by the state) for being the authentic voices of an active citizenry in Canada and for speaking out on behalf of numerous problems – and victims – in specific areas and issues around the world. This perception is far from new. The push towards increased participation by NGOs in the earlier social conferences was generated at least in part by the credibility question. Could state officials truly represent Canada at these forums without at least some consultation with NGOs? As the individual from the Canadian Institute of International Affairs (CIIA) who was delegated the task of facilitating this consultation process for the Bucharest population conference concluded: "The federal government has apparently come under pressure from several quarters to take a sounding of public opinion as part of its preparations for the world population conference" (Robert W. Reford, "Population", letter to the *Globe and Mail*, 13 May 1974). By the standard of the post–Cold War era, nonetheless, this earlier form of "partnership" was merely a token or cosmetic exercise without substance or serious intent.

The leap in credibility that NGOs began to enjoy from the late 1980s on reflected how much more thoroughly ingrained the notion of civil society had become. Although NGOs had existed within the UN constellation from the time of the San Francisco conference of 1945, few struggled to gain anything close to an equal status with states during the Cold War years. While NGOs challenged the monopoly of the state in a more assertive manner from the late 1960s on, the overall impression is that this early mobilisation did not activate an immediate shift in status. Instead, many critics interpreted the increased intensity in the activities of the NGOs as consolidating the "separate worlds" imagery; NGOs continued to operate (and were seen to do so) on the outside looking in at state behaviour with great disapproval. This image is certainly evident in Canada's case. Writing in 1983, Cranford Pratt asserted that there had recently emerged in Canada a substantial number of internationally minded public-interest groups that were "in serious opposition to many components of the present consensus which underlies Canadian foreign policy" (Pratt, 1983–1984: 118). Indeed, from this critical perspective, these groups derived credibility explicitly because of their exclusion from the decision-making process. Expressing ethical concerns on issues in areas such as "disarmament, human rights, international equity, and solidarity with oppressed peoples" (Pratt, 1983–1984: 118), these groups were labelled (with some pride) as part of a "counter-consensus".

Yet, while tensions between state and NGOs persisted, several factors were coalescing to counteract this "two worlds" approach. In part, the softening of this dualistic mindset was a consequence of the positive media and public response given to emergent expressions of state–NGO partnerships on a selective basis. The best illustration of such a positive response was felt during the Nairobi conference; both state officials and NGO representatives were bathed in a warm glow, and NGO representatives were seen to have enhanced their right to be included in specialised decision making (see, for example, Lynda Hurst, "Putting sisterhood on the map", *Toronto Star*, 27 July 1985; Michelle Landsberg, "Canada works stubbornly for international women's rights", *Toronto Star*, 26 April 1996). Furthermore, there were also signs that many NGOs were willing to test their credibility through organisational adaptation designed to enhance cooperation with the state rather than resistance. The degree of adjustment varied from issue to issue, but a generalised movement towards greater partnership can be located. Even before the UNCED negotiations, individuals with close ties to the environmental movement in Canada had been appointed to a number of advisory positions and NGO representatives were given elevated status on boards and commissions. Together with business representatives, academics, and scientists, the CEN, a coalition of environmental groups, was given a place on the National Task Force on the Environment and the Economy set up in preparation for the major debate at the United Nations on the report of the World Commission on Environment and Development in October 1987. Similarly, a significant feature in the history of the state–NGO nexus in the decade prior to the Vienna conference had been the formation of the Norwegian Institute of Human Rights (NIHR). The origins of this body can be traced back to 1979, when the head of the delegation to the United Nations Commission on Human

Rights (UNCHR) started consultations with human rights NGOs. By September 1992 this network had progressed to the point where it held consultations of its own on new models of effective relations between NGOs and the state, entitled "Transforming the Model" (Network on International Human Rights, 1992).

The gradual rebalancing of legitimacy in the connection between statecraft and society-craft cannot be calibrated solely on the basis of the activities of NGOs; the weakening credibility of the state needs to be factored in as well. From an external perspective, this shift had a great deal to do with the impact of transnationalism. Dealing with issues that were often interpreted as "cascading catastrophes" for which national boundaries had little or no meaning allowed NGOs to gain a credibility unavailable to national states. In Matthias Finger's words: "NGOs are more representative than are national governments [and therefore] draw their legitimation from citizens who no longer refer to national boundaries" (Finger, 1994: 34-35).

On the domestic front, the erosion of legitimacy for the state was associated with demands for change in the rules of the political game. Canadian NGOs gained momentum from a wave of public support for greater openness and transparency in decision making. But this decline in authority was also apparent on specific questions relating to who and what interests gained advantage through this process. To give just one example, NGOs pressed for greater transparency in the budgetary process.

Canadian circumstances at this time also contributed to the impact of this high degree of sensitivity. For one thing, the 1982 Charter of Rights and Freedoms had created a rights-based psychology. For another thing, the bitter controversies over Meech Lake and the Charlottetown referendum debates on the constitution had left in their wake demands for a more open and inclusive political process. At the very least, governments were induced to recognise the necessity of negotiating and bargaining with their publics more directly and comprehensively. As Denis Stairs reminds us, the breakdown of the old ways of doing things on foreign policy went hand in hand with a "populist array of expectations with regard to the conduct of government more generally. Such pressure doubtless came in part from changes in the Canadian political culture, encouraged among other things by the entrenchment of a Charter of Rights in the written portion of Canada's eclectically composed constitution. It may also have been aggravated by a growing public distrust of conventional political processes at a time of economic and constitutional malaise" (Stairs, 1998: 37).

Internal and external factors worked in combination to buttress each other. Public disenchantment with lack of transparency in institutional structures was not confined to Canada. On the contrary, in the 1980s the legitimacy crisis appeared to be a worldwide phenomenon (for one of the earliest expressions of this theme, see Crozier, Huntington, and Watanuki, 1973). And the high degree of sensitivity at the international level about deals made behind closed doors with little or no public debate helped galvanise the activities of NGOs determined to alter rules at the domestic level. As Alan Cairns points out: "The very identities of citizens, and the values they brought to their role in constitutional politics, were shaped by the international factors of which, especially in the case of group leaders, they were fully aware" (Cairns, 1992: 31).

Having built up the notion of an ascendant civil society and a weakened state, the flip side of the legitimisation question should not be ignored. On questions of principle, the notion that NGOs held a legitimacy unavailable to states remained contested. Indeed this claim provoked a strong backlash, with the NGOs' own defects in terms of accountability and representation being scrutinised in much greater detail (for good accounts of the NGOs strengths and weakness, see Edwards and Hulme, 1996 and Gordenker and Weiss, 1997). Some critics asked simply: "Who elected the NGOs?". Another cluster, along with Stairs, asked whether NGOs were not merely traditional "special interest" groups in a new guise (Stairs, 1998).

On practical grounds, NGOs were required to recognise (albeit grudgingly) that the state still possessed sources of legitimacy that were vital to their own agendas. Whatever progress the NGOs made in penetrating the UN system, the system itself continued to operate on an intergovernmental basis. As made quite clear in the case of the Rio and Vienna conferences, the access accorded to NGOs was still contingent on the willingness of states such as Canada not only to accord them that right nationally but to invest diplomatic capital to win this right for international negotiations. Success in this endeavour could not be taken for granted. True, the campaign to maximise NGO access in the Rio negotiations was abetted by Maurice Strong's enthusiasm for this project. But even with this wellspring of institutional support, NGOs' claim that they had a right to access at the conference was strongly resisted by a blocking coalition of states. In Vienna, without an ally with the mindset or reputational credibility of Strong, the struggle for NGO access was much tougher. The rules of procedure with respect to access to the Vienna negotiations were far more narrowly defined by Ibrahima Fall, director of the Centre for Human Rights and convenor of the conference. The participation of NGOs was severely restricted in the regional Prep Coms in the Americas. While many Canadian human rights NGOs were members of the Economic Commission for Latin America and the Caribbean (ECLAC) – and thereby qualified as being "active in the region" – they were denied access because they did not have headquarters in the region.

As such, they had to either join an umbrella organisation or work through another NGO that met this requirement. Similar obstacles existed at the Vienna conference itself. Although most international Canadian NGOs had indirect access through their parent bodies, only those with consultative status through ECOSOC (United Nations Economic and Social Council) were able to participate directly.

A second major reason for the change in the dynamic between statecraft and society-craft arises out of questions related to the possession of knowledge. The image of the state losing legitimacy goes hand in hand with an intellectual and psychological deficit: an inability to deploy skills, such as the evaluation and nurture of ideas, information gathering, and communication, that are needed to deal with a changing agenda. This erosion in capability largely reflects the new hierarchy among issues. Whereas during the Cold War, economic and social issues had been subordinated to the security agenda, in the post–Cold War era, the perception of threat had become far more diffuse. The new problem of issue-definition dictated a huge learning curve for government. As Jean Charest, the Canadian environmental minister during the Rio conference, stated: "No tanks or missiles can defend against the loss of security caused by a degraded environment" (quoted in "Rich–poor gap threatens security, Charest", *Globe and Mail*, 12 June 1992). The changed scenario linked the problem to a more sustained loss of confidence on the part of the state. The knowledge deficiencies of the state contrasted sharply with the putative expertise of NGOs in these areas, exhibited by their ability "to breed new ideas; advocate, protest, and mobilize public support; [and] do legal, scientific, technical, and policy analysis" (Mathews, 1997: 55).

There is much to back up this claim of a loss of confidence on the part of the state. The notion that societal as well as state interests had a stake in decision making became intertwined with enhanced forms of mobilisation. As the definition of security broadened, so did the premise that civil society had not only had the right but the duty to be involved in redefining and implementing the policy agenda on a continuing and significant basis. Galvanised by what they considered to be the neglect or the conscious destruction of the natural environment, NGOs carved out a space for themselves to act locally and to think (and campaign) globally. So did an array of human rights activists. As one prominent Canadian legalist proclaimed in the midst of the struggle to mainstream women's rights issues at Vienna: "Where human rights were once considered matters of purely domestic concern narrowly construed, global forces now mandate that they take on broader international dimensions, transcend borders, and command ever widening participation in their definition and implementation" (Mahoney, 1992: 556).

Fundamentally, of course, it was the substance of the NGOs' message that was the key to their success in breaking through the barriers of decision making. But the style in which they got the message across also contributed a great deal. Indeed, with respect to information gathering and ideas, NGOs benefited from having become essential components of extensive and well-honed policy and support networks (see, for example, in the human rights area Sikkink, 1993: 418). In scope, their message addressed the "new" security debate engaged in defining the rights of individuals and groups rather than supporting an exclusive state-centred focus. Their mobilisation of "on the ground" monitoring and witnessing techniques boosted their credibility. Rather than discussing environmental and human rights abuses only in the somewhat detached atmosphere of the diplomatic conferences, civil society activists brought to the table a wealth of case-specific anecdotal evidence. In terms of intensity, NGOs were able to deploy a sophisticated repertoire of tactics. As shown in the human rights case, traditional tactics such as petition gathering (with 65,000 signatures) were complemented by the flexible and agile use of new information technology. In Jessica Mathews' words: "Technology is fundamental to NGOs' new clout. In lowering the costs of communications, consultation, and coordination, [information technology favours] decentralized networks [such as NGOs]. Governments, on the other hand, are quintessential hierarchies, wedded to an organizational form incompatible with all that the new technologies make possible" (Mathews, 1997: 52, 54).

Notwithstanding the force of this set of arguments, the notion of a wide gap between the knowledge capabilities possessed by government and NGOs should not be taken beyond credible limits. As demonstrated most vividly (and controversially) by the Conservatives' push into the arena of peace-building and humane intervention – and the Liberals' warm embrace of a broadened concept of "human security" – Canadian governments are not necessarily hamstrung in the framework of "old thinking". On the contrary, they may be criticised for moving too quickly into new mindsets. More routinely, the application of what may be termed "just in time" diplomacy has become a fixture in the toolkit of official diplomacy. While rapid technological change within the electronic mass media unquestionably presents challenges for the Canadian state, it also provides opportunities for access and presence to a greater array of domestic and foreign audiences. Similarly, the state is presented with different (and creative) ways to build ideas and policy networks. Whatever its merits, this interactive approach suggests tactics based on an impulse to cooperate rather than to compete head-on with NGOs. Although far from being uncontested in the Canadian case, the suggestion, for example, that the

Canadian state possesses an abundant reservoir of "soft power" (linked to communication and information capabilities) makes this point in robust fashion.

A third factor behind a change in the relationship between statecraft and society-craft relates to the theme of resources. It has become commonplace to accept the notion of a decisive decline in the state's resources in the 1980s and 1990s. This trend was seen as a consequence of a financial contraction due to the overhang of budget imperatives and the shedding of responsibilities associated with decentralisation and offloading. In the context of diplomatic activity, this decline is taken to mean that state officials had to tackle all the complexities of the changing policy agenda with fewer personnel and/or monies. This trend was linked to the cuts in the foreign policy "envelope" suffered by the Department of External Affairs (DEA)/Department of Foreign Affairs and International Trade (DFAIT) since the early 1980s (Doern and Kirton, 1996: 256). Of the episodes under review for this study, signs of over-stretch are most visible in the Vienna negotiations. Although mandated to play a number of intricate roles, the cohort of state officials delegated to perform these tasks was much smaller than one might have expected. Headed up by Anne Park, the Canadian team during the negotiations consisted of three other foreign service officers, a junior officer to handle the Western European (WEOG, Western European and Others Group) dimension, and an official from the Justice department.

At the same time, the ability of a wide variety of NGOs to mobilise resources is taken to be a fundamental feature of the evolving international system. Operating on a transnational basis, groups such as Greenpeace, the World Wildlife Federation, and Amnesty International have built up their ability for task-related delivery as well as fund raising. The head of the UN Centre for Human Rights in Geneva is quoted, for example, as having exclaimed: "We have less money and less resources than Amnesty International, and we are the arm of the United Nations for Human Rights" (quoted in Clark, 1995: 517).

NGOs have in addition been able to fill gaps in areas of specialisation left by the erosion of state resources. A good example is found in the area of legal affairs. Simultaneously with the heavy cuts imposed on this area of state activity, several members of the legal community within civil society developed a higher profile. Experts with this background who played prominent roles during the Vienna negotiations included Kathleen Mahoney, Rebecca Cook, and Anne Bayefsky, all of whom enjoyed some access to the policy-making process through their inclusion in a round table meeting in early June 1993 and via other more informal routes (their individual contributions include Bayefsky, 1990, 1994; Cook,

1994; Mahoney and Mahoney, 1993; see also Linda Hossie, "Women want concerns raised at UN rights conference", *Globe and Mail*, 7 November 1992).

The state's loss of monopoly status, nonetheless, should not be equated in any way with the so-called hollowing out of the state. In some areas, the process of offloading may have had the effect of tightening rather than loosening the grip of state officials. A case in point is the area of task delegation in which a form of resource transfer takes place, which allows the state to have a grip on the purse-strings. In other cases, the more profound shift in governance has come through not a redistribution of tasks via transfer of responsibilities from states to civil society/NGOs but through an assumption of authority in cases where a vacuum in responsibility has been created. As Susan Strange phrased it, many of the dramatic changes in functional responsibility have come about not in cases involving transference of authority "to other actors – or levels" but in cases where responsibilities "are not being performed at all" (Strange, 1996b: 14).

Equally, the image of NGOs as increasingly influential actors should not hide the reality of their limits. The financial condition of the Canadian constellation of human rights NGOs is far from impressive. On the contrary, as Leslie Pal has laid out in a number of publications on the members of the Canadian Network on International Human Rights: "The financial situation for this segment of the NGO foreign-policy community was found to be, if anything, more precarious than the ODA [Official Development Assistance] segment" (Cooper and Pal, 1996: 222–223). To reinforce this point, it must be mentioned that a variety of NGOs have also suffered cutbacks and a loss of staff over the last decade.

Uneven contours of partnership

The respective needs of both state and non-state actors demand that they communicate, share information, and negotiate with increasing frequency on a growing list of issues. The contours of this nexus, however, remain uneven. There is no single script that fits all cases (see, for example, Higgott, 2001: 127–157) even when interaction takes place in similar contexts; that is, in cases when issues are pursued through the vehicle of UN social contexts by an analogous category of actors. The interface found in the case of the Rio UNCED and the Vienna Human Rights Conference creates very different narratives, which highlight the breadth and diversity of the emergent state–NGO partnership.

One means of classifying these relationships is to look at the nature of the state apparatus in greater depth. Teasing out the nuance of this machinery allows us to cut quickly into some of the operational realities of the case studies under review. The organisational feature that did the most to shape the nexus in the environmental arena was the fragmented condition of the Canadian state. From the time of the Stockholm conference, this condition had been affected by a high level of policy diffuseness and bureaucratic competition. The evolving relationship between the foreign ministry and the newly created Department of the Environment (1971) was particularly important here. The Stockholm conference offered the department an ideal opportunity to polish its reputation. Indeed, Jack Davis, the then minister of the environment, took a number of high-profile initiatives at the conference, including the proposal that the International Joint Commission (which the United States and Canada used to settle transboundary problems) be adopted as a model for dealing with environmental disputes at the global level.

To the old Department of External Affairs (DEA), environmental issues offered a test of its ability to adapt to changing needs and skill-sets and manage a more technically oriented agenda. Another test was how well it could adjust its coordination role within a changing bureaucratic structure. The key to meeting this test was the DEA's ability to move from a "lead" role patterned on past habits (the need to speak with a single voice to pursue a national interest) to one based on an instrumentality (the foreign ministry's ability to act as a valuable coordinator-manager) (on this theme, see Hocking, 1995).

The right to manage change in the environmental area continued to be contested up to and during the time of the Rio conference. As the foreign ministry moved to adjust to this type of agenda, it managed to meet some of these tests. From the time of the Law of the Sea on, the mark of success at the technical level meant according greater standing and responsibility to specialists, most notably foreign service officers in its legal division. But it also meant retooling its capacity to conduct intricate negotiations traditionally featured most prominently in the "high" security domain, into areas traditionally cast as "low" issues. A good indication of this success was the work of John Bell, who, as special advisor to the Secretary of State for External Affairs, chaired one of the most demanding committees through the UNCED process.

Passing the coordinator-manager test was much harder. In tactical terms, individual foreign ministry personnel made progress in building a solid relationship with the NGO community. This was true of Bell, who remained a central figure in the Canadian coordination mechanism. It was also true of Michael Small, who with Adrian de Hoog, ran a UNCED task force out of the foreign ministry. In the aftermath of the Rio conferences, several NGO representatives complimented these foreign ministry officials for the way they had provided opportunities to give input into specific issues being addressed by the department.

Strategically, however, the foreign ministry fell far short of its aim to be the central change agent. Notwithstanding the presence in UNCED mechanisms of foreign ministry personnel who had the ability to identify targets clearly, a number of serious constraints inhibited the foreign ministry from building a constructive and coherent nexus with the environmental community. If, as Stairs suggests, an expanded and strengthened client base provides a useful tool in administrative "turf" conflicts (Stairs, 1977–1978), the Department of the Environment retained a number of structural advantages which, despite all its efforts, the foreign ministry could not. In the bureaucratic campaign to "exploit the opinions of their respective constituencies as a source of leverage in the policy process", the Department of the Environment held a winning hand on the trust dimension. The Department of the Environment's record on recognition and access allowed it to avoid the charge of being "Johnny-green [NGO] lateiles" (Doern, 1992).

Environment Canada had earned kudos for its gradual if somewhat ad hoc incorporation of NGOs into the decision-making process prior to the UNCED process. Together with business representatives, academics, and scientists, the CEN was given representation on the National Taskforce on Environment and Economy in the preparations for the major debate at the United Nations on the report of the World Commission on Environment and Development (the Brundtland report) in October 1987 (World Commission on Environment and Development, 1987). And a close working relationship was forged between Environment Canada and the so-called Group of Eight cluster of environmental NGOs, which included the Canadian Arctic Resources Committee, the Canadian Nature Federation, the Canadian Parks and Wilderness Society, and the World Wildlife Fund.

This department–NGO partnership was consolidated through the UNCED negotiating process. At the bureaucratic level, the environmental CPCU worked out of the National Secretariat for UNCED at Environmental Canada, and the executive director of this "shop" was G.V. Buxton, who also served as the alternative head of the Canadian delegation. At the ministerial level, Jean Charest invited all the Canadian NGOs with official status – close to 1,000 – to the daily morning briefings of the Canadian delegation, which he chaired. Selected NGOs also had additional briefing sessions with Charest during the Rio conference. As Elizabeth May noted in her "Report on Participation", these meetings (albeit ad hoc) allowed close and ongoing contact: "Every morning I attended the delegation meeting, which was made open. These sessions provided an excellent opportunity for lobbying the Minister directly as well as the various government negotiators. Minister Charest also held a daily session with NGOs. These sessions were more intense than the morning delegation meetings, and attracted between six and a dozen NGOs" (May, 1992).

The human rights arena was also affected by this splintering dynamic (on this effect in comparative terms, see Cerny, 2000). Several bureaucratic elements within the state apparatus had a stake in this arena, among which were a cluster of actors on the women's human rights dossier. Unlike in the case of the environment, however, the foreign ministry was able to successfully hone its status as the coordinator-manager of the Vienna process. This position did not translate into absolute control, as the foreign ministry had to continually communicate and bargain on a range of issues. But, within this context of continuous interaction, the foreign ministry took on the role as lead actor on the human rights negotiations. While responsibility was shared with a number of other actors, including Status of Women Canada, Immigration, Justice, Indian Affairs and Northern Development, Multicultural Canada, and the Canadian International Development Agency (CIDA), DFAIT (Manfred von Nostitz, director general of International Organizations) was given the responsibility for chairing the Interdepartmental Planning Group for the Vienna conference.

To a large extent, winning this status was connected with the restructuring efforts embarked upon by the foreign ministry through the 1970s and 1980s. The department had strengthened its organisational competence on the human rights agenda in a number of ways. The clearest formal expression of this diversified focus was the creation of a section called Human Rights, Women's Equality and Social Affairs Division within the International Organizations Bureau. And greater salience of human rights was reflected externally by some changes in personnel management, most notably in the Canadian missions to the UN in New York and Geneva.

This organisational dimension was complemented by the department's application of its extensive repertoire of skills and reputation – both traditional and non-traditional. As in the environment case, the foreign ministry's ongoing source of comparative advantage was its ability to play (and to be seen to be playing) the diplomatic game at the international level. The foreign ministry was the classic insider in this game. One signal that the reputation of both Canada and the Canadian foreign service remained strong came with the selection of Anne Park as the chair of the WEOG in the lead-up to Vienna. From this position as coordinator of the Western group, Park was placed at the centre of the negotiations.

At the domestic level, the foreign ministry benefited considerably from the trust created at previous conferences in the domain of women's human rights. As noted in the previous chapter, this bonding exercise had been especially strong at the 1985 Nairobi Conference on Women and Development. Indeed, Nairobi reinforced the image of "femocrats" from different organisations working together – despite the potential for infighting. As at Stockholm, the foreign ministry faced a serious challenge from other bureaucratic actors, most notably Status of Women Canada. Maureen O'Neil, the coordinator of Status of Women Canada, served as the deputy leader of the Canadian delegation. What could have been a sensitive episode nonetheless turned out quite differently. In contrast with the image of intra-bureaucratic competition generated at the Stockholm conference, Nairobi became a model of bureaucratic harmony. The fact that Lindsay Niemann, Senior Adviser, International Relations, at Status of Women Canada, worked during the Nairobi process as Special Coordinator for the Nairobi Conference, External Affairs gives a good indication of how well the International Women's Equality Division in the foreign ministry and Status of Women Canada worked together.

Somewhat curiously, the most pronounced disagreement on the human rights dossier came between the foreign ministry and CIDA. This heated conflict cannot be separated from a wider struggle over status and domain. Until the mid- to late 1980s, CIDA had for the most part accepted a position subordinate to the foreign ministry. Since then, however, CIDA had tried to expand its decision-making capacity, not just in the development-aid dossier but on a wider spectrum of issues, including dossiers such as women and development. In doing so, CIDA raised its status and leverage. In the words of one respected observer of Canadian foreign policy: "Canada has a strong reputation for work on women's rights and development globally. Relative to other aid agencies, CIDA has taken an impressive stand on gender equality since the adoption in 1984 of a policy and implementation strategy for women and development" (Appel Molot, 1994: 39:36).

The foreign ministry appreciated the spill-over benefits from the promotion of this dossier with respect to its own organisational credibility. But it bridled at the degree of autonomy CIDA was forging for itself. This split in part reflected differences over policy issues, especially "conditionality", the insertion of human rights with the development agenda. These tensions were further complicated by the underlying divergence of views within the foreign ministry itself. Notwithstanding the integrative trend of the 1980s, the points of view of the foreign ministry officials still varied by department. The issue-specific interests of the International Organizations Bureau differed considerably from those of the geographic desks; and the Trade and Economic ("E") Policy Branch in turn had its own distinctive perspective and goals, based on the need to consider the commercial aspect of any activity in the human rights or social area.

Fundamentally, however, the disagreement was about turf. Fearing that CIDA was breaking completely free from its grip, the foreign ministry took the offensive in order to regain control. Any attempt to rein CIDA in on an issue-specific basis during the Vienna process, however, could only be made in an awkward and incomplete fashion. The foreign ministry, generally speaking, was not a department with programme delivery capabilities. CIDA, in contrast, had a mandate to distribute resources (Pratt, 1998). Until this relationship was rebalanced through a grab-back of the CIDA budget, therefore, CIDA could expand its own bureaucratic position by channelling funds to its own priorities and client-base. On issues such as the delegation of funds to selected human rights NGOs at Vienna, the foreign ministry could only complain about CIDA's lack of effective coordination and strategic direction.

In highlighting the cross-purposes of the Canadian state the degree of fragmentation found among NGOs as a conditioning factor for some movement towards the integration of statecraft and society-craft should not be overlooked. As one NGO expert cautions: "In focusing on NGOs as if they had a common role and common characteristics, we may conceal the failure of many to measure up to the ideal" (Pearce, 1993: 223). During the Rio process, the partnership dynamic did not incorporate the entire constellation of the NGO environmental community. Divisions that had long existed in the "green" movement were vividly demonstrated in the response of specific groups to the embrace of government generally and to the establishment of the CPCU more specifically. At one end of the continuum, Greenpeace and a number of other more direct-action oriented groups declined to participate in the CPCU process at all. Their resistant stance was due in a large part to the ideological and policy distance between the "dark" green element of the environmental community and the governance agenda of states. Interpreting Rio as a convenient gesture rather than a commitment, Greenpeace offered an alternative plan:

The challenge is nothing more nor less than to rescue the planet and its capacity to support human life; to seize this moment to set in motion the economic, political and technological transformation that the world plainly requires. However, UNCED seems set to fail to meet this challenge or seize this moment. In many areas the Earth Summit is clearly moving backwards from Stockholm. (Greenpeace International, 1992: 2)

Rejecting insider status, these critical voices found an outlet at Rio in two different ways. One was to direct an alternative message out through the alternative NGO conference – the Global Forum. The other, more controversially, was to mount ripples of guerrilla diplomacy focused at consciousness-raising (or disruption) of the mainstream conference.

Another impediment to unity among NGOs was the Mulroney government's push to make the integration of statecraft and society-craft as comprehensive as possible. Despite the environmental NGOs' higher standing in the negotiations, the definition of partnership was extended to other elements of civil society to include parallel representation in the Canadian delegation. The NGOs that joined the CPCU and took an active part in the process were therefore highly diverse in their structure and goals. On one side there were various components of the environmental movement, such as the Canadian Environmental Law Association, the Sierra Club, Pollution Probe, and Cultural Survival Canada. On the other side were various members of the environmental movement, such as the Canadian Council for International Cooperation (a coalition of 130 development NGOs in Canada), the United Nations Association in Canada, Indigenous organisations (most actively the Native Council of Canada and the Inuit Circumpolar Conference), youth groups (through the Canadian Youth Working Group on Environment and Development), and women's organisations (Women and Environmental Education and Development). This diversity of groups in itself reduced the opportunity for coherence. Adding to the severity of this problem was the presence of the business community in the Canadian delegation. At Prep Com III in Geneva, for example, representatives from the Council of Forest Industries of BC (Michael Apsey, president and CEO) and the Canadian Pulp and Paper Association (David Barron, vice-president, Production Services) were listed in the "NGO" category.

Suspicious of this extended embrace from government and business, several other environmental groups became disenchanted with the policy-making process. Their backtracking was most obvious in the behaviour of Friends of the Earth (FOE). Initially a member of the CPCU, the FOE left the umbrella group well before the actual Rio conference.[19] Even some of the NGO representatives who stayed in the process had had serious reservations about the Mulroney government's approach. While acknowledging the tangible advances made on specific issues such as biological diversity, NGOs were far less satisfied with the government's performance on the more ambitious items of the UNCED agenda. Some issues close to the NGOs' heart, such as consumption patterns, were left out entirely. On a wide spectrum of other issues, ranging from financial resources and developmental aid to preferential and concessional terms for technology transfer, few guarantees were made on targets and schedules, and the financial provision was weak (Bernstein, 1992).

Still, despite these general frustrations, the attitude of the NGOs that remained in the CPCU diverged markedly from the attitude of the resisters. If the determination of Greenpeace to stay removed from the entire process was strengthened, so was the impulse of the insider groups to accommodate. Indeed, individuals within those groups in the CPCU had come to believe that they could "best exert influence from within the system" (for a good journalistic piece on this theme, see Peter Gorrie, "Eco-summit losing lustre", *Toronto Star*, 25 June 1992; for further detail on the process, see Bernstein and McGraw, 1992). In doing so, they played down the attractions of grabbing the attention of the media and the general public, insisting instead on the need for greater professionalism if environmental groups were to have a meaningful impact on policy outcomes.[20]

The longer-term effect of this division was to open up a debate about tactics during Rio and about the strategic and political implications of an inside versus outsider approach. The insiders favoured instrumental advantage: gaining access to power centres. Notwithstanding the forces pushing them away from government, insiders saw both the pressures and the benefits of some degree of cooperation and even synergy from building a more constructive interface with government. Outsiders, conversely, saw the pitfalls of such an interface between statecraft and society-craft. They considered any approach based on the principle of accommodation with society-craft to be flawed in that it prioritised doing what was possible over what was right. In practice, any trade-off or concessions used in conducting negotiations challenged the bona fide pretensions of the accommodationists. From this perspective Stairs' point that "NGOs cannot make trade-offs" becomes a self-fulfilling proposition (Stairs, 1998: 41). Locked into such logic, any attempt to be flexible risked being labelled co-optation (see, for example, Marci McDonald, "NAFTA slid through cracks in green movement", *Toronto Star*, 11 October 1993).[21]

In line with its discrete attributes, the area of women's human rights issues featured more consistent behaviour by NGOs. This is not to say that a considerable ad hoc element was not built into a move towards partnership, with a great deal of short-term assessment about the value-added benefits of striking a constructive arrangement during the Vienna process. As with environmental NGOs at Rio, advocates of women's human rights at Vienna held many different assumptions about the role of government. The highest priority for NGOs was to protect the essential rights of individuals and groups. All attempts at updating and reinvigorating this thinking continued to locate this set of issues in statist terms. Even while acknowledging the eroded relevance of the concept of the national interest for NGOs, state (or former) state officials analysed the international social agenda through that lens. As the minister responsible for the Vienna process expressed the point: "Foreign policy defined as defending the national interest is not high on the agenda of most members of the public today in virtually any country. The components of national interest are of vital concern to separate and increasingly narrow but highly vocal sectors of the public" (Barbara McDougall, Secretary of State for External Affairs in the government of Prime Minister Mulroney from 1991 to 1993, "How interest groups are shaping foreign policy", *Globe and Mail*, 1 August 1997).

The difference with respect to the women's movement was that it was able to achieve a fine balance between concern with principle and pragmatism in getting results. In efforts to make a stark emotional appeal, advocates of women's rights adopted a form of society-craft that was quite similar to the direct-action behaviour used by other human rights activists. In the eyes of the majority of observers, the most moving event of the Vienna conference was the 15 June global tribunal on the violation of women's human rights at which an estimated audience of some 1,000 people listened to the heartfelt testimony of abuse by 33 women from 25 countries and all classes of society. The cases ranged from wife burning (Pakistan), systematic rape (the former Yugoslavia), female genital mutilation (Sudan), and sexual slavery/comfort women (Korea) to domestic violence (Europe and the United States) and acquaintance rape (Canada). A panel of judges representing all regions of the world, including Ed Broadbent from the International Centre for Human Rights and Democratic Development (ICHRDD), issued recommendations both to states and to the conference on how to establish mechanics to prevent, investigate, and provide redress for violations of women's human rights. Unlike other expressions of protest, however, this event notably did not in any way jeopardise the relationship with state officials. Organised through the NGO forum, the tribunal did not interfere with negotiations throughout the official world conference. Moreover, the wide publicity given to the tribunal by CNN and other media outlets gave a strong message that this event needed to be taken seriously (Bunch and Reilly, 1994; see also Alan Riding, "Women Seize Focus at Rights Forum", *New York Times*, 16 June 1993).

The sense of balance in this tribunal was contrasted, in the minds of Canadian state officials at least, with the guerrilla activities of other elements of the human rights movement in the style of Greenpeace. One sign of such disruptive behaviour was the booing of former president Jimmy Carter by some human rights activists at the NGO forum that preceded the official conference. Another was the controversy over the placement of posters showcasing individual cases of human rights abuse. From a UN institutional perspective, this type of activity went against the tenor of a decision taken at the Prep Coms not to engage in this form of publicity. From an NGO perspective, by way of contrast, the removal of these posters constituted a form of censorship. The sensitivity of this issue in the Canadian context was increased by NGO accusations that the WEOG states had pressed for this agreement on the parameters of NGO behaviour. As at the Rio conference, Canadian state officials attempted to keep the negotiations squarely on thematic issues. Issue-specific cases were treated as being unproductive and out of bounds.[22]

By this standard, the women's movement played within the rules determined and sustained by the state. Consistent with their goal of mainstreaming women's rights, the central focus of the agenda of the women's movement was the establishment of collective rights. Equally, on the question of means, the women's movement was prepared to work diligently and patiently in achieving the best possible outcome from the Vienna negotiations. Mobilised through the NGOs' women's caucus, through the United Nations Development Fund for Women (UNIFEM), the movement held regular strategy meetings to determine how best to keep an eye on the prize. Success was defined in tangible achievements, both in terms of technical gains (via the placement of specific forms of language in the text) and entrepreneurial diplomacy (through specific initiatives on war crimes, for instance).

Throughout the process there was an awareness of the need for political compromise and the acceptance of a less than perfect result, given the number of issues and actors involved in the negotiations. This willingness to play within the rules had not been derived exclusively from the exigencies of the Vienna moment itself, but had taken shape during the protracted negotiations. The working group on women's rights, for instance, met during the week preceding the world conference and issued strong recommendations to the government conference on the mechanics needed to strengthen and protect women's rights. Indeed, the women's working group was the only one of the NGO forums' thematic working groups to draft recommendations, using the draft world conference conclusive text that came out of Prep Com IV. While the NGO "broader conclusive" recommendations went well beyond the text agreed to an interstate level at the final stages of the Prep Com process, the NGOs' approach was marked by its willingness to build on the text agreed to by the states with the intention of making it very difficult to weaken the document. At the Vienna conference itself, the women's caucus debated whether to focus their diplomatic efforts on ensuring the adoption of the proposal from the WEOG, or to try to strengthen the concluding text on women with the risk that other countries might seize the opportunity to weaken it. In the end, however, the caucus accepted the view that ensuring the adoption of the existing text was the wisest course.

From a critical "outsider" perspective, this behaviour could be viewed as symptomatic of the kind of risk feared by Greenpeace in the Rio process. Being drawn so deeply into the negotiating process exposed society-craft to the dangers of manipulation. At the political level, the state stood to benefit considerably from having the women's movement "on side". As in the environmental case, many within the women's movement remained fully aware of the traps built into any closer relationship between state and non-state actors including both obvious and more indirect forms of control. Among the former were a variety of co-optation scenarios; among the more subtle devices was the naming of state practitioners as "gatekeepers" (Hocking, 1999a).

So strong did the presence of the women's movement at the Vienna conference become, however, that the "capture" hypothesis with respect to society-craft was rivalled by the notion of statecraft being held "hostage" to this component of civil society. Unlike the ad hoc and disjointed behaviour of the green movement or the wider human rights movement, the women's movement seemed coherent in its aims and organisation. As Shelagh Day, vice-president of the National Action Committee on the Status of Women in Canada, affirmed, although this internal dynamic contained some tense moments it resulted in a "document of consolidated recommendation". This view was strengthened, moreover, by the sense of triumph the women's movement enjoyed. In looking beyond Vienna, Charlotte Bunch, of the Center for Women's Global Leadership at Rutgers University, stated that the goal of the movement was "not to move from conference to conference, but to ensure that women's rights [were] infiltrated throughout the UN system on a daily basis" (Day and Bunch quoted in W. Parker and P. Comeau, "Women Succeed in Vienna Where Others Fail", *Human Rights Tribune*, November 1993, pp. 24–25; see also Linda Hossie, "Getting at governments the women's way", *Globe and Mail*, 9 July 1993).

The triumph of this achievement was further amplified by contrast to the mixed reviews Vienna received in other components of the conference. Unlike the women's movement, human rights organisations remained divided on their conclusions. Some, most notably Amnesty International, regarded Vienna with bitter disappointment as a missed opportunity. Just as Greenpeace had condemned UNCED, Amnesty's secretary-general, Pierre Sané, denounced the Vienna conference as a "slap in the face of humanity" and "a failure" (Sané quoted in Linda Hossie, "UN conferences subverted, Amnesty International says", *Globe and Mail*, 2 June 1993, and Linda Hossie, "Human rights groups find they lack cohesion", *Globe and Mail*, 29 June 1993).[23] Another human rights activist voiced a similar opinion: Vienna "epitomized everything that a UN world conference ought not to be" (quoted by Wiseberg, 1995:

177).[24] Other NGO participants, though, were more sanguine about the outcome. Reed Brody, director of the Washington-based Human Rights Group, for example, concluded: "While we have a long way to go before we can say the UN is serious about [human rights], NGOs were able to put the UN on the defensive; to force the UN to come up with responses which will hopefully have a ripple effect to the General Assembly, the Sub-Commission, etc." (quoted in Human Rights Internet, "States stand pat while NGOs face a revolution", *Human Rights Tribune,* November 1993, p. 9).

Debating the applicability of partnership

From these extended narratives of the character of statecraft and society-craft found vis-à-vis Rio and Vienna, it is quite clear that a partnership of sorts was forged between state officials and NGOs in the context of the UN world conferences. Notwithstanding the stylised traditions of orthodox statecraft and the preferences of hard-nosed realists, the "two-solitude" model of diplomacy was thoroughly supplanted. Interaction, rather than being the exception, has increasingly become the rule in Canadian international relations. In doing so, it has forced a greater intellectual effort to close the gap between the tempo of contextual transformation, policy, and procedural adaptation, and our longer-term understanding of these dynamics. Belying the realists' view that "nothing has changed", this type of interaction has forced a re-evaluation of this sort of framework, a re-evaluation that has meant delving more deeply into the substance rather than the style of the phenomenon of partnership.

Its portrayal as a big-bang transformation – as evoked by the proponents of "world society" – is no more justified than the mirage presented by those wishing away the signs of the state–NGO interface. The integration of statecraft into society-craft has moved in parallel with an adjustment of the state. But this departure from the status quo has meant a tactical retreat marked by a greater sharing of activities and distribution of resources, not a strategic withdrawal. Certainly it cannot be associated with the hollowing out or terminal decline of the state as predicted by critics of traditional diplomacy. Rather it has produced elements of both accommodation and creativity previously missing and untapped.

As intellectual formulations move to catch up with the fluidity and speed of contemporary diplomacy, signs of appreciation of this adjustment process have emerged in the literature. The need to see changes in diplomacy not as a zero-sum game, with winners and losers, has been recognised by some retired professional representatives of the state who are eager to make diplomacy work more effectively (Langhorne, 1998; Marshall, 1999; Talbott, 1997: 69). The expression of a need for more flexibility in the study of diplomacy has also become a marked feature of several more general works in international relations (Evans, Jacobson and Putnam, 1993; Risse-Kappen, 1995; Strange, 1996b).

Of course, the basis upon which this partnership hinges continues to be contested. The impulse to manage NGOs remains an instinct ingrained in state officials, even as their need to "bring NGOs in" is motivated by a decline in resources and a need to bolster their own credibility through extending the interface (and being seen to do so). At the same time, NGOs' willingness to take advantage of the space offered to them will be marred if their approach is perceived as being incompatible with their good name.

Another phase in the evolution of the relationship between statecraft and society-craft has been entered. Not only has the continuum of relationships between these actors been enhanced by the growing skill and reputation of the NGOs themselves, but it is also reflected in the way that professional diplomats perceive and discharge their roles and in the texture of the formulation and implementation of international policy. This array of forces and interests demands that the actors connect with increasing frequency and in a greater variety of forms. That interface manifests in a range of both cooperative and conflictual modes of behaviour as each actor vies to develop relationships on an issue-specific basis while retaining as much room for autonomous action as possible. This relationship is still characterised by fuzziness, awkwardness, tension, and conflict. What is apparent, however, is the richness of the milieu between statecraft and society-craft created by this interactive process.

4
Tests of leadership: the prime ministerial role

The fundamental test concerning diplomatic leadership at the UN world conferences arises from what Brian Hocking terms the tension between diffusion and consolidation (Hocking, 1999b: 26–28). It is common to see the UN world conferences as exemplars of the model of multiplicity in diplomatic activity. Diversity in society-craft is reproduced at the administrative level both within the UN apparatus and in connection with the structure of national states. One pull towards diffusion comes from the minutely detailed needs of the agenda. Multilateral diplomacy in its general orientation has developed a bias towards the technical, and hence toward those who possess technical expertise and administrative capacity. This is true of the international civil service that populates the UN secretariats. It is also true of national civil servants who operate outside of the realm of those traditionally endowed with the status of diplomats. Although foreign ministries and foreign service officers have done much to embellish their repertoire, their core skills remain in the areas of information-gathering, communication, and negotiation. Specialist knowledge on specific issues lies elsewhere in the machinery of government, most frequently in line departments and specialised agencies. The heightened complexity framed by the UN world conferences has contributed greatly to this impression of fragmentation.

Buttressed by its combination of reputational credentials and skill-set, the Canadian Department of Foreign Affairs and International Trade (DFAIT) retained some comparative advantages not only over many of its counterparts in the international system but also over its domestic partners and rivals. Among the bureaucratic entities involved in the diplomatic process, foreign ministry officials were the only ones able to hold some big picture awareness concerning Canadian participation at all these forums. Whereas other departments such as Environment Canada, the Department of Justice, the Department of Indian and Northern Affairs, Human Resources and Development Canada, the Canadian International Development Agency (CIDA), Status of Women, and Heritage Canada became intensely involved in one or two of these conferences, the foreign ministry remained engaged throughout the entire run. Foreign ministry officials, therefore, had the unique ability to retain some institutional memory that could override fragmentation. In more practical terms, they brought impressive qualities to the conference proceedings: they could integrate material and ideas throughout the span of conference proceedings; they could persuade from inside and put the best spin outside the negotiations; and, more controversially, they had the confidence to try to educate others about the lessons to be drawn from these events.

When put to the challenge, though, these qualities were not sufficient to maintain the foreign ministry in an unrivalled lead position. The severity of this test was increased in turn by the number of actors brought into the (extended) diplomatic process. A huge gap was exposed also between the thinking and operation of segmented client-based actors and the foreign ministry in its guise as the defender of the national interest and bearer of a long and sophisticated awareness of the functioning of the international system as a whole.

If one face of this test of diplomatic adaptation came through diffusion, another came through the impact of consolidation. It was one thing for diplomats in general, and foreign ministry officials more specifically, to maintain their "premium" over representatives from other departments and agencies in terms of their "awareness" and "perceptiveness" about the diplomatic game (Hocking, 1999b: 107), but it was another thing completely for these officials to get government leaders to pay attention to the game or to heed their advice in any systematic fashion. In Canada, as elsewhere, diplomacy had to adjust to being stripped of any form of insulation from domestic politics. In the immediate post-1945 period, Canadian professional negotiators may have been given almost complete autonomy over the negotiation process in multilateral forums. Regardless of the stripe of government, this was no longer the case. The political instincts of the prime minister (and his or her closest advisers) not only intruded into the process, but dominated proceedings.

Although considerable room was allowed for departmental officials to apply their ministerial responsibility to their day-to-day manager/coordinator roles, when it came to Canada's performance during the actual UN conferences, the ultimate direction came from the apex of power. When a prime minister decided to run hard with an issue at one of the UN conferences, the state apparatus was mobilised in support. Conversely, when a prime minister signalled that a conference posed more of a political problem than a solution, strict boundaries were placed around the activities of both ministers and officials.

Political leadership remains a key test of diplomacy. The Canadian prime minister, consistent with a worldwide tendency, has become surrounded by a court made up of the senior staff of the central agencies, with the Prime Minister's Office (PMO) and the Privy Council Office (PCO) accorded primacy. This consolidation of authority does not in itself trap Canada into a limitationist approach to international affairs (for variations on this theme, see Neufeld, 1995, Nossal, 1998–1999 and Rioux and Hay, 1997). It does mean, however, that statecraft will be thoroughly penetrated by highly personal political considerations.

The precise way in which these instincts will play out in international public policy does not follow any set playbook. As exemplified by Brian Mulroney, leaders most associated with bilateralism can become enthusiastic (if still idiosyncratic) multilateralists. Alternatively, an exponent of liberal internationalism in principle, such as Jean Chrétien, can become prisoners of more constraining instincts and imperatives in practice. Risk-prone leaders such as Mulroney were attracted to ambitious mission-oriented diplomacy within the UN domain. By way of contrast, Chrétien expressed a reluctance to embrace big ideas and vision without the promise of instrumental political opportunity and delivery. Unlike initiatives where Chrétien and Canada could build on the prospect of issue-specific or niche leadership cautious habits prevailed.

State officials had to work therefore within very different types of boundaries. As part of a wider test of diplomacy, the contours of statecraft had to respond to a changing landscape beyond the purview of the national government and build new and ongoing relations with internal societal forces at the same time as the logic of strict territoriality was undergoing continuous revision. The claims and influence of personality added very different ingredients to the test as diplomats had to respond to the demands of the UN conferences through the interpretative eyes of their political masters. When leaders and their advisers took up an enthusiasm – as occurred in Mulroney's embrace of the Rio process – they had to shift from a routine form of behaviour to a new more intense level of activity with attendant demands on their time, knowledge base, and resources. When there was scepticism and inertia over purpose at the leadership level – as there was for the most part under Chrétien – the task became reduced to warding off the enthusiasm of other actors both domestic and international. Under both versions of these tests of leadership, however, the logic of Canadian statecraft became a focused one: skewed either towards a maximisation of profile or the avoidance of embarrassment.

The centrality of leadership

Individual leadership matters in statecraft. Sometimes termed the "idiosyncratic factor"[25] (on this point, see Nossal, 1982, 1994), this component reflects the capacity of key personalities to make a difference. To be sure, this influence is grounded in the wider political and policy context. What is significant, however, is the manner by which this ingredient shines through in diplomatic activities. As John Ravenhill reminds us, "the personal interests, beliefs, personality, ambitions, energy and skill of the prime minister" (or, one may add, the lack thereof) largely determine "the extent ... and the issues on which their governments play activist roles in foreign policies" (Ravenhill, 1998: 322).

The fundamental premise of this chapter is that leadership (or indeed non-leadership) applied at the prime ministerial level adds a distinctive flavour to Canadian diplomacy as expressed at the UN world conferences. Moreover, this distinctiveness seems to be free from any entrenched loyalty or adherence to a political tradition. If the connection between the attitudes of a political party and policy behaviour is to have any meaning, it might be expected that it would be the Chrétien Liberals and not the Mulroney Conservatives who privileged these UN conferences. With reference to the multilateralist focus, the impulse to "be like 'Mike'" is contingent on a strong element of personal engagement. For Lester Pearson – the Canadian state official most identified with the rise of Canadian liberal internationalism – had been an active participantat forums such as the 1945 San Francisco conference. Continuing this direction both in style and substance, Canadian diplomatic activism in the earlier UN world conferences during the Trudeau years – whether the 1968 International Human Rights Conference in Teheran, the 1972 Stockholm Conference on the Human Environment, the 1975 Conference on Women in Mexico City, or the 1974 World Population Conference in Bucharest – was all related to the expansion of the role of the state. Although Trudeau did not attend any of these conferences, they all have his imprint. His concern for participatory democracy in the Canadian policy process, for example, came out strongly through the extensive consultations that preceded the Bucharest conference. The stamp of Trudeau's social liberalism on the Bucharest agenda can be found on a wide number of items ranging from the preference for choice on the abortion issue to the implicit link between population issues and immigration.

At odds with these common assumptions, nonetheless, it was the Mulroney Conservatives and not the Chrétien Liberals who became most closely identified with an assertive form of multilateralism as directed through these UN conferences. On the axis of participation, it is clear which prime minister was the most activist. Prime Minister Mulroney attended two major UN world conferences: the New York World Summit for Children in September 1990, and the 1992 Rio United Nations Conference. At the Children's Summit he took on the role of conference cochair. At Rio not only was he one of the first leaders to arrive but he made his presence felt throughout the proceedings. Prime Minister Jean Chrétien, on the other hand, attended none of the UN world conferences under review for this book. While Mulroney's high-profile position stood out among the 71 heads of state or government who took part at the Children's Summit and the 108 who attended the United Nations Conference on Environment and Development (UNCED), Chrétien's lack of participation was most noticeable at the 1995 Copenhagen World Summit for Social Development, where 117 other heads of state or government took part (including President Nelson Mandela of South Africa, Prime Minister Paul Keating of Australia, and Prime Minister Gro Harlem Brundtland of Norway).

A comparison of the two leaders' performances is even more puzzling and controversial because of a seeming reversal of expectations. A number of social activists, although acknowledging the blemishes in this record, have gone so far as to argue that in relative terms the Mulroney government deserves more credit than the Chrétien government for its work on social issues in these forums. Stephen Lewis has pointed out that the way the Chrétien government lost momentum on this dossier "says something about the ebb and flow of international social justice" (Stephen Lewis, 1998 Kerr-Saltsman lecture in Canadian Studies, University of Waterloo, quoted in *Globe and Mail*, 24 March 1998). In a more personal statement, Elizabeth May, a "non-Tory", stated that the performance of the Chrétien government even made her begin to miss Mulroney (Elizabeth May, "A non-Tory misses Brian Mulroney", *Globe and Mail*, 22 June 1998; in the run-up to Rio, May pushed Mulroney to take the "hero's" role at the conference: "Put on your Capt. Planet cape, Brian, and get busy", *Globe and Mail*, 7 February 1992).

It must be acknowledged that this type of judgement hangs largely on the record of the two prime ministers at the 1992 Rio de Janeiro Conference on Environment and Development and the Kyoto environmental conference in December 1997, a juxtaposition that may be more misleading than informative. It assumes that Mulroney's activism, by virtue of its out-in-front quality, was a positive form of diplomacy. A common theme picked up by several academic commentators has been the contrast between the "heroic" leadership shown by the Mulroney government at Rio and the retreat from leadership evidenced by the Chrétien government at Kyoto. Heather Smith, for one, contrasts the constructive internationalism of the Mulroney government with the defection of the Chrétien government: "Climate change ... was an issue marked for Canadian leadership by Brian Mulroney and yet the Chrétien government scrambled at the recent conference in Kyoto, Japan to cobble together an internationally credible position" (Smith, 2000; on the Mulroney approach, see Smith, 2001). Lorna Stefanick and Kathleen Wells similarly depict the behaviour of the two governments in terms of a fall from grace, in that Canada's behaviour degraded from "world leader" to "environmental laggard" (Stefanick and Wells, 1998: 252).

Mulroney's high profile vis-à-vis the Rio conference, however, does not appear to result from any coherent shift towards a principled form of leadership. Rather his embrace of environmental leadership had the hallmarks of a convenient or compensatory form of activity designed to deflect or distract attention. After all, the initiatives Mulroney is best known for are in the bilateral and the regional trade arena – implemented through the Canada-US Free Trade Agreement (FTA) and the North American Free Trade Agreement (NAFTA) – not the multilateral. Mulroney's initiative-oriented diplomacy at the UN social conferences may well have had some positive attributes. What should not be missed, though, is the manipulative nature of this form of behaviour. Claims that this activity advanced the agenda of global governance should not mask the opportunism embedded within it. Nor was Mulroney's behaviour consistent. While he earned considerable kudos for his role at Rio, the reaction to his performance at the Children's Summit was far from positive.

The salient aspect of Prime Minister Chrétien's approach to these UN world conferences, on the other hand, was its conformity with his government's overall record. Chrétien selected certain issues for his personal attention (most notably, the Zaire-Great Lakes initiative at the end of 1996). But this sort of mission-oriented diplomacy was a departure from his basic instincts and operating mode. The hallmark of the Chrétien government was its unwillingness to enter into international commitments that deviated from its core agenda of managing the economy. Bluntly put, less is more. Chrétien's diplomatic style was not the expansionary free-spending form associated with Trudeau (and indeed with Mulroney), but rather a functionalism marked by self-imposed limits.

Criticisms of this restrictive style, of course, go well beyond targeting particular cases such as the Kyoto agreement. This style can be said to lack breadth. It also subordinates the demands of global governance to the dictates of a narrowly constructed, top-down, policy agenda. At a political level, however, this back-to-basics approach smacked of convenience. If a low-key approach reduced Chrétien's exposure on the global stage, it also reduced the possibility of international scrutiny (and embarrassment) at a time of budgetary cutbacks.[26]

Any justification for this restrictive strategy rested on a combination of rationales. On a personal basis it allowed Chrétien – in principle – to concentrate on the small number of issues that mattered most to Canada's main game. On a national basis, it reverted to the modest presentation of Canadian diplomacy of the earlier post-1945 era when its core tenet was that "its reach ought not to exceed its grasp" (Holmes, 1970: vii). Operating within such confines, Canada placed great weight on selectivity. If this approach legitimised targeting diplomatic attention towards specific issue areas in which Canada had some special interest or skill, it rigorously avoided the dangers of overstretch where there was a growing discrepancy between commitment and capability.

It would be wrong-headed to raise the influence of personality to a status as the most important factor shaping the performance of the Mulroney and Chrétien governments in relation to the UN conferences. A wider view is needed, to take into account the conditioning effect of the domestic and international constraints as well as the circumstances and timing of engagement (or lack of engagement). Yet, the variable of personal leadership should not be discounted. At the level of heroic (or anti-heroic) gestures and more routinised activity, the behaviour of both these leaders was grounded in their political styles and policy orientations. A crucial element in shaping their approaches was a firm but differentiated appreciation of the stakes involved. "Larger forces" may well bend "the initial intentions and visions of those who assume power" (Nossal, 1988: 122), but there is still room for prime ministers to leave their distinctive personal mark on foreign policy.

Comparative leadership styles

A quick rehearsal of the leadership styles of the two prime ministers themselves may be helpful. For, as Leslie Pal reminds us, amidst all the complexity of decision making, the personality and individual talents of leaders stand out as a vital determinant of behaviour. In leaders' efforts to shape events, "the results of [these individual characteristics] vary, but their efforts must inevitably have some effect" (Pal, 1988: 16). While a concentration "on variables other than the individual is perfectly sensible in the Canadian case", Kim Nossal adds, "such a focus diverts our attention away from the effects that individual decision makers can have on policy change and innovation" (Nossal, 1994: 91).

When in opposition, Chrétien made some effort at the declaratory level to fit his approach on international affairs into the model of Pearsonian internationalism and UN-based multilateralism. This theme was the core ingredient in his major speech on foreign policy at Trinity College during his time as Opposition Leader (Chrétien, 1991) and it was elaborated in the Liberal *Red Book* and the Liberal Foreign Policy Platform (Liberal Party of Canada, 1993: 157).

Yet once in power Chrétien made little effort to push the notion of good international citizenship and UN-based multilateralism to the top of his agenda. By appointing a "stay at home" minister (André Ouellet) as foreign minister in October 1993, Chrétien created some room to run foreign policy himself. Yet he rarely seized this opportunity in a creative manner. The key policy advisers to the Prime Minister's Office continued to be cautious managerial types not bold entrepreneurs of ideas. They directed their attention to reducing not expanding Chrétien's agenda. Accordingly, the main initiatives during Chrétien's first term of office focused on procedure not policy, most notably attempts to allow some opening-up in foreign policy agenda-setting.

The innovative tone of these procedurally oriented measures stand out. An extensive dialogue about Canadian foreign policy was conducted through the channels of the special joint parliamentary committees on Foreign Affairs and Defence (with a wide-ranging mandate to hold public hearings) and through a Foreign Policy "National Forum" held in March 1994. These new features, however, had a limited impact. The Liberals adopted a different style in pursuit of a new direction in foreign policy making, but in substantive policy terms – or even in terms of more systemic procedural changes – the results were uneven. The overall impression was one of a government trying to recalibrate its foreign policy on the basis of a narrowing, not expanding, calculus of interests and capabilities. If there were some serious modifications around the edges of the Pearsonian model, Chrétien's interpretation of "being like Mike" meant sticking to a limited set of functionalist activities.

Chrétien's contribution to this more restrictive approach to foreign policy came about partially by default. His attempts to present an image of Canadian foreign policy in a more ambitious framework during his time in office were mainly rhetorical. In a major speech in Toronto in February 1996, inaugurating the Pearson Chair in International Relations at Oxford University, Chrétien emphasised that Canada must reject isolationism and avoid the tendency to "run away and hide" from the problems of the world. Canada must "either stay engaged, or ... allow others to determine our future for us" (John Gray, "PM offers antidote to Canada's naysayers", *Globe and Mail*, 23 February 1996). Although well intentioned, and well publicised, however, this speech fell well short of expectations. A major problem – as in the earlier Trinity College speech – was Chrétien's delivery. As his biographer reminds us, Chrétien is not at his best in speech making (Lawrence Martin, "Words don't define Chretien's character", *Ottawa Citizen*, April 29, 1999). He lacks the "rigour and command of language" to be a commanding orator (Greenspon and Wilson-Smith, 1996: 77). Nor does he seem inspired by a sense of vision; on the contrary, "great visions" are seen as causing "trouble" (Anthony Wilson-Smith, "When flexibility breeds success", *Maclean's*, 23 February 1998, p. 11). These traits may not be debits in terms of routine policy and political matters, but for image building or signalling a new direction for Canada in international affairs, they fall short of the mark.

For the most part, though, Chrétien's restrictive approach came about by design. If Chrétien was faulted for his lack of vision or oratorical skills, there can be no dispute about his work ethic or the force of self-discipline he imposed on the operations of his government. As in other areas, Chrétien's stamp as prime minister was most evident in his defining the government's foreign policy agenda by way of core competencies. Despite pressures to do more, there was no sense of a crowded agenda. Initiatives at the prime ministerial level certainly existed but they were severely rationed. While it would be wrong to say that Chrétien, like Ronald Reagan, was a disengaged leader, he was, rather, "highly selective in his engagements. Usually it was left to others to speak on his behalf" (Greenspon and Wilson-Smith, 1996: 249).[27] Minimalist and "bottom line" in his style, Chrétien's main concern was to avoid undue risks and mistakes.

Brian Mulroney stands out as a leader with far more volatile personality traits and talents. The orthodox treatment of Mulroney is that he is a classic brokerage type of politician, with a high quotient of willingness and ability to accommodate interests (Aucoin, 1986: 1–27). Examples abound of his eagerness to exploit his capability as a transactional agent. Internationally, Mulroney threw himself into the role of mediator in the GATT/agricultural as well as the South African/Commonwealth context. Domestically, as illustrated, for example, by the issue of the South Moresby National Park in British Columbia, he was a master of the charm offensive (May, 1990). These characteristics in themselves did not distinguish Mulroney from other prime ministers, including Chrétien. The difference was more in the gusto with which he threw himself into these endeavours.

This image of Mulroney as a broker is supported by a number of other traits. When he took office as prime minister, he had little interest in the "interplay of ideas" (Aucoin, 1986). Conrad Black, an entrepreneur of ideas in his own right, conveys the concern of more ideologically driven conservatives about the shallowness and inconsistency of Mulroney's intellectual toolkit. In Black's words: "The Pollyanna flippancy ... of his positions disconcerted his friends, including me.... His knowledge of how to get ahead was geometrically greater than any notion he had of what to do when he reached his destinations" (Black, 1994: 284n). What Mulroney possessed was not only the ambition but the acumen of a professional deal-maker. As one of his senior cabinet members is quoted by Donald Savoie: "Remember Mulroney was one of the most skilled labour lawyers in Canada before he came to office. He looks at problems one at a time and also, looks to one solution at a time.... He is not the type to add them all together to make sense out of the whole thing" (Savoie, 1994: 272).

What this orthodox take misses is Mulroney's impulse to gamble, to "roll the dice" on even the most sensitive and important of issues. He broke out of the pattern of cautious, incremental decision making associated with a variety of other Canadian leaders. Whereas Chrétien's transactional approach was marked by enormous self-discipline, for instance, Mulroney's leadership style was marked by a greater risk-taking. As a senior official commented: "Mulroney is not the most focused politician.... Once in a while, he would declare that one issue – say, the deficit – was the priority issue for the government. That would hold for a while, or until another issue that caught his attention came around" (Savoie, 1994: 190–191).

Although these instincts did allow him to become involved in a concerted effort on some particular issues for a certain time (the case of the Free Trade Agreement is the obvious illustration in the foreign policy context), what stands out is the way they added uncertainty to the decision-making process. From a negative perspective, the tendency to "roll the dice" made Mulroney come across as an opportunist and a manipulator. But seen more positively, this risk-taking ability allowed him to move out in front on issues in an unanticipated and unconventional manner. As Bruce Doern and Brian Tomlin describe Mulroney's "leap of faith" on free trade: "It was the prime minister alone who ultimately decided that the risks of pursuing the free trade initiative were worth the political candle" (Doern and Tomlin, 1991: 272).

The interplay of personality and circumstances

If it is accepted that leaders' personal styles affect the shaping of the policy agenda, their temporal circumstances help set the parameters of action. The timing of Mulroney's tenure gave him a far greater opportunity to make a difference in UN-based multilateralism with respect to the world conferences. As suggested earlier, the end of the Cold War provided opportunities for innovative forms of activity and association. Canada had a chance to be more than simply an idea-taker with little or no room to influence the intellectual or policy agenda on an issue-specific basis. With the new flatter power structure, the mainstream opinion was that Canada's special qualities and connections would allow it "to play an increasingly important role" in the "new multilateralism and evolving security systems" (Welsh, 1991: 86). As Doug Roche, the prominent anti-nuclear advocate, put it: "This new moment allows the middle-power countries to assert themselves. There is no middle-power country of a stronger capacity to do this than Canada, which is really a diplomatic switchboard for the world" (Roche, 1992: 50:15).

At the same time, the agenda of international politics was in transition. With the end of the Cold War and the reduced dominance of "high" security issues, the ascendant agenda could deal with economic well-being and a broad range of social issues. At one end of the spectrum of this extended agenda were the various forms of transnational activity (including joint ventures, and cross-border strategic alliances) embarked upon by companies. At the other end of the spectrum were the activities of a vast array of societal forces. Paralleling the transnationalisation of business culture, the societal groups found growing expression in the global political system during the late 1980s and early 1990s.

In many ways, the Mulroney government was a beneficiary of change during this period. As pressure for a transformed agenda built up among civil society and NGOs, there was a strong incentive for the government to "do something" different and be seen as catching the wave of change in a dramatic fashion. One incentive was the chance of capturing or co-opting political support. A symbolic incentive was the credibility and legitimacy to be gained by taking steps along these lines. In other ways, however, the Mulroney government became a more explicit agent of change. From 1985 (with the formal request for free trade negotiations with the United States) to the beginning of 1989 (when the Canada–US FTA came into effect), the image of the Mulroney government had been dominated by the agenda of trade liberalisation. Catching the wave of the UN world conferences was useful as a way of providing some form of indirect compensation for a perceived loss of sovereignty as a result of this extended trade initiative. One could argue that Mulroney's robust performances at both the New York World Summit for Children in 1990 and at the Rio UNCED in 1992 were forms of overcompensation for the FTA. Free trade with the United States, suggests John Whalley, increased "the pressure on Canada to elevate its middle-power diplomatic role [and] to demonstrate that Canada's sovereignty has not been impaired by the agreement, that Canada is a separate country that takes foreign policy positions independent from the United States" (Whalley, 1988: 176).

Even if Chrétien had visualised a UN-based multilateralism – directed through such forums as the 1994 Cairo International Conference on Population and Development, the 1995 Copenhagen World Summit for Social Development, and the 1995 Fourth World Women's Conference – as being at the core of his government's international profile, it would have been much more difficult for him to put that vision into action. Chrétien's circumscribed diplomacy meshed well with his own personal preferences. But this mode of performance was also grounded in a web of conditioning circumstances. Chrétien went to great length to distance himself and his government from the Mulroney record and style. Given some of the U-turns his government performed on core economic matters (such as NAFTA and the Goods and Services Tax (GST) an especially unpopular tax) (Greenspon and Wilson-Smith, 1996), the onus of his disassociative approach rested on the question of image. Whatever the success or failure of Mulroney's performances at the UN world conferences, any repetition of the same high-profile approach on Chrétien's part was extremely unlikely.

The structural context that continued to dominate the Chrétien years domestically militated against forms of ambitious commitments. Burdened by both a heavy foreign debt and a budget deficit, the Chrétien government no longer took the soft option of expansive promises but had to adopt the harder option of fiscal constraint. Unlike previous governments, it chose not to throw monies at what some have either realistically or cynically called the "residuals" (Stairs, 2001: 35). This atmosphere of streamlining and cost-cutting, while allowing innovation cost-sharing and decentralisation, was hardly conducive to a diffuse diplomacy via the UN or other forms of constructive multilateralism. As Evan Potter argued at the time: "The view from abroad of Canada's international role continues to be that of a country highly valued for its diplomacy on promotion of international justice, fairness and the rule of law. The problem is that Canada no longer has the governmental capacity to be so broadly engaged at the official level. It is not that Canada should not be globally engaged; rather, the means of this global engagement will have to change" (Potter, 1996: 47).[28]

In the diplomatic arena the Chrétien government operated in a context in which the UN suffered a painful recoil from the expectations of the new order. Neither of the serving Canadian officials who contributed to the 1996 volume *Canada Among Nations*, for example, offered any ringing endorsement for the UN as change agent. Robert Fowler stated simply that the UN had "yet to find its post–Cold War role" (Fowler, 1996: 35). Of more precise relevance to the topic of the UN world conferences is Louise Fréchette's comment on the UN's participation in the economic and social areas: "Often criticized as useless extravaganzas", she wrote, "these conferences, when well prepared, in fact serve the vital purpose of defining new priorities for the entire UN system, a task which regular meetings of other bodies simply cannot perform" (Fréchette, 1996: 159).

Ambassador Fréchette's criteria for success in the UN world conferences are illuminating. Not only do they have to be "well prepared", but they have to be more comprehensive in their agenda. Fréchette readily acknowledged the positive impact of the conferences embarked on during the Mulroney and Chrétien years as agenda-setting exercises. The 1994 Cairo Conference on Population and Development, she wrote, reached "unprecedented consensus on the issue of international migration where the need for cooperation between receiving and originating countries was stressed". And the "UN World Conferences on Women and the World Summit for Social Development, held in 1995 in Beijing and Copenhagen respectively, articulated a broad vision of development and human security and set the parameters of UN action continuing into the next century" (Fréchette, 1996: 160). What these conferences lacked, however, was a direct connection to the "role of the UN in economic affairs" (Fréchette, 1996: 161).

Even Fréchette acknowledged that any fresh opportunities emanating from the new extended agenda were mitigated by the risks attendant on this way forward. To open up the debate in this fashion meant also the possibility of reopening the North/South division on how reforms were to take place. In Fréchette's words: "Negotiations will likely be very difficult. And great care will have to be taken to avoid recreating the great North–South divide" (Fréchette, 1996: 161).

Prime ministers as summit diplomats

Brian Mulroney's performance as a summit diplomat remains controversial. The personal imprint imposed on Canadian statecraft during his time as prime minister was generated by his inclination to be an "avid summiter" (Kirton, 1988: 33). One of his strong character traits exhibited in these forums was his ability to connect with a wide variety of political leaders from different backgrounds and ideologies (Mikhail Gorbachev and Bob Hawke as well as Ronald Reagan and George Bush). Another strength was his skill at using summits as a means of overcoming (rather than reinforcing) cleavages between Ottawa and the provinces. A case in point was his success in reviving the summit of La Francophonie. Contrasting with the imbroglio found on the Kyoto negotiations between the Chrétien government and the provinces, Mulroney released blockages between the federal government and Quebec. As J.H. Taylor, the former Under-Secretary of State for External Affairs, comments: "Brian Mulroney believed that this was an issue that he could solve, a formula was found, the file was unblocked, and the series of francophone summits duly inaugurated.... This was clearly an important innovation, and was clearly one in which the prime minister's role was crucial" (Taylor, 2001: 217).

A further positive trait exhibited by Mulroney's summitry was his aptitude for mediation, as epitomised by his active diplomacy on the South African issue. As Nossal recounts: "At the [1986] biennial meeting of the Commonwealth Heads of Government in Nassau, the Prime Minister found himself as the centre of a major mediating effort between Margaret Thatcher of Britain, who was adamantly opposed to sanctions, and the rest of the Commonwealth" (Nossal, 1988: 119).

If Mulroney's personal leadership qualities surfaced through the medium of summitry, however, so did his weaknesses. The flip side of his enthusiasm was a perception of status seeking. A variety of observers saw his capacity for building connections as manifestation of self-indulgence. And his attempts at mediation could be interpreted as unwanted intrusions well beyond the purview of Canadian national interest.

The main context of this type of denigration, of course, was the realm of Canada–US relations. On substance, Mulroney was subject to a barrage of criticism for his eagerness in pursuing a regular schedule of these bilateral summits. On style, the cosiness of these forums (the 1985 "Shamrock Summit" in Quebec City comes immediately to mind) also set a tone that was unpalatable to many observers. Backlash increased as these efforts towards a renewed special relationship gained momentum through the FTA negotiations. Critics pointed to Mulroney's willingness to subordinate both principle and negotiating advantage to his desire "to get a deal" (Clarkson, 1991: 116).

What is most interesting about Mulroney's role in the UN conferences is the way his performance both elaborates and shades these basic impressions. At the September 1990 World Summit for Children in New York he showed not only his diplomatic agility but also the conditioning constraint imposed by the close links between the international and the domestic. Impelled by growing public interest in the issue of children's rights, Mulroney took the opportunity to play a personal and prominent role (as co-chair) at the summit. In keeping with the traditional Canadian practice of multilateral diplomacy, he emphasised the usefulness of this gathering as a catalyst, claiming "the summit has the potential to put children's issue on the top of the international agenda". The gathering was also seen as a facilitator for further technical and specialist work by public officials. As Mulroney stated: "Summits do what nothing else can do. Put leaders face to face with each other and raise public awareness of issues. There is nothing like [that] for galvanizing a bureaucracy" (quoted in Paul Lewis, "World Leaders Gather for Summit Meeting on Children", *New York Times*, 30 September 1990).

Mulroney's "heroic" role at this summit was nonetheless overshadowed by criticism at the domestic level. A common argument was that Mulroney was hardly well positioned to press for children's welfare at the global level given the condition of so many children in Canada. As a *Globe and Mail* editorial put it, Mulroney should set an example by his activities at home: "Brian Mulroney can show leadership at the summit by pledging money to fight disease and hunger at home, a shameful item of unfinished business that Canadian activists who have travelled to New York for the meeting will not let him (or other delegates) forget" ("A Better Start for the World's Children", *Globe and Mail*, 29 September 1990). Multilateral activism could only go so far in winning kudos. While it might well serve the international reputation of Canada and, by extension, its leaders, it also served to intensify the gaze of domestic scrutiny.

That being said, Mulroney's sobering experience at the Children's Summit begs the question of how and why his intervention at the Rio UNCED earned a decidedly more positive reaction. In some respects, the context of the Rio conference was little different from the Children's Summit. On the international front, the Mulroney government had been active in moving the agenda ahead on matters relating to the ozone layer and climate change. Most notably, it had hosted a number of conferences designed to stimulate international activity on atmospheric pollution. Begun in tandem with the activities of the World Commission on Environment and Development, this work was highlighted by a conference on the ozone layer in Montreal in September 1987. Despite such activity, however, the Mulroney government received little praise at home for its environmental policy. Environmental activists were highly critical of the government's claims to leadership in the international domain when its record on the domestic front was so weak. These activists emphasised inconsistencies between the government's international activity and its willingness or ability to address environmental issues at home. As one "green" activist bluntly put it: "Our international reputation as environmental advocates far exceeds our accomplishments at home" (David McRobert, "On global warming, Canada is full of hot air", *Globe and Mail*, 18 February 1991; for a good review of these issues and debates, see Boardman, 1992).

Why, then, against this background of cynicism, did Mulroney receive such positive response for his actions at the Rio UNCED conference?

One potential explanation relates to the increased access offered to NGOs during the Rio process. His success in getting many (although far from all) of the environmental activists "on side" provided a degree of credibility to his performance. Another explanation hinges on the management of Mulroney's image. As at least one commentator suggests, an array of "spin doctors" worked hard to present Mulroney and his state officials in a positive light: "More than 30 pages of the 100-page Rio strategy memo that the federal bureaucrats forwarded to Cabinet dealt with communication objectives. And of the more than 100 official Canadian delegates, well over a third (42 by one count) were with the Prime Minister's Office. A good deal of these PMO staffers were detailed to inundate the media with press releases and arranged interviews" (Boychuk, 1992: 35).

Still, to be effective, this elaborate exercise in image building (or re-pairing) had to communicate a positive signal or message from the Prime Minister. Here was a situation in which Mulroney's willingness and ability to gamble in terms of diplomatic style was decisive. Seizing the opportunity presented first by the indecision of George Bush Sr. about whether to attend the summit, and then by the US president's obstinate behaviour concerning the introduction of "timetables and tables" into the conference agenda itself, Mulroney made a series of high-profile gestures about Canada's (and his own) good international environmental citizenship. On 27 March 1992 a press release announced that Mulroney would attend the Rio Summit and revealed a package of Canadian initiatives designed to boost the "green" image of the prime minister and the Canadian delegation. Closer to the summit, Mulroney made a major speech establishing a five-point agenda for UNCED and defining a Canadian yardstick for success. These actions were then quickly followed by a press conference on 12 June pointing to progress on these points. As a climax to these efforts, Mulroney moved to have Canada become the first country to sign the Convention on Biological Diversity immediately on his arrival at Rio. All these gestures were political events designed to grab the attention not just of political insiders but of the media and the general public.

Without minimising the import of Mulroney's gambler impulse, we should note that in the particular case of Rio the odds of this approach failing were reduced in several ways. Mulroney looked carefully before he leaped. He had talked extensively to Bush about strategy and tactics with respect to Rio. He was comfortable also in the knowledge that Canada did not stand alone in departing from the United States on environmental issues, as other G-7 countries (in particular Germany and Britain) were also at odds with the Bush/US position (see, for example, Paul Lewis, "U.N. Opens Environment Talks; Europe spurs U.S. to Act

Urgently", *New York Times*, 3 March 1992). And, for all of Mulroney's show of working towards the ratification and implementation of the convention, the Canadian delegation to the Rio Summit had already made it clear that it had a number of reservations on US-supported issues such as patent protection.

It is nevertheless undeniable that Mulroney's initiatives played well in Canada. At one level, these steps created the impression that Canada was prepared to distance itself from the American position on many of the conference's key issues. And this impression was reinforced by Mulroney's decisiveness. His decision to sign and ratify the bio-diversity convention came only 24 hours after Bush announced that he would not sign. Moreover, Mulroney used the opportunity to make a bigger political point: "We don't subcontract our rights and obligations to the United States in any way" (quoted in James Rusk, "Mulroney signs ecopact", *Globe and Mail*, 12 June 1992).[29]

This sense of triumph was interpreted in the media almost exclusively as the personal success of the prime minister. Soon after the announcement that Mulroney would be going to Rio, John Hay wrote in his column in the *Ottawa Citizen*: "The 'Earth Summit' in Rio this June runs a fair-to-middling chance of being a foul-tempered failure. What a good thing, therefore, that Brian Mulroney will be there" (John Hay, "Earth summit may prove embarrassing", *Ottawa Citizen*, 13 April 1992). On the conclusion of the summit, the *Toronto Star* ran an editorial that conceded (somewhat grudgingly) Mulroney's diplomatic success: "His environmental record at home is nothing to boast about. But Brian Mulroney deserves full credit for his performance at the Earth summit in Rio de Janeiro.... [He] emerged as a progressive leader willing to do Canada's part" ("PM performs well at earth summit", *Toronto Star*, 15 June 1992).

Jean Chrétien's overall performances at summits, in contrast, have been far more discrete. During the early years of his tenure as prime minister, Chrétien was anything but an avid summiter. As part of his strategy to disassociate himself from the Mulroney diplomatic style, Chrétien downplayed Canada/US summits at the leadership level. As Nossal remarks: "It was not until 23–24 February 1995 that Clinton paid an official visit to Canada, addressed the House of Commons, and had his first bilateral summit with Chrétien" (Nossal, 1997: 206). Chrétien did not reciprocate with an official visit to the United States until April 1996. Although it is true that Chrétien and Clinton met quite frequently between the time they were elected into office (November 1992 and October 1993) and their bilateral summits, these earlier meetings were held in a multilateral context such as the Seattle Summit in December 1993.

This sense of distance was reinforced by Chrétien's determination to balance Canada's role as a partner to the United States with its role as an autonomous actor. Externally, this signalling device was ingrained, albeit often unintentionally delivered. An illustrative case is the "open mike" episode at the July 1997 Brussels NATO Summit, in which Chrétien revealed his double-edged feelings about the United States to the Belgium Prime Minister: "I like to stand up to the Americans. It's popular. But you have to be careful because they're our friends" (quoted in Richard Gwyn, "So what if PM's remarks smacked of Machiavelli?", *Toronto Star*, 16 July 1997).

Eschewing the symbolic expressions cultivated and enjoyed by Mulroney, Chrétien retained a highly instrumental focus at multilateral summits. Despite the political benefits he derived from the No. 1 status accorded to Canada in various UN "social" rankings, Chrétien kept a very low-key presence at functions such as the UN 50th Anniversary celebrations in October 1995. He stayed only one day, turning down invitations to take on other speaking engagements or stay to the formal conclusion of the ceremonies, preferring to devote his time and energy to those forums that promised to deliver tangible rather than symbolic results. The agenda-setting exercise of the 1995 G-7 Summit in Halifax, for example, was directed quite specifically at introducing reforms into the international financial architecture. His key concern at the December 1994 Miami Summit of the Americas was to restore momentum towards the free trade project within the hemisphere. The November 1997 Asia Pacific Economic Cooperation (APEC) Summit in Vancouver "meant business" as opposed to following a widened agenda that might have placated some of the protesters outside.

As the Vancouver APEC Summit demonstrated, this focus-oriented approach was not entirely politically risk-free, yet it meshed well with Chrétien's personal style. In terms of character and talents, Chrétien enjoyed the exchange of information more than ideas. He was most comfortable in one-to-one situations (either on the sidelines of wider meetings or on the phone), than he was with large "talking shop" affairs. Despite his brief spell as minister of external affairs, the common view of Chrétien was that he "came into office with a limited feel for foreign policy [and] lacked the same experience in External Affairs ... that he enjoyed in economic ministries.... His meetings with foreign leaders tended to be more about comparative domestic politics than any exploration of the intricacies of international diplomacy" (Greenspon and Wilson-Smith, 1996: 102–103).

Consistent with his cautious style, Chrétien's active participation in foreign affairs centred on what he considered the core competencies of government: economic competitiveness, trade politics, and jobs. As illustrated most vividly by his leadership on the Zaire/Great Lakes initiative, there were exceptions to this rule, but they occurred only in rare circumstances. Although versions differ about what was the primary catalyst for Chrétien's interest in the Zaire/Great Lakes, most interpretations mention the personal framing of the issue. One variant of this theme suggests that the trigger was a telephone conversation between Chrétien and his nephew, the Canadian ambassador to the United Nations. As special envoy to the Secretary General of the United Nations, Raymond Chrétien had been assigned the difficult task of addressing the crisis in the Central African region, and his message to his uncle was that the international community must act to deal with the "dire" situation (transcript, press conference, Prime Minister Jean Chrétien, CBC Newsworld, 16:00, 12 November 1996).[30] Another version highlights the influence of Aline Chrétien in drawing her husband's attention to the apocalyptic reports from CNN about the refugee situation, as they were spending a quiet weekend at their Harrington Lake retreat. A key litmus test for the actual mobilisation of any such initiative, furthermore, was the way in which it played to the "national unity" dossier. If an endeavour was positively received in Quebec, it would be given considerable weight.[31]

Chrétien's diplomatic forte was leading "Team Canada" initiatives to Latin America and the Asia-Pacific region. But he was highly competent as well at using relatively small or exclusive summits such as the G-7, the APEC forum, or even the Organization on Security and Co-operation in Europe (OSCE) or La Francophonie, to get to know individual leaders, so that he could take advantage of these connections "when it was time to call political leaders around the world to organize" a mission such as the Zaire initiative. As Chrétien explicitly put it: "The people I called were the people I knew.... You call a guy on the phone and generally speaking, because you met him a few times ... he returns your phone call" (quoted in "Rebels claim victory in Zaire battles", *Globe and Mail*, 3 December 1996; for further analysis, see Cooper, 2000).

By this instrumental set of standards, the 1994 Cairo Conference on Population and Development, the 1995 Copenhagen World Summit for Social Development (WSSD), and the 1995 Fourth World Conference on Women in Beijing held little attraction as sites for Chrétien's personal involvement. Massive rather than intimate affairs, none of them had much value in forging deeper connections with other leaders. In their focus on big ideas and sweeping visions for the establishment of new economic rules, they held at least as much potential for generating "trouble" as for guiding or explaining the government's agenda. By raising rather than diminishing expectations in a time of austerity, they were out of step with the tone of governance adopted by the Chrétien government. Try as they might, therefore, NGOs had little hope of triggering a renewed burst of high-level personal diplomacy at these social conferences. The cry of "Where is Chrétien?" at the Copenhagen WSSD might have been a fitting slogan for the extended mobilisation of civil society (or for domestic resistance to cutbacks in social policy), but it had little potential to activate direct forms of prime ministerial leadership (Paul Knox, "Chrétien blasted for summit absence", *Globe and Mail*, 7 March 1995).[32]

The delegation of authority to ministers

Leadership at the prime ministerial level constitutes more than just direct participation; it also applies to the more indirect methods of sailing the ship of state. Prime ministers act not only as the proverbial "pilots" guiding foreign policy but also as captains charged with overall responsibility for other ministers who are actually at the helm. As Nossal more succinctly depicts this shared responsibility: "While prime ministers tend to be the central figures in the development of many aspects of Canada's foreign policy – determining what the priorities will be, shaping the administration, policy making at the summit – they do not engage in the foreign policy process alone. They are assisted by, and must deal with, other ministers in cabinet, including those whose portfolios touch on the wide-ranging issues in foreign affairs" (Nossal, 1997: 219).

One of most interesting pieces of the puzzle of Canada's role in the UN conferences concerns the way the delegation of ministerial responsibility in these specific episodes fits the general pattern of governance adopted by prime ministers Mulroney and Chrétien. In Mulroney's case, given both his business background and his brokerage instinct, it is tempting to see him as either a chief operating officer or a CEO. In the evolution of policy towards these select UN conferences, however, this executive style allowed for an enormous range of outcomes. At one end of the continuum, it allowed a tightly centralised authority among the PMO/PCO and key advisers. In the run-up to the Rio conference, most significantly, Derek Burney took on a vital role in the agenda-setting process. As Mulroney's former chief of staff and lead official on the FTA negotiations, Burney had the confidence of the prime minister and direct access to him. As Canada's ambassador to the United States, Burney also served as the central conduit between Ottawa and Washington on climate change and other sensitive issues.[33]

At the other end of the continuum, with respect to the Rio negotiations, a tremendous amount of overlap can be found in the delegation of authority. This fragmentation dated back to the turf war between the foreign ministry and the environmental ministry at the Stockholm conference (Knelman, 1972–1973: 28–49; for a fuller discussion of the relationship between the Environment and Foreign Affairs ministries, see Doern, 1993). Nonetheless, the dispersion of authority was much more complex than this single historical divide would imply. As well as coordinating the UNCED Task Force, Michael Small in External Affairs was appointed Special Advisor to the Secretary of State for External Affairs. G.V. Buxton served as the alternate head of the Canadian delegation and as Executive Director of the National Secretariat for UNCED at Environment Canada. And to complicate matters even further, Arthur Campeau was appointed the Environment Minister's Special Advisor on International Affairs as well as the Prime Minister's Personal Representative to UNCED.[34]

In all this clutter, key ministers could still use the Rio Summit process to do some running of their own. As Minister of Fisheries and Oceans, John Crosbie served as an effective message-carrier for Canada's public information campaign on conservation with respect to high seas fishing. More comprehensively, Jean Charest proved well able to handle a sharp learning curve as environmental minister despite not being the same type of mission-oriented environmental minister that Lucien Bouchard had been (on this typology, see Savoie, 1990). Although eliciting a good press and media spin was a major concern (and skill) of Charest's, he came across also as an engaged participant with respect to the Rio negotiations. As the head of the Canadian delegation, it was Charest, not Mulroney, who handled day-to-day procedural matters and application of strategy. In terms of process, Charest's success as a communicator and handler of the Canadian delegation may be judged by the fact that Mulroney asked the minister of the environment to continue his large morning delegation meetings even after the prime minister had arrived. In terms of substantive diplomatic engagement, Charest was included as one of the cluster of 15 ministers included in the intensive negotiations over the wording of the final text.

This relative ministerial autonomy did not signify that the "thumbprints" of Mulroney and the PMO were not all over the dossier of the Rio Summit – and the thumbprints did not have to be applied very hard. The mere fact that "the Boss was going" to Rio was enough to mobilise and orchestrate the bureaucracy into unlocking problems and resolving turf differences. If problems remained, though, these thumbprints were applied more forcefully. The main casualty of this force was Monique Landry, the minister of external affairs with responsibility over CIDA. Although CIDA had moved to emphasise the theme of international sustainability, especially as it applied to environmental assessments, Landry was told by the PMO only the day before she was to leave to join the Canadian delegation that she was not going to Rio.

The pattern of delegated authority among Canadian ministers at the 1993 Vienna Conference on Human Rights seemed very different. Preparations for this summit were a good deal more coherent at the bureaucratic level. Despite some fragmentation with the federal-provincial committee chaired by Multicultural Canada, a sense of bureaucratic coherence was achieved when External Affairs and International Trade assumed the "lead" position on this dossier. Interdepartmental consultations were coordinated through a committee chaired by a foreign ministry official (the director-general of International Organizations). Anne Park took on the dual responsibility of heading the Canadian delegation throughout the preparatory process of the negotiations on the conference and chairing WEOG (the Western European and Others Group). The foreign ministry's lead position, therefore, allowed both a sense of domestic continuity and international status.

What was lacking at the Vienna conference was the sense of any focus being applied by short but intense bursts of prime ministerial or ministerial attention, as had been present at Rio. Somewhat paradoxically, this lack of high-level attention enhanced the sense of bureaucratic coherence in routine matters. The deficit was in the lack of political leverage to seize the moment of the Vienna conference in a more dramatic fashion. Foreign ministry officials kept trying to get the minister engaged in the process – to publicise the Vienna conference before the House of Commons Standing Committee on External Affairs and International Trade; to have a discussion of the dossier at the cabinet committee on foreign and defence policy; to put out a position paper on Canada's priorities; and to help break some of the deadlocks mounting up in the negotiating process. But these efforts appear to have fallen on disinterested ears.

In contrast to the activist role played by Jean Charest at the Rio Summit, Barbara McDougall was a passive (and increasingly distracted) observer during the negotiating process on the Vienna Human Right's Conference. Why there was such a difference in participation level invites some speculation. Running out of steam with respect to popular credibility, Mulroney became increasingly keen to take high-profile initiatives (most notably on peacekeeping and humanitarian interventions). At the same time, there was within the PMO/PCO central agency apparatus an obvious frustration with many of the traditional ways of doing things by professional diplomats. This combination left little space for innovation at the ministerial level.[35]

Chrétien was more of a "chairman of the board" leader than Mulroney, allowing considerable room for ministers to run their own show within the parameters of the government's core agenda (Greenspon and Wilson-Smith, 1996: 77; this theme is elaborated upon with great insight in Savoie, 1999). Guided by his own formative experience in the Pearson government of 1963–1968, Chrétien refrained from excessive micromanagement. As long as ministers did not make mistakes, they were usually allowed to run a long way with their own policy initiatives. In general principle, and usually in specific practice, the goal was not to tighten but to "relax central control over the government by farming power back to individual ministers" (Greenspon and Wilson-Smith, 1996: 46).[36] At the UN conferences, however, this approach translated awkwardly into action. In theory, individual ministers had considerable room to manoeuvre. The experience at the Kyoto conference on climate change imparted a ragged twist to the Chrétien government's approach of delegating authority between a number of different (often competing) ministers. In this case the Canadian negotiating team looked more like "a ragged flotilla" each responding "to wind and wave in peculiar and singular fashion" than part of a singular ship of state (Pal, 1988: 25). The announcement of Canada's position was repeatedly delayed. A face-saving consensus finally emerged only with considerable difficulty.

With such open (and embarrassing) divisions, Prime Minister Chrétien was ultimately forced to intervene on this important dossier. Once opened, however, the forces of fragmentation were very difficult to contain. Instead of managing the Kyoto agenda by prime minister intervention, the issue continued to swirl out of control up to the 2002 Johannesburg Conference on Sustainable Development. This aura of equivocation, if not outright retreat, triggered a number of scathing critiques. One scholar went as far as to term Canada a "rogue state" on climate change, defending a "bureaucratized, sterile, and commodified view of the natural world" (Broadhead, 2001; see also Macdonald and Smith, 1999–2000).

Chevrolet or Cadillac approach?

There can be little debate that Chrétien adopted a more muted approach to the UN world conferences than Mulroney. He made no bold initiatives in their direction that required substantial infusions of money. The Chrétien government resisted calls for any of these conferences to be made "pledging" forums with shares being allocated according to specific sectoral targets.

What is more debatable is whether this approach is evidence of a trend towards a complete erosion of the Canadian diplomatic tradition. The Chrétien government's no-frills approach to these UN conferences did not mean that it was turning its back to the world on these issues. As will be showcased in later chapters, high profile ministers attended both the Copenhagen WSSD and the Cairo conferences, and these ministers were eager to deliver a lot more in the way of tangible resources and policy outputs. Far from holding civil society back from participation, Chrétien allowed the diversity of Canadian NGO representation to be extended greatly. If Canada fell short of being a role model on programme delivery, it was a model both in terms of the pluralism of its participation and the nature of the relationship forged between the External/Foreign Affairs bureaucracy and the NGO community.

But it cannot be said that this stance was irrevocable. While Chrétien had plenty to be modest about during the span of his prime ministerial terms, agency could still trump the structure of constraint on an issue by issue basis, as shown by the signs that he was willing to contemplate a reversal of position on the Kyoto agreement. Changes in personnel within the bureaucratic apparatus of the Canadian state helped ease this reversal, as did the pressure maintained by societal groups. But these factors could not have effected a change alone. For a change of heart to take place on such a sensitive issue it had to come from the apex of power.

If the Chrétien style had the modesty of a "Chevrolet" approach, the Mulroney approach to the summits had some of the luxury and the overcompensation of a "Cadillac" model (see, for example, Cooper, 1997a: 13; Nossal, 1997: 184). Chrétien's approach made a virtue of returning to the sense of restraint that informed so much of the understanding of the practitioners of Canada's immediate post-1945 diplomacy. Mulroney's approach was more uneven and opportunistic. In terms of political/diplomatic image, it had considerable attraction; yet, in actually financial terms, the results were often more illusory than real. During the Rio conference, Mulroney made considerable noise about reaffirming the promise that developed countries reach the acceptable UN target of 0.7 per cent of GNP for development assistance. Generous but – as it transpired – empty words. Moreover, what was delivered had an unintended ricochet effect. Mulroney's commitment of CAN$4.8 million dollars as CIDA's contribution to UNCED necessitated an entire re-jigging of the programmes directed towards sustainable development.

Mulroney's characteristic opportunism is accentuated by a comparison of the relative wealth of resources devoted to the Rio conferences and the constraints at the Vienna conference. Without attention at the prime ministerial/ministerial level, the Canadian delegation was far smaller and more low-key at Vienna. With the cuts in the ODA (Official Development Assistance) budget, CIDA made a decision early in the process that it could not make a major contribution except possibly through advisory services. Canada's reputation for generosity, therefore, was diminished through these conferences well before the Chrétien government came to power.

This conclusion does not diminish the role of the prime minister in Canada's performance at the UN world conferences. Indeed in some ways it highlights the cycle from considerable enthusiasm at the Rio conference to a more muted approach at the Copenhagen and Cairo conferences. Yet, this impression of strong contrasts must be nuanced. The Mulroney approach appeared an exciting means to meet the leadership test, yet it ran on illusions and commitments were subordinated to convenience. Chrétien's role, on the other hand, appeared very restrained in terms of the application of the test of leadership. But it did bring Canadian diplomacy in tune with a more consistent approach. On many issues the constraints of discipline curtailed innovation from the top down. Still, in encouraging other forms of constructive multilateral diplomacy, Chrétien allowed margins for manoeuvre below the radar of leadership.

5
Tests of discipline: imposition or negotiations of the system of governance?

The primary normative test of UN world conferences relates to the question of what purpose they serve. To those who interpret UN conferences as part of a benign construct of the interplay between governance and diplomacy, the machinery of the conferences is central to the promotion of a stable international order. At the very least these conferences promote dialogue at the global level. More ambitiously they can become the motor by which settlements are brought about, maintained, and reformulated. With multilateralism at the core of a revised post–Cold War system, the potential of UN conferences as part of that repertoire deserves more attention. As elaborated by John Ruggie, the role of multilateralism as the "foundational architectural principle" of the new order has become thoroughly embedded in the literature (Ruggie, 1993a: 25). What gets less attention is the concomitant question: In what ways can multilateral instruments such as the UN conferences build on the incentive structure to "pursue interests via joint action"? (Ruggie, 1996: 20). While the norms and values at the crux of this new order matter, so do the techniques on which the order is reproduced and modified.

With this test in mind, academic scrutiny should focus on the UN conferences as a series of narratives that highlight the way in which these forums have led the internationalisation of public policy. Rather than abdicating under pressures for contraction of collective agency, this component of multilateralism can offer a site (and a face of governance) for attempting to grapple with – and to promote – an extension of the distributive and regulative components of the international order.

At its most all-encompassing, this test centres on the prospect of the UN conferences being mobilised to advance an authentically globally directed and inclusive expression of policy. One leading team of British researchers, although acutely aware of obstacles in the way of this mechanism adopting a "far reaching and radical" rather than reformist stance, has given the UN conferences a very high grade on both substance and style. Highlighting the role of the 1995 Copenhagen World Summit for Social Development (WSSD) in advancing the agenda of universality in global social policy, Bob Deacon and his colleagues claim that this event "represented the most significant global accord on the need to tackle issues of poverty, social exclusion and social development, North and South" (Deacon, Hulse and Stubbs, 1997: 87). They further underscored the legitimacy given to non-state actors: "The summit was where the role of global NGOs as a surrogate for UN democratic accountability was endorsed" (Deacon, Hulse and Stubbs, 1997: 89).

Other analysts, in a far more defensive mode, see the positive attributes of the UN conferences as part of a compensatory strategy. Whatever progressive spirit can be found within this shaping of governance and diplomacy does not come with an unconditional commitment to a new (and equitable) order but is rather a convenient means to deflect and offset momentum towards neo-liberal/market tendencies. That is to say, UN conferences represent a tactical device by a select combination of international and national (mainly Western) state and non-state forces to introduce some element of a welfare-oriented counter agenda to cushion the impact of the dominant trend. This theme of compensation is picked up in the work of Anne-Marie Burley (Burley, 1993). It also comes out in Sorensen's contention that revitalised forms of multilateralism represent an "attempt to regain some of the regulatory influence lost in the national political space" (Sorensen, 1998: 99).

The detractors of UN conferences (predictably) see its role in change in a very negative light. To them, rather than helping advance any positive agenda, these conferences have become part of a "frame-up" devoted to a very different and detrimental set of outcomes (Constantinou, 1996). Tearing away the secrecy of the negotiation process simply exposes the failure of traditional diplomacy to act in an enlightened fashion. From one critical outlook, a new form of multilateralism may have the potential to become "a means of promoting global co-operation" as well as being a "site of political and ideological struggle" in episodes such as the Earth Summit, the World Social Summit or the Women's Summit in Beijing (Gill, 1997: 7). However, the potential for diplomacy is held back because it has been captured by entrenched forces devoted to a narrowly based consensus on the accepted rules of the game. Rather than being a force of emancipation, therefore, the orthodox mode of multilateralism has become another tool of discipline or "coercive socialization" (Barry Jones, 2000: 97). As Gill declares, multilateralism from the top down reinforces the status quo "construct[ing] and codify[ing] sets of rules, norms and principles from the vantage point of established or predominant power" (Gill, 1997: 6–7).

In a subtle (or cynical) variation of this critical assessment, the "frame-up" by multilateral diplomacy vis-à-vis the UN conferences is made out to be part of a conscious design to offer symbolic cover as opposed to winning instrumental benefits through a global social policy agenda. Borrowing implicitly from William Robinson's "pushing polyarchy" argument (Robinson, 1996),[37] the vehicles of multilateral diplomacy in these episodes are cast as "gimmicks" intended not to nudge welfarism forward (Emmerij et al., 2001: 89) but rather to mask (and defuse the consequences of) the lack of genuinely constructive delivery. Instead of becoming part of the solution, they are at the core of the diplomatic problem.

Canada in the 1990s was poised for this test of purpose. In a variety of ways the decade was ripe for a renewal of Canadian commitment to the United Nations and a new world order. The logic of taking on a greater set of obligations beyond borders (Hoffmann, 1981) became more compelling, with the crises in the former Yugoslavia, Somalia, and Haiti fostering an acceleration of humanitarian intervention and the intensification of debate about values and rights. The end of the Cold War was also expected to bring some kind of peace dividend. Diplomatically, Canada could bask in the luxury of being secure, without explicit enemies or threats as commonly defined. The general intellectual tenor of the times and the fact that the ties of followership were not as tight as in the bipolar era enhanced the opportunity to exert keener voluntarism and initiatives.

While this leadership was still predicated on the political will at the apex of power, some space for action remained available through the overall apparatus of government. With an expanded international agenda state officials in a variety of ministries had some incentive to claim a tangible piece of that peace dividend. Not only was this an attractive political tactic, but it was irresistible in many areas because of incentives to cooperate to solve common problems in such areas as the environment and population. The exhortations of a constellation of societal forces, along with a desire to reaffirm their own technical abilities reinforced state officials' wish to influence the international agenda.

In the case of Canada this test of purpose was made more difficult, however, by the intrusion of a particular combination of international and domestic circumstances. More with wishful thinking than experience, Canadian state officials held out the hope that the United States would play not only a major but a constructive and coherent role in global management through the UN. Yet the United States adjusted to the post–Cold War realities – and even its own position of strength as the one remaining superpower – with some awkwardness. If the United States remained an uncomfortable multilateralist, neither did it exploit its unilateral capabilities to the fullest extent. It continued to be in – but not completely of – the multilateral diplomacy as practised through mechanisms such as the UN world conferences. Canada and a number of other like-minded countries were conditioned in consequence to play variations on their longstanding dual role: both nudging the United States forward from a laggard position and trying to restrain it when it became overzealous.

On the domestic front Canada's capacity to make bold statements about how it would "make a difference" (Department of External Affairs and International Trade, 1991) was stymied by the country's ongoing obsession with national unity and the question of Quebec's constitutional status. This condition intensified at that time following the failure of the Meech Lake agreement and the Charlottetown Accord, the revival of the Quebec nationalist/sovereignty movement under Lucien Bouchard, and the events relating to the 30 October 1995 referendum. Although these sensitive and emotionally draining domestic questions did not rule out foreign policy innovation, neither did they encourage a comprehensive dynamic of outward-looking involvement in reconstructing the global infrastructure.

Nor can Canadian foreign policy through the 1990s be separated from the twin crises of governmental legitimacy and organisational capacity. Along with most other Western countries, Canada faced multiple demands to recognise the need to negotiate and bargain with their publics in a new and inclusive fashion. This loss of confidence in the authority of government was accompanied by a serious – and widening – gap between governmental responsibilities and resources. Burdened with a rising foreign debt and a budget deficit, Canada could no longer undertake international commitments without checks of a disciplinary nature being exerted from within as well as without the country. The concept of extending the strands of a global agenda based on social welfarism – at this moment of fiscal crisis – came up against the ideas and interests of "market civilization" or the "transnational managerial class" (Cox, 1992a) as well as those of the powerful Department of Finance and its constituents in Canada. Any prospect of acting on the temptation to follow an expansive course meant contesting and overcoming the resistance of these constraining forces, which were driven by economic criteria rather than by international good citizenship.

Setting the rules of the game: the two faces of discipline

Questions of discipline invite us to focus more closely on the establishment of the rules of the game vis-à-vis global governance. Who (or what) sets the framework for rules of the game? Are the parameters of a system of governance imposed by the thinking and practices of a globalised business community? Or is there room available for an emergent pattern of global governance to be established through a "society" of states via negotiations on a multilateral basis?

The business face of governance privileges control by market forces and leaves individual states with little choice on how to formulate or implement the system of governance. It gives primacy to efficiency in adapting to the pressures of globalisation rather than to the cultivation of equity or justice, and it subordinates transparency of process to achievement of the desired result. The residue of state power is harnessed to a concentrated diplomacy of competitiveness in which individual nations and their leaders jockey for position – and approval – in "an international business civilization" (Strange, 1991: 260).

The "society of states" face of governance (Bull, 1977), for its part, allows a more robust form of multilateral diplomacy to take place. It assumes that the world turns through a pattern of economic and political interdependence not on a self-help basis. Any system of governance presently in train, therefore, must take as its starting point the need to create rules through a form of collective problem solving via salient international institutions (Keohane, 1989). States may have reduced space in which to operate, but they will have ample room for manoeuvre if they choose to maximise this option. At the domestic/administrative level, the onus remains on state/societal mobilisation and the creative deployment of a diplomatic skill-set.

Seen in their starkest contrasts, these two faces of governance clearly have different basic assumptions. The business face takes it for granted that any future system of governance will act as a receptor for the forces of "coercive socialization" Barry Jones talks of. Any attempt to offer alternative or critical policy guidelines from within the system will be effectively controlled. In this construct, the UN conferences may be well intentioned but their impact will be disciplined (as mentioned above by Falk) by the combination of market forces and corporate power, aided and abetted by the application of state coercion. As Susan Strange defines the power structure: "What is lacking in the system of governance

[is] an opposition. Where states were once the masters of markets now it is the markets which, on many crucial issues, are the masters over the government of states" (Strange, 1996a: 6).

Stephen Gill, through his notion of "new constitutionalism", has extended the analysis on this shadow of discipline. The discipline imposed at the core of a comprehensive business agenda gives little room for societal input. The autonomy of national governments on policy questions is eroded because of both indirect pressure (through socialisation practices) and direct pressures (enforced harmonisation). Indeed, says Gill, the differences between national governments and national policies have disappeared with consolidation of practices and tighter patterns of conformity: "An international regulatory regime that emphasises market efficiency and discipline, and limitations on democratic decision-making processes [ensuring] the insulation of key aspects of the economy from the influence of politicians or the mass of citizens by imposing, internationally and externally ... 'binding constraints' ... the conduct of ... policies" (Gill, 1995a: 412).

Elsewhere Gill further outlines the detrimental effect of such control, commenting on how such a system reinforces the crisis of the democratic deficit:

The new constitutionalism seeks to reinforce a process whereby government policies are increasingly accountable to [international] capital, and thus to market forces [and] to strengthen political discipline, in part to provide a more hospitable investment climate to attract production. Credibility with the financial markets is, for governments, becoming perhaps more important than credibility with voters. (Gill, 1995b)

Robert Cox, for his part, privileges the impact of a "transnational business élite" in the disciplinary process (Cox, 1992a). Indeed, Cox argues that the impact of this élite is often decisive because of the same combination of indirect and direct forces emphasised by Gill. That is to say: "Governments [have been] made to understand that a revival of economic growth depended on business confidence to invest, and that this confidence depended on 'discipline' directed at trade unions and government fiscal management" (Cox, 1994a: 46).

The key difference between Gill and Cox concerns the degree of choice they see in the disciplinary process. Gill maintains that privileging of structure not agency is crucial to understanding the form, scope, and intensity of this disciplinary system. Cox allows more leeway for individual differences, in that he gives considerable weight to the role of national governments in accommodating to globalisation through their functions as "managers of the national economies" or "mid-wives to globalization and international trading agreements" (Cox, 1991, 1992b). In other words, governments can at least to some extent plan their role as arbiters of the process. If firm in his belief that the "autonomous capacity of states has been reduced for all states" in the "emerging global economy", Cox concedes that this pattern of adjustment is uneven and nationally distinctive, taking place "in a greater degree for some [states] than others" (Cox, 1997a: 528).

The multilateral rules-based face of governance, on the other hand, offers a divergent take on the nature of discipline. Paul Hirst and Grahame Thompson see discipline in a "more complex system of power" as being more variable and constructive (Hirst and Thompson, 1996). The forces of globalisation and the new world economy reinstate "the need for the nation state as a crucial relay between the international levels of governance and the articulate publics of the developed world" (Hirst and Thompson, 1996: 191). From this perspective, national governments, rather than contracting under the weight of these forces, must not abdicate their responsibilities to the dictates of disciplines exerted by a narrow and confining business agenda. Rather, discipline must be applied via a new form of global governance on an ambitious scale.

A variety of scholars supports such an image of global governance. David Held sees recent trends in global governance as being conducive to the "requirements of nation-states to collaborate more intensively with each other" through intergovernmental cooperation and international agreements (Held et al., 1999: 89). Saskia Sassen envisages a substantive concept of international governance emerging via coordination (Sassen, 1996). Robert Keohane stresses the development of a new and more sophisticated form of bargaining in global affairs whereby states give up some form of control "in return for influence over others' policies and therefore greater gains from exchange" (Keohane, 1995: 177; Raustiala, 1996).

Notwithstanding their divergence on purpose and method, however, considering these two faces of governance in isolation distorts as much as it informs our attempt to gain a deeper understanding of events such as UN world conferences. As rehearsed in our description of the first disciplinary face, the economic or business agenda cannot be separated from the UN conferences. If, as Ambassador Fréchette suggests, these conferences lacked a direct connection to the "role of the UN in economic affairs" (Fréchette, 1996: 161), the conditioning effect and interplay between mainstream economic/financial/business policy making and diplomatic performance at the national level became thoroughly linked. Any account of negotiations on the way to a new architecture of global governance, therefore, must be broadened to allow material considerations (and limitations) to be brought into the picture.

This meshing of the two faces of discipline is apparent in the wriggle room allowed in the business face for some rebalancing towards a more benign form of global governance. At the statist level, Cox allows room for varied forms of autonomous action by national governments if they have the will to act. Although Cox acknowledges that "we live in a multi-level world that challenges the old Westphalian assumption that a state is a state is a state" (Cox, 1993: 263), he still leaves some (albeit diminished) room for the older "statist" expression in this re-balancing process, but he puts more emphasis on "societal" expression as a counter to the "destructive consequences ... of the self-regulating economy" for the purposes of "bringing the global economy under social control" (Cox, 2000: 25).

At the societal level, both Gill and Cox see the primary locus of resistance as being outside accepted structures and arrangements and operating through collective mobilisation of networks of citizens and other forms of agency. Yet, if they offer a secondary approach, UN institutions, together with the Bretton Woods financial institutions, continue to be accepted (and targeted) as a central "terrain of struggle" (on this theme, see Cox, 1997b). Far from dismissing the UN world conferences as irrelevant against the "dominant forces", Gill and Cox both grant them some potential for a "new multilateralism". As Gill notes:

How do we assess the potential for the further development of other, potentially countervailing types of national and transnational social forces? One way to approach this is through analysis of transnational linkages surrounding certain crucial social problems, such as the environment and social inequality, for example the focus of the Earth Summit, the World Social Summit or the Women's Summit in Beijing. (Gill, 1997: 15)

When we turn our attention to more detailed narratives of the UN conferences themselves, it goes without saying that to highlight the potential of these events in principle is not the same as praising their impact in practice. Some critics have interpreted these forums as events that have provided a mechanism by which energy could be drained away from potentially more substantive forms of mobilisation and resistance (see, for example, Dewar, 1995). Others have gone as far as to suggest that these forums were part of a disciplinary agenda, not just because of what or who was left out, but because they tipped the scales explicitly towards an economic/business bias. Such a process of hijacking by the élite is the central theme of the work, for example, of Pratap Chatterjee and Matthias Finger, who trace how: "UNCED [UN Conference on Environment and Development] set up a process through which TNCs [transnational corporations] were transformed from lobbyists at a national level to legitimate global agents, i.e., partners of governments. UNCED gave them a platform, from which they could frame the new global issues in their own terms" (Chatterjee and Finger, 1994: 112) Another illustration of this theme of business co-optation of the Rio process is found in Hildyard, 1995.

Commentators from the more benign face of global governance view these UN conferences alternatively as part of a top-down attempt to reconstruct forms of multilateral rule making. John Ruggie in particular, building on the notion that the practices and policies of states could be distributed – or "sutured" – upwards to the international level as part of a new design of governance, gives an enthusiastic assessment of this process of shape shifting. The UN world conferences serve as "town meetings of the world", he says, and prove "very influential as sensitivity training for governments on issues that had been neglected, doubtless because they required governments to think hard about the quality of life and values to be served by growth. There were also policy consequences" (Ruggie, 1999: 17). From a bottom-up perspective, these conferences have been portrayed by new multilateralists such as Gill as an important means for providing more inclusive (and effective) societal participation. Once released from the disciplines of the Cold War era, social actors mobilised on a transnational basis and played a prominent role as part of a constructive (albeit also suspicious) opposition to the dominant forces at these conferences (see, for example, in the human rights arena, Sikkink, 1993; Wapner, 1995). In Bjorn Hettne's analysis: "The market cannot liberate itself; neither can it organize society! It reflects, rather, the character of the society and its particular social order, or lack of social order" (Hettne, 1995: 24).

From a more specific perspective, civil society and NGOs in some of these conferences have been cast as major players in the larger drama of an effective "double movement". Cox himself offers the insight that while the substantive impact of the Earth Summit was inconclusive, the conference had another: "Social practices are called into question ... President George Bush was reported as saying, apropos [the] Earth Summit: 'Our lifestyle is not up for negotiation'". This comment seemed to smack of the opportunism of politicians involved in the immediacy of an election campaign. But it was condemned for its larger contradictions: "The relatively affluent are challenged to rethink their patterns of consumption and behaviour, in relation to the biosphere and to models they project to less affluent peoples" (Cox, 1995: 42–43).

This emergent dynamic goes some way, then, to confirm Gill's assessment of the potential of these world conferences (and the NGOs participating at them) to act as agents. On the one hand, this dynamic may be seen as part of a potential "counter-project" (see, for example, Falk,

1994) by which the globalisation of economic and social change can be rebalanced between a business agenda and an agenda that includes a social component. On the other hand, the process offers support for the hope that the UN could finally fulfil its promise by becoming not only a forum for deliberations about pressing international questions but a venue to "provide effective democratic mechanisms of political coordination and change" (Held et al., 1999: 268).

Tests of discipline in two case studies

Having sharpened the tests of discipline in the context of UN world conferences at the conceptual level, we can now cut more concretely into these questions by examining two specific case studies: the Mulroney government's handling of the Global Forestry Convention and the Chrétien government's diplomacy at the Copenhagen WSSD.

The Mulroney government and the Global Forestry Convention

The Mulroney government's performance at the Rio UNCED conference, with specific reference to the attempt to negotiate a forestry agreement, is interesting because at first glance it contradicts the perception of this government as a strong advocate of a business or market-driven disciplinarian agenda. Looking at the big picture, both Gill and Cox see the Mulroney initiatives as an exemplar of the hyper-liberalism or neoconservatism dominant in the 1980s. Cox asserts: "Neo-conservative ideology has sustained the transformation of the state in Britain, the United States, Canada and Australia in the direction of globalization" (Cox, 1994b: 49). And Gill adds that the Mulroney initiative on the North American Free Trade Agreement "can also be seen as a vehicle to extend corporate power in North America, and ... to 'politically lock in' neo-liberal reforms in Mexico, Canada and potentially in Chile" (Gill, 1995a: 72).

Through a narrower, more country-specific lens, this image is supported by a wave of commentary that depicts Canada (and Mulroney) as being trapped in the discipline of globalisation and hyper-liberalism. This image is captured by the stark words of two critical academics: "The Mulroney government's policies were driven by an ideological predisposition for neo-liberal economics, free trade, minimal state involvement in the economy and social policy retrenchment" (McBride and Shields, 1997: 12). Yet, this dominant perception was counteracted by another (albeit less common) image of the Mulroney-Conservative government as the proponent of international governance via multilateral agreements and conventions. As one respected Canadian non-governmental organisation reassessed the Conservative's record after its first term of office: "Canada's primary identification today is not that of a junior continental partner to a superpower, nor a second-tier actor in the Western Summit Seven or the North Atlantic Treaty Organization (NATO). Instead it is that of a vigorous, activist middle power" (North-South Institute, 1989: 2).

To which face of governance did the Mulroney government actually subscribe? The level of its commitment to international environmental reform provides an interesting test case. This theme was especially salient with respect to the negotiations on the Global Forestry Convention (GFC), a convention on sustainable forestry development. In many ways, Canada's push through these negotiations for a separate GFC reinforced the impression of Canadian multilateralism. Canada worked closely with traditional "like-minded" countries such as Sweden on the forestry issue. Canada and Sweden, for instance, together convened an informal consultation of some 25 major forestry nations in February 1990. It was largely thanks to this initiative that a declaration was made at the UNCED Preparatory Committee (Prep Com) II in March–April 1991 to develop a non-legally binding authorised statement on the management, conservation, and sustainable development of forests.

If forestry diplomacy reinforced a general commonality among like-minded countries, however, it also revealed a number of differences in style. Australia played down the forestry issue, choosing instead to focus (via high profile diplomacy) on the pursuit of a bio-diversity convention. Other potentially like-minded countries were considered too eager to use unilateral techniques of diplomacy to be willing to impose the immediate discipline of a global agreement. The Netherlands, to give the most interesting illustration, had already signalled its intention of imposing import restrictions on tropical hardwoods from countries that did not have sustainable managed forests, a tough official policy that restricted its options at Rio. Stylistic differences between Canada and Sweden stood out as well. The Canadian delegation complained in particular about Sweden's "overzealous" style on the forestry dossier, as Sweden pushed for an immediate start on negotiations towards a convention rather than first laying down a set of broad principles that could subsequently be used to build consensus for a convention.

Seen in context, this search for discipline through a new multilateral form of global governance reflected Canada's desire for a balanced international–domestic approach. On the domestic front, the Mulroney government wanted to defuse the mounting "green" campaign of the late 1980s and early 1990s, because of the Canadian practice of clear-cutting old growth forests and allowing pulp-mill effluent. Building on a variety of local eco-actions, the green campaign had progressed to the stage where exports of Canadian lumber were being targeted for sanctions by the transnational environmental movement. Faced with the threat of considerable damage to its reputation (the stigma of being labelled "Brazil North") and substantial material loss (tourism as well as trade, where Canada enjoyed a $20 billion net balance), the Mulroney government had a strong motive for promoting a balanced forestry convention at UNCED. However, Canada did not want to lead other countries, especially those in the developing world, in making sacrifices through conservation measures. It preferred discipline to be applied through international obligations in a comprehensive and even way.

From this initial discussion, it becomes clear that disciplinary action can be interpreted in opposing ways. According to the "society of states" face of governance, the discipline can be seen as being contracted and benign, with the Mulroney government playing the "crucial relay" role described by Hirst and Thompson above (Hirst and Thompson, 1996: 190). This discipline is consistent in turn with a rebalancing agenda based not just on a narrow business agenda and market forces but on an agenda filled with social purpose. By stressing "fulfilling Canada's responsibility to citizens of the world", and creating a new set of guidelines and binding international standards for the world's forests, the government hoped more easily to overcome resistance within the domestic forestry industry to the modification of their way of doing business. As Mulroney made clear at Rio: "Countries have a right to manage their forest resources. And humanity has a right to expect these management decisions will be ecologically sound" (Office of the Prime Minister, 1992).

What stands out about process of the forestry issue is the complexity of the "two-level games". Even the images such as "double edged" patterns of negotiation (Evans, Jacobson and Putnam, 1993) and "triangular diplomacy" (Stopford and Strange, 1991) do not capture the multi-faceted nature of this process. At the domestic level, business and civil society both took an active part in the forestry negotiations. On the business side, Rio extended the consultation process, already dating back over two years, by Forestry Canada in partnership with both the provincial forestry ministries and the forestry industry. In this process of consultation, representatives of the Council of Forest Industries of British Columbia and the Canadian Pulp and Paper Association (CPPA), together with the "peak" group of Canadian CEOs, the Business Council on National Issues (BCNI) and the so-called Friday Group[38] engaged with these issues as they attended the Prep Coms and became immersed with the UNCED agenda. On the civil society side, several NGOs with an interest in the forestry issue took part in the UNCED negotiations through the Canadian Participatory Committee for UNCED (CPCU). To give just one illustration of this hybrid milieu, a representative of the Western Canadian Wilderness Committee attended Prep Com III together with a representative from the British Columbia forestry industry.

Encapsulated by this diplomatic approach, the requisite amount of discipline could be applied to ensure the trade-offs necessary for a balanced and regulated framework. Business groups were willing to accept the need for this type of discipline for both domestic reasons (to stymie NGO protests about forestry practices) and international reasons (to allow a level playing field with competitors). The NGOs that remained within the CPCU accepted the discipline during the Rio process as a technique for maintaining their direct access to the negotiation floor and the channel of information.

From another angle, however, it may be said that this pattern demonstrated that both business and government in different ways were hostage to the actions of the NGOs on the outside of the process that were prepared to take direct action in the way of blockades and boycotts. Alternatively, the NGOs within the CPCU may be seen as having been "managed" to the extent that they were hesitant to criticise Canadian forest practices at the Prep Coms and risk losing their ability to present their concerns in the negotiations. Rumoured protests on the floor of the negotiations against Canadian forest practices did not transpire.[39]

This focus on disciplinary activity within the forestry negotiations does not mean that the attempt to introduce international governance through negotiated rulemaking was at all complete. A number of key environmental groups, most notably Greenpeace, declined to participate in the CPCU or the Rio negotiations at all. Suspicious of the embrace of national governments, and of the participation within the Canadian delegation of the Council of Forest Industries of British Columbia and the Canadian Pulp and Paper Association, these environmental groups opted to stay on the outside. Greenpeace provided an alternative plan of action on the environment that declared emphatically: "The challenge is nothing less than to rescue the planet and its capacity to support human life: to seize this moment to set in motion the economic, political and technological transformation that the world plainly requires" (Greenpeace International, 1992: 2).

Greenpeace's operational strategy was to concentrate on direct action. In the case of the Canadian forestry industry this option was built around a multidimensional public campaign involving both a local dimension (blockades of roads and other activity intended to disrupt logging in Clayoquot Sound, for example) and an international dimension (protests outside Canadian embassies, and threats of boycotts against forest products companies in general and MacMillan Bloedel, in particular, as well as the principal customers of these companies). Greenpeace was attempting to apply a very different type of discipline to the industry. This discipline was imposed not by a process of multilateral bargaining but by unilateral sanctions. The results were predicated on the scenario of far more intensive activity into the future. As Brian Hocking puts it: "New environmental pressures presented the prospect of more stringent – and expensive – regulations together with a consumer-directed international campaign led by Greenpeace ... [Canadian forestry companies] were subjected to what they regarded as blackmail, but which Greenpeace termed consumer education programmes directed towards alerting the public to the origins of the raw materials from which their products were manufactured" (Hocking, 1995: 30).

The attempt to introduce disciplinary action through a new forestry regime proved just as incomplete at the international level. From the outset of the Rio Prep Coms, the developing countries resisted any move in the direction of a GFC. This resistance stemmed in part from logistical considerations. Developing countries expressed reservations about entering into immediate negotiations on forests when their diplomatic and scientific resources were stretched to breaking point from the highly technical negotiations on climate change and the bio-diversity conventions, as well as the general preparations for UNCED. Opposition to a forestry convention also took on an equity dimension, as the developing countries were concerned that any move towards a legal instrument on forestry could be exploited by developed countries to deflect the need to control emissions of greenhouse gases which arise primarily from the activities of developed countries. Prime Minister Mahathir of Malaysia was particularly vocal in his criticism of the hypocrisy of the developed world. Having failed to tackle their own environmental problems – brought about by development "paid" for by the South – Mahathir argued, the developed North was now claiming the right to regulate the development of the South. He roundly condemned the activities of northern-based environmental NGOs for imposing (as illustrated by the Netherlands case) unfair additional unilateral constraints on the trade of developing countries.

Still, notwithstanding these obstacles, some momentum persisted for the introduction of a new form of rules-based global governance in the forestry industry. A year after the Rio conference, an agreement was struck among NGOs and some members of the forestry business to found a Forest Stewardship Council (FSC), and in October 1993 the first assembly of the FSC was held in Toronto. This form of discipline proved once again, however, to be both loose and incomplete. The FSC lacked an intergovernmental component. What is more, there remained a clear distinction between NGOs as insiders and outsiders. From within, the World Wildlife Federation supported a comprehensive push for a labelling system in order to promote sustainable forest management. From the other side, Greenpeace and Friends of the Earth removed themselves from the body (although continuing to be observers) in response to the representation of the forestry industry on the FSC (Peter Knight, "Timber watchdog ready to bite", *Financial Times*, 6 October 1993).

At the intergovernmental negotiation level, Canada pressed forward at UNCED and at a number of post-Rio conferences, the so-called Helsinki Process and the Montreal Process for an international convention (Grayson, 1995). The motivation for this active form of "forestry diplomacy" was expressed in the 1994 report of the Standing Committee on Natural Resources:

What is urgently needed to 'level the playing field' between various forestry countries is an international agreement on principles and standards of forest management that would be both transparent and scientifically defensible. Such an International Convention on Sustainable Forestry would address the management, conservation and sustainable development of all types of forests and, in so doing, provide benchmarks against which Canada's performance could be measured objectively. (House of Commons, Canada, 1994: 46)

Some sign of success came with the Malaysians' agreement on the need for at least a set of non-binding international principles, a shift in attitude signalled by a willingness to work jointly with Canada to develop compromise language for international guidelines for forestry products. This move was designed largely to redirect the pressure (or "scapegoating") on the practices of tropical timber producers alone to the global industry as a whole. It also helped reorient the debate to the question of the transfer of financial resources needed to achieve sustainable forest management. By November 1992 the Canadian government had built on this momentum by endorsing a statement of principles on forests as a first step towards defining sustainability in forest practices and establishing rules through a legally binding international convention. As encouragement for such a convention, Canada assisted with model forest projects (one of these being through the ASEAN Institute of Forest Management). Despite the Canadian and Malaysian co-sponsorship of an Intergovernmental Working Group on Forests in September 1993, a huge gap between the views of these countries and Canada has been the motivator for a push towards a new type of international discipline via concepts such as sustainable forestry management and "stewardship". Developing countries, conversely, continue to argue for the easing of other forms of discipline through "debt relief, reversal of net South-to-North financial flows, and other NIEO [new international economic order]-related claims" (Humphries, 1996; Kolk, 1996).

The Chrétien government and the World Summit For Social Development

The Liberal governments in Canada have traditionally appeared more balanced between the two faces of governance. Cox, for example, locates the Liberal record in the post-1945 period as being "more rooted in social policy and territorially balanced development" (Cox, 1994b: 49). Through a narrower, country-specific lens, Maude Barlow and Bruce Campbell similarly depict Canada's traditional governing party as representing "a compromise between conflicting visions of government. 'Business' Liberals and 'social' or 'welfare' Liberals have worked, ruled, and fought together for most of the party's history, reaching out to a diverse cross-section of Canadians to maintain power" (Barlow and Campbell, 1995: 8).

Throughout their years in opposition, during the Mulroney period, the Chrétien Liberals cast themselves as willing and able to continue this "double vision". Their 1993 *Red Book* criticised the Conservative government for its "tendency to focus obsessively on one problem, such as the deficit or inflation, without understanding or caring about the consequences of their policies in other areas such as lost jobs, increased poverty, and dependence on social assistance" (Liberal Party of Canada, 1993: 10).

After they were returned to office, however, the Liberals underwent a number of sharp reversals. For both "social" and "business" critics, the dominant theme of the Chrétien government's performance since October 1993 was its frequent U-turns. On the social side, Stephen McBride and John Shields argue that while "the Liberals were the national political party that oversaw and administered the construction of the Canadian welfare state, they have proven to be most effective and efficient architects of its dismantling.... Upon assuming office the Liberals became even more committed to deficit reduction, cutting much further and faster than their Conservative predecessors" (McBride and Shields, 1997: 13). On the "business" side, Andrew Coyne adds:

> There is no denying that, under Mr. Chrétien, or more particularly since taking power, the party has undergone a remarkable about-face; from opposing free trade to supporting it, from scrapping the GST to extending it, from denouncing the 'obsession' with price stability to entrenching it, from attacking privatisation to defending it, from decrying any and all spending cuts to enacting the steepest reduction in the federal budget since the Second World War. (Andrew Coyne, "Chretien's Third Way? Not quite", *National Post*, 15 December 1998)

The extension of these U-turns into the international arena became clear in several issue areas. Some critics point to the reversal of the

Chrétien Liberals from resistance to accommodation on NAFTA. Other critics highlight the shift in foreign policy from a diffuse orientation (with a high degree of priority on human rights) to one centred on narrower economic concerns (especially the Team Canada initiatives). A consensus opinion was that the profile of social welfarism in international affairs had been reduced.

The Chrétien government's low-key approach towards the March 1995 Copenhagen World Summit for Social Development (WSSD) appears to bear out this criticism. The WSSD did not attract the personal attention of the prime minister. Preoccupied with deliberations on the 1995 budget, Chrétien sent Lloyd Axworthy in his stead as leader of the Canadian delegation (Paul Knox, "Chretien blasted for summit absence", *Globe and Mail*, 7 March 1995). Nor, it may be added, did Chrétien show any commitment to the agenda of rules-based global governance in the course of these multilateral negotiations. While Axworthy displayed some bursts of innovation at the ministerial level, his initiative with substantive proposals was stymied by the short leash he was allowed by the confining apparatus of control. One's immediate impression of the WSSD, therefore, is of a discipline more akin to the first face of discipline suggested by Gill and Cox. In other words, the discipline imposed on Axworthy at the WSSD was exerted through the dominant power of a business agenda that conditioned the Chrétien government and prevented the introduction of an alternative agenda. Instead of being willing to apply the wriggle room still available to it, to redefine a form of new multilateralism, the Chrétien government conceded the primacy of competition and market efficiency.

Two clear narratives emerge from a detailed analysis. One is the struggle between Finance Minister Paul Martin and Human Resources Minister Axworthy. From this angle, Axworthy's inability to impose his will or an agenda at the WSSD is an extension of his "loss" to Martin on the domestic front. As detailed by Edward Greenspon and Anthony Wilson-Smith, this setback was made inevitable by the personal factors that affected Axworthy's capacity to act as an agent of change in his experiments to modify social policy. He was hampered by his own fluctuations between idealism and pragmatism, his impatience and hyperactivism, his lack of people skills, and his distrust of bureaucracy and subnational governments (Greenspon and Wilson-Smith, 1996: 229–251; see also Edward Greenspon, "Why a left-winger skated off side", *Globe and Mail*, 15 February 1995).

However, consistent with Cox's notion that concentration of power rests in state "agencies in closest touch with the global economy" – in the Canadian case, primarily the Department of Finance, whose role is to maintain discipline and thereby the confidence of markets and international business community (Cox, 1994b: 48–49) – the structural/ administrative limitations imposed on Axworthy and other "social" Liberals must also be factored in as a source of serious constraint. These impediments included the indirect and direct pressures towards a more comprehensive business agenda. Indirect pressures came about partially through a socialisation process, as illustrated by Martin's relationship with the Finance Department and newspaper editorial boards at home and in the Davos/G-7/OECD community abroad. More direct pressure was applied through the shocks reverberating from the 1994 peso crisis. As Greenspon and Wilson-Smith relate, the impact of the Mexican crisis was significant in tightening the disciplines imposed on the Canadian government: "The peso slide assured that [the 1995] budget would be forged in a crucible of crisis. With each successive turn of the screw – a critical editorial in the *Wall Street Journal*, an apocalyptic interview with an influential money trader, a debt warning by Moody's Investor Services – Martin was, ironically, bolstered in winning further concessions from his cabinet colleagues" (Greenspon and Wilson-Smith, 1996: 236).

The other narrative that emerges from this analysis is the struggle between the Department of Foreign Affairs and International Trade (DFAIT) and the Canadian International Development Agency (CIDA). The Liberal government had initially made considerable effort to distance itself from the Conservatives on development assistance. The main thrust of its approach was its promise in the February 1995 governmental statement on foreign policy, "Canada in the World", that 25 per cent of the Official Development Assistance (ODA) budget would be targeted for "basic human needs". Operationally, this represented a changed emphasis on a "human-centred" or "people-centred" activity. As this "basic human needs" agenda was given pride of place, the Liberals worked hard to alter the tone of discourse/action that had dominated the Mulroney years. Their quick fulfilment of their *Red Book* promise to organise a National Forum on Canada's International Relations, together with the establishment of the Special Joint Committee Reviewing Canadian Foreign Policy, served as particularly valuable devices for giving the impression of "openness" in foreign policy making. Many of the 277 NGO representatives submitting briefs to the Joint Committee came from development NGOs. A significant number of individuals associated with the NGO development community also participated at the National Forum on Canada's International Relations held in Ottawa in March 1994.[40]

In contrast to these expansionary sentiments, the Chrétien government also wanted to display its talents for operational efficiency. On the development assistance dossier they needed to show that better development assistance could be delivered with fewer resources. Notwithstanding the *Red Book*'s affirmation of "Canada's will to help the world's poor" (*Red*

Book, 1993, p. 108), the Liberal government had little interest (or, arguably, capacity) to devote more resources to the problem. On the contrary, Paul Martin's February 1994 budget imposed a cut of another 15 per cent from Canada's ODA. The Liberals were also struggling to incorporate commercial objectives into a renewed system of development assistance. A core commitment to "basic human needs" did not signify that the Liberals were prepared to jettison aid as an economic tool. Indeed, they became in some ways more forthright about their desire to mesh commercial goals with development assistance policies and programmes.

Integral to this process of renewal was an increased degree of control over the work of development NGOs within Canada. The blunt end of this control was a retreat from a number of activities previously regarded as being in the mainstream of the development NGO–government partnership. One activity so affected was the promotion of the work of international NGOs (INGOs). As part of the 1994 Martin budget, groups without a Canadian base were excluded from funding through CIDA's Partnership Programs. Among the hardest hit of these INGOs was the International Planned Parenthood Federation, which lost its annual grant of approximately CAN$8 million. Consistent with the "basic human needs" approach, financial support for family planning and population-education programmes in poor countries would continue, but it would be routed through multilateral and bilateral channels (Paul Knox, "Canada chops aid-agency grant", *Globe and Mail*, 4 April 1995). In the same vein, CIDA's Public Participation Program and Youth Initiatives Program and the funding of separate educational programmes about international development were eliminated. As one NGO representative complained: "We keep hearing from the government that we are being linked internationally in so many ways. Yet at the same time they are cutting one of the avenues for Canadians to understand these international links" (Debbie Culbertson, resource coordinator, Ten Days for World Development, quoted in Paul Knox, "Canada chops aid-agency grant", *Globe and Mail*, 4 April 1995).

The sharp end of this control mechanism consisted of a number of steps intended to rationalise the administration of Canada's development assistance policies and programmes. In the design of an "integrated" foreign policy (into which CIDA had little input), some of DFAIT's supervisory powers over CIDA were tightened. All of CIDA's major policy and programme decisions (with their funding requirements) had to be approved by DFAIT, and overall responsibility for CIDA was firmly placed in the hands of the minister of foreign affairs. DFAIT's own capacity to act as a "lead" agency over global governance, furthermore, was given a boost by the creation of a Bureau for Global Issues as part of a new branch on Global Issues and Culture. The trade-off for CIDA was that its own operational responsibilities with respect to the implementation of this design were extended. Control over assistance operations to Central/East Europe and the countries of the former Soviet Union was handed back from DFAIT to CIDA. Control over the commercially oriented development assistance programmes (with particular reference to those under the mandate of CIDA-INC) was also retained by CIDA – despite calls by many participant/observers for these functions to be hived off to DFAIT (see, for example, Cranford Pratt, "To ensure CIDA's humanitarian focus", *Globe and Mail*, 8 November 1995).

The onus on CIDA was to embrace the agenda of managerial efficiency, and it attempted to tailor its approach in a variety of ways. On the premise of a need for greater accountability at a time of reduced financial resources, CIDA was nudged to move to implement a "results-based" mode of operation (DFAIT, 1995). In response, it moved to establish a system whereby the activities of NGOs would be evaluated on a formal set of "measurement of results" criteria. Further, it adjusted its basic partnership programmes with Canadian development NGOs. In a new set of guidelines, CIDA reduced the autonomy of NGOs and other members of the voluntary sector to set their own priorities for activity as partners. CIDA itself was to identify exclusive areas for supported activity in this sector. As the vice-president of CIDA's Partnership Branch explained: "We have to ensure that the majority of resources go toward the development objectives that the Canadian taxpayer feels he or she is paying for" (quoted in Paul Knox and John Stackhouse, "Aid agencies compelled to dance to Ottawa's tune", *Globe and Mail*, 8 November 1995). These new and tighter forms of discipline spilled over into the WSSD. In tandem with the United Nations Development Programme (UNDP), CIDA put forward a number of big – and controversial – proposals for discussion and possible action by the Canadian delegation in the run-up to the WSSD. One of these was a proposal for debt reduction, a suggestion made on the assumption that it would facilitate social development in developing countries and increase global equity. A second proposal was for a new form of international taxation and a third was for a serious reform of the Bretton Woods institutions to encourage the UN system and the international financial institutions to adapt. Finally, the idea was mooted of offering trade concessions for low-income countries.

Each of these proposals was reined in by DFAIT officials during the process of agenda setting. Instructions to the delegation emphasised that no new commitments with respect to Canadian ODA would be made. Despite awareness that some support was building up within both international organisations (UNDP) and some like-minded national countries (such as Australia) for either a form of peace dividend or some form of new international taxation (most notably, the so-called Tobin tax), these proposals were dismissed for "lacking currency" in Canada and the major industrialised countries. The so-called 20/20 formula proposed by UNDP was viewed as being much broader than would be required by the "basic human needs" approach. It was therefore said to be in need of elaboration before it could be made operational. DFAIT showed itself more willing to bend on the issue of reform with respect to the Bretton Woods institutions. But rather than accepting the "fundamental transformation" urged by CIDA and UNDP, in the name of equity of process and policy the focus was placed on upgrading the multilateral role and mandate of these institutions to make them more effective. Unlike other like-minded countries such as Australia and Denmark, DFAIT did not propose forgiving the debts of developing countries.

A nuanced examination of Canadian diplomacy and administrative behaviour simply reinforces the impression that the WSSD was an important site for the imposition of the discipline of an "international regulatory regime" underscored by the values of "market efficiency" and "limited democratic" decision making. As revealed by its thinking and behaviour towards the WSSD, Canada became more attuned to the imperatives of global economic forces. Lacking resources and a consensus on the use of the resources it possessed, however, the Chrétien government contracted its efforts to alleviate poverty and to stop the polarisation between "winners" and "losers". Internationally, the government viewed expanding resource transfers on a North/South basis as a sterile solution, hoping instead to find more positive way ahead through a better system for the distribution of resources.

Nor did the advancement of a more comprehensive social agenda – with the introduction of alternative forms of discipline through new forms of rule-based global governance – receive much support either from Canada's partners in the OECD/G-7 or through the format of the WSSD itself. Ambitious ideas for policy reform did not fly at all. Most significantly the Tobin tax was vetoed in the Prep Coms to the WSSD process in a response led by the European Union. Of the G-7 leaders, only the gravely ill French president François Mitterrand expressed any enthusiasm for pursuing a tax on short-term financial transactions or for tackling global social problems and their causes more generally. And even his plea was more rhetorical than substantive: "Are we acting out a comedy before the world? Or are we actually resolved to put social questions on the same level as peace and the economy?" (quoted in Paul Knox, "Summit leaders' next task is to live up to their pledges", *Globe and Mail*, 13 March 1995).

In terms of procedure, the WSSD was in many ways a throwback to the "talking shop" model of the Cold War UN conferences. One restraint was linked to the budgetary crisis of the UN. The director of the secretariat for the WSSD was a former financial controller in the UN system who resisted strongly the idea of social development, with its corollary drain of resources, being elevated to the same level as economic development in the UN's agenda. Another constraint was imposed by the diffuse nature of the WSSD agenda, as many items among the broad range of issues relating to social development – such as poverty and employment – could have provided enough material and work for an international conference of their own.

Around the edges of this imposed disciplinary activity, though, there was space for the bubbling up of resistance, or even a "double-movement", at both the state and societal levels. This "probing the social and political foundations of a future order" was conducted largely by representatives of civil society. NGOs pushed for a new form of multilateralism via the WSSD. Consistent with Cox's themes, these forces sought to curb the "disintegrating and alienating consequences" of the ascendancy of the market (Cox, 1991: 335), a business agenda, and economic globalisation through re-regulation and a rebalancing social agenda. In pushing this countervailing agenda NGOs relied on both emotional passion and technical sophistication. Their calls for alternative forms of global control based on equity and justice were supported by sophisticated computer network linkages ("The Copenhagen Alternative Declaration", Declaration of Civil Society Organizations Participating in the NGO Forum of the Social Summit, 8 March 1995, http://www.pcdf.org/1995/cpendecl.htm).

We must not, however, overestimate the impact of civil society forces in this instance. For one thing, the influence of the NGOs was held in check by the concern of the organisers for "balanced" access. As NGOs moved out in front in terms agenda-setting preparations for the summit, considerable effort was made to bring the business community back in. Prominent international personalities such as Olivier Giscard d'Estaing, brother of the former French president, helped mobilise representatives of the business community who were interested in providing a consultative voice. Members of organisations such as the Business and Industry Advisory Group of the OECD, the International Chamber of Commerce, and the association of employer's organisations connected with the ILO were invited to participate. This concern with balance also affected the Canadian procedural approach. Three representatives selected by the Canadian Council for International Business attended the New York Prep Com meetings in January 1995. John Dillon, a senior associate of the BCNI was a member of the Canadian delegation to the Copenhagen Summit.[41]

Unlike the "triangular" or "double-edged" diplomacy that dominated the forestry negotiations, during the WSSD the business and NGO communities remained in their separate spheres. Rather than encouraging some creative activity as the two sides interacted with each other, the summit highlighted the distance between their agendas. Any move towards privileging a social agenda (especially one so open-ended as to address structural poverty and employment issues) was viewed as having a price tag that business would have to pay in some way or other. The priority was to complete the disciplinary measures at the national level not to dabble in social engineering projects. In the Canadian case, the need for continued emphasis on discipline remained a constant in the public messages of the business community. Well after the WSSD, for example, Tim Reid of the Canadian Chamber of Commerce (and a frequent representative of the International Chamber of Commerce at international summits) expressed the widespread aversion to re-regulation in the business community:

Our policy on regulation is very tough-minded to the government sector. We do surveys of our members [that ask] a very simple question. What is stopping you from hiring one more person next year? ... Three years [ago] when we did this there was no question that the debt question, the interest rate issue, and generally getting government finances in order in this country were the major concerns. (Reid, 1997)

A second procedural constraint was the ingrained dualistic organisational mode of the UN conferences. At the WSSD, as at Rio, there was a clear division between the "official" and the "non-official" summits. The official summit was held at the Bella Centre, a trade-show site near the Copenhagen airport, whereas the unofficial part, the NGO Forum, was held a few kilometres away at a disused naval base. In one respect, this division made good sense: it reduced the clutter that would inevitably have been part of a holistic summit (the NGO Forum had close to 10,000 participants) and it allowed autonomy for the NGOs that wanted it. This separation was especially inviting for the NGOs that appreciated their outsider status and concentrated on consciousness-raising "stunts" rather than on direct policy influence. One of the major features of the NGO Forum, for example, was a clock that ticked off the number of children who were born into abject poverty.

In another respect, however, this dualism invited tensions by accentuating the differences between individuals and groups that chose to work as "insiders" and their "outsider" counterparts. This was especially true for countries such as Canada, which made a serious effort to include NGO representatives in its official delegations, with an impressive array of representatives from the Canadian Labour Congress, the Council of

Canadians with Disabilities, the Canadian Council for Community Living, and two other NGO representatives, John Foster of OXFAM-Canada, and Josephine Grey, director of Low Income Families Together (LIFT). This approach earned Canada praise, as it was one of the 14 among the 187 official delegations that had any NGO representation. However, within the delegation tensions surfaced as well, as "insiders" wanted more say both in process and in policy than the Canadian government was prepared to allow.

The public comments of the two NGO representatives on the Canadian delegation featured a marked critical tone. Grey expressed the sense of exclusion felt by immigrants in Canada: "The most frightening thing is that your life is profoundly controlled by systems. You live in another country with a different set of rights and laws" (quoted in Paul Knox, "Not many poor at UN summit to deal with poverty", *Globe and Mail*, 9 March 1995). Foster pushed the Canadian government to act more firmly on an alternative global agenda centred on debt relief, a greater balance between structural adjustment programmes and social development goals, and income transfers to offset the social cost of economic adjustment. Although gratified that the WSSD, at least in declaratory terms, had signalled a willingness to address global poverty issues, Foster urged that the substance of this agenda be moved ahead more rapidly: "I wish it were there more strongly" (quoted in Paul Knox, "Summit pledges to end world's poverty", *Globe and Mail*, 11 March 1995).[42] These strands of criticism revealed the uneven and fragmented nature of the Canadian NGO community. As noted above, the international development component of the NGO community dominated the agenda-setting process in the run-up to the WSSD. Aided by their close contact vis-à-vis CIDA, these NGOs pushed issues of primary importance to "others" in the international community. As with CIDA, their list of priorities included greater sharing of resources internationally (including the cancellation and swaps of debt for social programmes, with a special priority for Africa); support for new forms of taxation, including the Tobin tax; the wish that Canada take a greater lead in emphasising the need for a review of structural adjustment policies, multilateral aid, and the global economic rules and financial activities controlled by the Bretton Woods institutions; a release of the discipline imposed on multilateral international financial institutions and the internal governance and process of decision making in the UN system either through moral persuasion or under the umbrella of a new international body; and strong support for the so-called 20/20 proposal in development assistance.

The self-confident style in which the international development NGOs in Canada advanced their agenda (despite cuts and policy setbacks) may be contrasted with the tentative approach of Canadian social policy activists across a number of axes. While international development NGOs still felt connected with strong networks at the societal and governmental level and advanced a relatively coherent alternative agenda, the social activists felt isolated and were scattered in their emphasis and internally divided among a host of groups. Whereas the international development assistance NGOs were enthusiastic globalists who still enjoyed client status, with all the attendant benefits, the social activists were underfunded and for the most part highly defensive about internationalism. Their high-profile actions, whether on the bilateral free trade agreement signed between Canada and the United States or on NAFTA, had been campaigns of resistance not accommodation.

It is not surprising, then, that the social activists were less influential than the international development NGOs at the WSSD, as noted by Keith Banting in his review of the internationalisation of social policy: "Canadian social-policy groups did participate actively; over 60 organizations attended, and several representatives of NGOs were included in Canada's official delegation. However, international-development groups, which have more experience in such settings, tended to take the lead and to exert the strongest influence on the Canadian delegation and, through it, on the conference proceedings and recommendations" (Banting, 1996: 45).

Turning towards the state dimension of this double movement, it is worth examining Axworthy's own efforts to probe the social and political foundations of a future order. His tactic of going on the offensive by playing up the international dimension of social policy at the WSSD had some immediate political benefits. Although seen as the loser in the budgetary/policy struggle with Martin on the home front, Axworthy could draw some symbolic and compensatory benefits by playing up his initiatives on the world stage. The WSSD also helped to alleviate the image of isolation that had become associated with him. While in the short run Axworthy's close contact with NGOs had very little instrumental value, in the longer run it was useful in anticipation of his later work on land mines, the International Criminal Court, and other initiatives. Indeed the WSSD may be taken to be a turning point for Axworthy. Instead of the critical attitude he had adopted (and had received from social activists) when he had tried to reform the domestic social agenda at Human Resources Development, he now became enthusiastic about the potential of NGOs in new forms of diplomacy. A later profile highlights this triggering effect, in that the NGOs he encountered at Copenhagen were not part of "just another lobby group ... they were a highly organized, highly connected international network that really had some clout ... and were putting these issues on the agenda.... There is the emergence of a global political process ... with the same ingredients and the same players that you deal with at the domestic level" (Jeff Sallot and Paul Knox, "The young Axworthy believed he could change the world, friend says", *Globe and Mail*, 1 January 1999).

Axworthy was also exposed to some of the constructive features of the Canadian foreign service. He worked closely with a number of DFAIT officials with respect to the WSSD, most notably with Marius Bujold, a Canadian coordinator for the summit. The episode opened the possibilities of his working with like-minded countries on an issue-specific basis, and touched on some of the themes he would follow up as minister of foreign affairs. As Axworthy commented in his report on the WSSD for the parliamentary Committee on Human Resources Development:

The summit on social development was one of a series of seven summits that have been organized by the UN over the past several years to basically redefine the role of the world organization in its post–Cold War era.... What we're really seeing taking place ... is an attempt by the UN and its member states to change the mission of the United Nations from the emphasis on the security of nations, which is its original mandate, to security of individuals. (Axworthy, 1995: 5)

This positive take on the WSSD, once again, should not be overestimated. Axworthy praised the summit as a forum for ideas, but little progress was made in translating any of the ideas into action. To counteract the volatility imposed on the market "by people in red suspenders moving money around" (on the push for the Tobin tax, see McQuaig, 1998; see also ul Haq, Kaul and Grunberg, 1996). Axworthy tried to pick up the idea of the Tobin tax and run with it, playing up his own credentials as an intellectual change agent and painting himself and Chrétien as populists. This idea did not travel well, however, despite being floated to the Department of Finance at home and the G-7 abroad (Axworthy, 1995: 9–10). On the other hand, Axworthy tried to take the lead in addressing some of the big themes dealing with the impact of information technology on jobs and employment. But in the absence of the hard quantifiable measures and data, this mission bogged down.

Nor did Axworthy's contact with NGOs at the WSSD translate into closer NGO support for the Chrétien policy agenda. On the contrary, using the greater transparency allowed through the UN Economic and Social Council (ECOSOC) and other UN forums, these social NGOs increasingly used international organisations as sites of resistance to this agenda. While the voices of these groups are still discordant, the groups have caught up in their awareness of where to effectively locate their concerns. Instead of being "managed", social activists such as Josephine

Grey of LIFT who had been on the official delegation at the WSSD, were among the harshest critics of the Liberals' record on poverty and social inequality.[43] As she asserted in Geneva:

> Canada uses its reputation as a champion of human rights as leverage in many ways in the international arena and boasts about it at home.... You can't claim [to do so] and only in fact respect a couple of small rights that are under the declaration that are about civil and political rights.... Your right to vote is meaningless if you don't have a roof over your head. (quoted in Helen Branswell, "UN to scrutinize Canadian welfare policies", *National Post*, 26 November 1998)

Images of fragmented authority

This study has reinforced the impression that there is no single image through which the complexity of the international system may be captured. Rather, there are a plurality of images that reveal fragmentation of authority. To be sure, the forces of economic globalisation have bent, if not completely broken, the "balanced" system associated with the post-1945 settlement. New and tighter disciplines have been applied on national governments concerning the limits of their policy agendas.

Yet the degree and intensity of the disciplinary activity imposed by the global "business agenda" and the "transnational business élite" should not be taken to an extreme. The alternative face of global governance is encouraged by the greater prominence in the international system of multilateralism, institutions, and bargaining, negotiating, and rule making. This rebalancing effort is aided, at the domestic level, by the efforts of civil society and NGOs towards a countervailing agenda with a greater onus on social policy. Moreover, if there has been a decided shift to decrease the autonomy of states, national governments still search for wriggle room within this discipline. As Richard Higgott and Simon Reich put it:

> It is more accurate (albeit less parsimonious for theorising) to see state and non-state authority existing in a more contingent, interactive and dynamic manner. Firms, social forces, international regimes and institutions, and NGOs do not always operate in either ignorance of, or defiance of the state. Similarly, the state is not always too weak to combat activities it does not like. (Higgott and Reich, 1997: 3)

In the forestry case, the willingness and capability of international institutions, the Canadian government, and selected NGOs and business groups came forward. All of these actors shared some motivation to establish new rules of the game in the multilateral domain. Although messy, these negotiations were able to be sustained in the post-Rio context; although complex, the discrete nature of the issues allowed continued movement to take place.

The WSSD was far less amenable to bargaining and negotiation, as business and NGOs remained almost completely polarised. The issues under discussion (or non-discussion) were not only more diffuse, but the stakes in opening up the agenda were extremely high, in that poverty and employment were among the most central and sensitive issues to all concerned (UN, 1995). Any concrete decision could be used as either a signalling device in the vanguard of a social agenda or as the "thin edge of the wedge" away from economic "rationality".

On neither issue, however, was the Canadian government locked in. Using the Rio conference as an opportunity, the Mulroney government focused not only on the forestry issue as a problem to be solved but on the environment more generally as a dossier that offered some compensation in the interplay between the economic and the social agenda. Disciplines imposed though the bargaining process would be shared with other actors in the international domain, and alternative forms of discipline (through NGO direct action) would be avoided.

With less space to operate in the Liberals treated the WSSD more as a challenge than an opportunity. NGOs had less incentive to be managed because of the Chrétien government's unwillingness or incapacity to advance any tangible policies necessitating a transfer of resources. Yet, even in accommodation to disciplinary forces, gestures could be made that indicated that the traditional Liberal commitment to a balanced economic and social approach was not forgotten completely. Biding his time until the moment of opportunity became ripe again for new initiatives,[44] Axworthy used the summit to reiterate his government's commitment:

Our central theme clearly expressed time and time again is [that] the fundamental link between economic and social policy or development, and the notion that focusing on one to the exclusion of the other is bound to be a failure for both, within individual countries and the globe itself. It means you have to address both fiscal deficits and the human deficits at the same time. The two are inextricably linked as part of a broad attack. (Axworthy, 1995: 9)

6

Tests of sovereignty: an evasive and estranged diplomacy?

An extended test of the UN world conferences stands at the intersection between purpose and means in relation to the debate over sovereignty. To consider sovereignty as legal authority places the onus on more than international standing alone. It emphasises the protection of domestic territory as "bounded and marked social space" and the integrity of national political borders. Affirmation of boundaries, control, and the prevention of transgressions take precedence over negotiation on new rules for global governance (Immerfall, 1998). Self-help by individual states, rather than collective problem solving, is maximised. When sovereignty is relocated as autonomy, on the other hand, the instrumental aspect of diplomatic relationship becomes paramount. Symbolism with respect to the status of participants gives way to a flexible use of sovereignty as a "bargaining chip in intra-organization negotiation" (Terpstra, 1999: 212). Either/or prescriptions have less weight than negotiations over a continuum of options. States choose where, how far, and with whom to deploy their own freedom of action as part of a bargaining process (see, for example, Keohane, 1995).

Any overview of the UN conferences underscores the salience of – and the tensions between – these differing connotations of sovereignty. On the territorial axis the contest is marked by rigidity based on fundamental divisions between states still wanting to maintain a hard shell around their participatory and territorial privileges and those wishing to bend (albeit not break completely) some aspects of this orthodoxy. Along the autonomy axis, room opens up both for cooperative problem solving and for antagonism in the coalition building and bargaining process.

What this image cannot capture, however, is the complexity found within the positions of individual states as revealed through the cycle of UN conferences. In an extension of the analysis of the Canadian case in particular, what stands out is the way in which these tests of sovereignty bifurcated its diplomatic personality. In many respects these conferences reinforced Canada's image (and self-image) as an actor ready and able to adjust to the realities imposed on it, recognising that it could only exploit its limited room for manoeuvre by strengthening its legitimacy across the state–societal divide and maximising its skill in working through the institutional fabric of the conferences. In doing so, Canada was seen to be moving forward in rebuilding its identity as an entity less interested in power and territorial control than in opening up the processes and searching for issue-driven outcomes. Although the fuller parameters of these tendencies can be much debated, they contained some positive implications from the perspective of global governance.

Yet, amidst evidence confirming this standard version of Canadian diplomacy with a reduced emphasis on territory, selected narratives from the UN conferences clash with this image (Scholte, 2000: 15–16). The expression of sovereignty as legal authority continued to matter a great deal to Canadian state officials. To the symbolic and sometimes status-seeking aspect of this concern must be added an instrumental concern with reinforcing fixed boundaries and territorial integrity. One of these narratives, which illustrate significant tension between these images of sovereignty, relates to the issue of women refugees. Through one lens, Canada is cast as the champion of a progressive new and universally applicable regime shaped by its move to implement gender-based guidelines for refugee claimants as part of a general "relocation of sovereignty" onto supranational and non-governmental forces (Sassen, 1998: 92). A territorially-based lens, however, reveals an initial governmental opposition to a differentiated gender-related protection regime – and the reality that the Canadian state remains the ultimate arbiter on asylum decisions (Baines, 2002).

The hard face of Canadian statecraft as the protector of Canadian sovereignty is witnessed most clearly in the narrative about Indigenous or Aboriginal rights at the Vienna Human Rights conference. When the agenda of Indigenous groups conflicted with Canadian territorial jurisdiction and integrity, Canadian state officials drew the line between sovereignty as a device designed to manage complex interdependence (Biersteker and Weber, 1996) and sovereignty as the final authority within a given territory (Krasner, 1999). In doing so, they marked off the area where the Canadian state retained its prerogative to decide rather than to bargain. Unlike in the case of women refugees, where some adjustment took place within the state apparatus, in the case of the Indigenous challenge this hard face showed no sign of flexibility from within. Nor was it softened by the assertive campaign of Indigenous groups at the Vienna conference to make their own claim of sovereignty. The stakes, the degree of polarisation, and the obstacles to any formula for sharing sovereignty (see, for example, Ignatieff, 2000) were simply too deeply entrenched.

These two narratives show both the capabilities and the limitations of diplomacy in rising to the test of sovereignty. Consistent with the core functions of diplomacy, the refugee case demonstrates the flexibility of diplomatic practice to build dialogue and consensus on even the most controversial "two-level" games within domestic and international negotiations (Putnam, 1988). Even if the result fell short of the expectations voiced by women's groups and other members of civil society, it was at least predicated on the need for the government to change its mind. On the Indigenous case, conversely, diplomacy helped block rather than facilitate the negotiating process. Instead of living up to the expectations of the advocates of a new and inclusive diplomacy, the style adopted by the Canadian delegation reinforced the notion of diplomacy still being trapped in its older (and most problematic) character.

The territorial/autonomy dichotomy

Tests of sovereignty tease out the distinction between the ability of states to determine and their ability to bargain. Debates about sovereignty shadow discussions about discipline. As the discipline applied either by market forces or new multilateral rules tightens, the nature of national sovereignty becomes less distinct. States may retain the formal attributes of sovereignty with respect to legal authority; yet, de facto, the state moves into a very different position as sovereignty changes from a formal concept relating to "legal supremacy within a given territory" (Keohane, 1993, 1995) to being an open-ended concept that is an evolving "social construct" (Barkin and Cronin, 1994: 109). In contrast to the traditional and exclusionary notion of sovereignty being founded on a top-down hierarchy, whereby states make determinations on the basis of a delimited national interest, a more flexible and autonomous approach can allow a bargaining component to take place not only among states but between state and non-state actors.

In its territorial mode, sovereignty rests on the privileging of a fixed set of tangible aspects related mainly to a state's physical integrity and the possession and use of property within distinct parameters. Sovereignty as autonomy, by contrast, is linked to performance pertaining to control over public policy and decision making. The key test is whether a state can act with a degree of success, or relative independence, in pursuit of its national objectives (Held, 1991).

To set out the territory/autonomy dichotomy in this fashion reinforces the polarisation found in much of the literature and applications of sovereignty. Attention to the physical or territorial aspects of sovereignty highlights legal, fixed, and state-centric components that make sovereignty seem like a shell, shaping who and what is within or beyond the boundaries of the territorial unit. It can also be characterised by a sense of the state having exclusive rights over a territorially demarcated area; or put another way, an established claim to determine rules within a fixed geographically determined political community. The condition of autonomy, by contrast, shifts attention away from authority to management. It matters less whether a state has legitimacy in principle over its domain than how effectively it can use the leverage it possesses to shape its course of action. Autonomy, for a nation, includes a psychological element – an attitude or state of mind about being the master of its own fate.

There are further fundamental differences. The potential for bargaining in the exercise of autonomy is far greater than under the umbrella of territoriality, where more either/or lines are drawn in the sand. Because of its association with intangible qualities, the practice of sovereignty as autonomy is more amenable to give and take or to nuanced solutions. Although the diplomacy of autonomy may not make boundaries irrelevant, boundary issues are increasingly ambiguous as transactions become disconnected from territorial concerns (Ansell and Weber, 1999; Ruggie, 1993b: 152).

There is considerable room for merger between the two dimensions of sovereignty as the nature of the authoritative shell is influenced by the level of state capacity and vice versa. Indeed, these elements can be seen as part of an extended (and often complementary) continuum. The territorial imperative is not only associated with the right to make rules but is often assumed to be the main organising principle of the international system (Caporaso, 1989). Autonomy suggests a sense of social purpose as well as the ability to exercise control (see the debate between Waltz, 1979 and Ruggie, 1983). States – such as Canada – may well push to transcend national borders in accordance with the tenets of an expanded guide for good international citizenship. At the same time, they may express reluctance, or even exert explicit resistance, when their right to make rules within their territory is challenged.

The first of our case studies from the 1993 Vienna Human Rights Conference examines the challenge to the territorial imperative in state sovereignty posed by the campaign of women's groups and their supporters to have gender persecution and violence taken into account with respect to refugee claims and entry into Canada. A study of policies determining who is accepted or denied entry into Canada is crucial for an understanding of the question of sovereignty from a territorial perspective, as it goes to the heart of fundamental assumptions not only about territorial control but about where the right to make rules originates.

In meeting this challenge, Canadian diplomacy proved evasive. On the question of control, it continued to focus on thematic categories rather than on specific cases. On the question of authority, an attempt was made to turn attention away from national policy making to external/international sources. The emphasis of the Canadian response, while not entirely avoiding the issues wrapped up with these human rights and immigration policies, was to deflect the question rather than meet it head-on.

The second – and more detailed – case study concerns the issue of Indigenous or Aboriginal rights in Canada. Although not entirely separate from the wider human rights agenda, the basic controversy on this issue was related to the question of territory as expressed through land claims. The test for Canadian diplomacy was, as a consequence, even more difficult. The Indigenous challenge contained awkward elements of recognition and status, and spilled over into more sensitive issues around "national" self-determination. What is revealing about Canadian diplomacy in this case is how estranged state officials became from the Indigenous community at the time of the Vienna conference. Although skilful (and often successful) in the art of interstate mediation, when put to the test at the domestic level, Canadian diplomacy came up short.

Sovereignty in turbulent times

The restructuring associated with the post–Cold War era intruded on the sovereignty debate at several different levels. One telltale sign of this intrusion was the weakening of hitherto unyielding tenets of non-intervention. The role of transnational NGOs and policy networks in challenging this taboo was crucial. Encouraged by the pace of change presented by the new order (or disorder), civil society would no longer allow the sovereign dimension of politics to dictate the terms by which international affairs were played out. Their stance was predicated by morality and a sense of duty, as well as being prompted by a changing sense of problem/opportunity definition. As sovereignty became identified not just with the defence of differences but with practical obstacles impeding deliverables on a global scale – whether through the diffuse push for universal rights and justice or through the targeted delivery of famine relief – the concept was cast in a far more negative light. The conditions of transparency opened up in the 1990s obliged states to come out of their mental (if not their physical) shells and respond to demands from civil society. As Kathryn Sikkink states: "The work of NGOs make states' repressive practices more visible and salient, thus forcing states that would otherwise have remained silent to respond" (Sikkink, 1993: 414).

From above, the UN's adoption of the principles and practices of humane intervention focused the spotlight more intensely on the debate. Intellectually, the boldest salvo in the campaign to define the limits to state sovereignty came with the publication of Boutros Boutros-Ghali's *An Agenda for Peace*. This document called for a more balanced approach to the concept of sovereignty. Trying to avoid giving the impression that its intent was to tilt the emphasis completely over to the side of a "sovereignty-free" world, the UN Secretary General reassured his prime constituency (the member states): "The foundation-stone [for international organization] is and must remain the State. Respect for its fundamental sovereignty and integrity are crucial to any common international progress" (Boutros-Ghali, 1992: 6).

At the same time, however, Boutros-Ghali made it clear that the rules of the international game were in flux and that the orthodoxy of the post–World War II era could no longer be unconditionally accepted. Although still central to international governance, states could no longer do what they pleased within their sovereign confines with no regard for the implications with respect to human rights and basic human needs. As *An Agenda for Peace* declared: "Sovereignty is no longer absolute. Sovereignty must be kept in its place" (Boutros-Ghali, 1992: 11).

The resonance of this rethinking process was heightened, of course, by the attempts of the UN to act according to these guidelines. A test of their practical application came with United Nations Security Council Resolution 688 of 5 April 1991, which sanctioned intervention to provide "safe havens" for the protection of the Kurds in northern Iraq. By allowing UN member states to send humanitarian personnel inside Iraq without the permission of the Baghdad government, this resolution provided a stimulus (if not a precise model) for other forms of interventionist activity in a wide range of cases, including Cambodia, Somalia, and the former Yugoslavia.

Challenges to sovereignty were also posed by emergent patterns of regionalism, whose trajectories, in terms of scope, pace, and form, have been widely divergent. While the members of the European Union (EU) have made substantial movement towards pooling their sovereignty in an elaborate and dense set of external institutions, NAFTA and Asia Pacific Economic Cooperation (APEC) have lagged in comparative terms

(Smith, 1999). Still, for all of their varied architecture, these experiences have in common a degree of development or movement involving integration or harmonisation of formal and informal contracts, conventions, or understandings, at least on an issue-specific or sectoral basis.

While this layer of analysis provides very different takes on the sovereignty debate, it raises similar questions about motivation and effect. From a standpoint within the national context, we need to better understand the reason why Canadian state and domestic-oriented societal actors moved so comprehensively in the immediate post–Cold War years to take up the search for a balance between state sovereignty and international obligations. At a declaratory level, the enthusiasm of this embrace shone through as a theme in a cluster of statements made from the prime ministerial level down to the ministerial/bureaucratic apparatus. In the best-known evocation of this sentiment, Prime Minister Mulroney stated in his convocation address to Stanford University in September 1991, that Canada was receptive to "re-thinking the limits of national sovereignty in a world where problems respect no borders; [and] invocations of the principle of national sovereignty are as out of date and offensive ... as the police declining to stop family violence simply because a man's home is supposed to be his castle" (Office of the Prime Minister, 1991).

State officials in the foreign ministry, consistent with their image as upholders of tradition, were more cautious about the implications of the post–Cold War world for the concept of sovereignty. But even they conceded that something was happening to the Westphalian pillars that was seriously modifying the ways issues were thought out and dealt with. As a head of the ministry's Policy Planning Staff noted

There are limits to sovereignty, there are limits to inviolability, and we have seen them crossed in the past little while.... But I don't think the international community has completely understood or worked out all that this might mean. We are seeing it in Yugoslavia, and we are going to be testing it, I suspect, again and again in the years to come. None of us really understand where this is going to end and how it may lead to the development of ... case law, if not codified understanding of how the world is going to manage those changes in the future. (Balloch, 1992)

In practice, the push towards some pooling or sharing of sovereignty was reflected by the Mulroney government's across-the-board support for multilateral codes and firmly established rules. In the trade domain, this support could be seen in the Canadian government's advocacy for a revamped World Trade Organisation. In the economic/social intersect, the approach came out on both the forestry and the fishing issues. In the forestry case Mulroney repeatedly emphasized "Canada's responsibility to citizens of the world" (quoted in James Rusk, "Mulroney signs eco-pac", *Globe and Mail*, 12 June 1992). Despite a build-up of frustration by domestic interests in regard to results, however, the foreign ministry firmly upheld its faith in international negotiations. Barbara McDougall laid out her department's attachment to these principles in a March 1992 radio interview: "We abide by our international commitments. I don't believe in gunboat diplomacy. We believe in multilateralism. We work with our allies" (transcript, L'Agence France Presse, Ottawa, 17 March 1992).

The Mulroney government's willingness to stretch the boundaries of sovereignty can be interpreted as the logical (and accelerated) extension of Canada's traditional approach. Rather than shedding the cloak of Pearsonism, Canadian behaviour became seemingly more tightly wrapped in the mantle of good international citizenship. It signalled "a new internationalism [that] place[ed] human rights above the absolute right of sovereign right of sovereign states" (Wirick, 1993; see also Keating, 2002: chap. 7).

Seen through a different lens, the Mulroney approach to sovereignty contained a strong element of convenience. On specific issues (such as the forestry case), it shifted the focus away from requiring unilateral sacrifices from Canadian producers to reaching a more universally applicable settlement. And this outward-looking orientation allowed some compensation for the drawbacks commonly associated with the costs to sovereignty incurred by the FTA and NAFTA (on this point, see Cooper, 1993). An excellent way to sell the notion that Canada must move to continental free trade in order to become more economically competitive in global markets was to balance the onus on efficiency with an appeal to the need to extend good governance globally. Whereas sharing sovereignty on the economic side was deemed to be full of risk, the concept of a more sovereignty-free world tapped into a reservoir of approval for its non-economic ramifications (on this dynamic, in comparative terms, see Streek, 1996).

As well as allowing the Mulroney government to associate itself with some popular issues, however, this rejigging of the debate exposed the division within the NGO community on the question of sovereignty. An ascendant component of civil society was ready to break with the territorial dimension of politics. The main criticism levelled at the Rio UNCED conference by Greenpeace International, for instance, was that UNCED lacked a vision that was based on "a new global sovereignty on behalf of environmentally sound and socially equitable development" (Greenpeace International, 1992: 25).

Still, if the critically-minded segment of the NGO community saw the principle of state sovereignty as a strategic impediment to effective global action, there remained considerable room for compromise in case-specific problem-solving exercises. Across a range of issues, NGOs on the ground wanted more not less government action. The worst-case scenarios for these NGOs would be for the state to abdicate responsibility or show a reluctance to get involved in the complex challenges of the post–Cold War era. This was true of relatively discrete issues, such as global warming and the depletion of the ozone layer in the environmental dossier, as well as gender discrimination and violence against women in the human rights dossier. It was also true in the less defined arena of peacemaking and humanitarian intervention. While wishing to extend their own sets of activities, NGOs also wanted state officials to do more in crisis situations, especially in non-permissive environments such as Somalia and the former Yugoslavia where unilateral action was not possible. The most striking feature of these missions, in terms of the manner in which state sovereignty became intruded upon, was the way in which they were extended from parallel operations to forms of viable (if extremely awkward) civil–military cooperation (see, for example, Duffield, 1997; Slim, 1997).

As the range of cooperative action between state and societal actors was extended, the defensive agenda of the societal groups resistant to the FTA was tightened. True, this ongoing contest did not remain static; conceptually, the expression of societal interests focused increasingly on the theme of societal or popular sovereignty. Practically, many of these groups became transnationalised through broadened links and communication networks with their counterparts in the United States and Mexico (for example, through the Common Frontiers project). As Jeffrey Ayres summarises: "Economic integration created new opportunities for transnational collective action" (Ayres, 1997).

Despite the willingness and ability of activists to cultivate new alliances, though, the continuity needs to be stressed as much as the points of departure. Ingrained in the argument that society is the ultimate source of authority was a sense of grassroots localism. Despite their tactical adjustment, the political, economic, and social particularities of these groups remained their core ingredients. Instead of making a bold leap to a universalistic framework, as did a variety of outward-looking groups within the environmental and human rights domains, economic resisters shifted their thinking in a series of short, disjointed – and often contradictory – steps.

Do borders matter?

A fundamental question that persists throughout this discussion about the reconfiguration of sovereignty is whether borders matter. To certain types of observers the answer is clear: national boundaries have been reduced to irrelevance. As Jessica Tuchman Mathews expressed this thinking in the early stages of the post–Cold War era, the cluster of issues that "transcend national borders are already beginning to break down the sacred boundaries of national sovereignty" (Tuchman Mathews, 1989). Focusing on the acceleration of a multi-faceted dynamic of globalisation, at least one leading scholar of international political economy has suggested that we have already arrived at a moment in which the territorial component of sovereignty has become a remnant of the past: "In economics where capital, labor, and information are mobile and have risen to predominance, no land fetish remains. Developed countries would rather plumb the world market than acquire territory. The virtual state – a state that has down-sized its territorially-based production capacity – is the logical consequence of this emancipation from the land" (Rosecrance, 1996: 59–60).

Forceful rhetoric is no substitute, however, for careful analysis. The sense of absolutism that Mathews interjects into this debate suggests an either/or dichotomy that is simply not accurate. While sovereignty has been severely bent it is certainly not broken. Even a robust post-sovereignist such as Joseph Camilleri pulls his punches with a healthy drop of relativism: "Boundaries, whether underpinned by law, culture or physical force, have not withstood the tidal flow of change; national and other boundaries may persist, but they are increasingly porous" (Camilleri, 1995: 211; see also Camilleri and Falk, 1992). If the general trend is towards an erosion of state capability, significant exceptions exist.

The crux of the argument for the demise of sovereignty, furthermore, is a holistic perspective on sovereignty that simplifies reality. Few would reject the claim that the position of states has been more deeply compromised in the last decade by changes in problem-definition and by gaps between commitment and capabilities. As James Rosenau suggests: "The boundaries of states no longer confine the flow of information, goods, money, and people" (Rosenau, 1995: 193). To conflate territory and autonomy, however, goes too far in a unidirectional or even a reductionist path. While important components of state capacity have been (and will continue to be) eroded, questions about authority have not been laid to rest.

Migration and gender: refugee issues

Of the two significant cases at the core of this chapter that shed light on questions of sovereignty, the first relates to migration, or more specifically the issue of women refugees. As Saskia Sassen has rightly asserted, the cluster of questions around immigration provides "a sort of wrench one can throw into theories about sovereignty" (Sassen, 1996: 63; see also Freeman, 1998). On the one hand, these issues provide a key test of a state's capabilities, since the level of a state's physical control over the flow of peoples across its borders gives a good indication of where the state lies on a continuum between a hard shell and extreme porousness. On the other hand, migration issues raise the question of the sources and justification of a state's authority. A nationally based citizenship within fixed territorial limits has been both a symbolic and a tangible cornerstone underpinning the entire Westphalian structure. Consistent with the premise of a bounded national community, state officials have maintained exclusive authority over the right of entry to a state. They determine who belongs and who does not – they define citizens and aliens.

What makes the case of migration even more interesting in the context of the international social conferences is the disjunction among the challenges made to the both dimensions of sovereignty. This disjunction was particularly evident in the issue of whether gender discrimination and sexual violence should be taken into account with respect to refugee claims into Canada. Pressure to make these criteria a legitimate claim for refugee status had built up among societal groups since the late 1980s (see, for example, Ptolemy, 1989: 21–24; Seward and McDade, 1988). Throughout this period the National Action Committee on the Status of Women (NAC) had built up a coalition of groups pushing for a new refugee determination process that would prioritise women in danger.[45] The breakthrough in attracting attention to this issue, however, came when the focus shifted from the thematic to the personal. The case of Nada, a Saudi Arabian woman facing deportation from Canada, galvanised this agenda-setting effort by raising a name (and a persona) to the front pages.

The most intriguing aspect of the women's groups' framing of this case was the way in which they rebalanced the standard formulation of the capability/authority dimensions of sovereignty. Their primary aim was to ratchet up the level of capability and downplay the issue of authority, urging Canada to move beyond accepted practices of governance. Women's groups – and their allies in civil society – accepted the notion that on this issue the state had a high degree of capability in terms of its control mechanism. Indeed, with its emphasis on deportation, the state apparatus was painted as being closer to a hard shell than a porous entity in its use of its enforcement power.

What the women's groups and their allies challenged head-on was the Canadian state's legitimisation of its actions on the basis of authority (see, for example, Linda Hossie, "Knowing when to provide asylum",

Globe and Mail, 12 March 1993) (on this wider point, see Jacobson, 1997). They argued that the traditional gatekeeper role of the Canadian state was out of date because of the state's unwillingness to extend the parameters of qualification for refugee status. From early on in the preparation stages for the Vienna conferences, the Mulroney government was cast as having subordinated justice to order. Furthermore, this portrayal seemed appropriate, given that the state's reflex response moved it towards a harder-edged position, with state officials insisting that the definitional limits for acceptance were not negotiable. As the Conservative immigration minister, Bernard Valcourt, stated before the Law Society of Upper Canada in January 1993: "Some people want to forget and to ignore that it is millions and tens of millions of people who are on the move daily around the globe. And Canada cannot act unilaterally – or even argue – against the principles of the United Nations to which we subscribe" (quoted in Estanislao Oziewicz, "Canada not planning to widen refugee rules to cover sex bias", *Globe and Mail*, 15 January 1993; Allan Thompson, "Canada spells out stance on refugees", *Toronto Star*, 15 January 1993).

As with other campaigns of this nature, shaming and embarrassment were used to get the state to change its mind. Appealing to Canada's wish to be seen as a leader not a laggard, the women's groups and their allies (including most vocally Ed Broadbent and Gordon Fairweather) addressed gender violence as a phenomenon that needed innovative and fair-minded solutions. If the Canadian government could make a value judgment against a country such as the Republic of South Africa for its state-sanctioned policies on apartheid, why, they asked, could it not similarly treat the Kingdom of Saudi Arabia for its state-sanctioned policies of gender discrimination? (Mahoney, 1992: 573).[46]

They also appealed to alternative sources of authority. At the level of norms formation, the role of UN specialised agencies such as the United Nations High Commissioner for Refugees (UNHCR) made this a viable approach. Since 1985 the UNHCR had shown a high level of interest in women's refugee issues. By 1990 the UNHCR executive committee had requested that guidelines for the protection of refugee women be drafted in order to put an effective policy into action. These guidelines provided instructions for UNHCR field staff and their implementation partners to help them identify the particular needs of refugee girls and women. The willingness of select bureaucratic agents to think differently added further weight to this effort at the domestic policy-making level despite the fragmented structure of the Canadian state apparatus. Whereas the Immigration Department was slow in opening up the criteria for refugee claims, the Immigration and Refugee Board (IRB), which had the task of actually determining refugee claims in Canada, played a more facilitative role. Under the catalytic leadership of its chair, Judge Nurjehan Mawani, the IRB had produced a discussion paper providing an analytic framework for board members to consider refugee claims by women.

Stimulated by all this activity, small steps towards a more inclusive approach were made over a number of years. By as early as February 1988, in the domestic context, Canada had formally implemented a Women at Risk programme to focus on women in particularly difficult circumstances who required assistance in adapting to life in Canada. In the international context, Canada did a great deal to encourage and financially support a senior position at UNHCR, with a mandate to coordinate and monitor the integration of refugee women issues into all stages of planning and implementation of its programmes. A still bolder step was made in March 1993 when the IRB issued *Guidelines on Women Refugee Claimants Fearing Gender-Related Persecution*, a comprehensive document that would allow its members to grant refugee status to women on the grounds that they faced gender-based persecution (Immigration and Refugee Board of Canada, 1993).

Despite tangible evidence that this action offered a model for other countries to do the same (Australia and New Zealand, for instance, quickly moved to replicate the approach), these steps earned little kudos in Canada. Some critics interpreted this breakthrough as a reflection of how successfully a concentrated lobby in Canada, centred in the Canadian Council for Refugees, had been able to co-opt the adjudication process (Adelman et al., 1994). Others criticised it as a manoeuvre of militant feminism that weakened the traditional function of the gatekeeper on ideological grounds. The opinion piece by Eric Margolis "Creating Feminist Haven?" captures the tone of this criticism: "Attention all females around the world. Do you suffer from domestic abuse? Does your husband or mother-in-law yell at you? Are you forced to wear a veil? If you are, then rush over to Canada" (Eric Margolis, "Creating Feminist Haven", *Toronto Sun*, 11 March 1993) (for a very different appreciation see Mawani, 1993);[47] on the change in approach itself see the Immigration and Refugee Board of Canada, 1993).

The women's groups who pushed a more inclusive approach on refugees, conversely, still found the delivery function problematic. While acknowledging the value of the shift in the IRB guidelines, they realised that the net to be used for cases of women persecuted on the basis of gender remained full of holes. Above all, they perceived a mismatch between the actions of Canadian state officials at home and abroad. Although the Women at Risk programme was intended to encourage resettlement in Canada of refugee women in especially dangerous situations abroad, the catch was extremely small. Only 50 women and children came to Canada through the programme in 1993 and about 30 women in 1994.

During the Vienna conference process, Canadian diplomats played up what they considered the positive features inherent in such an evolutionary process. These included UNHCR's ability to develop new institutional/ multilateral or policy strategies to provide prevention and temporary protection measures for crises such as that in the former Yugoslavia. Where their behaviour proved evasive (Der Derian, 1987; George, 1994), however, was in their reluctance to stretch the limits of sovereignty. They opposed the promotion of any large-scale scheme for the resettlement of displaced peoples in third countries. Even the UNHCR's proposal to resettle small numbers of refugees in countries such as Canada was seen as exceptional, applicable only to individuals at particular risk (including women) whom it would be most difficult and costly to repatriate (in the words of Peter Harder, "repatriation and local integration", *Globe and Mail*, 16 July 1992).

While a humanitarian impulse shone through in this approach (particularly in the emphasis on the search for safe havens), a self-defence mechanism based on crisis management remained ingrained. Justice was also finely balanced with order, in that all recommendations were to include a reference to the 1951 Geneva Convention and Protocol, which established guidelines for refugee status according to "well-founded fears of persecution due to their race, religion, nationality, membership in a particular social group, or political opinions". In this context international agreements could not serve as mechanisms to push for action but acted as inhibitors that bound state officials to a set of restraining arrangements. The formidable practical obstacles to potential multilateral grounded solutions must be factored in as well. It was a difficult task to find safe havens, as acceptable sites such as Germany had become crowded. It was also difficult to make a clear distinction between bona fide refugees and asylum-seekers and irregular migrants (on this issue, see Gerald Shannon, Address to the Plenary Session of the 42nd Executive Committee of the UNHCR, Geneva, 7 October 1991, quoted in Adelman and Cox, 1994; for journalistic commentary, see Linda Hossie, "Migration increases as search for good life grows", *Globe and Mail*, 22 June 1993). And family reunification raised sensitive issues about definitions of a family.

To be fair, this evasiveness reflected a growing disconnect between the foreign ministry's administrative role and the development of domestic policy on migration issues. The foreign ministry's resources (and authority) on this dossier had been depleted by departmental reorganisations carried out in the late 1980s. In addition, the conclusions of leading migration experts within the foreign ministry (Shenstone, 1992; see also Shenstone, 1997) coincided more closely with those of the Department of Immigration (as revealed by its sponsorship of Bill C-86 in 1992) than with the IRB. From their bureaucratic perspective, the emphasis should be placed on tightening the structure for controlling immigration and the movement of people through new legislation.

To complement control with legitimacy (Simmons and Keohane, 1992), two themes were given heightened prominence during the actual Vienna negotiations. The first highlighted the national differences between Canada and the EC/EU, Australia, and the United States. Although cast in the general framework of harmonisation and the dynamic of intergovernmental consultation among these industrialised countries, Canadian diplomats emphasised that Canada's approach was far more balanced than those designed by the other countries. The control function imposed by Canada, unlike the Schengen and Dublin agreements (1993) designed to regulate entry into Europe, was taken to be grounded not just on deterrence but in efforts to share responsibility among a wider group of countries (Adelman and Cox, 1994; Stoett, 1996). Nor, unlike the United States, did Canada resort to immediate (and explicitly politically directed) solutions, such as processing migrants on boats. If migration issues were to be successfully managed, Canadian state officials maintained, solutions could only be found in thoughtful longer-term multilateral or regional agreements not in short-term opportunism.

The second theme, which extended from Vienna to the Cairo conference, focused attention on creating the conditions necessary to allow migrants to safely return home, as the dominant test of diplomacy (Young, 1991). From one perspective, this strategy hinted at making a serious commitment to countries from which refugees came (Gurtov, 1993). From another perspective, though, it accentuated the evasiveness within Canadian diplomacy. Considering repatriation as a solution deflected attention from the needs and interests of specific categories of refugees. It also begged the question of how a strategy linking migration and development might operate. Alleviating the initial pressure that caused refugees to move in the first place held some attraction in principle for developing states in that it addressed problems across the spectrum, from brain drain to loss of capacity to control borders. But in application, an approach of this type had to pass a demanding means test with respect to resources. For the causes of migration (especially the material ones) to be successfully targeted and addressed, new pledges from recipient and donor countries would be required. As such a scenario was unlikely at a time of declining aid budgets, it was unrealistic to expect that the locus of concern could be re-directed away from the responsibilities of "recipient" countries.

Indigenous rights

The second study, which cuts into the tests of sovereignty as territory in an even more profound and emotional fashion, is the issue of Indigenous rights in Canada. From one perspective, the challenge to the Canadian state, as posed by the Indigenous peoples through the Vienna process, can be interpreted as a struggle over authority. Not only did they challenge the state's determined tactics to assert and maintain its authority, they also contested the historical basis for that authority itself. In demanding both fundamental redress for their structural condition at the domestic level and recognition of standing at the international level, this Indigenous challenge undercut some of the core traditional organising principles on which the Canadian state was based. The assertion of the right to self-determination assumed importance in the diplomatic engagement of the Indigenous peoples. But if it was a goal, this demand served also as a means. Underpinning the form, scope, and intensity of this struggle was the ultimate question of who had exclusive and final possession and jurisdiction of land.

Faced with this challenge, Canadian diplomats used a variety of evasive methods. As with the refugee/migration issue, their approach was largely designed to deflect attention onto other actors and sources of activity. One tactic was to relegate the activities of Indigenous peoples to the status of NGOs. In similar fashion to civil society generally, Indigenous groups were to be allowed (and encouraged to have) greater access in the international system and the UN negotiating process. Although special concessions might be made in terms of symbolic expression, however, these groups were not to have any special or distinct status.

Another tactic was to try to regulate the purview of the UN institutional architecture over the domain of Indigenous rights. In declaratory terms, at least, the Canadian government was an enthusiastic proponent of the extension of UN mechanisms into this domain, having regarded the establishment of the UN Working Group on Indigenous Populations, for example, as a constructive way forward in 1982. The Canadian government also worked hard throughout the 1980s for the entry of Indigenous representatives into the wider operational machinery of the UN, most notably through the drafting of international legal standards in the working group and through the drafting group of its parent body, the Sub-Commission on Prevention of Discrimination and Protection of Minorities. It also supported its commitment by delivery, making a contribution through the UN Voluntary Fund for Indigenous Populations to enhance the capabilities of the Indigenous groups to work the system (the most complete source for this topic is Barsh, 1995: 107–134; for interesting insights see also Cairns, 2003).

As Indigenous groups moved more autonomously and deeply into the UN system, though, Canada backed away from this commitment and chose instead to try to impose limits and restrictions on the extension of the UN's institutional apparatus vis-à-vis Indigenous groups. The Canadian government resisted the Working Group's push for a comprehensive legal study of treaties signed with Indigenous peoples. It did its best as well to stymie and restrict the parameters of the initiative for an International Year of Indigenous Peoples in 1992.

From this overview, one might observe that the dynamics witnessed in the Indigenous rights issue shared some common characteristics with the migration/gender refugee issue. In both cases, Canadian diplomats directed most of their efforts towards widening the focus of attention from issue-specific to thematic and universal concerns. An essential difference between the cases, however, was that the level of controversy on Indigenous rights reached the point where the two sides became thoroughly estranged from one another. Instead of employing the positive attributes of the traditional diplomatic culture, with special reference to mediation, diplomatic engagement produced heightened tensions and alienation. At a point when there was a strong incentive and opportunity to mobilise more skilled and sensitive techniques of diplomacy – both internally directed and externally directed – this test was failed (Der Derian, 1987).

It may be argued that this failure of diplomacy was unavoidable, as the stakes inherent in the Indigenous rights issue were even higher than in the migration/gender refugee issue. Rather than being a debate about citizenship and the porousness of borders, the Indigenous rights question entailed considerations about the actual physical integrity of Canada. The diplomatic controversy over Indigenous self-determination became associated with a set of domestic debates over the occupation of native lands. The issue spilled over into ancillary questions about national unity that targeted Quebec as much as native peoples. On this second front, the state became preoccupied with the search for balance between sending a signal implying some demonstration effect for Quebec secession and putting out a more provocative signal in which Quebec interests were subordinated to Indigenous self-determination.

Canadian diplomats were reduced to a reactive position. The substance of the Canadian approach on Indigenous rights was set largely at the political/ministerial level, and the tone of the bureaucratic input was legalistic, whether from the Department of Justice or the legal bureau at the foreign ministry. Both contexts were recipes for trouble. At the political and ministerial level, the initiative on constitutional reform through the Charlottetown process had raised expectations among Indigenous groups. The rejection of this arrangement, accordingly, released a wave of frustration and anger that crashed up against established institutions and interests. At the bureaucratic level, the prime concern was to limit liability on the part of Canadian state.

As policy taker not policy maker on Indigenous rights, the foreign ministry was obliged to defend a narrow and rigid position. Justifying their stance as being part of a forward-looking not a backward-looking approach, Canadian diplomats rejected any notion that there was a need to address the legacy of colonialism or the effects of "past injustices" (Barsh, 1995: 109). Despite an acknowledgement of the salience of the native experience in Canada's heritage, Indigenous groups were treated merely as scattered minorities. Although it was accepted that they had grounds to press forward with land claims, they were not accorded any intrinsic right to possession of territory. Instead of working towards collective rights based on common cultural characteristics and/or treaty obligations, the onus was placed on the need to enhance the individual rights of Indigenous peoples to allow them equal status with "other national citizens" (Barsh, 1995: 122). This lesser objective was equity and non-discrimination, with adequate control over their own development.

Canadian diplomats were placed at a further disadvantage because of two additional contextual factors. The first was the fragmented organisational structure within the Indigenous groups, made up, as they were, of hundreds of tribes and communities. The Mulroney government had chosen to circumvent this diversity by privileging particularistic forms of representation, limiting consultation on the constitution to four national organisations, most notably the Assembly of First Nations (AFN), led by Ovide Mercredi. This decision had some immediate advantages in shaping the form and the content of Indigenous participation (for some insights, see Mercredi and Turpel, 1993). In the longer term, however, the restrictions inherent in this option became another serious impediment to a more inclusive form of diplomacy. Fatigued by the long (and ultimately unsuccessful) experience of the constitutional process – and stung by charges of manipulation – the AFN hung back from being a major player on the international human rights dossier and showed little interest in getting ready for the Vienna conference. In January 1992, when numerous NGOs were getting involved in the first consultations, AFN representatives were noticeably absent.

From the perspective of many other Indigenous representatives, state officials were perceived to be practising a not too subtle "gatekeeper" role, picking and choosing among representatives on the basis of a co-optation scenario. The resulting sense of frustration gave additional impetus to autonomous diplomatic initiatives. Spearheading this activity were the Cree of Quebec, the Mohawks, the Lubicon Cree, and the Mi'kmaq, all of whom had specific grievances against the Canadian state based on the control of land. Through the 1980s these groups had established the practice of externalising their actions by taking their complaints to the UN Human Rights Committee and the Working Group on Indigenous Populations. Formalising this behaviour as a legitimate part of the UN process, the Grand Council of Cree (of Quebec) obtained accreditation within the UN's Economic and Social Council (ECOSOC). Symbolically to highlight this status and to work this system as effectively as possible, Ted Moses, a former chief of the Grand Council, was established in Geneva as the ambassador of the Cree to the UN.

The second contextual element that posed a dilemma for Canadian diplomats was the sideswipe effect of Quebec issues entering into the international arena. Many of the most controversial sources of debate were found between the Quebec government and Indigenous groups. At the outset of the proceedings on the Human Rights conference, Ted Moses recounted the history of "intrusions" on the "Cree" territory and way of life by the building of mega hydro-electric projects in the north of Quebec (see, for example, "Briefing by Ambassador Ted Moses on Indigenous Issues for the Heads of Foreign Posts", External Affairs, Canada, 20 June 1991, available from http://www.gcc.ca/Political-Issues/international/briefing_to_external-affairs.htm). The first of these intrusions came in the early 1970s with the La Grande 1 power project, a series of super-dams designed to harness hydro-electricity from Quebec's northern watershed (Bourassa, 1985). It was soon followed by the Great Whale project. In counteracting these intrusions, the Cree transformed their tactics completely. Initially they tried to use Quebec's own institutional apparatus; indeed, Moses had been the Cree's principal negotiator on the James Bay and Northern Quebec projects. Over time, however, this inward-directed approach was discarded, as the Cree became disillusioned with the negotiation process (denounced by Moses as asymmetrical and meaningless) as well as environmental deliberations and other legal challenges. Their efforts then became more outward-directed through public relations and international lobbying.

Relations between the Mi'kmaq and the Mohawks and the Quebec government were no less contentious. The Mi'kmaq challenge to the Quebec government had been long-standing; as early as 1980 they had submitted a complaint to the UN concerning the "unlawful violation" of their territory (Barsh, 1995: 108). The demands of the Mohawks, both during and after the 1990 Oka crisis, provided a crucial flash point. The immediate issue, from the perspective of the Mohawks who lived on the Kahnawake and Akwesasne reserves, was their need to defend themselves against intrusion, whether by state officials in the form of police (especially the Sûreté du Québec) or by private developers and local townspeople. Below the surface, nonetheless, as with other developmental issues, lay deeper tensions over the future of Quebec and the place of Indigenous minorities within the province. Indigenous groups became increasingly forceful in their assertions that they would strongly resist any imposition of Quebec sovereignty (for a critical assessment, see Joffe, 1995).

Faced with this volatile situation, Canadian diplomats had little room in which to operate tactically. As suggested above, they had no competence (or mandate) to deal constructively with the substantive aspects of this set of issues. In any case, to condone the Indigenous defence against the intrusion of the Quebec government would risk provoking a nationalist backlash in Quebec. The status quo might change with the extension of self-government; but, even if flexible, these measures had to accord with the overall framework of Canadian federalism. The line in the sand was drawn at the model of internal self-determination as understood by the international community.

Under these circumstances, obstruction, delay, and deflection were inevitable in the response of Canadian statecraft. What is striking, however, is the determination with which Canadian diplomats defended not only what was judged to be the national or sovereign interest but their own professional standing, for the outward-directed campaign of the Indigenous peoples constituted a fundamental challenge to the activities of professional diplomats as well as to existing constitutional arrangements. In some ways, the diplomatic defence may be interpreted as the instinctive response of the established machinery to "outside" forces determined to do things differently. After all, Indigenous diplomacy performed very differently on the world stage. It showed little of the self-imposed constraint characterised by official diplomacy. Through the 1980s and 1990s Indigenous representatives went beyond the accepted boundaries of activity. They were willing, on the one hand, to join with the "South" group of countries, and at the same time they were prepared to work with representatives of isolated countries such as Cuba. (This was most controversially evident in their close cooperation with Professor Miguel Alfonso Martinez, a Cuban legal expert on the treaty study for the UN Commission on Human Rights). They also tended to deploy any tactics that were necessary to achieve results, including concerted efforts to shame the Canadian diplomats away from what was considered recalcitrant statecraft.

The international dimension of the Indigenous response to the Oka crisis was played out through a formidable repertoire of tactics. Relying on their access to the Working Group, the Mohawks called for censure of the actions taken by the Canadian state (invoking the National Defence Act and the deployment of troops). This complaint inflicted considerable public relations damage on Canada's reputation for "patience and moderation" (Barsh, 1995: 123). It also placed Canadian state representatives in the embarrassing position of having to scramble to avoid – if not formal censure – at least some expression of concern from the Working Group about the Oka episode, and Canadian representatives had to spend a great deal of diplomatic energy to wriggle free from this dilemma. Moreover, quite sensitively, they had to agree to the presence of outside observers to report back to the Working Group and the chair of the Sub-Commission (for warnings about Canadian sensitivity about foreign observers, see Michael Bliss, "Let's not get carried away by zeal for intervention", *Toronto Star*, 7 January 1993; Richard Gwyn, "Canadians are beginning to get pushy in foreign affairs", *Toronto Star*, 20 January 1993).

This process of estrangement was exacerbated by the Indigenous peoples' appropriation of some of the traditional techniques of Canadian diplomacy. During the run-up to the Vienna conference, the representatives of Indigenous groups demonstrated that they could in their own right use certain forms of technical and entrepreneurial diplomacy. As attested by their role in the Working Group on Indigenous Populations and other components of the UN machinery, these representatives moved appreciably from an outsider an insider status. True, they continued to protest about "colonialism" and "unlawful occupation", and to use traditional regalia and garb to accentuate their differences, but rather than depending exclusively on these older tactics, groups such as the Cree of Quebec, the Lubicon, the Mi'kmaq, and the Mohawks (assisted by a number of legal advisors) became immersed in the minutiae of UN conventions and proceedings. They frequently referred to Article 1 of the International Covenant of Civil and Political Rights, and other international human rights treaties, as well as to section 35 of the Constitution Act 1982, and an array of other Canadian legal decisions and precedents. And they made skilful use of opportunities to widen the scope of UN conventions. Prime illustrations of this approach came in relation to the revision of the International Labour Organization (ILO), the treaty study, and the campaign for an Indigenous Year.

Through their ability to build multi-layered forms of support, Indigenous groups showed that they could provide entrepreneurial leadership. One layer of this coalition-building activity consisted of enhanced ties of solidarity with other Indigenous groups on a transnational basis. This transnational movement included, inter alia, the World Council of Indigenous Peoples, Indigenous Survival International, and the Indigenous Initiative for Peace. Another layer was formed of tighter networks of activity with key individuals within the UN human rights system. In this category fell the Indigenous groups' dealings with officials such as the Greek legalist, Erica-Irene Daes, the chair of the Working Group, Halima Warzazi of Morocco, and the Cuban legal expert, Miguel Alfonso Martinez. Still another layer was the good working relationship Indigenous peoples had built up with Canada's preferential allies of choice, especially with the classic set of like-minded countries (Australia, and many smaller European countries including Norway, Denmark, the Netherlands, and Austria). Although there was extensive mutuality of interest in extending Indigenous rights, however, there was no common point of application among these countries. Australia, like Canada, was trying to work out a new comprehensive deal with its own Indigenous peoples. The European countries, on the basis of the imprint of history or out of good international citizenship, got involved in Indigenous affairs on a more selective basis. The Dutch were especially interested in the effect of NATO low-level flights on the Indigenous way of life in Labrador. The Danes focused on the extension of Indigenous rights and the ILO. The Austrians, to the consternation of Canadian diplomats, picked up and ran with the issue of the legitimacy of the term "Indigenous peoples".

It would be misleading to suggest that the official response to this appropriation of the imprint of Canadian diplomacy lacked considerable skill of its own. Canadian diplomats made a vigorous defence of Canada's historical treatment of its Indigenous population in comparative terms, and its more recent efforts to correct matters. They also became far more responsive in drawing selected Indigenous representatives into the work of the UN, a pattern that continued in the Vienna process. At the same time, the application of these skills began to take on a hard edge. Canada was accused of working to oust Australia as the Western Group's coordinator at the UN Human Rights Commission, because of that country's activist and more forthcoming stance in redressing Indigenous grievances. Canadian diplomats were portrayed as using muscle tactics to stall proceedings, such as threats to curtail the Working Group's activities if it targeted Canada.

Over time, Canada was surpassed in diplomatic leadership on the international dimension of Indigenous affairs not only by the like-minded cohort but by a number of other countries (including Colombia on the ILO) whose records on the Indigenous dossier had not previously been outstanding. To compensate, Canada was drawn closer to countries that it deemed "troublemakers" in other aspects of the human rights agenda. It teamed up with countries such as China and Bangladesh to incorporate the inviolability of the UN Charter in terms of "sovereignty and territorial defence of States" and stymie the treaty study. As Moses charged during an appearance before a special committee reviewing Canada's foreign policy: Canada "sought and established alliances on Indigenous issues at the United Nations with states that are notorious for their lack of respect for human rights and their ill-treatment of Indigenous peoples and whose interests are inimical to Canada and to the Indigenous peoples of Canada" (Moses, 1994).

This hard edge in Canada's diplomacy was revealed most clearly during the Vienna negotiations on the acceptability of using the term "Indigenous peoples" rather than "people" or "populations". From the perspective of the Canadian government, the question of the "s" reflected the high stakes invested in the Indigenous dossier. According to some strands of international law, and especially Article 1 of the Covenant, the word "peoples" opened up the prospect of unqualified acceptance to self-determination. This potential scenario was problematic in terms of its specific application to Indigenous groups. It also raised the possibility that Quebec sovereignty might implicitly be defensible. As the head of the Canadian delegation working on drafting the declaration on Indigenous rights during the Vienna process claimed: "We would not be serving the people of Canada as a whole if we did not ask for a rider (a legal definition of self-determination).... We would not be serving Canadians if we allowed anything that would imply the splitting up of Canada" (Ross Hynes quoted in Rudy Platiel, "Ottawa out to sabotage native rights. Leaders say", *Globe and Mail*, 23 June 1993; see also "Aboriginal groups call for rights protection", *Toronto Star*, 19 June 1993).[48]

The Indigenous considered this official stance unworthy of serious negotiation. Although an acceptance of the term "peoples" would have considerable instrumental value, this value was largely tactical. Few, if any, Indigenous representatives considered secession from Canada to be a realistic option; indeed, some explicitly denied that independence was the objective. Rosemary Kuptana, the president of the Inuit Tapirisat of Canada, accused Ottawa of "scaremongering tactics" by making the connection (Rudy Platiel, "Ottawa out to sabotage native rights. Leaders say", *Globe and Mail*, 23 June 1993). To reinforce this point, a comparison may be made with Australia, where a vocal minority of Aboriginal activists was calling for independence (Australian Provisional Government Council, 1990; Fletcher, 1994). And Mary Simon, member of the board of the Inuit Tapirisat, declared: "We wish to emphasize again that the Inuit agenda for the exercise of our right to self-determination is not to secede or separate from Canada but rather that we wish to share a common citizenship with other Canadians while maintaining our identity as a people, which means maintaining our identity as Inuit" (Simon, 1994).

If the threat of secession was to be used at all as a bargaining tool, this card was more likely to be played against the physical integrity of Quebec than Canada. Recognising this possibility, the concern of the Canadian government became sensitive to the potential spill-over effect of conceding the legitimacy of the principle of self-determination, or at least of creating gaps and ambiguities that could be exploited in the context of national unity. At a news conference well into the Vienna conference Canadian diplomats specifically warned that groups such as the Cree of Northern Quebec could potentially use their recognition as "peoples" to declare their sovereignty.

Strategically, the direct implications of winning this concession would have been twofold. On the one hand, Indigenous groups could use the legitimacy of the "s" to buttress their case in the series of land claims negotiations that were building momentum. International law permits peoples to control resources. Accordingly, the use of the term "peoples" was operationally significant because it would give Indigenous groups additional powers to control their resources (Smith, 1993a). Indeed, the security of such a land base was the essential factor differentiating "nations" from minorities. As one Indigenous representative spelled it out:

We, the world's Indigenous peoples, have lived on our lands before colonization and we continue to reside there, manifesting distinct characteristics which identify us as nations. We must emphasize the importance of land to Indigenous peoples. The most important of these issues is the right to obtain our land, the right to retain our land, and the right to live as people on our land. (quoted in Smith, 1993a: 1)

In addition, the legitimisation of the "s" would allow Indigenous groups ascendant standing in the diplomatic arena. Since the late 1980s organisations of Indigenous peoples had been gaining status with (and in certain respects beyond) NGOs in the international system. Official Canadian diplomacy was quite supportive of these endeavours, however, boundaries were drawn between reform and transformation. Internationally, the Canadian government was reluctant to allow the Indigenous peoples any special arrangement beyond the ad hoc and subordinate Working Group. Domestically, there was a tendency to still lump Indigenous groups into the wider category of civil society. This tendency surfaced during the Rio negotiations, as a number of Indigenous representatives (including Dan Smith of the Native Council of Canada, Cindy Gilday from Indigenous Survival International, as well as Simon and Moses) were brought into the process at one stage or other. A repetition of this model was expected for the Vienna conference. Indigenous members were sought for the Canadian delegation, alongside women's groups and other NGOs. Some Indigenous representatives were willing to get on board on this basis, however, a variety of others preferred a completely autonomous stance. Indeed, many Indigenous groups pushed for a parallel forum to that of the NGOs to provide guidance for the direction of the conference during the Prep Com process.

Tensions over style intersected closely with substance during the Vienna conference. With the question of the "s" hanging uncomfortably over the negotiations, the proceedings on the entire Indigenous dossier stalled. Indigenous groups such as the Cree, Lubicon, Mi'kmaq, and Mohawks were unwilling to give credence to the Canadian government's agenda, which emphasised economic development and universal standards. Nor did the advancement of the theme of a unique Indigenous cultural identity offer enough symbolic compensation. A commemorative session at the world conference, complete with spiritual invocation and speakers such as Rigoberta Menchu, was necessary but it was far from sufficient.

The full extent of the evasiveness of Canadian diplomacy and its estrangement from the Indigenous peoples peaked in the midst of the most crucial phase of the Vienna process. Because of the way the negotiations at the fourth Prep Com had taken shape, and thanks to the wording of documents prepared for the world conference, Indigenous groups had raised expectations about their ability to win out on the "peoples" issue. The Working Group's Chair, Mme Daes, had taken pains to downplay the breadth of the practical implications of moving forward on this principle, focusing on the need to work out new formulae for political arrangements and representation within the existing state structure rather than on the potential demand for Indigenous independence. She argued that the onus should be on bargaining in good faith about power devolution not on maintaining barriers to secession.[49]

Expectations about the inevitability of a breakthrough nonetheless received a serious setback when the latest version of the UN's draft document, issued just one day before the conference was to start, reverted to the term "people" not "peoples". Indigenous representatives interpreted this setback not only as further evidence of Canadian official recalcitrance to the question of the "s" but as a sign of the divergence between declaratory and operational policy with respect to a "new" form of inclusive diplomacy. Canadian diplomats may have been fully prepared to open up in an exploratory direction on many routine procedural matters. On issues with meaning and bite, however, they were accused of working to consolidate the logic of a traditional state-centric world. Perceiving the Indigenous challenge as a threat, they warded it off by power-based tactics. Evidence to support this interpretation was quickly assembled in the Indigenous-oriented media, which portrayed this episode as a betrayal of Indigenous interests behind closed doors. Not wanting to be seen as the obstacle in public, they claimed, the Canadian government had mounted its opposition safe from the scrutiny of non-state actors. As Dan Smith in the *Windspeaker* summarised: "They went into the meeting in Geneva, the fourth preparatory committee, with the 's' there. That was scheduled to be a two-week meeting that was later stretched to three weeks. The third week, during secret sessions that were closed the 's' went out" (Smith, 1993b: 1).[50]

With growing confidence in their international standing, Indigenous groups spent little time on repair work with Canadian diplomats. A meeting between the Canadian head of delegation was first postponed and then cancelled. Instead, the Indigenous representatives raised their offensive on the "s" question another notch.[51] Employing the skill-set they had assembled, they concentrated on closer networking with their list of allies. By extending the coalition-building exercise, they could count on an impressive cluster of "like-minded" countries on the "peoples" issue, ranging from Australia and New Zealand, as well as Norway and Denmark, to a number of Latin American countries. The Austrian foreign minister, Alois Mock, added impetus to this mobilisation process with his expression of sympathy for reopening the Indigenous "peoples" issue. In his capacity as chair of the conference, Mock sent a clear signal that he intended to ask the final plenary to amend the drafting committee's language to re-insert the "s" ("Austria opposes Canada to back indigenous peoples", *Toronto Star*, 24 June 1993). Mock added: "These are nations we should recognize". The Indigenous groups sent a letter of gratitude to Mock – which was handed out to all delegations in the plenary – professing the hope that he would meet this commitment to get the term "peoples" instead of "people" into the final conference document.

As this campaign built momentum, the Canadian government was backed into an increasingly isolated corner. Non-Indigenous sympathisers such as Max Yalden and Stephen Lewis, taking their cue from the Indigenous groups, vociferously played the "shame" card. Arguing that such obstructionist behaviour was detrimental to Canada's reputation as a good international citizen, they expressed regret that this fight had been pursued. The question was not about semantics and possible worst-case scenarios, the question was about right and wrong. As Stephen Lewis put it: "If you have a large indigenous population and you don't say yes to this kind of initiative it is clear where your instincts are" (quoted in Rudy Platiel, "Ottawa out to sabotage native rights. Leaders say", *Globe and Mail*, 23 June 1993).

In the face of this awkward position, the official Canadian approach was to resort to procedural imperatives and hardening coalitions of the "unlike". Caught off guard by the Austrian foreign minister's attempt to reopen the "s" issue, Canadian diplomats regrouped to remind Mock, inter alia, that in terms of process no language whatever could be re-opened in the plenary. They emphasised the political risks attached to such a move. Raising the "peoples" question again as a centre-piece of the Vienna conference, they suggested, would precipitate an acrimonious fight pitting the supporters of the "s" against hard-line countries such as Brazil, China, Bangladesh, and Malaysia. One spill-over effect of this fight would be to immobilise a variety of other human rights issues.

On the direct question of the "s", in the context of the Vienna conference, this official stance stood up to the diplomatic test. If willing to bend on the issue of how self-determination was to be defined and practised, Canadian officials were not willing to sever the connection between self-determination and the preservation of the territorial integrity of Canada.[52] While Indigenous representatives might challenge the authority of the state to operate according to this organising notion, their ability to cut into the state's capacity in a still primarily state-centred context was limited.

Where the Canadian state lost ground was not along the grid of effectiveness but on the contours of legitimacy. The more resistant the official approach was to the inclusion of the "s", the more importance the Indigenous groups attached to a breakthrough on this question. If the build-up of momentum made no immediate difference in winning the unqualified right to self-determination entrenched in a UN document at the international level, at the domestic level the results featured palpable changes in the political landscape. Any hope held out by the Mulroney government that it could replicate the Rio model of building and sustaining a partnership with non-state actors in each and every domain of the UN conferences was severely dashed. Some Indigenous representatives who had come on board became disenchanted with the process. Marc Leclair, the representative of the Métis National Council on the Canadian delegation, for example, resigned from the delegation during the controversy, complaining about the pro-forma consultation used by the government (Leclair, 1994). Other Indigenous representatives, who had at least been partially integrated into the Vienna process, became thoroughly alienated. Rosemary Kuptana, for instance, although continuing to work on the inside as well as the outside of the conference, had become frustrated that Canada had not embraced the world conference as an "opportunity to reach a consensus on some substantial and practical measures". Expressing her disappointment with the Canadian government's performance, she remarked at one meeting: "To be perfectly frank, there is no true dialogue between Indigenous peoples and Canada on these issues despite our efforts to do so" (Kuptana, 1993: 1, 4). The refusal of the Canadian government to accede on the "s" issue, however, precipitated an open and complete break. Going public with her view that Canada's position on Indigenous issues had become an "adversarial" one (Kuptana, 1993: 4), Kuptana told the Canadian media: "Canada's done a very good job of trampling on our rights at this conference" (quoted in Rudy Platiel, "Ottawa out to sabotage native rights. Leaders say", *Globe and Mail*, 23 June 1993).

The contradictions of sovereignty

The two cases studies explored in this chapter not only highlight layers of double-meaning involved in the concept of sovereignty but expose some of the contradictions that arise when this organising principle is applied in the context of autonomy and territoriality. When sovereignty is viewed as it relates to the physical integrity of a state, it becomes clear that we need to see sovereignty as a continuum. When facing outwards, Canada has shown considerable leeway in countenancing expanded forms of intervention. Even in select issue areas dealing with intrusion from external forces, Canada has met the need to be flexible in the application (if not the symbolism) of national sovereignty. This behaviour is especially evident where Canada lacks not authority but the ability to exercise clear control. A more rigid line is drawn in areas where the challenge moves beyond intrusion to contestation about jurisdiction over territory.

As expressions of societal demands for a reconfiguration of sovereignty, both cases under review share common characteristics. Challenging the foundational and assumed nature of the Westphalian model of sovereignty, the advocates for women refugees and the Indigenous representatives both assert that the ultimate source of authority lies beyond the state. Whereas state authority (and the exclusivity of national jurisdiction) was seen in earlier decades as the solution, it has become a source of problems. In relocating this debate, these groups not only attempted to redesign the political debate within Canada but also expanded their transnational links. Their appeal is largely based on their emphasis on social particularities along with their ability to embarrass or "shame" state officials as a result of their traditional unequal treatment.

In many ways, nonetheless, the differences between the two cases outweigh their similarities. The refugee advocates certainly had a diminished respect for territorial attitudes. Not only did they associate increasingly beyond borders but they denied the legitimacy of the state's making decisions pertaining to the right (or denial) of entry and citizenship. That is to say, they denied established entities' "externally recognized right to exercise final authority over [their] own affairs" (Biersteker and Weber, 1996: 2). While questioning the authority of the state, however, they did not seriously question the capacity of the state. If anything, they overexaggerated the hard shell of the state in order to delegitimise it. The image of a coercive state provided a much better target for attack than an internally divided and quite porous state.

The Indigenous groups combined the transformative component of identity politics with the push for self-determination over land and resources. The dilemma for the state, therefore, not only extended further into its policy dimension but intruded on an overall (and long-accepted) ideal of national physical integrity. Given the sensitivity of a potential break with this model, this robust challenge met much stronger resistance. On both issues, Canadian diplomacy tried to deflect the challenge by evasion. Only on the refugee issue, however, could these countermeasures be used without completely damaging the sense of partnership established between women's groups and the Canadian government in the Vienna process. On the Indigenous dossier, by way of contrast, this technique proved not only to be a failure but appreciably raised the level of estrangement.

The question of the "s" became the litmus test for the struggle between the fixed assumptions of a state-centred perspective on sovereignty and a world in which no single structure can encompass all its components. From the Canadian government's perspective, any formalisation of a multi-dimensional model – with "unbundled territoriality" (Ruggie, 1993b: 173–174; Slaughter, 1997) – held enormous risks. Domestically, it risked sending the wrong message to Quebec about its own claims to independence and about scenarios involving internal partition. Internationally, it raised the spectre that Canada was in a condition of endemic (and immobilising) instability with its fragmented entities becoming a harbinger of a Yugoslavia-like conflict (see, for example, Ignatieff, 1993).

From the perspective of Indigenous representatives, the Canadian government's hard line on the "s" during the Vienna process reflected what Stephen Krasner terms "organised hypocrisy" (Krasner, 1999). At the domestic level, the Canadian government was not averse to the word "peoples", including its use in the Canadian constitution. It was only externally that a more rigid line was drawn. Similarly, Canada's general support for transparency and openness in the UN system contrasted with its specific efforts to deflect any negative attention on its own record through censure, sustained scrutiny, or monitoring.

All this being said, though, the Indigenous case is as much a prototype as an anomaly. The Indigenous groups in no way considered themselves to be in a similar situation to ethnic minorities in Canada or "national minorities" searching for autonomy or independence in other parts of the world. Yet, for all of the tension between them and the Canadian state, the struggle over Indigenous sovereignty has become highly contingent. The bending in terms of recognition was highly politically constructed and had been in train for some time. The "s" controversy at Vienna represented not the beginning but the culmination of a long struggle.

The crucial difference between Indigenous sovereignty and nonterritorial issues was that the question of Indigenous sovereignty still needed to be determined by a clash of will, underscored by power resources and appeals for public support. On issues for which the stakes concerned other dimensions of authority than the physical integrity of the state, the room for bargaining widened considerably. As a variety of other issue areas demonstrate through the UN world conferences, an expanded bargaining mechanism does not necessarily reduce discord (Keohane, 1995: 182–186), but at least in such cases, resort to coercion and threats of violence are excluded. It is to these less exceptional but nevertheless highly salient tests that we now turn our attention.

7
Tests of the civilisational divide? The Cairo International Conference on Population and Development

How can the UN world conferences serve as a means of dialogue within and across boundaries of identity in international politics? This test, the sixth in our study, is undergone in the context of the relationship between sovereign-bound states and sovereign-free societal groups, whether members of transnational NGOs, the transnational managerial class (Cox, 1992a), different categories of refugees, or asylum seekers. It also encompasses the "encounters" between officials of "settler" states and representatives of the colonised "First Nations" (for a sophisticated analysis of these encounters in the international relations literature, see Dunne, 2000). All of these cases, while allowing for huge differences of interpretation, hinge on the core question of "Who is us?" (for an elaboration, see Reich, 1991), and, in related form, on the question: how should the lines between 'insiders' and 'outsiders'? (Walker, 1993).

Another important variation of this test comes out in the twin questions: "Who on the outside are we similar to?" and "Who are we most different from?", the difference between "we" and "they". In the Canadian case, the "we" group constitutes what have been termed like-minded countries. Their clubbishness must be differentiated from Canada's relationship with a core set of partners in NATO and the G-7 industrialised countries. The like-minded constellation constitutes a loose network of countries with roughly similar worldviews and diplomatic styles – the traditional candidates being Australia, New Zealand, and the Nordic countries. The hallmark of this like-minded group has been its established bias towards institutionalism and multilateralism. More specifically, among them the instinct for cooperation has forged a healthy regard for the ability of states to solve problems collectively. Unlike the pivotal powers, and especially the "indispensable" United States, they remain optimistic that even the most contentious or complex issue can be handled through cooperative efforts and collaborative arrangements. If it is somewhat far-fetched to suggest that these states acted, as Hedley Bull claims, as "the local agents of a world of common good" (Bull, 1983–1984: 14), it is not too much of a stretch to say that the diplomatic practices of these countries did at least demonstrate interest in seeking creative solutions on salient issues at specific times.

The questions of whom we differ from, and how we differ – who constitutes the "non-we" – are far more tortured. Whereas the identity of the non-we was defined during the Cold War by differences (and the connotation of being the "other"), the new order allowed a greater sense of community and cosmopolitanism of attitude and values. As in the case of the Indigenous peoples, an ideology of assimilation has become ascendant since the end of bipolarity. New like-minded entities could come into being, and long-standing differences between the "like" and the "unlike" could be tempered and deflected as the spirit of market-based liberal democracy took firm hold.

From the viewpoint of some commentators, however, the world is seen as becoming more polarised, not more homogenised. The most sombre of such assessments is expressed by Samuel Huntington in his argument about *The Clash of Civilizations and the Remaking of World Order*. "To the extent that non-westerners see the world as one", Huntington contends, "they see it as a threat" (Huntington, 1996: 66). For them, the ideological divide of the Cold War years has simply been replaced by a cultural conflict pitting the West against the Rest.

A negative perception on the way these debates have been informed by the UN world conferences is that multilateral diplomacy has increased the political, economic, and cultural space between the "we group" and the "others". This clash was particularly imposing on the human rights agenda and spilled over into environmental and population issues (Evans, 1997). Consistent with Huntington's view that "conflict does not necessarily mean violence" (Huntington, 1996: 25), issue-specific diplomacy at the UN conferences became a prime vehicle through which such differences of identity could be magnified. On top of entrenched cleavages, such as the one between political rights and the right to development, came additional layers privileged by Huntington and proponents of cultural relativism based on rigid divisions between the ethos of individualism and community-based values, secularism versus spirituality, and the universalistic coercive influence of the American way of life (Buzan and Little, 1999: 99).

If one turns attention from the constraints of this structural deterministic posture, the opportunities provided by multilateral diplomacy – especially through the use of the UN as a forum for talk and mediation – become apparent. The weight Huntington accords to particularistic identities conditioned by fundamentalism and tradition is offset by the room for manoeuvre provided by economic self-interest and the opportunism of state-based officials. A rigid definition of "us and them" is made more ambiguous and multi-dimensional (Cox, 1993: 263; Cox and Schechter, 2002) as the images of the West and the Rest (and the likeminded and the unlike) are reconfigured to conform to internal diversity within these blocks. The social space between the two groupings is not magnified – but shrunk – through diplomatic interaction. Dialogues of the deaf can be superseded by a more creative process characterised by a willingness to think and act beyond the "civilizational" box in order to deal with "issues of common concern" and search for "common ground" (Evans, 1997; for a good critique of Huntington, see O'Hagen, 1995).

Contextualising the civilisational divide

Tests of civilisation inject an element of added volatility into the diplomacy of UN world conferences, which leads us to ask: "Has a new type of division been interjected into global affairs?". With the East/West cleavage no longer dividing the world along ideological economic lines, new (or perhaps more accurately older) points of difference based on cultural identity arise as replacement sources of tension. As rehearsed most provocatively by Huntington, the ascendancy of differences along a clearly marked cultural fault line provides a paradigmatic shift of profound import: "The fundamental source of conflict in this new world will not be primarily ideological or primarily economic. The great divisions among human kind and the dominating source of conflict will be cultural. Nation states will remain the most powerful actors in world affairs [but] the fault lines between civilisations will be the battle lines of the future" (Huntington, 1993: 22; this argument is expanded in Huntington, 1996).

Huntington's flagging of a civilisational ingredient in international politics needs to be taken seriously in light of recent global change. Stifled by the domination of objective strategic and material concerns, subjective and cultural features defining "self identification" (Huntington, 1993: 24) have been given too little attention as elements that bind groups of people. Karen Mingst and Craig Warkentin note the need for us to rethink our assumptions to compensate for the fact that the cultural element was "silenced by the dominant paradigms of international relations" through the Cold War years (Mingst and Warkentin, 1996).

Here again, the UN world conferences provide an ideal opportunity to examine this test of world governance as it unfolded in the interplay between global change and diplomacy. It immediately becomes evident, however, that a fundamental difficulty with privileging the cultural dimension is that it is so difficult to pin down in situational terms. To gain the insight that the cultural dimension can offer us into post–Cold War politics, we need a structured environment that encourages contrasting views and values to be voiced – a site of multilateral negotiation that allows close interaction among large numbers of actors across a marked rift in values. The UN world conferences meet these criteria.

Discord across civilisational lines can be found right across the spectrum of UN conferences. The 1994 Cairo International Conference on Population and Development (ICPD), however, brought cultural clashes into much starker relief ("Clash of cultures mars formal start of Cairo meeting", *The Times* [London], 6 September 1994, p. 17). The most sensitive issue was undoubtedly abortion, but a focus on this single question belies the range of contentious questions entwined with it. The debate about the definition of the family demanded a great deal of time and emotion. Should the title of "family" be reserved exclusively for one recognised model (whether nuclear or extended) or should it refer to several models extending to single-parent families or same-sex families? Questions about sexual rights and education, especially in terms of adolescents, were equally contentious. All focused attention squarely on issues pertaining to moral respect and well-being.

One line of division ran along the axis between individual and group rights. An individualistic perspective gave primacy to sexual and reproductive choice, which could only be enacted at the individual level not by government or community. From a group-centred perspective, adherence to a well-defined set of local standards remained a necessity; to act outside such standards smacked of "permissiveness" and an abdication of responsibility. Another division followed the axis between the secular and the spiritual. The individualistic perspective celebrated certain "Western" liberal and humanistic principles that held men and women to be the supreme arbiters of their universe. The group-centred perspective, on the other hand, became consolidated along religious lines. Much of the "Islamic" opposition to an expanded definition of the family and to "permissiveness" in sexual matters was based on a cultural particularity premised on readings of specific religious texts. Several countries with exclusive or majority Muslim populations, including Saudi Arabia, Syria, Sudan, and Lebanon, boycotted the ICPD, alleging that it contravened

Islam and the teachings of the prophets (Michael Georgy, "Saudis boycott population conference", *Globe and Mail*, 30 August 1994). Other Islamic countries such as Iran and Yemen did attend but emphasised that in putting Islamic law first, they objected to the idea that discussions over individual rights in sexual matters were included at the conference.

"The West"

To build up the image of the civilisational Western/non-Western divide, and more specifically a Western–Islamic cultural clash, does not mean we must accept the reality of that image without rigorous questioning. A quick appraisal of the ICPD conference, as suggested above, may lend itself to a confirmation of Huntington's hypothesis of distinct civilisational–cultural polarisation. Many of the media stories on the conference highlighted the theme of a bitter clash between a secular West and a theocratic (and uniform) pan-Islamic front. Even a far more detailed account of the ICPD negotiations by a conference insider had warned prior to the actual meeting in Cairo:

There can have been few international conferences where the opening barrages have been quite so ominous. With only a few weeks to go before the opening of the Cairo meeting, the Islamic world appeared in open hostility to the concepts set out in the draft programme and indeed to the very idea of holding such a conference in a predominantly Muslim country. (Johnson, 1995: 72)

Yet, when looked at more closely as a test of the structural power of the putative civilisational clash, the case of the ICPD is less than a "whole and intact" illustration of this phenomenon in operation. As foreseen by some of Huntington's more sophisticated critics (see, for example, Ajami, 1993: 2–9), an episode such as the Cairo conference appears to be far more ambiguous and unpredictable than the "clash of civilizations" hypothesis would suggest. Instead of a being predetermined set-piece struggle between dichotomous and competitive worlds, the Cairo conference illustrates just how freewheeling and disjointed the craft of diplomacy had become in the post–Cold War years. Attempts to clarify "who is us" and "who is them" became entangled and disputed. Public declarations of partisan support through appeals "to common religion or civilization identity" (Huntington, 1993: 29) were contradicted by private behaviour. Behind the scenes, channels of communication and negotiation among the various actors remained open.

The first set of questions revolves around what is meant by West and non-West. Huntington, in his survey of the cultural divide, assumes the West to be a monolithic entity requiring only cursory analysis – "the

West" becomes shorthand for "the United States". Yet, a close reading of the Cairo conference (as with Rio and Vienna) reveals just how misleading this assumption is. On the debates at the core of these conferences, the United States stands out less as a prototype than an as exceptional country featuring a very different (and superior) mindset and mode of debate. On the international human rights dossier the United States did epitomise a zealous commitment to individual rights (see, for example, Donnelly, 1993). Because of its own issue-specific domestic record, however, it lagged as much as it led – witness its continued massive use of capital punishment and its tendency to resort to coercive administrative measures such as forcibly returning Haitian "boat people" without a hearing.

This exceptionality became more pronounced in the United States' application of unilateral psychology and its level of volatility. As a great power the United States proved itself an awkward multilateralist. In none of the major UN-sponsored conferences did the United States demonstrate any great skill in diplomacy. Threats and bluster were used repeatedly on the environment and human rights. At the Rio UNCED, Bush senior's protracted status as a no-show was the classic expression of this behaviour. At the Vienna Human Rights Conference Washington's claim (exerted by Secretary of State Warren Christopher and other members of the American negotiating team) that it would prefer no agreement to one watered down to achieve a consensus further demonstrated United States high-handedness.

The volatility of the United States' performance had also been seen on the population dossier. During the Reagan era, the United States' traditional enthusiasm for international activism became subordinated to domestic concerns on the abortion issue. At the 1984 Mexico City population conference, the US delegation (led by well-known conservative James Buckley) announced that it would end its aid to international population programmes if their activity financed or supported abortion. President Bill Clinton dropped this policy immediately after his inauguration. There had also been a reversal of the market-oriented approach to population issues favoured by the Reagan administration. Nudged along by Vice-President Al Gore's personal interest in this dossier, the United States' official position moved back in synchronisation with the UN and the programme of action developed by the ICPD (Johnson, 1995: 43; Brad Knickerbocker, "US assuming Major Role at Cairo Population Talks", *Christian Science Monitor*, September 8, 1994).

Overlapping with this push–pull dynamic at the state level was the tremendous fragmentation of societal interests within the American political fabric. US-based organisations were at the heart of the women's caucus during the Cairo process (Higer, 1999). Some of these organisations, such as the Women's Environment and Development Organization (WEDO), particularly through the work of veteran activists like Bella Abzug, linked the societal activity of the UN world conferences of the 1990s to the earlier wave of conferences stretching back to the 1970s. Other organisations, such as Rutgers' Center for Women's Global Leadership, headed by Charlotte Bunch, rose to prominence at the Vienna human rights process. Paralleling this societal activity, American representatives also formed a prominent component of the religious caucus constituting both formal religious groupings and "pro-life" activists.

If a US-centric take is a necessary starting point for any discussion of what constitutes the "West" it should not have the last word. Indeed, a strong case can be made that at Cairo, as at the other UN-sponsored world conferences, it was not the United States but a loose consensus of "like-minded" countries that more consistently represented the image of the West as the bastion of progressive and individualist secular values (on some aspects of this divide, see Jurgensmeyer, 1994). Allowed more space in this domain than in the more traditional disciplined area of security, the leadership of these like-minded countries took on the role of agenda-setters based on this model. The best-known advocate of this cause was without question the Norwegian prime minister at the time of the Cairo conference, Gro Harlem Brundtland. At the opening session of the Cairo conference Brundtland unequivocally championed the cause of individual choice on issues of morality. And she was ready to defend that position against any counterclaims. Drawing the limits to religion's mandate to influence public or private activities, Brundtland argued: "Morality becomes hypocrisy if it means accepting mothers suffering or dying in connection with unwanted pregnancies and illegal abortion, and unwanted children living in misery" (Brundtland quoted in Johnson, 1995: 89; see also Bob Hepburn, "Religion assailed as threat to women", *Toronto Star*, 6 September 1994).

Again, however, this association of like-minded countries with secular Western values must be considerably nuanced. In looking more closely at the influence of national cultures, it becomes evident that a number of countries identified as like-minded in fact had extremely strong religious traditions that influenced their behaviour at Cairo. To give just one illustration, the Republic of Ireland diverged considerably from the Brundtland approach to the legalisation or the legitimisation of abortion. Rather than going along with the Western consensus, Ireland supported choice on the abortion issue not on an individual but on a national basis (Johnson, 1995: 106).

This division was exacerbated further by additional differences on the individual/collectivist dimension, the most serious of which were over migration issues. The traditional "settler" countries among the like-minded (including Australia as well as Canada) were more receptive to establishing regimes for family reunification, albeit within the parameters of a restricted definition of the numbers that comprise the family. From an opposing point of view, a grouping of mainly European countries rejected the notion that family reunification was a universally recognised human right and insisted that this component of the Programme of Action did not establish any new rights (Johnson, 1995: 172).

Given these disagreements, the potential for close cooperation of the like-minded was quite limited. As in the established pattern going back to the 1970s, the main vehicle of this common set of activities was the process of informal consultation. Any additional stimulus for this dynamic was created by the structural design of the United Nations, in which the West European countries, together with Canada, Australia, and New Zealand, continued in the catch-all "Western Europe and Others Group" or WEOG. In terms of agenda building, what stands out is the degree of segmentation. The loose association of the like-minded did not translate into a coordinated mode of operation. Rather, it manifested more as tactical coalitions in ad hoc responses to an agenda that was broken down into smaller (and more manageable) items. Like-minded diplomacy partners were sought on an issue-by-issue basis.

As indicated by the division on abortion, the extent to which the like-minded countries actually shared common values should not be overestimated. Their divergent interests must be taken into account as well. On a variety of issues, such as family reunification, these interests were predicated on identity; that is to say, on the basis of whether a country defined itself in exclusively ethnic terms or as a multicultural territorial entity. Even among countries that had a great deal in common, however, dissimilarities persist. As at the Vienna conference, for example, at Cairo as well Australia and Canada had differing positions on Indigenous issues. Whereas Canada was still not ready to abandon its rigid stance, Australia had embraced the term "Indigenous peoples". Nor of course can the "West" as the repository of a set of selected values be reduced to a state-centric monolith. As R.B.J. Walker has made explicit, contemporary patterns of cultural politics suggest a very complex field of possibilities that cannot be captured simply in overlapping compartmentalised statist images (Walker, 1993: 13–14). To be sure, a key conviction of the society-craft pursued by NGOs and civil society throughout the Cairo process was that their promotional activity – and not statecraft – was the authentic expression of the values of individual equality, autonomy, and dignity (Donnelly, 1989; Donnelly and Howard, 1986).

The Roman Catholic Church, for its part, acted on both sides of the state–societal interface. In institutional terms, the Vatican/Holy See had the attributes of a nation-state, with official status as a sovereign entity;

its diplomatic corps were widely located, well connected, ample in resources, and highly experienced (see, for example, Hanson, 1987; Vallier, 1972). Unlike the NGOs represented at the periphery of the UN conferences, its delegation to the Cairo conference had the right to speak at all open and closed sessions. In activity that placed a high premium on consensus, it had the power to shape the ICPD's outcome to its own will.

When examined conceptually, the role of the Vatican during the Cairo conference supports the validity of Robert Cox's point of the need to take a pre- as well as post-modern perspective on the existence of a "multi-level world" (Cox, 1993). In terms of privileging universal values as well as cross-border identities and loyalties, the Vatican resembled a large transnational NGO more than a territorially-based state. In its claim to speak to and for a universal constituency on the basis of core values, it more closely resembled the functioning of some NGOs. It considered ethical or moral leverage as a more appropriate tool to shape the craft of diplomacy than national interest. Strategically, this perspective subordinated pragmatic problem solving to a higher ethical or religious stance; tactically, it allowed the limits of action to be stretched on the grounds that the end justified the means.

Akin also to the world of NGOs was the Vatican's ambiguous position vis-à-vis "the West". Both were targeted by some voices in the South as agents of Western political and cultural influence. At the same time, both shared an anti-materialistic and anti-technological bias that was decidedly out of step with mainstream Western thinking and actions. Throughout the cycle of UN conferences, the Vatican's attacks on the excess of the Western lifestyle stand out as a fundamental theme. The Vatican's demand in the lead-up to the Rio conference that the "scandalous patterns of consumption and waste of all kinds of resources by a few" be replaced by the assurance of "justice and sustainable development to all, everywhere in the world" found resonance in views manifested throughout the NGO community ("Vatican defends position on population growth", *Globe and Mail*, 5 June 1992). Although targeted at a number of the key strands of the Cairo agenda, this common cause held up. On the migration dossier, for instance, the Vatican and NGOs together championed the cause of the displaced as well as the need to extend the right of family reunification. The Vatican also pushed hard with the NGOs to realign the priorities of the Cairo conference away from the entrenchment of opulence towards equity, with a greater distribution of "Western" resources and access to technology.

But the loose kinship of the Vatican–NGO relationship was transformed into antipathy in the controversy over abortion and reproductive health. On these issues the values advocated by the Vatican – "the most fundamental right of any human being to life" (Johnson, 1995: 44) – were expressed with an entrenched calculus of interest. With respect to technically oriented diplomacy, the Vatican took full advantage of its official insider status to block the ascendancy of values based on the primacy of personal choice and the right to abortion. The texts under negotiation, from the Prep Coms to the committee work of the Cairo conference, were heavily bracketed with specific reservations on language and sentence structure, particularly in the paragraphs dealing with reproductive rights and family planning as well as health, morbidity, and morality.

With respect to entrepreneurial diplomacy, the Vatican showed interest in building issue-specific coalitions where and when it could. As might be expected, many of the Vatican's strongest allies were countries with "Latin" roots, such as Argentina, Malta, Ecuador, Peru, and Honduras. Significantly, however, numerous other erstwhile supporters within this constituency were either willing to soften their stance or defect completely on abortion. By default as much as design, therefore, the Vatican spent an impressive amount of time attempting to extend its support across cultural boundaries as well as reinforcing its campaign inside its own civilisational orbit.

Contrary to the thrust of Huntington's thesis, this diplomatic offensive translated into strong overtures towards the Islamic world. Building on its own credentials with respect to anti-materialism and its ambivalence about Western sexual morality, the Vatican defined the struggle as a polarisation along a secular–religious fault line as a West/non-West split. As Joaquin Navarro-Valls, the main Vatican spokesperson, said before the Cairo meeting: "The positions of some of the delegations going to Cairo, coming from different countries, different backgrounds, and certainly not from a Catholic and even Christian background, are now closer to the position of the Holy See" (Johnson, 1995: 79; see also John Hooper, "Pope makes holy alliance with Iran", *Manchester Guardian*, 17 August 1994; Gustav Niebuhr, "Forming earthly alliances to defend God's Kingdom", *New York Times*, 28 August 1994).[53]

The NGO community responded to this manoeuvring in two different ways. The Vatican's characterisation of the struggle as an antipathy based on religion was countered by charges that the Church was out of touch with modern realities. In the lead-up to the Cairo conference Jessica Mathews from the Carnegie Endowment on International Peace entertained a scenario in which "the only dark cloud" was the Vatican's efforts to stymie "international momentum on an endeavour vital to human hope and individual fulfillment" (Jessica Mathews, "Now we know that population control can work", *International Herald Tribune*, 5 April 1994). At the Cairo conference itself, NGO representatives made frequent comparisons between the recalcitrance of the Vatican and their own flexible skills in practising creative society-craft. Joan Dunlop of the

International Women's Health Coalition voiced NGOs' indignation at Vatican attitudes: "Whereas [we] have gone a long way to compromise, far further than we would have preferred, I think the Vatican is behaving outrageously" (Johnson, 1995: 117; see also Dunlop's CBC radio interview "Women: the new discovery of the United Nations", available from www.hsph.harvard.edu/Organizations/healthnet/sasia/depop/chap15.html7).

With respect to the agenda for action, the Vatican's offensive pushed the NGOs in the same direction. Determined to belie their image as creations and agents of the West, the NGO community participating in the Cairo process broke with the older consensus on the need for externally imposed demographic quotas and controls in population programmes. As part of a wider transformative process associated with the empowerment of women, they gave pride of place to policies integrating the right to family planning and abortion with the achievement of a much wider set of development goals, emphasising the right to health, employment, and participation (Hartman, 1987; Heschel, 1995). In organisational matters, priority was given to enhancing the effort to establish genuine cross-cultural links. The drive to build a "Women's Voices '94 Alliance" was one signal of this effort. Another was the campaign for the "Women's Declaration on Population Policies" (Johnson, 1995: 135–136).

"The non-West"

A need for nuance must also govern the discussion of the contribution of the non-West to the ICPD process. Signs of a possible working arrangement at Cairo across the West/non-West religious divide point to the flaws in buying into an analysis that is too structurally determined – as does any cursory treatment of the divisions found within the Islamic cultural world. As the more sophisticated analysis of James Piscatori suggests, there emerged at Cairo "no such thing as a monolithic Islam, let alone a monolithically anti-western Islam" (Piscatori, 1984: 313).

Some impressive forces of resistance could be mobilised against the "Western-imposed" agenda dominated by secularism and individualism, but any potential sense of unity among this grouping was hampered by internal differences. Although individual religious and government leaders denounced the ICPD, no collective plan emerged either to boycott it or to coordinate a common strategy. The result – in complete contrast with the monolithic image proposed by Huntington – was an extreme fragmentation along national lines. Some resistant countries chose to be no-shows on the outside looking in at the conference. Others, such as the high-powered Iranian delegation, chose to oppose from within by stalling or deflecting the process of negotiation.

Highlighting these types of resistance on the part of non-West participants should not minimise the extent of the support for the ICPD process that was visible within the Islamic world. Egypt proved to be an indefatigable host of the proceedings, with a huge material and public relations investment in a successful result. Exceptions to the "us and them" fundamentalist/radical image of the Islamic world also abound among other participants. Pakistan, whose prime minister, Benazir Bhutto, grabbed a high profile at the opening session of the conference, not only chaired the small working group established to settle on a compromise solution on paragraph 8.25 dealing with abortion but also lined up with some quintessentially liberal countries (including Norway) in endorsing the possible wording of a consensus text. Individual change-agents at the core of the meeting, most notably Dr. Nafis Sadik, the ICPD's secretary-general, had a solid grounding and considerable standing in the Islamic world. A gynaecologist and pioneer in family planning from Pakistan, Sadik served for a number of years as executive director of the UN Population Fund. In her advocacy of an activist programme of action on population in tandem with a renewed drive for equality and development, she transcended West/non-West differences.

Just as the claims of a West versus Islam division are off the mark, other manifestations of a "West versus the rest" conflict are not realistic guides to the Cairo process (Mahbubani, 1992). Extending the counter-argument to Huntington's thesis further shows even more clearly that the image of a deeper cultural fault does not fit accurately into the case of the ICPD. This deficiency is particularly obvious when Huntington's claim of a "Confucian-Islamic" challenge to "Western interests, values and power" is presented (Huntington, 1993: 45). Consistent with one of Fouad Ajami's criticisms of Huntington, there is little evidence of an alliance of this nature present at Cairo (Ajami, 1993: 6). Asian countries opposed the West in a number of ways, not least on the need to legitimise the right to development, but this cleavage did not mean a "West versus the rest" gap in their attitude to population policies.

The Asian states, as affirmed by their support of the Denpasar Declaration of November 1993 in the run-up to the Cairo conference, were stalwart defenders of the population "stabilization" regime based on demographic targets and quantitative controls which was developed from the time of the Bucharest conference. They aligned themselves with the orthodox approach traditionally espoused by the United Nations Population Fund and its allies. However, they bridled at an operational model that valued universal consistency over nation-state differentiation. Throughout the debate China argued that it was essential that a global population regime encompass the right of individual states to respond to their own social conditions in selecting their population policy.

What more accurate view of the Cairo conference emerges? Instead of being seen through the lens of cultural or identity differentiation, this dimension of the Cairo conference is better portrayed as a cross-cultural struggle of interests between defenders of state-centrism and advocates of a more porous model with space and legitimacy for societal actors. As on the human rights and environmental agendas, appeals to self-determination were increasingly interpreted by NGO representatives as opportunistic and self-serving tools that could allow states to hide from different sorts of value-based obligations. Intensifying criticism was directed particularly at the coercive elements of China's population policies, but the programmes implemented by other countries such as Indonesia and Bangladesh became targeted as well.

The NGO community did contain a variety of groups that had been strongly associated with the global population stabilisation regime. The International Planned Parenthood Federation (IPPF) was the most prominent of these actors, both as a generator of ideas and as a provider of services. What was striking about the IPPF's role at the Cairo meeting, nevertheless, was its performance as a catalyst for change. Challenging the consensus on which the global regime had been grounded, the IPPF agreed to stretch the bounds of its agenda. It more directly championed the needs of the excluded, focused more explicitly on the empowerment of women, and supported the perception of abortion as a health care and not a legal issue (Johnson, 1995: 117).

NGOs from the West chose to disassociate themselves from the older consensus and were careful not to lay the blame exclusively on the South. The former consensus had been problematic on a number of counts. First of all, a uni-dimensional approach meant jeopardising potential cross-regional partnerships within the wider NGO community. Activist NGOs from the South shared the counter-consensus perspective that crimes had been committed in the implementation of the population stabilisation regime (see, for example, the statement by Farida Akhter, of the Asian Women's Human Rights Council, quoted in Norma Greenwood, "Women demand control of bodies, lives", *Ottawa Citizen*, 8 September 1994). Their target, however, was not their own government but the actions of the international system at large, the global population lobby made up not only of the United Nations Population Fund (UNFPA), and the IPPF but of other influential private bodies such as the Rockefeller and Ford Foundations through to the Population Council, and Western donors – that is to say, the actors that had provided much of the drive for the regime in the first place (on this regime, see Crane, 1994). Others blamed the combination of Western aid and corporate interests, which had made the South both "a dumping ground" and a testing site for reproductive technology (see, for example, John Stackhouse, "Best laid family plans sometimes go awry", *Globe and Mail*, 9 September 1994).

On top of this internal problem there was also a risk that an overly critical outlook on the part of Western NGOs would encourage an alternative alliance between the Vatican/Holy See and a wider area of the South. Having distanced itself from the international population stabilisation regime from the outset, the Vatican/Holy See had some credibility at Cairo in its advancement of an anti-technological approach to population control. Indeed, the attractiveness of this approach was enhanced by the coincidence of interest between the Vatican and the South on a number of other issues. They shared views on the need for an equitable distribution of the West's resources. They also agreed on family reunification. When the working group with the mandate to hammer out an agreement on this issue failed to do so, the Holy See sided with 34 developing countries in their expression of "frustrations, sadness, difficulties and even reservations" (International Institute for International Development, *Earth Negotiations Bulletin*, 06/39, 14 September 1994).

Finally, to single out the state apparatus in the South as an obstacle to a revitalised agenda on the population dossier neglects the opportunities it offered for innovative ideas and capacity building. Heightened sensitivity to questions of sovereignty did not immobilise the South; on the contrary, it provided added impetus for select initiatives from these forces during the Cairo process. A group of 10 developing countries, for example, used the ICPD experience to try and forge a new form of South–South partnership for sharing knowledge on how to balance best international practices with traditional values ("Partners in Population and Development: A South-South Initiative", available from http://www.south-south-ppd.org/). These countries encompassed Bangladesh, Colombia, Egypt, Indonesia, Kenya, Mexico, Morocco, Thailand, Tunisia, and Zimbabwe.

Bridging the gap? Opportunities and limits for innovative diplomacy

In detailing the role and impact of Canadian diplomacy at the ICPD, the space allowed for leadership and innovation by the changing international policy environment and policy agenda must be taken into account. In keeping with our theme of the ascendancy of agency over structure, the diplomatic opportunities presented in the context of the Cairo negotiations played up some well-honed Canadian strengths. This landscape encouraged the type of association among the "like-minded" that Canadian officials felt most comfortable with. Extensive consultation free of a heavy overlay of institutionalisation was considered vital to the process of sounding out ideas and procedural directions.

The entrepreneurial side of like-mindedness had come forward on various issues at the Rio and Vienna conferences. During the UNCED process, Canada had concentrated on building a coalition on fisheries with a small group of coastal countries, including Iceland, New Zealand, Argentina, and Chile, with Norway and Peru joining later on. This core group agreed, to some extent at least, on a diagnosis of the problem and a framework for solution. After a number of meetings (Buenos Aires, in October 1993, for example) these countries co-sponsored the so-called Santiago Resolution prior to the Rio meeting. Maintaining this coalitional effort, John Crosbie, as Minister of Fisheries and Oceans in the Mulroney government, convened a forum explicitly labelled the "Like-Minded States Meeting" in January 1994 in St. John's, Newfoundland, to work through a draft convention on high seas fishing.

During the Vienna process, as the coordinator of the WEOG Canada was well positioned to shape the agenda on the human rights dossier. Anne Park, the Canadian diplomat chosen to be chair, proved effective as an organiser and negotiator within this group in its preparations for regional meetings and Prep Coms, its liaison with UN bodies (such as the UN Centre for Human Rights), and the proceedings of the Vienna conference itself. Canada worked closely with those countries it considered "like-minded" on the issue areas that it prioritised. With Australia, the Netherlands, and Sweden, among others, it pushed for greater participation for NGO institutions within the Vienna process. The Nordics, New Zealand, and Australia remained steadfast "like-minded" partners on agenda items for the advancement of women's rights.

At the Cairo conference, this habit of innovative diplomacy was still in practice. Canada worked hard to build a like-minded coalition to target the causes of migration (or push factors) as opposed to its effects.[54] On population and reproductive questions per se, Canada participated in a campaign to extend the definition of the family to encompass a diversity of family structures and composition. Working with Sweden and Australia, among other countries, Canadian diplomats contributed to the fine-tuning of Chapter V of the Cairo programme of action to include a reference to the changed composition and structure of families in many societies and to express support for "the plurality of family forms" (International Institute for International Development, *Earth Negotiations Bulletin*, 06/18, 6 April 1994). Canada also took part in the campaign waged by the EU, Norway, and Sweden against forces wanting to downgrade the word "partnership" in the title of Chapter XV, "Partnership With Non-Governmental Sector", with the phrase "on a consultative basis". In some areas of diplomacy, the Canadian approach showcased opportunities for assembling larger cross-coalitions. Besides the traditional trio of "like-minded" countries referred to in the pattern of association found above, Canada found allies among other – very different – countries. Bangladesh, for example, supported Canada's position on the question of family definition, and Nigeria and Jamaica moved onside with respect to the language of the "partnership" issue.

Still, the development of a credible and effective form of like-minded diplomacy proved a difficult test. In many ways Canadian behaviour reflected a dilution of traditional Canadian diplomatic habits. This was particularly noticeable, for instance, in the way Canada subordinated policy development to procedural matters. With its wealth of experience on how to run a smooth conference, Canada took on the role of navigator or guide for the conference process. At the pre-negotiation stage, it stood out in its role as discussion leader (with Indonesia and the Netherlands) on a specific set of themes. Prior to the conference, Canada had worked on the draft preamble (Chapter 1) and principles (Chapter 2) as prepared by the chair of Prep Com III. Looking forward to the follow-up stage, Canada released a document with suggested mechanisms for coordinating the 23 United Nations system units, bodies, and organisations involved in population activities (International Institute for International Development, *Earth Negotiations Bulletin*, 06/25, 15–18 April 1994). Canada called as well for the use of holistic and consistent methods in this post-conference evaluation phase, together with more effective resource management within UN agencies and the Bretton Woods institutions.

Canadian state officials showed that they were ready to use their expertise to help cut through (or circumvent) the procedural obstacles presented at the conference, and chose the tactic of joining new informal working groups to address outstanding issues. One illustration of this type of behaviour was Canada's effort through the working group to reach a consensus on Chapter VII of the programme of action, with a particular focus on paragraph 7.1, dealing with "sexual and reproductive rights". This working group included Canada's traditional "like-minded" partner, Sweden, but it also contained the Holy See as well as Iran and a host of other "unlike" countries. An analogous case existed in Canada's close association with the "Friends of the Chair", an informal subcommittee of the main committee.

From another perspective, this attention to procedure also meant an ongoing focus on the clarity of language. Canadian officials carefully watched for deletions or misprints, in order to privilege favoured words and phrases. Canada pushed to maintain the phrase, "sexual and reproductive rights embrace certain human rights", in Chapter VII against the objections of Iran, Argentina, and Malta. Over the wishes of Iran, Libya, the Dominican Republic, and a number of other countries, Canada pushed for the phrase "couples *and individuals*" in terms of reproductive rights. Contrary to the aims of Honduras and Bolivia, Canada sought in association with Japan to substitute "equality" for "equity" in the title of Chapter IV on the empowerment of women.

What Canada lacked was the vision and the courage to move beyond this low-key approach to address more directly the central (and highly controversial) issues at the core of the ICPD. Canada would not stick its neck out too far on questions relating to population stabilisation. Rather than serving primarily as a source of diplomatic innovation that might encourage casting off inhibitions, Canadian coalition building increasingly became a protective device to hide behind. Nowhere on this dossier was there any evidence of the burst of inspiration that had done so much to raise Canada's profile in other aspects of multilateral diplomacy.

Even on procedural matters Canada showed a distinct disinclination to raise its level of participation beyond a point where it put itself under intense scrutiny. In contrast to its performance at the other UN world conferences, no Canadian personnel were appointed or elected to key positions with respect to the Cairo conference. Nor, just as significantly, was any frustration or dissatisfaction expressed at this outcome. At odds with its long-standing dual image as a good international citizen with an elevated profile combined with status-seeking, Canada seemed content to be lost in the crowded sea of actors and agenda details during the ICPD episode.

The only endeavour on which Canada played any sort of mediative role was the search for consensus on the chapter (VIII) dealing with sexual education and reproductive health services for adolescents. Here again, however, far from demonstrating Canada's ability to raise its game when needed, this illustration reveals Canada's risk aversion. Instead of following the lead of the advocates of open access for adolescents to contraceptive information and supplies, Canada was more concerned with achieving a balance between the reformers (most visible among the "like-minded") and those with traditional attitudes. Working behind the scenes, Canada forwarded a proposal to the Holy See, which blended concern with select forms of confidentiality (most notably, in cases of rape and incest) with respect for parental rights and responsibilities regarding their children's involvement in sexual and reproductive health education and services.

A quick comparison of Canada's approach with the style adopted by Dutch diplomat Nicolas Biegman can give a taste of how muted Canada's approach became during the Cairo conference. At the first negotiating session on the abortion issue, Biegman, who as vice-chair of the main drafting committee took the prime responsibility for the final text, showed the traits of a classic problem solver. Calling on the delegates to discard their moral and ethical preconceptions on this issue, Biegman proposed that they concentrate exclusively on questions relating to the medical aspects of unsafe abortions. After two days of intense debate on the single paragraph (8.25) about abortion, however, Biegman's frustrations became painfully obvious. At a news conference on the third day, he chastised the participants for their issue-specific preoccupations: "We have just a week and a half to attract the attention of the world and all we read is abortion, abortion, abortion" (Biegman quoted in Bob Hepburn, "150 nations, Vatican in showdown on abortion", *Toronto Star*, 9 September 1994).

What Biegman had expected was a process of "mediation between states" (Watson, 1982: 19) played out according to a variation of the diplomatic method whereby all the players acknowledged that by now "the world [had] established an international diplomatic culture [that] socializes its members into similar behavior" (Zartman and Berman, 1982: 226). Instead he had to deal with a key actor that refused to compromise. Although the Vatican agreed that the reworked language represented an improvement, it pronounced that it could not accept any text that accepted the legality of abortions or promoted the use of abortion as a method of family planning.

Rather than interpreting these fundamental differences as manifestations of a clash of interests (or even cultures), Biegman aggressively questioned the very legitimacy of the Vatican as an international actor. He stated that the Vatican could not continue to possess dual status in diplomatic negotiations, as both sovereign state and religious institution. If it was unwilling to play by the same rules as other members of the society of states, Biegman challenged, the Vatican "should think twice" about attending future conferences "as a full participant" (quoted in John Stackhouse, "Cairo conference called victory for individuals", *Globe and Mail*, 13 September 1994).

Canada's stance on the abortion issue, by contrast, demonstrated its attachment to quiet diplomacy. At the outset of the Cairo process Canada committed itself with some enthusiasm to paragraph 8.25, which stated: "All Governments, intergovernmental organizations and relevant non-governmental organizations are urged to deal openly and forthrightly with unsafe abortion as a major public health concern" (Johnson, 1995: 110). Along with Norway, Finland, and the United States, it had resisted the EU's proposal during Prep Com III of alternative language to shift attention away from concern with universal "access to quality health care services" towards an emphasis on "national" considerations reflecting "the diversity of views" on the issue.

Once serious negotiations started at the Cairo meeting, this sense of commitment became tinged with elements of convenience. With its original allies, Canada indicated a desire at the first negotiating session to adopt the alternative language on 8.25. Later the same day, it moved with most other countries to delete the reference to the promotion of abortion as a means of birth control. What remained solid during these negotiations was its concern with women's access to public health: at the first session Canada reasserted its call for "reliable health care services"; at the second it highlighted the need for pre- and post-abortion counselling. But Canada also made concessions on the abortion issue. Although it worked hard to maintain the phrase, "in circumstances in which abortion is not against the law abortion should be safe" (Norma Greenway, "Canada adamant on need to fight unsafe abortions", *Ottawa Citizen*, 7 September 1994)[55] under pressure from the Vatican and its allies, it accepted the deletion of the mention of "legal" abortions in the final text.

Unlike Biegman and a number of other actors (including the Egyptian population minister who asked rhetorically whether "the Vatican rule[d] the world"), Canadian negotiators papered over differences in their declaratory statements. Sergio Marchi, the head of the Canadian delegation, downplayed the notion that Canada wanted to impose certain principles on the abortion issue beyond its concerns with women's health: "We don't come to this conference pushing our morality on anybody" (quoted in Norma Greenway, "Canada adamant on need to fight unsafe abortions", *Ottawa Citizen*, 7 September 1994). The only public indication that Canada had conceded to pressures came from Ruth Archibald, Canada's deputy head of delegation, who hinted that although Canada had had to shift on language it had stood firm on substance: "We've spent a lot of time in the last seven days talking about words. Words are important, but generally speaking, the concepts we were interested in seeing in the document have not been changed" (quoted in John Stackhouse, "Reluctant Vatican agrees to back part of global pact", *Globe and Mail*, 14 September 1994).

External logic/internal fragmentation

Adherence to a cautious mode of operation seemed logical from an outward-looking perspective. Why alienate the Vatican/Holy See on a single issue when its backing was needed for other goals? Certainly, the differences among like-minded and unlike-minded forces across the continuum of agenda items helped shape this attitude, but Canada's shying away from a confrontational stance against traditional forces did not constitute a complete change of identity; rather, it indicated Canada's close association of statecraft with what Harold Nicolson termed – many decades previously – "social banking", the management of trust, confidence – and credit – among the society of states (on this theme in the particular context of Cairo, see for instance Alan Cowell, "Negotiators Push for a Truce Over Population", *New York Times*, 5 September 1994).

By operating according to this orthodox understanding of diplomatic practice, Canada carved itself some additional room to lead on the migration issue. With their shared profiles as "immigrant" countries, for instance, Canada and its CANZ partners could work effectively towards a more liberal regime on asylum and family reunification issues (International Institute for International Development, *Earth Negotiations Bulletin*, 06/01, ICPD, Prep Com II, nd), but Canada could not count on support from the EU in this area. Retaining their historical self-images as "non-immigrant" countries, EU members had little interest in opening up debate on the migration dossier. Whereas Canada acted as the motor force in the negotiations on the text on international migration (Chapter X), the EU provided the brakes. In the paragraph dealing with "alleviation of uncontrolled migration" (10.3), Canada suggested the need for humane government policies. The EU, on the other hand, defensively requested deletion of the reference to the unwillingness of destination countries to admit more documented migrants. It also proposed that governments should make potential migrants aware of the legal conditions for entry and residence in host countries. On the paragraph (10.12) dealing with the "right of family reunification" Canada reaffirmed its commitment to the objective of family reunification, although it wanted to keep control of the means of implementing this policy. The EU, however, in keeping with its defensive posture, maintained its view that family reunification was not a universally recognised human right and insisted that the Cairo text not try to move in this direction.

Canada's flexibility (or lowest-common-denominator approach) on abortion earned it the prospect of a quid pro quo from the Vatican on migration. The intransigence of a solid core of its western European allies in regard to the movement of people forced Canada to search for alternative allies where it could. The Vatican responded eagerly, wishing both to project a progressive face in compensation for its stance on abortion and to maintain its close ties with developing countries. Capitalising on its go-between activities with respect to the issue of parental responsibilities and the provision of contraceptives and family planning information to adolescents, Canada worked in tandem with the Vatican on migration issues. They teamed up to write global principles for international migration, sharing a common concern with family reunification and the needs of women and children in the category of undocumented migrants (International Institute for International Development, *Earth Negotiations Bulletin*, 06/19, 7 April 1994).

This segmentation of diplomatic like-mindedness did not separate Canada from the EU on other issues (International Institute for International Development, *Earth Negotiations Bulletin*, 06/20, 6 April 1994). If Canada and the EU did not share common attitudes on migration, there was a sense of convergence on the structures and cultures of health care. Accordingly, they found it easy to cooperate in negotiations about health and mortality (Chapter VII). On the issue of primary health care and the health-care sector, both Canada and the EU (together with the Holy See) objected to fee-for-service programmes, since they discriminated against the most needy. On the section dealing with HIV infection and AIDS, both the EU and Canada agreed on the need to make condoms as widely available as possible.

Although there can be little doubt about the contribution of an externally oriented logic to setting the parameters of Canadian statecraft, separating this logic from the dynamic of domestic factors provides an unduly constricted view of the way the overall pattern of Canadian diplomacy took shape at Cairo. The salient feature of Canadian statecraft at Rio, Vienna, and Copenhagen had been the way an initial dynamism gradually ebbed with changing political and economic conditions. At Cairo the pattern was rather one of bifurcation. It was not that Canadian state officials were entirely reluctant to take on leadership at the Cairo conference, they simply wanted to make clear distinctions between areas in which Canada chose to move out in front and those that it earmarked for more cautious involvement.

As head of Canada's delegation, Marchi's fundamental goal at Cairo was to extend the migration regime to encompass "push" factors on the migration dossier. Preoccupied with this objective, he could not undertake any ambitious measures on the wider population agenda. What is more, Marchi's personal beliefs were not amenable to his pressing for an extension of the boundaries of the population regime in a secular or individualistic direction. A practising Roman Catholic with an electoral constituency made up heavily of Italian-Canadians, Marchi was uncomfortable with an agenda burdened with controversy about abortion, adolescent sexuality, and reproductive health. He had little to gain politically from trying to raise Canada's profile as a mediator. From a policy standpoint, the framing of Cairo "as a conference on abortion" (John Stackhouse, "Abortion main topic in Cairo", *Globe and Mail*, 6 September 1994) had the effect of crowding out his initiatives on migration. Earning him few votes at home and little diplomatic kudos in the international arena, population issues (apart from migration) were best left alone.

Complicating the scene still further was the contrast between the roles of CIDA (the Canadian International Development Agency) as champion and DFAIT (the Department of Foreign Affairs and International Trade) as a disengaged supporter of the international population stabilisation regime. Through its development assistance mandate, CIDA had become intimately involved with maintaining this regime. DFAIT, on the other hand, adopted a hands-off approach. As one parliamentary backbencher, an enthusiastic advocate of an extension of this regime, differentiated the two approaches: "I find our Department of External Affairs is very skittish, very shy, very reluctant to enter the domain of even suggesting [to other countries that] they might have a population policy appropriate to their situation, their culture, and so on. [Conversely] I know CIDA does take an interest" (Halliday, 1992: 16–21).

In its policy orientation, CIDA had bought into the concepts of quantitative targets and controls as well as the concept of "carrying capacity" – the ability of a particular eco-system to sustain a given population. By the mid-1980s, CIDA had become the world's second-largest bilateral population sector donor and the fourth-largest donor overall for international population activities (CIDA, 1987). Canada's greatest financial contribution went to the Bangladesh Population and Health Program, a project coordinated by the World Bank. As laid out in a 10-year plan, the aim was to spend more than $100 million for population activities in Bangladesh between 1986 and 1996, about $28 million of which was to be directed to contraceptive pills. Indeed, Bangladesh became the only country for which CIDA explicitly mentioned the reduction of fertility as an objective of its programme (CIDA, 1992; see also Gillespie, 1991).

CIDA's expertise was bolstered by the addition of population specialists to its staff (two of whom were members of the Canadian delegation at Cairo). In addition, the appointment of Margaret Catley-Carlson, one of its former heads, as president of the Rockefeller-funded and New York-based Population Council, was an indication of some movement of personnel between the upper echelons of CIDA and the central pillars of the population stabilisation regime. However, CIDA had also made forward strides in its own thinking and application. Through its policy redesign of the early 1990s, CIDA had clung to the orthodox position that rapid population growth was the main barrier to sustainable development and an improved quality of life, but it began to loosen its association with the coercive elements of the population control regime by evoking sympathy for the principles of free and informed consent, human rights, choice, and the empowerment of women (CIDA, 1993: 192–193).

Moreover, fiscal austerity cut into CIDA's capacity to support the regime. Canada's population assistance funding was severely reduced in the 1991–1992 cuts not only in absolute terms (Gordon Barthos, "Uproar threatens progress in ending poverty", *Toronto Star*, 3 September 1994), but also as a proportion of the total (and shrinking) aid budget. Whatever else altered in the policy context, the days of generous funding for overseas population stabilisation projects were over. The most generous gesture of the Canadian government during the Cairo conference was the announcement by the Canadian Secretary of State for Latin America and Africa of a contribution of $14.9 million to support primary education for girls in 15 African states (John Stackhouse, "CIDA to boost education", *Globe and Mail*, 9 September 1994).

From the standpoint of society-craft at Cairo, Canadian civil society's talent for leadership had to be filtered through the increasingly crowded field of individuals and groups who laid claim to the population agenda. As at Rio and Vienna this aspect of society-craft can be placed on an axis running from quiet insiders to vocal outsiders. Lorna Marsden, for example, fit quite well into the "quiet insider" category. A Liberal senator from 1984 to 1992, whose experience went back to her leadership of the Canadian delegation to the Mexico City population conference, Marsden worked assiduously at Cairo to promote and legitimise the compromise solution on abortion, whereby abortions were treated as a health concern but not as a means of family planning. From Marsden's vantage point this trade-off was as good a deal as could be expected under the conditions of polarisation found at the Cairo conference: "Given the strong views on the subject, it's a very good compromise" (Norma Greenway, "Vatican stance on abortion bogs down talks", *Ottawa Citizen*, 10 September 1994; see also Alan Cowell, "Vatican Rejects Compromise on Abortion at UN Meeting", *New York Times*, 7 September 1994).

Stephen Lewis best represents the category of "vocal outsiders". Although his resumé included appointment by Prime Minister Mulroney as the Canadian ambassador to the UN, Lewis remained a provocative gadfly, using his sophisticated language skills and well-cultivated access to the media to frame the Cairo conference not as a site for compromise but as a battleground between good and evil. Repelled by the spectre of Vatican and Islamic fundamentalists working closely together to stymie an agenda based on a woman's right to choose, Lewis accused these religious elements of "thinly veiled misogyny" with no sense of the moderation that would be induced by "an affirmation of the rights of women to literacy, employment and so on" (quoted in Norma Greenaway, "Lewis slams 'misogyny' of UN critics", *Ottawa Citizen*, 4 September 1994; see also the CBC's Quirks and Quarks documentary written by Anita Gordon, "Population: The Vatican Versus the People", 3 September 1994).

Cast in this dichotomous fashion, the hybrid nature of the agency of these individual performers is inevitably lost. Notwithstanding the tone of his public rhetoric, Lewis nevertheless continued to have a standing that allowed him to work inside the perimeter of the UN establishment. Although a vocal critic without status as an official delegate, the scope of his influence was far wider than that of unofficial participants who were restricted (whether by choice or not) to the parallel forums. Nor should the privileges of insider status be necessarily equated with a defence of the procedural status quo. Marsden, although more in tune with diplomacy as the art of the possible as opposed to simply doing what was right and necessary, was quite prepared to break through the older closed world of diplomatic consultations. If her means were quite flexible, her goals remained steadfastly emancipatory (see, for example, Marsden, 1992).

Locating NGOs on a continuum of activity is an even more elusive task. At one level, this complexity is a function of the sheer number of NGOs involved in the ICPD process. Galvanised by the Rio model, NGO interest had soared across the entire spectrum of women's health, development, and environment groups. The parallel Forum '94, held at Cairo's indoor sports stadium complex adjacent to the conference site, was attended by 260 NGOs. Sixteen Canadian NGOs were accredited to the conference (United Nations, 1994). At another level, this complexity arises from the structure of the conference arrangements themselves. As in the past a fundamental split emerged between NGOs with status and those that focused their activities on the alternative NGO forum at the perimeter of the official conference.

But beyond this single line of demarcation, the Cairo conference revealed a further layer of differentiation. Although the NGOs with status were technically limited to the main committee and the plenary session, if they were members of official state delegations their restrictions were eased. Extended access was thus opened in the Canadian case to selected members of the Canadian National Advisory Council for the ICPD, the Planned Parenthood Federation of Canada, and NAC (National Action Committee on the Status of Women), with alternative standing for representatives of the United Nation Association in Canada and Inter Pares. Although official and unofficial NGOs could meet and develop society-centred positions in caucus format, the barriers created through differentiation in status hung heavily over the society-craft developed through the conference.[56]

Along with this sense of procedural fragmentation came multiple sources of polarisation on policy. One dominant theme that surfaced was the tension between those who wished to reform the international population stabilisation regime and those who preferred to tear it down completely. Most prominent in the reformist camp were the representatives of the Planned Parenthood Federation (PPF) of Canada. As with CIDA and the international pillars of what had become the population establishment, the Canadian arm of the IPPF reflected the growing concern among civil society that population controls place a greater emphasis on self-determination and empowerment for women. As Bonnie Johnson, the executive director of Planned Parenthood affirmed: "Family planning doesn't mean just throwing birth-control pills at women" (quoted in John Stackhouse, "Cairo conference called victory for individuals", *Globe and Mail*, 13 September 1994).

Akin also to the experience of CIDA on the state side, the privileged position of the Canadian PPF among societal actors showed signs of slippage as population politics underwent a tectonic shift in the early 1990s. No longer operating from the peak position it held during much of the Mexico City process (a standing highlighted by its responsibility for organising the Canadian Task Force on Population in the pre-conference consultation phase), at Cairo the PPF of Canada had to operate in a much more pluralistic and competitive environment. Within the Canadian National Advisory Council it had to co-exist with NAC and other groups; outside, it faced challenges from groups at the opposite end of the political and policy spectrum.

What is equally striking about the Canadian experience, however, is the asymmetry between individualistic/secular and religious/traditionalist forces. During the Mexico City conference, the Canadian delegation was acutely aware of the need to hold consultative sessions with "problem" church groups. Similarly, at Cairo they held informal talks (albeit on a more ad hoc basis) with the Catholic Conference of Bishops and the Catholic Women's League. Neither of these religious groups, however, was given equal standing with the NGOs on the Canadian National Advisory Council. Nor did this channelling process give these churches any unique advantage, as meetings were also held with representatives from the more "liberal" United and Anglican churches and the National Council of Jewish Women.

One explanation for this lack of profile may be that religious groups most out of step with the international population stabilisation regime preferred to work on a transnational basis, as in the case of the Roman Catholic Church's alignment with the Vatican. Indeed, it could be argued that this transnational strategy was a more effective route for influencing the UN conference. From another perspective, however, these elements of the religious community may simply have recognised the limitations of the federal government's agenda. Despite the Canadian PPF's continuous pressure, Canada remained a country without a national population policy. On the highly emotive issue of abortion, furthermore, Canada (and Canadians) kept safely to the middle of the road. Unlike the massive swings between the Reagan/Bush and Clinton administrations' approaches to the issue, Canada maintained its eye on the goal: it worked towards the removal of legal impediments to safe abortions but would not support language that recommended abortion as a governmentally funded service.

This search for balance allowed a coincidence of identity on issues as well as dissent. The religious counter-consensus continued to oppose the targeting of ODA (Official Development Assistance) funds towards family planning programmes, but the Canadian state was also increasingly reluctant to submit to international (or other domestic) pressures to commit specific dollar amounts or set percentages in this fashion. Meeting the goals formulated through the Cairo process meant distributing resources across a wide spectrum of priorities.

Whatever the cause, the effect of Canadian efforts was to more fully triangulate the struggle. The third force that added to the polarities of the secular/religious divide was the powerful presence of the women's movement, which wanted to demolish the international stabilisation regime on the basis of feminist critique and principles. This movement shared with the more conservative elements of the religious community a deep-set hostility to the technocratic-bias of the stabilisation regime. A coincidence of view also appeared in their common antipathy to the coercive methods used in applying the regime, whether through its support for China's one-child policy or Indonesia's method of communal persuasion, or in its funding for tests of new reproductive technology such as the hormonal contraceptive implant Norplant, immunological contraceptives, or anti-pregnancy vaccines.

Where the women's movement broke completely from the religious counter-consensus, of course, was on the nature of an alternative birth control system. Instead of working to gain release from the grip imposed by demographers and family planners in order to return to an older order, the women's groups worked to establish reproductive security (or a reproductive bill of rights) for women, based on a system of individual and group justice. In pursuing this vision they would make no accommodation with forces interested in "curtailing, rather than supporting women's rights to reproductive and sexual health" – simply replacing one form of coercion with another, with its own formula for the "violation of women's human rights" and "the denial of reproductive freedom" (National Action Committee, 1994). Women, their robust argument went, must be given health rights on the basis of free and informed consent and dissent (quoted in Bob Hepburn "Canada faces fight", *Toronto Star*, 7 September 1994). Only by creating this type of woman-centred population plan could a guarantee even be contemplated that freedom from compulsion and violations could be combined with the choice to accept contraceptive and abortion services.

The National Action Committee on the Status of Women invested considerable energy on its own "in-between" status as an organisation with standing on the Canadian delegation as well as a transformational agenda. Its position as a recognised entity on the Canadian National Advisory Council with a representative appointed to the Canadian delegation at both the Prep Coms and during Cairo, earned NAC heightened attention as an agenda-setter. Still, NAC consciously chose not to take on the attributes of the classic conference insider. Its representative on the Canadian delegation, an executive member of NAC as well as a reproductive technology specialist at McGill University, praised the Canadian delegation both for its role as a "consensus builder" and for its leadership on specific issues (see, for example, John Stackhouse, "Best laid family plans sometimes go awry", *Globe and Mail*, 9 September 1994), but at the same time she was critical of Canada's record of abuses perpetrated by new reproductive technology (Mulay, 1994). As an organisation, NAC expressed continuous frustration at the restrictions placed on it by the Canadian National Advisory Council for the ICPD. This frustration came to a head in the preparation of recommendations for the Canadian National Report on Population, as mandated by the ICPD. Feeling that Canadian policy was falling well short of its expectations, NAC took action in forming the Canadian Women's Committee on Reproduction, Population and Development.

This combination of insider and outsider positioning allowed NAC considerable freedom of action during the Cairo process. On the one hand, it continued to have access to the Canadian Inter-ministerial Committee as well as the wider Canadian delegation and the ICPD secretariat. On the other hand, it still had the means and the credibility to revert to a purer form of advocacy when its goals were being compromised (if not completely silenced) through mainstream diplomatic channels. Drawing on its horizontal societal links rather than its vertical contacts with state officials, NAC used the opening of the Cairo conference to offer a Canadian feminist manifesto on population issues. While this "Canadian Women's Report on Policies and Practices in the Area of Reproduction, Population and Development" made a host of recommendations, at its core was a Bill of Reproductive Rights. The emancipatory tone of its agenda stands out:

In contrast to those who argue that government population control programs should be the focus of and a precondition to development, we argue that to bring about improvements in health, the lead must come from the women whose lives are most directly affected.... Women must be allowed to determine their own needs and solutions in relation to fertility control, health and development within their own contexts. (Canadian Women's Committee on Reproduction, Population and Development, 1994: 21)

This division within a societal movement became even more marked with the intrusion of two other conflicts. The first of these overlapped with the question of state control but redirected attention from reproductive issues back to the debate about migration. As a corollary of the women's movement's critique of a state-backed apparatus of population control, feminists had challenged sovereignty-based border controls. This interconnection again touched a sensitive nerve. As noted in our chapter on sovereignty, any inside–outside debate about where obligations lay was rife with controversy. From the perspective of statecraft, this debate centred on questions of management; that is to say, the best ways by which Canadian citizens could be protected from shocks, whether "irregular" movements of people or the more systemic and sustained pressures that exacerbated the "push" effect on migration. From the perspective of society-craft, the debate raised questions of a more fundamental ethical or moral nature: the need to do away with the "artificial" distinction between citizens and non-citizens.

This debate exposed raw nerves not just between state and society but among societal groups. Extending the argument that population controls should be applied not just in the external arena but "at home", some societal groups moved to have the concept of environmental "carrying capacity" applied to the number of people allowed into Canada. From a position inside the Canadian National Advisory Council, the Conservation Council of Ontario (CCO) pushed hard to have this framework accepted by the Inter-ministerial Committee. When that tactic failed to deliver results, the CCO went over the head of the committee by making an appeal to the Canadian public that there was an urgent need to incorporate numbers and controls into the Canadian agenda for Cairo (see, for example, Mohamed Urdoh, "People, Ecology Divide Representatives to Population Meeting", *Now*, 18–24 August 1994).

This tactic succeeded only in alienating almost all the other groups with a stake in the Cairo outcome, albeit for extremely diverse reasons. Some environmental groups took offence at the CCO's linkage of a stabilised global population to a restrictive immigration and refugee policy. Women's groups took offence at the emphasis on controls, because of their view that population targets are by definition coercive. Human rights and refugee groups found the whole tone of the CCO agenda offensive and were ready to say so outside the confines of the Canadian National Advisory Council. Nancy Worsfold, the executive director of the Canadian Council for Refugees, most explicitly accused the CCO of being shallow and insular in their attitude: "Playing with mere numbers does not shed any light on the issue at stake. We have an obligation to humanity" (quoted in Mohamed Urdoh, "People, Ecology Divide Representatives to Population Meeting", *Now*, 18–24 August 1994).[57]

Another element of this extended societal divide showcased a very different sort of polarisation. Up to Cairo a sense of solidarity had prevailed in women's politics. Although the women's movement was far from monolithic, differences between state and societal actors and between insiders and outsiders were not obstacles to achievement. "Femocrats" were influential within the state bureaucracy as well as among their network of connections with a wide variety of NGO representatives and members of civil society. They held joint activities, such as Canada's hosting of a UN roundtable on women's perspectives on family planning, reproductive health, and reproductive rights, as part of the preparatory process for Cairo (International Women's Health Coalition, 1994). As a proportion of insiders, cutting across the state–societal divide, women' participation increased appreciably in Cairo (17 women and 16 men) from the 1984 Mexico City conference (5 women and 11 men). As demonstrated by the efforts of NAC and its allies on the Canadian Women's Report, horizontal alliances could be built not only between women's groups and social justice organisations but with women in disability rights groups, visible minority women's organisations, women's health and family planning centres, and academics.

The most open challenge to this unity came in a more unanticipated fashion, on the question of who represented the mainstream in women's politics. Although shape-shifting where, whom, and how this mainstream was defined and encompassed, both the "femocrats" and NAC took it for granted that they represented the majority. Female state delegates assumed a coincidence of interest and identity, as shown by Ruth Archibald's statement at the end of the Cairo conference that: "Women should be quite happy with the programme of action" (quoted in Bob Hepburn, "U.N. summit approves plan to curb population", *Toronto Star*, 14 September 1994). NAC was equally confident that it voiced the views of "Canadian Women". The populist, conservative backlash of "REAL Women" against this sense of solidarity came, therefore, as an unexpected and uncomfortable intrusion.

Unlike the women's movement, however, REAL Women did not enjoy any institutional entry to the conference at either the national or the international level, and had relatively little influence (REAL Women, 1994a, 1994b: 7–9). Although granted accreditation for Cairo, after having missed the Prep Coms, its official function was strictly limited to a single 90-minute special session. Nor could its base of support or representation match at all the large presence of the women's movement. The Women's Caucus, for example, the largest of its type, had some 400–500 participants daily. Each morning, after an overview of the negotiations in the conference's main committee, priorities and tactics were discussed. In recognition of their collective role, the ICPD secretary-general, Dr.

Sadik, visited the Women's Caucus to show her appreciation of their work. The caucus responded by giving her "a tumultuous welcome, with five standing ovations, sustained applause, foot-stamping and whistling" (International Institute for International Development, *Earth Negotiations Bulletin*, 06/18, 6 April 1994).

Yet neither should the impact of REAL Women be entirely written off as irrelevant. Turning the agenda-setting process on its head, REAL Women tried to make its appeal on the same basis as movements in the counter-consensus had done in the past – through attention-grabbing media stunts. Although limited in terms of its vertical alliance building, REAL Women could frame their arguments horizontally – not only in negative terms (as an alternative to "radical feminism") but in more positive terms, by portraying themselves as the authentic voice of the traditionalist and religious orientation, with a focus on family values. Its isolation from the women's caucus was compensated for to some extent by its linkages to the religious caucus ("REAL women assail 'feminist imperialism'", *Globe and Mail*, 10 September 1994; see also REAL Women, 1994c: 1–15).

Inter- and intra-cultural clashes

The multi-layered patterns traced out in this chapter belie the stark "us and them" scenario favoured by Huntington. Conflictual patterns along cultural lines did mark a good deal of the ICPD process, but we neglect the subtleties of interaction if we use the *Clash of Civilizations* framework exclusively to analyse how and why tensions played out at Cairo; one could fail to appreciate the more complex patterns of divergence and convergence on both the negotiating arena and outcomes.

What makes the ICPD such a compelling test is its potential for tensions to manifest themselves along the lines Huntington suggests. Indeed, unlike the conferences at Bucharest and Mexico City, signs of a clash of social values did emerge in the Cairo process along the fault line between the Western secular and the Islamic religious cultures. This was true with respect to issues pertaining to sexual rights and respect for religious values. These differences became personalised, most notably, in the juxtaposition between Prime Minister Brundtland of Norway and Prime Minister Bhutto of Pakistan.

Instead of Cairo entrenching these differences even further, as might have been expected, however, the meeting reinforced the primacy of communication, diplomatic engagement, and compromise within the text (United Nations, 1995). After a week of strenuous negotiations, none of the Islamic states participating at the conference rejected the final document. Some agreement was reached one chapter at a time, by modifications in language such as the subsuming of the phrase sexual health (a term not well translated into Arabic) under the definition of reproductive health. In terms of overarching principles, acceptance was facilitated by the inclusion of a chapter in the final document that acknowledged the need for balance between international human rights and religious, ethical, and cultural values. Considerations of this type gave states flexibility in their national implementation of the document.

The most formidable "civilisational" clash at Cairo was not an intercultural struggle between the West and elements of the rest but an intracultural secular/individualistic–traditional/religious divide within the West. Currents of this struggle dominated the public face of the conference, both at the state level (because of the Holy See's status as a sovereign entity) and in societal terms (with both the Vatican and transnational NGOs claiming to represent normative and universal values). The core of this dissension was the abortion issue. Whereas Pakistan and other Islamic countries worked hard to reach accommodation, the Vatican subordinated diplomatic culture to its deeply held values. If a holy alliance ever developed between Islamic countries and the Vatican, as was pending prior to the conference, it broke down when the Vatican refused to join the consensus reached in the working group on paragraph 8.25, which recognised abortion as a dimension of primary health care.

If there was divergence, however, there were also important elements of convergence across this divide. The intractable disagreement on abortion should not obscure the other areas at Cairo where agreement opened up. As the international population stabilisation regime changed shape, with a marked de-emphasis on what were deemed to be coercive practices, the Vatican moved away from its total opposition to the Bucharest and Mexico City documents to at least a partial consent on the Cairo text. Moreover, as witnessed in the Vatican's relationship with Canada, disagreement on the abortion issue did not spill over into other areas. In a compartmentalised and self-contained fashion, allowing the search for balance to prevail, coalitions were able to be developed on issues such as family reunification.

Generally speaking, therefore, the practices of diplomatic culture were maintained between individual states. Contrary to Huntington's assessment, state delegations were able to act as well as speak across cultural lines. Trade-offs were possible on individual issues in the West/non-West context, even among countries that could be assumed to be the most dyadic. One illustration of this power to accommodate came in the interaction between Norway and Pakistan. Another, behind the scenes, came between the United States and Iran, whereby Iran supported the United

States on abortion and the United States supported Iran on issues relating to the "corruption of youth".

Signs of the same impulse appeared as well in the intra-West context. Although Biegman and other participants portrayed the Vatican's behaviour as undiplomatic, the ultimate decision of the Vatican not to dissociate itself entirely from the conference's work was a major step. Getting what it wanted on some important principles played a part here, but so did a fear of potential isolation if it did not move with the consensus on some items. The Vatican made one concession in agreeing to include "individuals" in the term "individuals and couples". Another came with its declaration that it had no fundamental disagreement with the concept of reproductive health.

The lessons from Cairo about the evolution of society-craft were less clear. The Canadian case shows just how far society-craft penetrated the ICPD proceedings. Not only was the women's movement instrumental, through a combination of resources, access, knowledge, and legitimacy, in getting women's empowerment embedded fully into the agenda of the conference (including Chapter IV explicitly on this theme), but it was a voice and a player in influencing that agenda. While determined to maintain its autonomy, the women's movement developed appropriate strategies and structures to building dialogue and interaction.

The salient characteristic of the type of diplomacy brought out by the Cairo conference was its volatile, multi-dimensional nature. NGOs worked with governments with different degrees of intensity and closeness. They also stood apart, criticising, cajoling, and embarrassing. The precise nature of their status remained unsettled, their input contingent. Claims of representation were challenged by the shape-shifting policy milieu and political environment. Delays were precipitated by societal infighting (as in the formulation of Canada's National Report on Population, which was released only a few days before Cairo). The erosion of boundaries and the reconfiguration of the landscape in which societal actors had to work nevertheless provided new opportunities in terms of strategies and outcomes. Success at the Cairo conference, however, did not become embedded in the overall process of UN world conferences. When the site or the moment of those conferences changed, diplomatic gains and long-held positions could be contested and clawed back. The instruments and rules of the game continued to be shaped by the interests of statecraft, and change within came only slowly and painstakingly.

8
Tests of difference: women's ownership of the Beijing conference

Can diplomacy be conducive to a fundamental alteration in the rules of the game for international affairs? Can it act as a conduit for doing things differently in forums such as the UN world conferences? A study of the role of women and women's rights can shed light on this test. For if claims that diplomacy can facilitate such change have any validity, greater credit must be given to women's participation in the process of these conferences and to their insistence on extending the boundaries of a women-centred agenda.

The view that the UN world conferences did in fact constitute a break from accepted practices in regard to women has much to support it. In terms of the institutional dynamics, the Vienna Human Rights Conference, the Cairo Population Conference, and, in its fullest expression, the Beijing Conference on Women (or more precisely the Fourth World Conference on Women) showcased the enhanced centrality of women in multiple sites – not only as politically active outsiders but as process-savvy insiders. Indeed, many features of this "actorness" that had been assumed to be a stretch for the international system in earlier conferences became the standard mode of operation at Beijing. The question "Diplomacy for whom?" took on new meaning. Women's rights as human rights, reproductive rights, and the connection between gender and security – issues that could be discounted or deflected in other conferences – could no longer be kept out of diplomatic discourse and negotiations. The traditional separation between public and private space became completely eroded in both procedural and policy dimensions.

One cannot go as far as to suggest, however, that any consensus on women and women's issues arose as part of the post–Cold War order. On a global scale, the advancement of new principles and operational contours was strongly resisted by those who saw them more as problematic departures from the past than as bold and needed improvements. Under such delicate conditions, the diplomatic processes were protracted and heated. Disagreements could sometimes be smoothed over, but, both at Cairo and at Beijing, crosscutting disparities persisted.

At the national level, this test of diplomacy is further complicated by the political interplay between state officials and societal forces. The exercise of society-craft – in this area perhaps more than any other – demonstrates how far women's groups had moved away from the authoritative ambit of traditional forms of statecraft. The mobilisation by women's groups at Vienna, Cairo, and Beijing was an unprecedented measure of the extent to which transnationalism had become implanted in global politics. Still, it must be underscored that this form of transnationalism does not mean de-territorialism. While the UN world conferences exposed the limitations of the state, they did not constitute a denial of its role.

What stands out at the societal level, as we have discussed, is the degree of diversity embedded within the women's movement, as it was not a monolithic entity but essentially a loose cluster of individuals and groups. Their differences rested on divergent assumptions about sovereignty, the legitimacy of the state, the merits of public protest and consciousness-raising over mainstream policy making, and priorities for agenda-issues at the conferences. Segments of the women's movement also had entirely different responses to the question "Who is with us?" both inside and outside politics (Doty, 1996: 126).

In a style similar to that developed by state officials, the women's movement placed great emphasis on developing trust and building coalitions. However, the movement was characterised by alternative loyalties and hybridisation of identity (for a fuller discussion, see Steans, 1998: 170). Wherever they sat in the structure of power, distinct individuals and segments of the movement could multi-task, take on varied roles, and use "the multiple terrains and spaces producing and produced by politics" (Dean, 1997: 2). Activists had many faces: insiders and outsiders, élite-oriented and populist, compromise-oriented and confrontational, localists and universalists, collaborators with "femocrat" state officials and outspoken critics of government policies, advocates of special interests and campaigners for comprehensive change in global governance, representatives of distinct and compartmentalised social forces (whether based on race, region, or sexual orientation) and authentic voices of the larger women's movement – and they could be both tolerant and intolerant of these internal differences. This constellation of contrasts engendered considerable awkwardness and ad-hocism. However, it also contained many of the ingredients for success.

How different was the Beijing conference?

As in all the UN-sponsored conferences under review, the concept of "difference" may be interpreted primarily in terms of their subject matter: did they make a difference in terms of their perceived impact on the global agenda? Beyond this instrumental aspect, any study of diplomacy and difference in the case of the Beijing conference needs to encompass two other unique questions. The first of these is: "Did the conference embrace a sense of ownership by women?". Or, put another way, "Did the diplomatic character of the conference have a distinctive quality because it was devoted to women's rights and empowerment?". The vast majority of participants at the official conference as well as the parallel forum were women, but the extent to which it was in any sense a conference of women's own making remains in question.

The Beijing Conference on Women cannot be isolated from the conferences that preceded it; indeed, its celebratory air derived largely from the opportunities accrued from earlier occasions. Whereas women's conferences had previously been concerned mainly with the extension of women's rights or the theme of women and development, the Beijing conference focused on human rights as applied to women (Bunch and Fried, 1996: 200). As such, there was a firm linkage and sense of spillover between the Vienna Human Rights Conference and Beijing '95. Similarly, the Beijing conference built on the objectives derived from the Cairo conference with respect to health and reproductive rights, and the education and overall equality of the girl child.

Still, despite this progression, the Beijing conference remained enclosed (if not trapped) by the UN system, the society of states, and the highly gendered structures endemic in the institution and its diplomatic structures. Instead of reaching a uniform view, therefore, participants differed over the significance of the event. Optimists, glad of the attention given to the comprehensive and interconnected nature of the Beijing platform, successfully confirmed that all issues related to global governance were women's issues. The legitimacy of women's rights as part of the overall human rights framework was validated. Pessimists, on the other hand, stressed the incomplete and exclusionary aspects of the Beijing process; they defined the conference by what was left out. This contrast in understanding was particularly evident in women's economic concerns as they related to globalisation and structural adjustment. As Sunera Thobani, the then president of the National Action Committee on the Status of Women (NAC) in Canada declared: "The Beijing Platform for Action [PFA] broke no new ground. The PFA is seriously flawed in its approach to women's economic rights. There is no recognition that the existing global economic system is increasing women's inequalities" (Thobani, 1995; see also Bakker, 1994a,b).

The second dimension of difference at Beijing emerged from within the women's movement itself. At the core of the mobilisation process building up from Copenhagen to Nairobi to Beijing was an image of a global sisterhood whereby the conference "processes and mechanisms" helped galvanise "women's grassroots activism into a reasonably coherent, truly international movement" (Capeling-Alakija, 1996: 24). As indicated by the internal tensions at this site of interaction, however, this perception of solidarity was never completely accurate. Several fractures were visible through the overlay of unity. To some these internal differences were based on ideological or geographic polarisations akin to the dynamics and context of other social movements. But beyond these generic factors were other expressions of difference quite distinctive to the women's movement. An alternative perspective favoured the multiplicity and contradictions found within a fragmented and incomplete identity politics based on a "partial understanding of the world" (Steans, 1998: 173) rather than encouraging a goal of universality. Through this lens, there could be no single authentic woman's experience – rather a diffuse range of experiences that had to be differentiated, validated, and struggled with.

Differentiating the women's movement

V. Spike Peterson and Anne Sisson Runyan acknowledge that it is "sometimes difficult to separate the women's movement from other political movements agitating for social, political, and economic transformation" (Peterson and Runyan, 1993: 22; see also Dorsey, 1997). This conflation is the subject of major internal debates about objectives and strategies. An analogous controversy has raged over the extent to which these forces should act as critical and transformative movements or responsible and problem-oriented NGOs. The first approach maintains an outsider status and carries on what can be termed counter-consensus activity. Its operational onus is on developing transnational coalitions both to enhance solidarity in terms of society-craft and to maximise pressure for extending the boundaries of agenda setting with respect to statecraft. The second approach focuses on winning access to policy negotiations by lobbying and providing a complementary mode of technical and entrepreneurial leadership.

While locating the women's movement within this wider framework offsets a tendency towards excessive essentialism, the unique style and outlook of the women's movement warrant closer study. For a start, the inside/outsider divide is blurred and complicated in a number of ways. Besides its oppositional aspect, the outsider approach contains a component explicitly devoted to self-development, self-realisation, and self-discovery. Women's individual experiences are "valourised" as part of the consciousness-raising project of cultural feminism. Not only does the political become the personal but this dynamic is proffered as the key to emancipation (Goetz, 1991).

Although elements of the second approach endorse a constructive, problem-solving orientation through established ties to both the UN system and to national policy-making forums, the women's movement avoided many of the tendencies associated with the shift to insider-directed activity. The sheer numbers of women involved in the official conference as well as the NGO forum provided ample testimony to the fact that it was a mass – not an élite – movement. Numbers of participants in official conferences and parallel forums, as well as NGO participants, had risen steadily between the 1975 conference and the 1995 Beijing conference (Riddell-Dixon, 2001: 18).[58]

What is more, these dimensions of internal difference did not play out in strictly demarcated manners. Unlike the environmentalists at UNCED most notably, components of the women's movement appeared far more reluctant to make an either/or choice between positions as insiders or as outsiders. Particularly at the individual level, they searched for hybrid roles. Bella Abzug's work through the Women's Environment and Development Organization (WEDO) is an interesting case in point. Much of the organisational activity of WEDO was directed towards enhancing women's access to decision making by providing technical and entrepreneurial leadership. WEDO paid careful attention to procedural matters, concentrating its lobbying efforts on draft resolutions and the development of the text through all the preparatory stages (Alter Chen, 1995). Its coalition building was multi-faceted: at one level, WEDO presented itself as a channel between the official conference and the parallel forum; at another, it was instrumental in creating a women's caucus within the women's movement, as well as the so-called caucus of caucuses, for coordination across the spectrum of social movements (or NGOs).

Notwithstanding their determination to work from within the system, Abzug and WEDO maintained a populist outside-oriented quality. The organisational fabric of WEDO was kept loose; lobbying at the official conference coexisted with strong participation in the workshops and demonstrations at the parallel forum. As shown by its declaratory statements as well as its operational practices (Abzug and UN Department of Public Information, 1995; Clark, Friedman and Hochstetler, 1998; WEDO, 1996), WEDO balanced a concern with the desire to insert women "into a modified male world of politics" with some sense of the need for "separation and renegotiation" (Arneil, 1999: 153). From at least the time of the Rio conference, it demanded entrée on the basis of differentiation as well as equality. As Abzug exclaimed: Rio was "deciding the fate of the earth without input from 50 per cent of the world; and not only 50 per cent of the world, but the earth's primary caretakers" (Abzug quoted in Christina Nifong, "Women link up from Austria to Zambia", *Christian Science Monitor*, 27 April 1995; for Maurice Strong's complementary view of Abzug, see Strong, 2001: 223).

A similar pattern runs through other divisions within the practice of both statecraft and society-craft. Tensions existed in the women's movement between those who saw statecraft as a formidable problem to be surmounted and those who were willing to harness themselves at least tactically to the state apparatus in their search for solutions. Indeed, it may be that the very form of particularistic discourse and the set of interpretations that animated the women's movement exacerbated these tensions. For one thing, succeeding waves of the movement (its chronological/ideological dimension) played a role. Arguments about the status and role of the state – and the level of autonomy of societal forces – were interconnected with the ongoing debate over the most appropriate framework for analysing and positioning the movement.

Transformative elements of the movement, especially those that can be clustered together as radical or socialist feminists, were often quick to denounce other elements as being the residue of the earlier (first or liberal) wave. A striking illustration of this phenomenon surfaced in the run-up to Beijing in Canada, when the president of NAC criticised the presence of a representative from another group (the National Council of Canada) on the Canadian delegation on this basis: "They are from the first wave of feminism in Canada. Once in a while they do surface and do something, but they are not part of the mainstream women's movement right now" (Thobani quoted in Paul Watson, "Ottawa stacking forum, feminists charge", *Toronto Star*, 6 September 1995).

For another thing, these tensions all cut into the rich set of questions surrounding the public/private divide. The proponents of a concerted lobbying approach justified it because it allowed the women's movement to claim more of the public space traditionally denied it. Paralleling the contours of their struggle in the domestic domain, women needed to move from the margins to the nerve centres of global political decision-making process so that the boundaries of participation and delivery could be extended. Conversely, the advocates of the self-development approach were more concerned with finding and organising safe public spaces. Rather than seeking effectiveness in gaining specific policy outcomes this arm of the women's movement sought primarily to share and assess experiences, express emotions and creativity, and forge common bonds (see, for example, Young, 1990). The relationship of the women's movement to the state was characterised, however, by finer degrees of paradox, fluidity, and contradiction (Pettman, 1996: 22). As will be seen more fully below in the specifics of the Canadian case, NAC sought an autonomous stance beyond the control and dictates of the state apparatus, but at the same time it resented other organisations being given a similarly privileged position with respect to the same state structure.

On the public/private divide, the borders between lobbying and self-development were often quite porous. Networking was a common feature of both approaches, as it had the advantage of adding "muscle" to the bid for access. In the words of one activist: "It's what the old boys have done for so long" (Jill Meric, communications director, Women's Center for Research, quoted in Christina Nifong, "Women link up from Austria to Zambia", *Christian Science Monitor*, 27 April 1995). When a strict division between public and private spaces was maintained, it could have a distorting effect on policy debates. As made clear on the issue of violence against women, the need was to recognise that this problem stretched across the public–private intersect and that the public and private are intimately connected. If private activities are sanctioned through the public domain at either the state or the societal level, they can be structurally related to the problem of violence. Equally, pressure on the public side can be used to implement reforms, based on the premise that the state is a potential source of solutions to this problem.

Geographical differentiation reinforced the disparity between fragmentation and integration within the women's movement. Because of the complexity involved in analysing where women came from and why their location mattered, a good case could be made that physical placement was the severest challenge to universality. This test encompassed the entire continuum of demographic differences along the urban–rural divide as well many of the more overtly political fractures of a geopolitical nature. The basic question here was: "Had the women's movement had become dominated by Western/Northern values and social forces?". Charges of this nature had surfaced in the context of the United States–third world divide as far back as the non-governmental tribune at the 1975 women's conference. What was championed as the authentic guide for action by American feminists such as Gloria Steinem was rejected as coercion by voices from the South (Stephenson, 1995; Stienstra, 1994; Whitaker, 1975).

Far from easing with the changes at the end of the Cold War, these tensions simply took on different shapes. With the new attention to civilisational concerns, charges of cultural interference or even cultural imperialism were intensified and embellished. The consensus among Western feminist theorists and practitioners has been that one of the greatest strengths of the women's movement is the extent of its transnationalism and solidarity across borders (Ashworth, 1995). Some within the movement portray the melting of borders towards a sovereignty- and territorial-free existence as a fundamental hallmark of a liberated existence. To others this concept seemed more like a pragmatic tool for mobilisation. As one prominent Canadian activist articulated it:

Raising women's issues in an international sphere is still a very, very new thing.... Most of us used to work at domestic issues. But we don't think that way any more. Issues just don't stay within borders of nation states any more. We have to work with international women around the world. Events in the South affect events in the North. It's quite different, and all domestic women's organizations in Canada feel the same. (Day, quoted in Rod Mickelburgh, "Women seek deeds, not words", *Globe and Mail*, 4 September 1995)

From the perspective of the South, the desirability of such universalism has been challenged and the entire concept of a "global sisterhood" is deemed problematic (Mohanty, 1991; Steans, 1998: 164). Factors of place and time command more recognition than the illusion of universality. From their more differentiated stance, women from the South act in a less passive and dependent way. In some cases, the expression of their concerns has meant a degree of identification with conservative practices (including collective societal values rather than individualism and the strengthening of the traditional family). In other cases, such as the issue of violence against women, however, their differentiation could entail a search for more holistic approaches. As Charlotte Bunch and her colleagues commented on these different linkages: "Women from the South tended to understand the economy as connected to other problems like violence, while northern women more often approached these as separate issues" (Bunch, Dutt and Fried, 1996: 9).

Proponents of another perspective raise the question of "matronising" behaviour on the part of Western/Northern women (Spivak, quoted in Steans, 1998: 164). Far from considering the UN-sponsored women's conferences as sites for making a difference, in their view these forums were irrelevant. Rather than treating learning as a two-way process, they saw it as a form of socialisation in which Southern (or rural) women take on the Western/Northern model for doing things. Gayatri Spivak stated this position most forcefully: "Serious activists" should stay away from these events "because the real work is to be done elsewhere" (Spivak, 1996: 2–3).

Despite the impact of these geographical tensions, however, such differences were not intractable; they could be muted or entirely transcended. Although the question of who legitimately spoke and acted for the North and the South remained hotly debated, strategic alliances could still be forged on a crosscutting basis. Both the caucus structure and the onus on networking helped in this process. So too did the presence of members of the diaspora among the ranks of "northern" NGO representatives and state delegations.

Making a difference

The conditions were ripe for the women's movement to take ownership of the Beijing conference. The main geopolitical considerations that had distracted attention at the earlier women's conferences were no longer on the scene. The US–USSR rivalry had ended and the apartheid system in South Africa had come to its demise. In this very different atmosphere the spotlight could be turned to issues of concern to women on their own merits and not as a sub-set of a larger debate. Although the Arab–Israeli conflict persisted in its intensity, the Oslo Accord allowed some (albeit brief) openings in that context as well. As one Israeli participant, a member of the City Council of Jerusalem commented: "I was really impressed that the consultations and dealings were done peacefully and calmly and in an understanding manner. For the first time in the history of women's conferences, when the representatives from Israel spoke, sisters from my neighbouring countries did not walk out" (quoted in Seth Faison, "Departing China, Women hold hope but see obstacles", *New York Times*, 16 September 1995).

The women's movement sought ownership of agendas that had been out of their hands in the past, particularly in the security domain. During the Cold War years, women's voices and interests had been absent from the ideology and institutional development of the national security apparatus. The enormous structural reconfiguration associated with the shock of the new allowed a less hierarchical and more diverse security discourse to emerge. Concepts and constructions previously taken for granted were no longer accepted as orthodoxy, in a process of reframing that had the effect of "rendering women's insecurities visible" (Peterson, 1992: 32). Room opened up for security to be framed as if women's experiences really mattered. As witnessed most dramatically on the theme of violence in the Beijing Platform of Action, with the softening of rigid distinctions between the national and the personal, responsibility for the prevention of violence was no longer placed solely at the level of the individual. Recognition of public accountability was elicited from the state.

The question of ownership extended also to the issue of whose conference it was. In terms of representation, a strong case can be made that the site belonged to women to an extent well beyond the practices and positioning of the past. This sense of ownership was greatly due, of course, to the mass participation of women in the Beijing process. This gathering was impressive both in its numbers and in the extraordinary scope of activities spanning the conference and forum, as well as many preparatory events. Approximately 1,500 women attended the regional Prep Coms held in Argentina and Vienna, and 5,000 turned out for the meeting in Dakar, Senegal (Christina Nifong, "Women link up from Austria to Zambia", *Christian Science Monitor*, 27 April 1995).

Women dominated the élite, high-profile positions attached to the conference. Within the UN system as well, women occupied almost all the administrative functions having to do with the Beijing process. The secretariat of the Beijing conference, operating out of the UN Division for the Advancement for Women in New York, was led by Gertrude Mongella (Tanzania), who also served as secretary-general of the conference. The preparatory committees stayed in the hands of the UN Commission on the Status of Women (CSW). Irene Santiago took the role of executive director of the NGO Forum on Women '95, and Supatra Masdit acted as convenor. Through the official conference, all the major working groups or contact groups were chaired by women. Patricia Licuanan (the Philippines), chair of the CSW, served as the chair of Working Group I, and Working Group II was chaired by Irene Freudenschuss-Reichl (Austria). Olga Pellicer (Mexico) became the chair of the Contact Group for Working Group II, and Mervat Tallaway (Egypt) chaired the contact group on the health section. The three vice-chairs were Freudenschuss-Reichl, Zelmira Regazolli (Argentina) and Natallya Drozd (Belarus). Selma Ashipala (Namibia) acted as the rapporteur. The only exception was the role accorded to Ismat Kitani as Secretary-General Boutros Boutros-Ghali's trouble-shooter and representative at the conference.

Although women did not have a complete monopoly on the state delegations, they did occupy the vast majority of these roles both as members and leaders. Only 40 of the 189 delegations were headed by men. The two best-known women leaders who had attended the Cairo conference – Benazir Bhutto and Gro Harlem Brundtland – also headed their countries' delegations at Beijing. The US delegation was led officially by Madeleine Albright, with Hillary Rodham Clinton as the honorary head. Even the Vatican/Holy See broke with precedent and selected a woman (Mary Ann Glendon) as leader of its delegation to the Beijing conference as well as including 14 women in a 22-person delegation.

Yet, despite this evidence of ownership, several factors constrained women's ability to embrace the official conference (as opposed to the NGO forum) as their own. Although Beijing was far more than a conference to which women were added and stirred, their sense of ownership was never complete. The bottom line was that this system was neither created by women nor designed for their needs. This reality was the crux of why many women were hesitant (or completely unwilling) to try to work within this system. Many insiders themselves remained sceptical about how far they could nudge or cajole the system in order to promote change. As a well-known Canadian UN official expressed this concern about structural limitations: "We're at the table [but] it's not even our own table. Like many women working in international agencies, I'm deeply cognizant of the contradictions involved in this work. I am acutely aware of the fact that we are trying to create change for women with instruments and institutions designed by and for men" (Capeling-Alakija, 1996: 23).

Further, when faced with any serious challenge, the state system fought back, and could use harsh measures when they were used by determined entities to defend their prerogatives and perceived territorial well-being. The relationship of China to the NGO forum, for example, reveals the extent to which a host country, concerned about the presence of an unpredictable form of society-craft on its soil, would go to control (and thereby silence) the voices. Although desirous of the international status that accompanied the role of conference host, Chinese authorities wanted to manage contact between its own population and the conference participants as well as to weed out any "troublemakers". For the most part it was not the "mainstream" women's movement but human rights workers (including Tibetan, Taiwanese, and lesbian activists) that the Chinese authorities targeted in this fashion (for one of these scenarios, see Jane Macartney, "Half-naked activists China's worst nightmare", *Globe and Mail*, 24 August 1995). Nonetheless, this campaign of containment imposed severe inconveniences on all the societal participants.

The physical space allotted to the participants was carefully manipulated. At the level of logistics, irritants arose from the choice of site and the facilities of the NGO forum. Instead of having this parallel event close to the official conference, as had become the norm, the Chinese authorities unilaterally moved the site 40 miles outside of Beijing to the tourist town of Huairou. Not only did this distance (at least an hour's trip) make interaction between the forum and the conference difficult but it made the forum participants more dependent on links through phones and faxes, closed-circuit television, and electronic mail. Participants' movements were closely monitored throughout the proceedings. Visas, hotel confirmations, and accreditations were often issued at the last moment and only after intense scrutiny and weeding-out. Demonstrations, public protests, and processions were allowed only within the tightly controlled and compact complex. Journalists and selected NGO representatives were put under surveillance, and access to news conference facilities and translation services was curtailed on occasion because of sensitive material.

The power of the state system also was manifested in a smoother and more sophisticated – but no less resistant – diplomatic format for negotiation. As at the Cairo conference, one of the greatest sources of leverage enjoyed by states most resistant to the influence of the women's movement was the use of brackets to delay and to muffle. Through the third and fourth preparatory sessions held at UN headquarters in March and April 1995, a very high proportion of the draft text was bracketed. While some of this bracketing could be considered of the "soft" variety (illustrating a degree of flexibility or a lack of time for discussion), the extent of the "hard" bracketing pointed to the depth of fundamental differences on issues of concern to women. As one prominent Canadian activist said on the eve of the conference: "The question is: are we going to be able to move forwards or are we going to have to fight just to maintain what governments agreed to less than a year ago?" (Day quoted in Rod Mickelburgh, "China steps up pressure on women's conference", *Globe and Mail*, 30 August 1995). Hopes of a breakthrough to allow a more holistic mode of analysis and agenda delivery changed during the run-up to Beijing into a defensive mindset determined to hang onto the gains at Vienna and Cairo on equality, reproductive rights, and other issues.

Another tactic relied upon at the intergovernmental level was to resort to procedures that were closed off to forms of society-craft. These exclusionary devices included the extensive use of "informal informals" to cut down on the level of transparency. So formidable had these practices become by the time of the Prep Coms that the organisers of the conference openly voiced concerns about the risk of a credibility gap between what was expected in terms of state–societal interaction and what was actually taking place. As Secretary-General Mongella pictured it, the scene had become one in which "the delegates, as hosts, invited the NGOs into their sitting room, but then disappeared into the kitchen to cook, keeping their guests waiting and hungry" (Summary of the Fourth World Conference on Women, 4–15 September 1995 in International Institute for International Development, *Earth Negotiations Bulletin* 14/21, 18 September 1995).

Critical attention also was focused on the UN system itself for being complicit in maintaining the status quo. If on the one hand the UN was acknowledged by the women's movement as a channel for transforming the international agenda, it was on the other hand perceived as too easily accommodating the accepted practices imposed by states. The UN's weak response to China's displacement of the forum to Huairou did much to fuel this negative attitude. Instead of standing up to the Chinese authorities and insisting on the need to have the forum close to the official conference, the responsible UN officials immediately put their energy into making the alternative Huairou site work. To many within the women's movement this stance constituted an abdication of responsibility whereby the organisers put their own "diplomatic careers" ahead of their "grassroots constituency". As one prominent American feminist contended in a scathing attack on this theme: "It's disingenuous to pretend, as did forum executive director Irene Santiago, forum convenor Khunying Supatra Masdit, and Gertrude Mongella, secretary-general of the UN Conference, that the Chinese government was 'trying to do its best'" (Morgan, 1996: 47).[59]

Further accentuating these tensions was the gendered analysis of the women's movement's appropriate response to this state-imposed predicament. To some women, these types of constraint at least highlighted their differences from men in a positive light as "outsiders" or the "other" (Arneil, 1999: 155). Secretary-General Mongella went as far as to say that the security regulations should remind delegates of the restrictions placed on women around the world: "The discomfort of being trapped is imposed on many women every day of their lives. So I am glad men and women are experiencing it for two weeks" (quoted in Rod Mickelburgh, "Broadbent blasts police at women's conference", *Globe and Mail*, 9 September 1995; see also Ed Broadbent, "Will next month's UN conference set back women's rights?", *Globe and Mail*, 10 August 1995). At the very least, these new obstacles generated a reaffirmation of many of the traits that had been devalued over the years: tolerance and the capacity to persevere against detrimental structural deficiencies and prejudice. To many other activists, conversely, these very arguments ran counter to the struggle for equality and against exclusion. As Robin Morgan bluntly argued: "The plain truth is that men would never have tolerated such treatment. Women did. And that's not necessarily something to be proud of" (Morgan, 1996: 46).

This reference to gender was not unique to this specific situation; the appeal for a gendered analysis sweeps through this entire case study. At the level of discourse and agenda setting, what stands out about the Beijing conference is the explicit debate that emerged about the meaning of gender. Because of the number of delegations that objected to the term being used in the platform, a contact group was set up to report on the question. The subsequent report tried to sidestep the issue by presenting a "non-definition". As with a variety of other controversies, the result in procedural terms was an ongoing struggle of bracketing and unbracketing very much along the lines of the divide found at Cairo. Unable to prevent the term from creeping into the text on an issue-by-issue basis, resisters such as the Holy See resorted to the power of reservation.

At a conceptual level, there is a need to more adequately locate the dynamics of the Beijing conference within the context of the structural conditions established by gender relations. Indeed, for some feminist activists, even quantitative and qualitative advances in terms of women's involvement were interpreted as a charade or "theatre", masking the retention of power in established hands. Taking as their cue the way the conference intersected with the society of states and the UN system, male-dominated institutions were privileged as the locus of control. What stood out, from this perspective, was the continuity of diplomatic practice. Any engagement with negotiations in the intergovernmental domain, rather than being considered a liberating process, would be long and protracted. Many of the women taking on official responsibilities for the conference were treated as a "subaltern" class, hemmed in either by being part of a restrictive diplomatic practice or by their relationships to powerful men. Moreover, when decisions were ultimately due, the focus moved to the way in which male diplomats wielded ultimate decision-making authority (see, for example, Dianne Rinehart, "Agenda being run by men", *Calgary Herald*, 15 September 1995).

This take on the Beijing conference can be backed up with a solid body of evidence. A number of the women in lead positions for the conference were career diplomats with a blend of loyalties to the women's movement, national states, and/or the UN. Secretary-General Mongella, for example, had experience both as a Tanzanian cabinet minister and a diplomat. Masdit, the chair of the Forum, was a Thai politician seen as a potential candidate to become prime minister. Tallaway was a high-ranking Egyptian diplomat, as evidenced by her appointment to serve as her country's ambassador to Japan. Several others had close personal ties to national politicians through family or marriage. Rodham Clinton, as honorary head of the US delegation, drew most attention from this type of connection. But she was far from alone in fitting this image. Mongella's Chef de cabinet, Leticia Shahani, was the sister of then President Ramos of the Philippines, and Nana Rawlings, Ghanaian leader Jerry Rawlings' spouse, led Ghana's delegation.

What this structural analysis misses, however, is the potential for agency at the individual level. Although Rodham Clinton's ability to influence the discourse and agenda was made exceptional by her status and profile, her role illustrated the capacity of key actors to seize the opportunity of Beijing to enhance their own reputations and that of the international women's movement. Rodham Clinton not only condemned violence and coercion against women generally but the Chinese family planning programme more specifically. She went out of her way to express sympathy for the troubles that forum participants had experienced at Huairou and urged women's groups to continue working towards the goals being discussed at the Beijing Conference: "You will be the key players in determining whether this conference goes beyond rhetoric and actually does something to improve the lives of women. What will be important is that you hold governments to the commitments that they make" (quoted in Seth Faison, "Thousands Jostled by Security Officers at Forum in China", *New York Times*, 7 September 1995).

The ability of the diplomatic cohort to make a difference should not be underestimated either, even though their responsibilities for the negotiations were quite routinely applied. Consistent with an essentialist interpretation of women's behaviour, it was claimed that the conditions under which this process took place were made more palatable because of the gender-specific attributes of the individual participants. According to at least one negotiator: "Because the vast majority of delegates are women they are more likely to listen closely to what the other side is saying, and try to accommodate them" (quoted in Rod Mickelburgh, "Consensus filters through the air at Beijing", *Globe and Mail*, 13 September 1995). In addition, the posturing and loss of temper so evident in the Cairo process were absent at Beijing (Boulding, 1988; Sylvester, 1994). Although the format of the two conferences was very similar, with informal groups and evening and weekend sessions to try to come to terms with the bracketed components of the text, the difference was one of tone. No parallels existed between the critical outbursts of Nicolas Biegman at Cairo and the problem-solving approach taken by the chairs of the working groups and contact groups at Beijing.

A deterministic analysis of this sort not only negates the constraints women negotiators had to work under, but it assumes one consistent operating style. Women with authority at the conference did make a difference but they did so in highly diverse ways. Although Secretary-General Mongella drew some criticism because of her idiosyncratic style; for example, her leadership provided a fascinating mix of forthrightness and tolerance on organisational matters. Others, more directly involved in the detailed process of negotiation, practised the classic diplomatic skills associated with diplomacy in building trust among the different parties. For all of their differences, when time was running out they were able to make decisions. Most notably, Licuanan, as the chair of the main committee, decisively concluded that the bracketed references to "sexual orientation" would be deleted from the text because of a lack of consensus.

The influence of the women's movement through the parallel forum cannot be so clearly framed. Symbolically, the presence and attention given to the counter-consensus contributed to surges of empowerment in

Huairou. Unlike the official conference, the parallel forum was punctuated by activities directed at breaking out from participants' sense of physical entrapment. Vigils, silent protests, marches, and petitions were all part of this repertoire. Instrumentally, the main contribution of this parallel activity was to energise and hold up to the light the work of the NGOs working on the details of the text. Pride in being part of the real action permeated the psychology of this side of the movement. As one activist phrased it

I felt discomfort at the official conference because although progress was being made, it was never enough. I was pleased, yet frustrated. Here at the forum was the energy, the action, the future. They were the ones breaking new ground. It was not the diplomats making the news, but the individuals out here, forty-five miles from the conference site, who held the world's attention. (Rife, 1998: 15)

Nor, to take the gendered analysis a step further, should the role of men at Beijing be neglected. By concentrating exclusively on the role of women we risk exposing men to the same fate women have traditionally endured – being relegated to the status of the "generalized other" (Seyla Benhabib, quoted in O'Gorman and Jabri, 1999: 10). A more complete view will include some of the diversity found in the male as well as the female roles. This is not to say that the "man question" cannot be differentiated completely from the caricature ascribed to it (Zalewski and Parpart, 1991). The placement of women in the delegations of the resistant actors did not mean that the "mask" of male authority was lifted. The appointment of Mary Ann Glendon as leader of the Holy See delegation, although greeted with a good deal of fanfare, did not keep the Holy See from registering its reservations on sexual and reproductive rights as well as in other areas. As at the Cairo conference, the most reliable guide to the position of the Holy See came not from the delegation but from the Pope's official spokesperson, Joaquin Navarro-Valls.

Male roles were far from undifferentiated. At the official conference, male negotiators were often credited with making a difference on an individual basis. The impact of this dynamic is underscored by its scope across the like-minded/unlike-minded continuum. Representatives from like-minded countries might be expected to take on the tasks of bridge builders. Given the fierce resistance of their countries to many of the initiatives at the heart of the Beijing agenda, representatives from the unlike countries were assumed to be blockers rather than helpful fixers. At odds with this typecasting, however, particular diplomats stand out for their creative statecraft. The best example of such a creative role was arguably the deal-making function taken on by a senior member of Iran's delegation, in forging compromise wording on the issue of sexual rights of children, parental rights, and the role of the family. As one Canadian NGO activist enthused: "He's a wonderful man, absolutely incredible. He's brought all of the Arab countries along on these issues" (Katherine McDonald, a board member of International Planned Parenthood from Halifax, quoted in Rod Mickelburgh, "Consensus filters through the air at Beijing", *Globe and Mail*, 13 September 1995).

Selective room for a multi-faceted participation by men also existed at the parallel conference, predominantly in the area of human rights. The role of Pierre Sané, the Secretary-General of Amnesty International, as a lightning rod for the linkage of women's rights to the wider spectrum of human rights (and the attention of the Chinese authorities) stands out. One sign of the strength of the linkages between the movements was the presence of Sané as a judge for the Global Tribunal organised (as at Vienna) by the Center for Women's Global Leadership at Rutgers University. Another area where an individual's ability to make a difference was recognised was in the area of micro-credit as the foundation of women's independence. The star actor here was Muhammad Yunus, an economist at the University of Chittagong, for his catalytic role in the establishment of Bangladesh's Grameen Bank (for more information see http://www.ebbf.org/woman.htm).

Finally, we must acknowledge the contested nature and the limitations of gender in greater depth. Gender relations must be viewed in the context of a plurality of identities and the multiplicity of both women's and men's experiences, rather than as a homogeneous international movement. This interpretation is no less transformational in its potential. The subtlety and complexity of differences among women is highlighted, not a collective standpoint (Lennon and Whitford, 1994). In this highly differentiated context, the opportunities for group action must be juxtaposed with images of tension and fracture in which inclusiveness was subordinated to instability and diversity.

Canada making a difference

Questions of difference vis-à-vis the Canadian contribution to the Beijing conference circumscribe two interconnected sets of questions. The first centres on whether Canadian diplomacy took on a different shape not only because of the agenda but also because of the actual conference participants. Or did a women-centred conference simply add women to the established habits of Canadian diplomacy? Alternatively did the conference privilege women as the dominant element in a reformulated mode of state/society-craft? And if so, did this privileging contribute to a universalistic tendency showcasing the solidarity of the women's movement, or did it allow for diversity and multiple identities? (Keeble and Smith, 1999: 14-19).

The second set of questions asks whether Canadian diplomacy made a difference in the process and outcome of the Beijing conference. These questions also focus on the generic attributes of Canadian statecraft and society-craft which provide it with leverage. Was Canada's lack of structural power compensated for by its particular toolkit of diplomatic skill? More pointedly, did these skills provide an excellent fit between style and subject matter? That is to say, did Canada's unique diplomatic toolkit contain attributes of negotiating style that can be associated with a gendered frame of analysis? (Keeble and Smith, 1999: 23-25).

The different faces of the women's movement

At first glance the case for privileging women in Canadian diplomacy at the Beijing conference seems extremely strong. Both the Canadian delegation to the official conference and the unofficial forum were highly women-centric. In terms of individual personnel, Canadian statecraft directly represented at the conference perhaps illustrated a role reversal – with a few men "added" as opposed to the standard token addition of women. The only male on the Canadian delegation who stood out was Ross Hynes from the Department of Foreign Affairs and International Trade (DFAIT), who shared the responsibility for negotiating sections of the Beijing text. Coincidentally, the hierarchical breakdown reflected the ownership of the conference by women. Unlike at the Nairobi conference, Canadian women were not placed under a male head of delegation. Selected to head up the official Canadian delegation at Beijing was Sheila Finestone, the Secretary of State for the Status of Women, supported by Ethel Blondin-Andrew, Secretary of State for Training and Youth.

This predominantly female leadership was reproduced within Canadian society-craft. Canadian NGO representation at Beijing spanned the layers of the women's movement, across the generations and including also an array of voices in terms of regional representation, ability and disability, sexual orientation, race, and ethnicity. The most visible male in Canadian society-craft at Beijing was Ed Broadbent, the former federal leader of the New Democratic Party (Canada's social democrats) and the then president of the Montreal-based International Centre for Human Rights and Democratic Development (ICHRDD). In a similar fashion to Stephen Lewis at the Vienna and Cairo conferences, Broadbent played a gadfly role in attracting media attention to Beijing. But he was a male "exception" to the overwhelming dominance of women in Canadian societal participation.

In bureaucratic terms, the women-centric nature of the Canadian delegation was reinforced by the situation of Status of Women Canada (SWC) as the "lead" agency for Beijing. Of all the bureaucratic entities in Ottawa, SWC enjoyed the greatest sense of ownership on the part of the Canadian women's movement. A number of officials from the SWC had an enormous wealth of experience from earlier UN-sponsored conferences. Louise Bergeron-de Villiers, deputy head of the SWC, stands out here, as does Valerie Raymond, coordinator of Canadian preparations for the World Conference on Women in Beijing. Although the timing might have been better, the integration of the Women's Program from Human Resources Development Canada into the SWC in the midst of the Beijing preparations provided SWC with a greater range of resources and administrative potential.

The appearance of a well-developed network of state-based women officials (or "femocrats") willing and able to coordinate a common approach on Beijing beyond the confines of inter-bureaucratic rivalry replenished the talent pool within SWC. The Nairobi women's conference had given an enormous boost to the professional reputations of several individual administrators. As Elizabeth Riddell-Dixon ably documents in her recent book on the conference, Beijing provided a similar opportunity to Rhonda Ferderber, director of Inter-governmental and Non-governmental Relations, Sheila Regehr of the Beijing Secretariat, and Jackie Claxton, the director of the Women's Program (Riddell-Dixon, 2001: 36–39). Among these "femocrats" was a small but determined cohort of women officials within DFAIT. These individuals included Adèle Dion, the departmental coordinator for International Women's Equality, Ruth Archibald, director of Refugee, Population and Migration, and Kerry Buck, who had earlier experience with the Legal Operations Division. While all had acquired an impressive issue-specific knowledge base, Archibald added an element of seniority (having served as deputy head of delegation at the Cairo conference). The final ingredient came from the participation of the Canadian International Development Agency (CIDA) in the Beijing process. Because of the extensive interaction between its policy priorities and the Beijing agenda, CIDA coordinated its involvement through the establishment of an in-house "1995 Network" (Riddell-Dixon, 2001: 42). It complemented its domestic-oriented networking focus with efforts to integrate southern NGOs into the Beijing process.

This configuration did much to inculcate an image that there was something different about the bureaucratic process. Riddell-Dixon gives an impression of an interdepartmental dynamic based on collegiality and even sisterhood. She details how "positions were developed collaboratively" and the "range of differences" was relatively small (Riddell-Dixon, 2001: 48). A collective push was made across departmental divides to comprehensively bring women and gender inequalities into the centre of governmental practice. As Riddell-Dixon elaborates: "During the process of preparing for the Beijing Conference on Women, cabinet approval was sought, and received, for a formal mandate to promote the equality of women and men and to ensure that gender-based analysis was used in the development of all future Canadian policies" (Riddell-Dixon, 2001: 47).

Notwithstanding the level of inter-connection and success that the interdepartmental committee enjoyed, however, neither its level of autonomy nor its room for manoeuvre was complete. André Ouellet, the then minister of foreign affairs, demonstrated on some key issues that he was quite ready to use his power to manage the process, in particular to rein in the commitment of financial resources to the conference (Riddell-Dixon, 2001: 47). He also applied direct leverage to the process of selecting NGO representation for the Canadian delegation.

Top-down state control was a problem that compounded the disjunction between the solidarity developed by state-based women officials and the fragmentation found at the societal level. In principle, the most visible difference between the experience of the Beijing conference and that of Rio, Vienna, Copenhagen, and Cairo might have been the development of a solid and viable relationship between the so-called femocrats and the mass women's movement. In practice, though, any hopes of a shared identification along these lines were dashed. In particular, the worldview of the state-based women officials was radically at odds with that of the putative umbrella group for the Canadian women's movement, the National Action Committee on the Status of Women (NAC). The barriers of "social position and experience" were too formidable to be overcome (Steans, 1998: 171). Both sides were equally engaged, but their differing types of identity formation and preferred methods of activity caused deep rifts.

NAC claimed recognition as the umbrella organisation of the Canadian women's movement. Recognition of this sort would mean the expectation of some form of special position with respect to the Beijing process, both through the Canadian Beijing Facilitating Committee and the Canadian Preparatory Committee. Indeed, in preparing for a lead role, NAC had broken the conference agenda down into issue-specific areas and assigned responsibility to individual representatives on that basis (Riddell-Dixon, 2001: 57). The problem was that the relationship between the Liberal government and NAC was not conducive to such an enhanced status. While NAC sought validation, it did so on its own terms. Although wanting the benefits of an insider, it was far from comfortable with the potential implications (especially the stigma of being co-opted) of taking up this position.

The government for its part was wary of both the political style and the ideological orientation of NAC. Some coincidence of interest had developed between the Liberals and NAC during the struggle against the Mulroney government and the free trade agenda. Since the 1993 election, however, NAC had become one of the Chrétien government's most open and severest critics. They missed few opportunities to embarrass the Liberals for their austerity measures. At the macro-level, NAC's campaign was directed towards reform of Canada's unemployment benefits system. At the micro-level, it targeted the closing of the Canadian Advisory Council on the Status of Women and the loss of CIDA's funding for educational organisations (NAC, 1995).

The Canadian government's goal was to extend the bounds of the liberal international order, based on Robert Cox's notion of "problem-solving" (Cox, 1986). As evidenced by the Plan for Gender Equality introduced by Finestone and SWC immediately prior to the Beijing conference, a necessary component of this approach was some form of demonstration effect. Still, they continued to push externally for the global good based on a concern for women's individual rights. NAC, by way of contrast, consistently adopted a more critical tone framed by an awareness of the "social and political complex as a whole" (Riddell-Dixon, 2001: 208–209) associated with women's collective rights and their systemic concerns related to globalisation, economic liberalisation, and structural adjustment. Whereas the state-based approach was incremental and compartmentalised, NAC's society-craft was transformative.

These lines of division made the Liberal government and NAC extremely wary of each other's motives and methods. But, as shown by the case of the Cairo conference, these divisions in themselves did not rule out the potential for some further (albeit awkward) working arrangement. What put the Liberal government and NAC on a collision course were two additional situational factors. The first of these was the conflictual relationship between NAC and Minister Finestone. A former president of the Fédération des femmes du Québec (and executive member of NAC), Finestone had distanced herself from NAC as the organisation underwent a process of radicalisation and transition (Vickers, Rankin and Appelle, 1993). Vibrations from this purge continued to reverberate through the Canadian women's movement.

The second factor, arguably related to the first, was the fundamental difference between the treatment accorded to NAC at Cairo and at Beijing. Notwithstanding its critical stance, some accommodation had been made to NAC with respect to both status and access to the official Canadian delegation to the ICPD. While in no way enjoying a monopoly position, NAC had been granted certain privileges consistent with its claim that it was Canada's "peak" women's organisation with over 600 member groups. The arrangements for Beijing were very different. Although it had had been given entrée to the Canadian Preparatory Committee (in similar fashion to the Cairo committee) and the Canadian Beijing Facilitating Committee, NAC was excluded from direct representation to the official Canadian delegation. The reaction of Thobani, NAC's leader, was as quick as it was predictable: "[The Liberal government] is trying to shut the women's movement in Canada from playing an effective role in lobbying" (quoted in Paul Watson, "Ottawa stacking forum, feminists charge", *Toronto Star*, 6 September 1995).

There had certainly been a tough calculus behind the selection process. As in past conferences, several of the positions were given as rewards for loyal or constructive service in the past. Individuals in this category included Glenda Simms, the former president of the Canadian Advisory Council on the Status of Women, Lucie Pépin, a pioneer in the birth control movement and a former president of the Canadian Advisory Council on the Status of Women, Madeleine Dion Stout, the director of the Centre for Aboriginal Education at Carleton University, and Gisèle Côté-Harper, a prominent professor of international law and founding chair of the ICHRDD. Pat Beck represented the National Council of Women of Canada, an organisation that Minister Finestone also belonged to. Caroline Anawak, the wife of the Liberal MP for Nunatsiaq, represented Canada's parliamentary spouses' association, and, just as controversially, the two youth members were selected after an essay-writing contest in *Homemaker Magazine*.

This distribution of service benefits was complemented by an appeal to diversity. From a list of 30 potential non-governmental observers with expertise, the final selection for the Canadian delegation was made on the basis of extensive representation.. Several of the chosen members had impeccable credentials, including Lorraine Michael from the Ecumenical Coalition for Economic Justice and Nancy Riche from the Canadian Labour Congress. Rebecca Cook, a high-profile human rights legal scholar and feminist activist, was added to the delegation as an academic advisor. This strength in the composition of the delegation did little to ease NAC's condemnation of the exclusionary nature of the delegation, but it did made it harder for the organisation to sustain its attack that the government was trivialising the conference.

The way the government chose those eligible for funding to attend the NGO Forum on Women '95 reinforced the perception that diversity was being taken seriously. While at least two of these delegates did come from NAC (with several others having either a regional or some form of cross-affiliation), their presence was overshadowed by the diffuse nature of the overall representation. Funding was provided to a host of individuals covering the entire spectrum of women's groups across the country. These ranged from The Métis National Council of Women, the National Association of Women and the Law, L'R des centres des femmes du Québec, the Congress of Black Women, the Native Women's Association of Canada, to the Public Service Alliance of Canada, and the Canadian Federation of Business and Professional Women Clubs.

This wide mix of interests and grievances made inevitable a polarisation in thinking and an operational clash between Canadian statecraft at the official conference site and NAC's type of society-craft. NAC transferred its well-practised mode of public advocacy – designed to embarrass the Canadian government and provide a "counter-consensus" awareness – to the Beijing conference. It was far from oblivious to the realities of state coercion as practised by the Chinese government. The release of a banner by Winnie Ng and other activists with the words "June 4, 1989. We Will Never Forget", signalled its members' efforts to stretch the limits of free speech at the Huairou site (Rod Mickelburgh, "Canada backs platform boosting women", *Globe and Mail*, 7 September 1995). At the same time, NAC showed an ongoing frustration with the Canadian media's tendency to concentrate on the host country rather than the conference itself. As Thobani exclaimed: "The stories pouring out focused on security problems, harassment of delegates and on and on. And, as many of us feared, the substantive issues were thrown by the wayside" (Thobani, 1995; on this theme, see also Rebick, 1995: 27–36).

From NAC's position, the main "us" and "them" differentiation was between the Canadian state and the authentic Canadian women's movement. Repeating the experience from the Mulroney years, NAC used Beijing as a vehicle to go on the offensive against the record of the Chrétien government. Its release of a document entitled "A Decade of Deterioration in the Status of Women in Canada" at a press conference in the midst of the Beijing conference generated a great deal of publicity (Riddell-Dixon, 2001: 132–133). The spill-over effect was a redirection of attention from the negative record of the resisters to the flaws of the "progressive" actors pushing for change.

By identifying itself as a "self-determining" agent "capable of challenging and resisting structures of domination", not as a co-opted organisation eager to be an insider under any conditions, NAC was able to claw back some ownership of the conference. Transnational networking trumped lobbying with national delegations. As Thobani concluded: "Workshops and discussion groups provided much needed space for exchanging information with sisters from different countries. The coalitions which were formed as a result will serve women's groups well in coming years" (Thobani, 1995).

The price paid was a loss of ownership over the official conference. Instead of being at the centre of the debate on women's issues, NAC was almost completely marginalised. Conceptually the dichotomous framework produced by NAC left little room for nuance and "straddling borders" (Arneil, 1999: 212). The hybrid role offered to other more dynamic elements of the women's movements took second place to dualities and rigid segmentation. Instrumentally, the "us" and "them" position gave permission to the state-based women to withdraw completely from engagement with NAC. As Riddell-Dixon relates, the contrast between the kudos garnered by Canadian state officials from the international NGO community and their lack of "accolades from the NAC" could hardly be ignored (Riddell-Dixon, 2001: 130).

Differences in Canadian diplomacy

Overall, the case for claiming that Canadian diplomacy made a tangible difference at the Beijing conference seems weaker. A survey of its diplomatic performance suggests that Canada reproduced many of its less innovative habits of statecraft during these negotiations. As opposed to moving out ahead of other actors, Canada sought an approach whereby international responsibilities would be balanced with domestic constraints. The most obvious illustration of this caution came on the issue of resources. Consistent with the "disciplinary" straightjacket adopted at the Copenhagen Social Summit, no offers of new spending were brought forward at Beijing. Even if Finestone wanted to provide additional means to help meet demands for promoting women's equality as the conference's proposed Platform for Action laid out, she lacked the clout to deliver an agenda of this magnitude. What emerged as a result was a conformist line in step with the tenets of fiscal orthodoxy. As the Secretary of State for the Status of Women, she kept repeating: "This is not a pledging conference. I didn't come here with a big cheque" (quoted in Paul Watson, "Canada won't add funds to fulfill U.N. women's platform", *Toronto Star*, 10 September 1995).

This lack of generosity was in itself enough to place Canada uncomfortably on the defensive throughout the conference, moving it additional notches away from the identity it had earned at Rio as a country ready to "put its money where its mouth was" to its later sobriquet of acting "on the cheap". This transition was made more noticeable by comparison with the expansive efforts of the Clinton administration. In a reversal of the positions taken at Rio, it was the United States not Canada who moved out in front with a series of initiatives (requiring richer funding) to advance women's rights. Externally, the US Agency for International Development was given an extended mandate to enable women in developing countries to possess legal rights and positions of political power.

Internally, the United States concentrated on efforts to combat domestic violence and create a new council on women (Paul Watson, "U.S. plan for women steals show", *Toronto Star*, 7 September 1995).

The lack of substance in the Canadian domestic political context made the Liberal government a far easier target for NAC as it had been for the social critics at Copenhagen. Instead of making good on their electoral plan to develop a programme of action that would make a positive difference in the lives of women, the Liberals were portrayed as sacrificing these promises on the altar of cuts to social spending, austerity, and structural adjustment. The Canadian delegation, trapped by this doctrine, accordingly had little room for contradicting the Department of Finance's dictates that any recommendations coming out of Beijing must come out of existing budgets. As Thobani eyed these structural considerations, she retorted: "I think it is [Finance Minister] Paul Martin who is calling the shots from home" (quoted in Dianne Rinehart, "Women said plenty, but the message was 'No'", *Calgary Herald*, 16 September 1995).

Reinforcing the perception of retreat still further was Canada's refusal to countenance the notion that Beijing be a conference of commitments, whereby countries would put in writing exactly what they would do to implement the Plan of Action and each country's pledge would be included in the annex of the conference's platform. Such a proposal contained, not surprisingly, enormous positive considerations for forces that wanted a strong document. Not only would it facilitate the process of cross state/societal mobilisation at Beijing (NGOs being readily on side with this proposal as a means to "bring Beijing home", according to one NGO activist quoted in International Institute for International Development, *Earth Negotiations Bulletin* 14/13, 7 September 1995), but it would allow for greater transparency in monitoring post-conference results.

One basic thrust of Canada's objections was quite legitimate. The risk of making written commitments open to scrutiny was that it might encourage national-specific minimalism; that is to say, a country would be tempted to implement only its specific promises rather than using the entire document as a guide or action. A second thrust smacked of avoidance. By focusing on the Plan of Action as a whole, Canada gave itself room to pick and choose among issue areas and to favour a form of selective delivery.

As at the other UN-sponsored conferences, the Canadian delegation put the onus on means as much as ends. It continued to be a priority for Canadian statecraft to be at the centre of action in terms of taking on functional responsibilities for the conference. Secretary of State Finestone became involved as the high-level group charged with dealing with the most difficult issues was enlarged to include heads of delegation in the final stages of the conference. Canadian state officials took major roles on several important bodies handling the negotiation. Ruth Archibald chaired both the contact group on parental rights and on women's sexual rights; Hynes, her colleague at DFAIT, chaired the contact group on the Beijing Declaration; Diana Rivington from CIDA chaired the contact group delegated to handle issues relating to the girl child; and Regehr from SWC chaired the contact group on unpaid work (Riddell-Dixon, 2001: 100–101).

Another official Canadian priority was to maintain constructive lines of communication with as many other actors as possible. Canadian diplomats based in China took their administrative and consular responsibilities extremely seriously. They offered help to groups especially vulnerable to restrictions and intimidation by the Chinese authorities. The small number of Canadians of Tibetan origin attending the conference were at particular risk. Canadian officials carefully monitored the situation when members of this community were detained and questioned for holding unauthorised meetings or demonstrations during the conference, and Canadian consular staff escorted the Canadian Tibetans to the airport to ensure their safe exit. This facilitative activity was not done, though, at the cost of alienating the Chinese government. Canada tempered the provocative element in its reactive behaviour, joining with other countries to register complaints about the location and treatment of groups represented at the Forum. It was the Danish, not the Canadian, embassy that organised a press conference for Tibetan activists that ended up being shut down by hotel security.

It should be mentioned here that the Canadian delegation did not employ the aggressive tactics of Rodham Clinton in excoriating the Chinese record. Finestone went out of her way to differentiate her attitude to the host country from that of the American first lady. In her official presentation she glossed over the logistical "inconveniences" facing non-governmental actors at the Huairou Forum (Statement of Secretary of State, Status of Women and Multiculturalism of Canada, Hon. Sheila Finestone, at 4th UN World Conference on Women, 6 September 1995). Nor did she directly tackle the sensitive issue of how China's one-child policy had been implemented. While refusing to acknowledge that this non-response meant condoning coercion, she justified her approach as one that allowed room for autonomous problem solving. Replicating the hands-off tone developed at Cairo, she said: "It's not for me to determine whether that's right or wrong" (quoted in "China's women back one-child policy, Canadian minister says", *Toronto Star*, 10 September 1995).

The material attractions of this ambiguous positioning were evident. By not challenging the Beijing regime head-on in a public fashion, she safeguarded the commercial aspect of Canada's relations with China. Some wriggle room was retained, at the same time, between non-governmental actors at the opposite ends of the continuum advocating a hard or a soft approach to the Chinese government. Canadian state officials could win approval from Amnesty International and Broadbent's ICHRDD for its support of dissenting groups such as the Canadian Tibetans,[60] but this facilitative role could not be interpreted as taking Canada off-centre in terms of the development of the conference's Plan of Action. Significantly, the refusal to play the anti-Chinese card was one of the few points on which the interests of the Canadian government and its critics intersected: Finestone expressed her concern that undue focus on China would detract from the substantive message of the conference (Rod Mickelburgh, "Broadbent blasts police at women's conference", *Globe and Mail*, 9 September 1995; see also Jonathan Manthorpe, "Finestone defends not blasting China directly", *Calgary Herald*, 7 September 1995). NAC and other alternative voices objected to the "anti-China bias in the media coverage of the conference" (Thobani, 1995; see also Rebick, 1995: 28).[61]

A similar awkward balance arose in Canada's relationship between forces pushing for a progressive agenda and forces of resistance. In keeping with the long-standing Canadian practice of associational diplomacy, special attention was devoted to coalition building with like-minded countries. Rich possibilities for this method of statecraft could be found at Beijing. The informal group to which Canada had the strongest attachment during the negotiations was JUSCANZ, a group that, in addition to the core CANZ trio of countries, contained the United States, Japan, Iceland, and Norway. Canada's own status in terms of the Beijing negotiating process was given a boost through the formation of this group. Indeed the enthusiasm with which Canada embraced this group may be judged by the fact that the Canadian delegation took on the task of chairing the daily coordinating meetings for this group. The expanded membership of JUSCANZ gave it the collective weight not only to pursue its own interests but to play the role of bridge builder on selective issues.

If this form of engagement had its predictable advantages, it also had its unintended risks. One of these risks was that any formalisation of the group could take the Canadian government in a direction it did not want to go. The tensions that surfaced between Canada and Australia on the issue of whether Beijing would be a conference of commitments demonstrated the limits of this form of coalition building. As on a variety of other issues, Australia epitomised the "heroic" style of middle-power diplomacy. With the solid backing of the NGO community – and at least the declaratory support of conference secretary-general Mongella – Australia pushed hard to have this goal established in some way (most notably, via a report to the UN secretariat) even after its original proposal was dropped (International Institute for International Development, *Earth Negotiations Bulletin* 14/11, 5 September 1995; 14/21, 18 September 1995). By impeding Australia's initiative, Canada was placed in an acute dilemma. Diplomatically, Canada's reluctance exposed the looseness of the coalition and changed the parameters of its effectiveness to act as a negotiating group. Politically, Canada's image as leader was compromised by its attitude to the Australian initiative. In contrast to Canada's reluctance to dislodge itself from a thematic orientation, Australia went forward by example with specific commitments in a number of the platform's critical areas of concern. Among these commitments were promises to establish working women's centres in all states, a task force on women and communications technology, and an initiative to address health inequalities for Indigenous women.

These risks were exacerbated by the different interpretations of the policy bias of this "like-mindedness". To many of Canada's critics within the NGO community the country's association with the JUSCANZ group was a sign of not moving towards a progressive agenda. It was taken to be a mask covering up the full extent of the Canadian government's reversal on financial resources. Certainly, on the issue of new allocation of financial resources JUSCANZ did not play a bridge-building role at Beijing. It became entrenched as part of a broader tactical alliance made up of the JUSCANZ countries and the EU membership. These rich countries emphasised the need to strengthen political commitment to the final document, with special attention to moving forward on equality of women in all areas of discussion. But they steadfastly refused to budge on the issue of change in terms of financial commitment to the Beijing Platform of Action (International Institute for International Development, *Earth Negotiations Bulletin* 14/21, 18 September 1995). As Thobani pronounced: "Nowhere was the hypocrisy of the governments of the north, including Canada, more evident than on this question. While these governments are quick to condemn the countries of the south on women's rights, it was the countries of the north that blocked committing new and additional resources to advance women's rights. Without these resources, the commitments made in both the FLS (Forward-looking Strategies for the Advancement of Women to the Year 2000) and the PFA remain nothing but hollow words" (Thobani, 1995).

To its partisan opponents on the conservative side of politics, the association of the Canadian government with these "like-minded" partners was taken to represent a very different sort of bias – a pronounced shift to a radical "feminist" agenda.[62] Such charges should not be taken too far, however. After all, the Canadian delegation kept up the good contacts with the Vatican/Holy See that it had developed during the Cairo negotiations. In the detailed work of finalising the consensus language of the Beijing document, Canada and the Holy See enjoyed a positive working relationship. Canada, for example, supported the Holy See in its proposal to replace a reference to inequality "among women" with language from the ICPD, adding mention of different geographical regions, social classes, and Indigenous and ethnic groups (International Institute for International Development, *Earth Negotiations Bulletin* 14/12, 6 September 1995).

What distinguished Canada's statecraft at Beijing from its diplomatic style at Cairo was a willingness to combine this behind-the-scenes constructive engagement with public disagreement. The clearest illustration of this boldness came on the question of the indivisibility of human rights and women's rights. Canada's endorsement of this theme by way of Finestone's speech ran counter to the opposition of the Holy See (and some Islamic countries), which continued to maintain that woman's fundamental role was that of mother and wife (quoted in Manthorpe, "Finestone defends not blasting China directly", *Calgary Herald*, 7 September 1995; see also Finestone, 1995).

Canada's shift to a more combative diplomatic approach was even more apparent with respect to the Islamic resisters. Consistent with its relationship to the Holy See, Canada did not back away from opportunities to act as a mediator between secular and religious-oriented actors. Capitalising on the Cairo experience, to be sure, Canada stepped in as a bridge builder on the sensitive issue of the rights of adolescents and parents. A central difference from Cairo, however, was that at Beijing Canada did not pretend to be an unbiased interlocutor. Under the compromise agreement worked out in the contact group chaired by Archibald, the rights of parents and guardians to give direction and guidance were balanced by an explicit recognition of the legitimate rights of children to evolve and to be provided with adequate information and confidentiality. The transformative NGO community, while concerned about the potential for backsliding, took the wording of this compromise as a victory for the primacy of "the best interests of the child". Correspondingly, conservative defenders of the traditional family regarded this deal as a bitter loss (quoted in Dianne Rinehart, "Canadian negotiators praised for major policy breakthroughs", *Calgary Herald*, 13 September 1995).

Nor, unlike at Cairo, did the Canadian delegation at Beijing show much restraint over going public with its "us and them" views. Finestone personally endorsed this behaviour by her remarks at the end of the conference. Although allowing that the Islamic states could react to the Beijing document as they chose, she emphasised that they would be on the wrong side of history: "Like the Berlin Wall fell, there will be a change in the walls that surround those women who do not have the opportunity to express themselves freely" (quoted in Dianne Rinehart, "Women said plenty, but the message was 'No'", *Calgary Herald*, 16 September 1995).

A lead-lag dynamic could also be detected in Canada's issue specific statecraft. On some issues Canada was caught defending a position not because it was right but on grounds of its feasibility. A case in point was Canada's reluctance to support the proposal that women should be equally represented in all national and international bodies that set peacekeeping policies, and in all stages of operations. Canada agreed with this proposal in principle, but wanted to preserve its own autonomy to put a peacekeeping operation together as quickly as possible on the basis of the personnel available on the ground, not according to the dictates of a quota system. As a spokesperson for Finestone cautioned: "There is a concern about the practicality. Would it delay peacekeeping while you stirred up enough women participants?" (Angela McLaughlin, quoted in Jane Gadd, "Canadian policy in line with UN plan, official says", *Globe and Mail*, 16 September 1995).

In a variety of other cases, Canada moved out in front with issue-specific initiatives knowing that this leadership role was based on a comparative advantage in terms of reputation or diplomatic leverage. One significant initiative of this type took place in the area of institutionalising sexual violence and gender-related persecution as legitimate criteria for refugee status. While still subject to criticism that progress in this area was not as comprehensive or as effective as it should be, Canada consolidated its standing both as an innovator whose domestic regime had moved well out in front of international norms and as an effective diplomatic actor instrumental in winning new recognition for these criteria in a UN document.[63]

Another Canadian effort featuring the same spirit of boldness came forward on categorising wartime rape not only as a war crime (and hence under the jurisdiction of the international courts) but, under certain circumstances, as a form of genocide. These initiatives developed their profile at UN-sponsored conferences through parallel timeframes, in that both had been ascendant since Vienna and the background of the Bosnian conflict. There were also obvious parallels between the two issues in the way they linked a justice-based domestic campaign with a tenacious and skilled cohort of legal advocates and transnational bureaucrats. The rape issue was given added impetus, however, for a number of reasons. Whereas the European Union and the United States continued to express formidable resistance towards any major innovations in the migration/refugee regimes at the multilateral level, the states that opposed the rape in wartime initiative gradually acquiesced. Russia, most notably, was silent on the proposal despite its earlier objections. The issue of wartime rape was externalised, in the sense that the campaign against violence against women was waged on the international front. The refugee issue, on the other hand, was internalised, in that any change in the rules determining refugee status had direct consequences for domestic policies and politics.

A third set of initiatives constituted those cases at Beijing where Canada tried to move out ahead in areas where it had little record of innovation at the international level or where its domestic regime was less advanced than its diplomacy. A pertinent case in this regard is Canada's effort to have sexual orientation included in the diversity clause, a long list of types of discrimination hindering women (as part of gender-based discrimination) from the full expression of their human rights. By taking up this cause, Canada reaffirmed its readiness to publicly confront those who resisted the extension of rights on religious grounds. Unlike on the issue of parental/adolescent rights, the language on sexual orientation was not conducive to compromise. Sexual orientation was either included in the list of barriers to equal rights or it was not. As one official put it, the problem was not with the language but with the concept of "sexual rights" itself (quoted in Jonathan Manthorpe, "Sexual-rights issue stumps delegates", *Calgary Herald*, 11 September 1995; "Islamic/Catholic countries resist push for 'sexual rights'", *Ottawa Citizen*, 15 September 1995; see also International Institute for International Development, *Earth Negotiations Bulletin* 14/20, 15 September 1995).

Moreover, the tough stance adopted by the resisters (a group that included not only Iran but "moderates" such as Egypt, among a large group of countries, 23 of which filed objections or interpretive statements) left no room for manoeuvre. This grouping of countries opposed the mention of sexual orientation in the text on the grounds that such an inclusion contradicted their religious and cultural values. On procedural grounds, they emphasised the break in practice: not only would the term "sexual orientation" be used for the first time in a UN document but the debate itself was renewed, given the fact that this terminology had not previously been aired. Finally, the site as well as the nature of this controversy ensured that any resolution would arrive with a bang not a whimper. The trend in dealing with most of the sensitive issues at Beijing was to move them out of the spotlight into informal groups where the precise wording could be decided in closed-door negotiations. The issue of sexual orientation was dealt with in a reversal of this procedure: after discussion in the informal group had become immobilised, this issue was moved back to the main committee on the last day of the conference.

Given Canada's usual risk-averse statecraft, its strong identification with this initiative begs further analysis. Unlike on other issues where it acted with boldness, Canadian state officials were operating without a great deal of experience. The sexual orientation issue was also different because of the domestic political calculus. Opposition from conservative forces at home compounded the international obstacles presented by the resisting countries. The Canadian delegation had not only to deal with NAC's criticism for not going far enough in its support for a progressive agenda but it also had to respond to the objections of REAL Women that it was going too far down the road of a "worldwide feminist revolution" (quoted in Rod Mickelburgh, "Canada backs platform boosting women", *Globe and Mail*, 7 September 1995). Objections from both sides had come out in force on other issues such as parental/adolescents rights; the sexual orientation issue simply hardened the lines of this divide.

International factors in isolation go a long way towards explaining why Canada was willing to move decisively on the issue of sexual orientation. Extending the concept of like-mindedness beyond the confines of CANZ or JUSCANZ, Canada worked closely with the EU, South Africa, and a number of other countries for the placement of sexual diversity in the diversity clause. After the chair of the main committee had eventually ruled against the inclusion of this term in the PFA, Canada, along with many of these countries, added an interpretive statement emphasising its understanding that the term "other status" remaining in the text included discrimination on the criteria of sexual orientation (Riddell-Dixon, 2001: 151). With a general confirmation of Canada's high-mindedness in adopting this positioning came a further bonus; it regained reputational advantage by catching up with countries it had been unfavourably compared with in other areas (in particular, Australia). This initiative also took some of the heat off the Canadian delegation for not promising additional funds at Beijing.

Domestic considerations also deserve further analysis. As NAC found out, diffuse pressure tactics on the government had little effect in re-crafting the Canadian approach to Beijing. Pressure from the outside along with a more sophisticated issue-specific focus, however, was more effective. Indeed, it was through this combination of approaches that lesbian activists gained credibility and access in the negotiating process. Lesbian activists from Canada, as elsewhere, were quite sceptical about how different the Beijing conference actually was from the standard male-dominated model. Allison Brewer, from the group Equality for Gays and Lesbians Everywhere, was quoted in the mainstream media as stating: "There's a woman's face on this conference, so when you walk in here, everything in you tells you that the show is being run by women. But when you see the decisions that are being made, then it's very clear that it's in fact being run by men" (Brewer quoted in Dianne Rinehart,

"Agenda being run by men", *Calgary Herald*, 15 September 1995). Whether in front or behind the scenes, men continued to be seen as exerting disproportionate power over the conference. When these activists were stalled in their efforts to work within the confines of the negotiating procedures, they took direct action. Brewer and Shelagh Day were detained by UN security officers after participating in a rally at the main conference, displaying a banner that read "Lesbian Rights Are Human Rights" in several languages (see http://www.egale.ca/~egale/pressrel/950914.htm). By taking such action they risked losing their accreditation to the conference. As in the case of Rio, Vienna, and all other such events, public demonstrations were strictly against the rules of UN-sponsored conferences.

The role of Day stands out as a prime illustration of what can be termed a hybrid style in this form of society-craft. As a member of NAC, Day served on the Canadian Preparatory Committee for the Beijing conference (as she had at Cairo). As with other members of NAC, she could take a dissenting tone on the record of the Liberal government as well as the UN negotiating rules and procedures, but her objection was framed discreetly with far more nuance. Instead of implying that Canada ultimately gave up the fight on the "sexual orientation" provision as part of a general retreat, Day suggested that this shift was part of a calculated approach on the part of the Canadian delegation. Far from suggesting that Canadian statecraft was simply weak, Day credited its strategy for being at the core of the trade-offs made in the final stages of the conference (Day, 1996).

In contrast with the all-or-nothing approach adopted by NAC, Day, as chair of the lesbian caucus at the conference, adopted more incremental tactics. While acknowledging that the lack of recognition for discrimination on the criteria of sexual orientation constituted a setback, Day put a positive spin on this outcome by referring to the number of countries that promoted this proposal. The high visibility of the issue reinforced this image of advancement. As Day weighed up the result: "The debate reported here was a landmark in United Nations history. It revealed disturbing bigotry. But it also revealed that there is support for recognising the human rights of lesbians in many regions of the world" (Day, 1996).

This overview is not to suggest that lesbian activists had no qualms about the validity of this approach. As Day admitted in her own assessment of the Beijing events: "I sometimes wondered about the usefulness of these intense struggles over words and phrases". Her conclusion remained, nonetheless, that while "the negotiation of the text can seem picayune and remote from the oppressive conditions of women's lives", this option remained "vital" (Day, 1996: 53).[64]

Similarly, a focus on the hybrid role of the lesbian activists should not obscure other political or policy motives for the Canadian delegation's embracing the "sexual orientation" proposal. At the political level, the redefinition of the Beijing conference along an ideological continuum imparted a partisan dimension that had been absent in the other UN conferences. As the Reform Party positioned itself in tandem with REAL Women as the champion of family values, the Liberal government could play the diversity card in a more muscular way. Finestone made little effort to hide this partisan dimension in her public declarations on the "sexual orientation" proposal, justifying the Canadian position as "a recognition of the diversity of women" and the "reality" of Canadian life (quoted in Paul Watson, "Canada won't add funds to fulfill U.N. women's plans", *Toronto Star*, 18 September 1995).

This aggressive counter-movement was quick to reap benefits. Whereas the Canadian delegation had been put on the defensive for its lack of commitment early in the conference, by the end it was the Reform Party that became isolated and moved into retreat. Sharon Hayes, the Reform Party MP for Port Moody-Coquitlam, left the conference saying she had become totally isolated in the Canadian delegation (Sharon Hayes, "Gagged in Beijing", *Globe and Mail*, 15 September 1995; see also Rod Mickelburgh, "Perturbed MP leaves UN meeting early", *Globe and Mail*, 11 September 1995). If successful in fending off the "sexual orientation" proposal, the conservative forces failed completely in rolling back the agenda on a host of other issues, including reproductive rights and the balance between parental and adolescent rights.

Taking the offensive with regard to the sexual orientation proposal opened up (as Day suggested) greater room for a "package deal" (Day, 1996) involving a number of other issues that the Canadian delegation and its allies valued. One of these was the reaffirmation of the concept of universality in terms of women's rights. Another was the maintenance of the policy pertaining to women's sexual autonomy, with freedom from coercion, discrimination, and violence. Viewed in this way, Canadian statecraft at Beijing may be seen less as a departure in terms of style. While it presented a more heroic face, behind this profile it employed focus and hard work, the long-familiar ingredients of Canadian diplomacy.

Degrees of difference

The most acute difference between the Beijing and Rio, Vienna, Copenhagen, and Cairo conferences appeared on the claims of ownership. Previous conferences had featured much contestation over the nature and parameters of the partnership between statecraft and society-craft.

NGOs were integrated into the decision-making process on a selective – and often self-selective – basis, and they brought a great deal of talent and energy to bear on outcomes. Few if any of these non-governmental actors believed, however, that these conferences were *their* conferences. The sites were not of their choosing; nor were the rules of the game. The agenda items were increasingly attractive but full of gaps and compromises. For all the progress in bringing NGOs in, an asymmetry still existed between their ownership of the parallel forums and their uneven and limited presence in the mainstream events.

Even a cursory analysis reveals that Beijing was not completely free of these tensions. As in the other conferences, an important segment of the women's movement rejected the notion that Beijing represented any substantive progress in the struggle for equality rights. The difference at Beijing was the intensity with which the collective voices of women spoke out, and the degree of mobilisation that took place among women. Any constraints imposed on the participation of women, whether by the host country or by national governments, were less significant than the opportunities for enhancing the process of interaction at the societal level. The stance of NAC serves as a prime illustration of this meaning of ownership. What was important for NAC was not making a difference in the text of the Beijing Declaration and PFA but celebrating solidarity and the politics of resistance. While its members remembered Tiananmen Square, they also organised demonstrations against the policies of the Canadian government and other members of the G-7.

Other segments of the women's movement made a different assessment. For them, ownership over the conferences had not been achieved. Yet Beijing was judged as a success not only because of the degree of "networking" and the sense of "fortitude" among the women (Bunch and Fried, 1996: 7). The real difference was in the results obtained. The key breakthrough was the expansion of the agenda to encompass "women's rights" as "human rights". Unlike at previous women's conferences, the legitimacy of this mainstreaming framework was accepted. On specific issues, these engaged critics and problem solvers shared the rejectionists' view that "clear gaps" remained, especially in terms of women's economic concerns (Bunch and Fried, 1996: 11); however, they accepted that these failures were balanced by an impressive list of achievements.

Furthermore, they interpreted the ongoing test of ownership quite differently. For the rejectionists, the objective could be nothing less than what was right: "transforming current power structures" (Thobani, 1995). For the engaged critics and problem solvers, the key function was to maintain the necessary forms of delivery. Following up the notion of Beijing as a "conference of commitments" (with a nod to Australia), the focus turned to improving the mechanisms both at the UN and national levels. The devil was less in the structural impediments imposed at the systemic level than in the development of "concrete strategies" as "a basis for demanding accountability" and for ensuring that "promises are carried out" (Bunch and Fried, 1996: 12).

Canadian diplomacy both reproduced and went beyond this contestation over ownership. The Canadian performance at Beijing was the culmination of a long track record of statecraft. Extending the speculation by Edna Keeble and Heather Smith that Canadian diplomacy contains a variety of non-masculine features (particularly in the privileging of mediation over muscle and multilateralism over unilateralism; Keeble and Smith, 1999: 24), it may be contended that a UN conference designed to promote women's rights was a propitious occasion for Canadian entrepreneurial and technical leadership. Style meshed with subject matter in the application of Canadian statecraft. Without too much overstatement, it may be said that Canadian diplomats gained ownership of specific issues on particular aspects of the Beijing negotiations. In complexity of the process, with its contact groups and line-by-line sensitivities, the familiar strengths of Canadian statecraft shone through. Although short on its commitment of resources, Canada took on a heavy workload in seeking compromises. Even on high-profile issues such as sexual diversity, where Canada took a lead role, it was accepted that progress would be slow and full of obstacles. As one Canadian diplomat stated, signs of "real progress" had to be judged against the background that "we move incrementally at the UN" (quoted anonymously by Paul Watson, "Long talks get compromise on U.N. women's action plan", *Toronto Star*, 15 September 1995; see also Jonathan Manthorpe, "Delegates resolve sexual rights issue", *Calgary Herald*, 12 September 1995).

The shape of Canadian statecraft was also influenced by the presence of a number of women diplomats whose experience on this set of dossiers went back to Nairobi, before catching the wave forward with Vienna and Cairo. In keeping with the reality of incremental movement, the shadow of the DFAIT socialisation process had an impact on the way this learning was translated into action. Gains were assessed through paragraph-by-paragraph progress on consensus wording, and attendant debracketing. Abetted by the presence of negotiators from a group of quintessential "femocrats", this cautious problem-solving orientation was mixed with a sense of critical engagement that became embedded in the Canadian approach. In the words of one negotiator, even compromise solutions were valuable: "The effort to get such a wide-ranging deal, and the attention it's getting around the world, has given the feminist movement new strength that a shrinking group of conservative countries can't beat" (see also Jonathan Manthorpe, "Delegates resolve sexual rights issue", *Calgary Herald*, 12 September 1995).

A long-standing assumption of Canadian statecraft was that ideological divisions at the international level were compensated for by a prevailing unity at the domestic level. With the mantra of a "global sisterhood" radiating out of the Nairobi conference, the similarities (not the differences) between women's experiences were taken to be the dominant characteristic in the process of mobilisation. By the time of Beijing, such a claim no longer held up. The very notion that there was an "authentic" women's standpoint serving as a locus of "identification, political action and knowledge claims" was subject to serious challenge (Steans, 1998: 171). The route to emancipation was only one entry point to this larger debate. The critically engaged problem solvers acted on the basis that they could make a difference by opening up space in the mainstream through transnational coalition building and lobbying on the inside. The rejectionists, while remaining active on the margins of the negotiating process, considered their main game to be a campaign of resistance to structural inequalities.

Concerns about the ends of emancipation revealed more starkly the fiction of universality. REAL Women and other political forces at one end of the political spectrum served as the cutting edge of a backlash against the entire project of women's equality on the basis of what they viewed as "radical feminism". To a much greater extent than in NAC and its associated groups, these groups remained on the outside of the Canadian negotiating process. Still, by appealing across the North/South divide, they could cut into the notion that the forces of tradition were isolated in geographical origin and on the defensive in organising "silenced" voices and an array of well-organised allies. In the words of Gwen Landolt, a vice-president of REAL Women: "We really don't waste time with Canada's delegation, or try to change it. We go after where it counts, the delegations of the developing world" (quoted in Paul Watson, "REAL Women target Third World delegates", *Toronto Star*, 8 September 1995).

At the other end of the continuum, the question of who the "global sisterhood" consisted of (and whom it benefited) nudged lesbians and other decentred groups to test alternative and more diverse strategies. From this perspective identity was more complex than a simple dualistic or dichotomous construction of gender (Arneil, 1999: 212). A multiplicity of identities and organisational affinities are possible. To give a practical example, Day could serve as a member of the Canadian Preparatory Committee as a representative of NAC, be involved as a participant on the Canadian Beijing Facilitating Committee as a lesbian representative, act as the chair of the lesbian caucus at Beijing and a highly publicised representative of Equality for Gays and Lesbians Everywhere – and also receive government funding to attend the NGO Forum on Women '95 as a member of the National Association of Women and the Law.

The risks inherent in this expanded "politics of difference" exacerbated tensions within the women's movement. Indeed, by breaking down representation systematically not only along lines of sexual orientation but along racial/ethnic and geographic/linguistic lines, the Liberal government might be portrayed as playing a sophisticated game of division within the women's movement. The Canadian Preparatory Committee contained members, for instance, from the National Council of Women of Canada, NAC, the Congress of Black Women, Réseau national d'action éducation femmes, the National Organization of Immigrant and Visible Minority Women, and l'Association des collaboratrices et partenaires en affaires. At the very least, this multiplicity of representation provided protective covering for NAC's exclusion from a peak position in the preparation and structure for the Canadian delegation at Beijing.

What stood out about the participation of the lesbian activists, nonetheless, was their capacity to promote differences at the same time as managing the contradictions: an approach that meant "straddling the borders" of identity and operating as "hybrids" (Arneil, 1999: 212). This connecting role was important, as it gave added momentum to the issue-specific diplomacy. Instead of adopting a rigid position in these negotiations, the lesbian activists were careful to appear flexible and constructive. The compromise on parental/adolescent rights was deemed to be a "positive" step (Day, quoted in Rod Mickelburgh, "Conference runs on compromise", *Globe and Mail*, 12 September 1995). The debate on sexual orientation, at the heart of their concerns, was acknowledged not as a defeat but as a "real advance" (Day, quoted in Dianne Rinehart, "Women said plenty, but the message was 'No'", *Calgary Herald*, 16 September 1995).

As a guide to future activity, therefore, this accent on differences rides a wave of possibilities predicated on a sense of creative tension. The presence of multiple identities as a source of conflict should be accepted. But the need for accommodating this multiplicity is also made explicit. Through its emphasis on diversity, Canadian diplomacy at Beijing contained some of this requisite metamorphosis through different forms of tactical coalition building. The downside, as in other areas of Canadian activity, was that this movement towards reconciliation between statecraft and society-craft was overwhelmed by controversy about what and who was left out. Beijing showed signs of advances in the form and the scope of Canadian diplomacy. But this reformulation, played out quietly behind closed doors, became lost amidst the polarisation of the government from both NAC and REAL Women. Moreover, to break down the feelings of manipulation, a high premium was placed on speed and intensity in diplomacy. Given the fundamental differences that remained between government and the entire range of NGOs as to the limitations of good international citizenship, the mix of identity and interests, and the relative salience of engagement versus resistance, opportunities for taking advantage of this variable environment were available only fleetingly and on an issue-specific basis.

9

Tests of value with respect to Durban and beyond: anomaly or end of the life cycle?

The World Conference against Racism (WCAR) – or more precisely the World Conference against Racism, Racial Discrimination, Xenophobia and Related Intolerance – held in Durban, South Africa in August and September 2001 raised serious questions about the value of UN world conferences. More than any of the preceding conferences, the Durban meeting put the fundamental purpose of the entire project, and the manner of implementing it, to a very public and acrimonious test. While earlier conferences had aroused enormous debate about their symbolic and instrumental meaning with respect to their implications for the delivery of global public policy (see, for example, Reinicke, 1998) and the trajectory of the international architecture, they were all seen as legitimate and even path-breaking exercises. The Durban conference, in contrast, ignited a firestorm of a reaction that put in question not only the effectiveness but the necessity and the authenticity of such enterprises. In a departure from the long-standing Canadian commitment to this form of UN conference, Canada's foreign minister (who had already distanced himself from Durban) was blunt in his condemnation: "I hope we don't have to see this again" (John Manley, quoted by Corinna Schuler, "Proceedings have descended into farce", *National Post*, 7 September 2001).

Questions of course can be asked about how representative such sentiments were. After all, the Durban conference was anomalous on many counts. In focusing so strongly on the Palestine–Israel question, it can be considered a return to the pattern of much earlier UN conferences in the

1970s and early 1980s when the geopolitical agenda dominated all else.[65] Whatever the merits of the actual arguments about the Middle East situation, such a singular preoccupation had the effect of bringing any substantial discussion of the overall agenda to a halt. Moreover, the issue of reparations for slavery, the other item that managed to grab the spotlight, was too controversial and beyond the comfort level of too many delegates – including many who supported other notions and forms of global welfarism – to serve as a counterpoint for consensus. In this atmosphere, meaningful problem solving was impossible.

Nonetheless, the conference still serves as a compelling episode through which we can return to – and evaluate – the major themes framing the entire ambit of UN conferences. Through its combination of intense style and a reductionist and ambitious substantive element, Durban can tell us a great deal about where and how the tests of global governance have become sited, displayed, and reconsidered. In tandem with the World Summit on Sustainable Development, held in Johannesburg from 26 August to 4 September 2002, it invites us to take a look at the scope and limits of the ideational and process-oriented space for this cycle of events.

Reprising the tests of global governance

Tests of transition

Critics were highly vocal in their denigration of the misguided ends and flawed means of the Durban conference. They differed, however, in their views about the implications of these deficits. For realists, the ingrained instinct was to portray the Durban conference as an episode that was highly problematic but one where the stakes were ultimately not terribly important. Unwilling to concede that anything had changed in international relations, beyond the fact that the "froth" was more visible, these critics clung – at least before the events of 11 September 2001 – to an orthodox, state-centric, and rigidly hierarchical worldview.

To them, the only actors that needed to be examined closely at Durban were states, but even among states there was little equality. When all was said and done, in fact, the only state actor that really counted was the United States. Other leaders could appear at the Durban conference, such as Fidel Castro, Yasser Arafat, and the presidents of Latvia and Bosnia-Herzegovina, but these figures were just sideshows to the US main game. As long as it seemed that Secretary of State Colin Powell would lead the American delegation to Durban, the event had some weight. This condition changed, however, when the United States downgraded its representation. And the ultimate decision by the United States to walk from the conference – because of the way Israel was treated – merely reinforced the farcical nature of the event. It may have provided interesting theatre, but talk did not translate into action.

From this orthodox perspective, the ideas brought out at the conference could not be taken seriously. What was true of all the other UN world conferences was also true of Durban: past errors in judgement were repeated, and irrelevant ideas were recycled. Although there was some serious questioning of US state tactics (concerning the walkout) there was unanimity that the Conference on Racism would not "accomplish much except rhetoric" (Angela Stephens, "Washington snubs a Conference on Race", *National Journal*, 1 September 2001, p. 2686). Civil society was relegated to the margins, with no right to participate with anything approaching the status of states. As one defender of the status quo bluntly put it: "What constitutes a legitimate non-governmental organization is highly elastic" (Puddington, 2001: 31).

It was only in the shadow of the tragedy of 11 September that realists – suddenly and without deep consideration – took the UN conferences seriously. In searching for causes they found it convenient to turn their gaze to Durban as an intellectual breeding ground for the terrorist strikes. In a dramatic volte-face, they no longer treated the world conferences as benign events that could be safely ignored but as manifestations of evil. In the words of Arch Puddington: "Durban does deserve to be remembered – not, as some would have it, as evidence that the world is unable to come to grips with prejudice and discrimination, but as an ideological prologue to 11 September. Durban must be recorded not necessarily as a farce and a failure, but as an event whose message, whose achievements, and whose legacy were uniquely monstrous" (Puddington, 2001: 34).

Critics of the populist neo-liberal persuasion were far more consistent and contextual in their evaluation. In terms of process, Durban, like the other UN conferences, was never treated as being irrelevant. Like many of them, it clearly demonstrated the ongoing capability of "illiberal" forces to hijack the agenda of such major international events. As in the past, the main actors in this constellation were leaders or countries in the South that objected to any internal opening on either the economic or political front. The presence of Castro and Arafat, and their roles as arbiters of political correctness, went well beyond farce to tragedy. Compounding the problem, though, was the case-specific coalition between these state actors and the representatives from a variety of transnational NGOs – about 4,000 of which were in attendance in one way or another at the conference.

Unlike the realists, therefore, this school of critics did not simply ignore – or attempt to marginalise – the NGOs. They targeted them through an aggressive counter-offensive. NGO representatives were not only castigated for being unelected and thus lacking in authority, as they had been since the Rio and Vienna conferences. In a manner similar to the tactics they used themselves, the NGOs were "named and shamed" for their willingness to do deals (especially on the Palestine–Israel question) behind closed doors (in the Canadian case, this tactic was adopted most explicitly by the *National Post*; on "naming and shaming" by NGOs, see Kaul, Grunberg and Stern, 1999: 451).

As with select countries from the South, on material matters, NGOs were condemned for their regressive tendencies that reverted to the compensatory strategies of the 1970s and early 1980s associated with the new international economic order (NIEO). The attempt to seek compensation for slavery and colonialism – not just through an apology from the West or through the branding of these activities as crimes against humanity but to get the West to pay direct financial reparations – was viewed above all in this light; that is to say, as another means to apply a coercive form of tax or redistributive payment from the rich to the poor. Initiatives of this sort were cast as dysfunctional and dangerous to the advance of the international order.

Paradoxically, however, those aspects that were interpreted as defects by the critics of Durban received the most laudatory treatment by its friends. And these friends had often been among the most vehement critics of the practical operation of the UN system through the cycle of past UN conferences. This was true of such NGOs as Amnesty International in the human rights domain and of a variety of groups engaged in the development domain. Many individuals within these constituencies fully shared the sense of failure evoked by Marie-Claude Smouts in 1997: "The UN is as ineffectual as it has ever been and attempts at reforming it have been more 'a strategy of avoidance' than anything else" (Smouts, 1999: 29).

Although constrained in scope, Durban had the effect of releasing new energy from below and beside the state level. As exemplified by the slavery reparations issue, Durban participants were amenable to putting issues of governance dealing with global disparities squarely on the agenda in an unanticipated manner – an approach that could be carried forward into other forums, most notably the Johannesburg World Summit on Sustainable Development. What was regressive to the populist neo-liberals for societal groups was a necessary and fair form of catch-up in terms of the equity/solidarity agenda.

One significant corollary to this overarching set of goals was the opportunity to try to embarrass the United States (in its absence) as the one remaining superpower in the global hierarchy. For, as most NGOs were highly aware, including those most sympathetic to its position on the Middle East, the United States' walkout from Durban left a gap in the realm of discourse and intellectual space if not, of course, structural power. As Michael Posner, the executive director of the US Lawyers Committee for Human Rights suggested, it amounted to an abdication of responsibility at odds with even its own best interest: "Damage has been done by the United States. For the United States not to play a leadership role but instead be dragging the conference down is distressing" (quoted in James Lamont, "Racism accord could set back enforcement of human rights", *Financial Times*, 4 September 2001).[66]

Tests of diplomacy

All of the critics noted above shared a scepticism about the value of diplomacy as it applied to Durban, as they had at the other UN world conferences. Where they parted company was on the question of where diplomacy had gone wrong. To realists and populist neo-liberals the problem lay in the expansion of the form, range, and intensity of diplomacy in the course of the conference process. Whereas older forms of statecraft had limited numbers of participants and were parsimonious in format and discrete in scope, the UN conferences had operated on the basis of a very different model: universalist, infused with society-craft that intruded on the intergovernmental bias, and robust in ambition for institutional change and the application of ideas. The archetype for these critics was the mark set by Maurice Strong at the 1992 UN Conference on Environment and Development:

The Earth Summit is not an end in itself, but a new beginning. The measures you agree on here will be but first steps on a new pathway to our common future. The road beyond Rio will be a long and difficult one; but it will also be a journey of renewed hope, of excitement, challenge and opportunity, leading as we move into the 21st century to the dawning of a new world. (Quoted in a round table on "The Years after Rio: Globalization and Sustainability", at the annual conference of the International Studies Association, New Orleans, 24–27 March 2002.)

For more traditional – and activist – representatives of civil society the problem was not that the UN conferences had done too much (by way of what Mandelbaum (1996) calls "foreign policy as social policy") but that they had not met the heightened expectations attached to them. As recounted through this study, they blamed this shortcoming on the laborious and consensual methods of the UN system. This slow-moving approach allowed the UN to flag issues of import to the agenda of global governance, but prevented it from following through in a timely fashion with implementation systems that worked. Diplomacy became an end in itself, rather than a technique for producing new forms of welfarism. As even experienced, and conceptually sophisticated, UN experts noted on the eve of the Durban conference, this subordination of substance to style had an enervating effect: "Delegates blithely play the game they have mastered; tactical jousting over ideologically charged issues, generally without much hope or expectation of affecting the world at large. At best, their speeches demonstrate superb debating skill. More often, they are consigned, at huge expense in six official languages, to the dustbin of history" (Ramesh Thakur and David Malone, "We need dialogue, not dysfunction", *Globe and Mail*, 24 August 2001).

At the national level, the main frustration of the activist cohorts was their inability to get governments to act on the promises they had made through the UN conference cycle. If conference diplomacy was not to be cast as a frame-up, with NGOs and civil society being co-opted into a system not of their own making, tangible results had to emerge. It was one thing to have somewhat closed the "democratic deficit" (see, for example, Higgott, 2001: 137–138; Prakash and Hart, 1999) in terms of their increased formal participation in these conferences, but access was no substitute for delivery.

These national and systemic problems become intertwined (Ono, 2001). Faced with a variety of issues, especially in the environmental area, which are by definition transnational, national governments could use the lack of interstate agreements as excuses for non-action on the domestic front. As seen in the Canadian diplomatic approach to Rio, Kyoto, and Johannesburg, this variant of Putnam's two-level game allowed non-action at the international level to reinforce non-action at the local level. A similar shortfall has been evident in the forestry case, where dialogue about best practices has been caught in the ongoing struggle between the advocates of a legally binding convention and the UN Forum to promote existing agreements. In many other areas, formulas and agreements that had been reached remained non-binding and contingent on a sustained political and policy commitment. Certainly this problem is pervasive in the human rights domain (see, for example, Dias, 2001) and women's rights (Cook, 2001; WEDO, 1996) as well as the environment.

In all these areas, considerable advances have been made in norm construction, which, as John Ruggie has made us so aware, has the potential at least of "imping[ing] upon 'national' laws" (Ruggie, 1988: 159, 169). The obstacle nonetheless remains: How to ensure that these norms become operational? (on this problem in specific issue areas see, for example, Conca, Albert and Dabelko, 1998; Forsythe, 2000; Young, 1999).

Prior to Durban, civil society activists were tightly pulled between two options. The first was to express continued – though often grudging – loyalty to the process of the UN conferences. This choice meant in effect resigning themselves to all the frustrations inherent in the negotiating process and continuing to push within the UN system for better ways to monitor compliance and enforcement of agreements. A salient example of this tendency was the ongoing response of NGOs central to the implementation of the Beijing Platform. In replying to the UN's *2000 Outcome* document the Rutgers Leadership Center, for instance, carefully balanced its support for the "positive aspects to this review process" and its applause for delegations that had fought to advance commitments to women with its disappointment at the lack of "political will on the part of some governments and the UN system to agree on a stronger document with more concrete benchmarks, numerical goals, time-bound targets, indicators, and resources" ("NGOs Respond to Women 2000 UN Outcome Document", New York, 10 June 2000, available from http://www.cwgl.rutgers.edu/globalcenter/ngorespondw2000.html).

The other option was an exit strategy incurring a more pronounced use of an autonomous form of society-craft. Acting on the premise that there was little to be gained from connecting their own activities with statecraft, rejectionists of this type increasingly condemned hitherto targeted conferences as a waste of time. Elizabeth May, a significant actor at Rio, for instance, refused to take part at the Johannesburg Conference on Sustainable Development, claiming that it was a "useless talk-fest" (May quoted in Kate Jaimet, "Summit a 'useless talk-fest'", *Montreal Gazette*, 28 August 2002). Such defectors preferred to focus their ongoing activities on mobilisation and demonstrations at the grassroots level. Rather than following the Rio, Vienna, Copenhagen, or Cairo model, they took their rallying cry to the experiences generated from the protests directed at the 1999 WTO Forum in Seattle, the campaign against the Multilateral Agreement on Investments, and the "Jubilee 2000" attempts to bring about debt relief. Through these connections and rerouting, then, we see "a whole new range of alliances, actors and agendas at work that has taken us beyond the traditional scope of international politics and diplomacy" (Newman, 2000: 10–11; see also Korbin, 1998).

In principle, Durban held out the prospect of becoming a boundary-stretching event. Its content, its wider context, and the relationship between its central participants encouraged the possibility that this conference could provide a fresh re-articulation of multilateralism. Because there were few precedents for dialogue (a key ingredient of global governance) on issues related to racism, an opportunity opened up for establishing and internationalising a key cluster of innovative norms (on the more general question of norm development, see Finnemore and Sikkink, 1998). Indeed, when Kofi Annan opened the Durban conference (http://

www.un.org/WCAR/pressreleases/rd-d14.html) he urged the delegates not to focus on one country or region but to use the meeting in an ideational but constructive fashion to draft a universally applicable resolution to combat racism in every country of the world.

The opportunity structure was also suitable for the advance of a new type of thinking and moral leadership. The host South Africans were determined to showcase their peaceful transition from apartheid. Key South African leaders, most notably President Thabo Mbeki (who spoke at the conference only two days after the death of his father, Govan Mbeki, a prominent anti-apartheid activist in his own right) and foreign minister Nkosazana Diamini-Zuma (the president of the conference) were eager to put their own diplomatic skill into action by introducing the Durban Declaration and Programme of Action. Opportunities for creative forms of middle-power activism, suitable for building coalitions not only with like-minded states but also with NGOs, were available as well in the effort to broker a compromise text. During the Preparatory Committees (Prep Coms) leading up to Durban, Mexico acted as the facilitator on the issues of discrimination and victims. Norway handled the Middle East dossier, going through every clause of the draft declaration. And finally, it must be mentioned, greater space had been given to NGO activists through a conjunction of circumstances: the presence of Mary Robinson (UN Human Rights Commissioner and a strong proponent of an expanded role for civil society), and hence a flatter diplomatic surface on which to work, and the willingness of many members of the NGO community to work with countries they might have labelled "un-likeminded" at previous conferences.

The ancillary question relates to how these expansive conditions were manifest in operational terms. To their credit, many NGO representatives proved able to act as enlightened entrepreneurs of new norms. Some in this cohort, such as Adrien-Claude Zoller, director of the Geneva-based International Service for Human Rights, warned of the danger of applying "concepts with well-established meaning like 'genocide' or 'crimes against humanity' in an attempt to emphasise existing political conflicts" such as those in the Middle East. Instead of helping to forge new international standards, he argued, this agenda would slow down the momentum built up through such mechanisms as the UN Declaration of Human Rights and the Convention on the Elimination of All Forms of Racism (quoted in James Lamont, "Racism accord could set back enforcement of human rights", *Financial Times*, 4 September 2001). In a similar vein, Irene Khan, the new secretary-general of Amnesty International, engaged creatively with the issue of slavery not only by tackling the question of reparations for past wrongs but by drawing attention to the evils of the contemporary slave trade (quoted in James Lamont,

"Racism accord could set back enforcement of human rights", *Financial Times*, 4 September 2001).[67]

Other NGOs, by choosing not to focus on extending such universal norms, risked being trapped in a society-craft that raised the bar of victimhood only in regard to specific issues. It is instructive vis-à-vis the Middle East issue, for example, to compare the wording of the declaration produced in the intergovernmental negotiations with the document proposed by the NGO Forum. Although the negotiations referred to the "plight of the Palestinians under foreign occupation" and the right of refugees to "freely return to their homes", the final declaration condemned both anti-semitism and anti-islamophobia and excluded references to the Israeli occupation of the West Bank and Gaza (http://www.unhchr.ch/html/racism/02-documents-cnt.html; on this point, see also Pamela Constable, "Racism Meeting Reaches Accord", *Washington Post*, 9 September 2001). Without the apparent tempering influence of the culture of statecraft, the process of society-craft arrived at a document couched in far more emotive and one-sided language. Conspicuous were its paragraph 418, which called for the reinstitution of UN resolution 3379 on "Zionism and racism" and paragraphs 422 through 425, which called for global solidarity to "impose a policy of complete and total isolation of Israel as an apartheid state" (http://www.racism.org.za/index.html).

Tests of partnership

As these illustrations suggest, the pattern of state–societal partnership at Durban followed no distinct pattern. The Canadian case exemplified the continued incentives for states to build close associations with societal partners in the NGO community. All the strands that originally made up the central Canadian strategy at Durban depended on this nexus: to take a "leadership role" on outcomes at the conference via "forward-looking recommendations to combat racism and discrimination", "to share the Canadian experience of diversity" or "valuing difference", to "influence world progress on fighting racism and related intolerance", and to "advance Canada's domestic agenda to combat racism". As the public document outlining Canada's participation at Durban put it: "Civil Society participation at the World Conference against Racism is an international priority for Canada" (http://www.unhchr.ch/html/racism/02-documents-cnt.html).

In contrast with its image as a "penny pincher" the Canadian state (or at least segments within it) showed a readiness and capacity to contribute considerable resources to the Durban conference. The Canadian Secretariat for the UN World Conference against Racism was created within the Multicultural and Aboriginal Programs Branch of Canadian Heritage "to oversee and manage the process of preparing the Canadian positions". This secretariat formulated the guidelines for "client groups" on civil society participation (including travel to South Africa) giving priority to groups whose activities focused on promoting social change and the government's agenda for social cohesion ("Multiculturalism Project Funding Related to the UN World Conference against Racism", http://www.crr.ca/EN/WhatsNewEvents/SR/eWhaNew_SR_links.htm).

Under the direction of Dr. Hedy Fry, the Secretary of State for Multiculturalism and the Status of Women, Canadian Heritage prepared a background booklet for domestic consultations in preparation for the conference. Meetings in support of this process, in which approximately 65 NGOs took part (Canadian Secretariat WCAR, 2000) were organised during 2000 in Edmonton, Vancouver, Winnipeg, Halifax, Toronto, Montreal, and Iqaluit, leading up to a national conference in November, 2000.

Partnership through this formula understandably raised more questions than it settled. One source of tension was a lack of clarity about who the partners actually were. A number of Canadian activists working in the human rights areas had built up constructive (albeit not symbiotic) relationships with Canadian state officials on the basis of their shared experience of working during the Vienna process. This was particularly true of several prominent members of the Canadian Jewish community who expressed mounting concern about the anti-Israel bias at Durban, and among whom were David Matas of B'nai Brith Canada and Anne Bayefsky, affiliated at Durban with the International Association of Jewish Lawyers and Jurists.[68] The lead role given to Heritage Canada/Multiculturalism restructured this relationship. To showcase Canadian diversity, heightened status was given to a very different set of actors – older NGOs (including the African Canadian Legal Clinic) and new groups (such as the African Canadian Coalition Against Racism) established to facilitate community participation at the Durban conference (http://www.aclc.net/un_conference/conference1.html).

Another crosscutting source of volatility related to the motives for a state–society partnership. Consistent with their long-standing approach, representatives of established human rights NGOs generally, and representatives of the Canadian Jewish community more specifically, directed their attention to expanding universal – and legally enforceable – norms to combat racism. In the words of Irwin Cotler, the respected legalist and parliamentary member of the Canadian delegation, the aim of the conference should be to concentrate on the "real issue, which is the struggle against racism in the global sense" (Cotler quoted in Daniel LeBlanc, "Rhetoric threatens UN meeting", *Globe and Mail*, 30 August 2001).[69]

The representatives of the anti-racist coalition mobilised through the Heritage Canada/Multiculturalism consultation process had a divergent set of goals. Internationally, their priority was to become a key member of the transnational anti-racist network animated by the Durban conference. The inevitable external consequence of this form of global activism was to push the issue of reparations for slavery and colonialism to the heart of the discussion. Domestically, as conceptualised by Margaret Keck and Kathryn Sikkink, this coalition's move to "multiply" its "channels of access" had a built-in boomerang effect that brought the Canadian record and reputation on racial issues into the spotlight in a more dramatic and emotionally charged fashion (Keck and Sikkink, 1998; see also Khagram, Riker and Sikkink, 2002). A representative from the Canadian Race Relations Federation complained that Canada had two faces, one for the outside world and a harsher one for its own ethnic minorities: "We're trying to deconstruct the myths and address the issue that there is racism in Canada" (Mark MacKinnon, "Canadian delegates blast homeland", *Globe and Mail*, 31 August 2001).

The notion of diplomatic partnership, therefore, was severely tested. At the state level, DFAIT (the Department of Foreign Affairs and International Trade) projected a growing discomfort with the entire Durban project, although it held to the prime rule of the Canadian diplomatic culture: being there. Amidst all the controversy and stress, John Manley evoked the mantra that it was better for Canada to stay the course: "Canada sees it as one of our duties in the international arena to stick with it in conferences like this, to make our points, to argue them and to try to persuade people" (quoted in Joan Bryden and Daniel Feist, "Manley praises Canada's 'guts' at UN forum", *Ottawa Citizen*, 9 September 2001). That being said, DFAIT signalled its negative attitude in a number of ways. Manley announced – just on the eve of the event – that he would not be attending the conference. And despite his appreciation of the "guts" it took to hang in, he did not try to hide his feelings about the counterproductive nature of the gathering. To reiterate the comments quoted at the outset of this chapter, the minister's conclusion was: "[Durban] hasn't been a good experience for the world community. It has not been a good experience for the United Nations and I hope we don't have to see this happen again" (quoted in Rachel L. Swarns, "After the Race Conference: Relief, and Doubt Over Whether It Will Matter", *New York Times*, 10 September 2001).

Fry, on the other hand, steadfastly hoped that an "acceptable outcome" could be squeezed out of Durban ("Canada hangs in at summit", *Toronto Star*, 4 September 2001; see also Corinna Schuler, "Fry defends decision to stay at racism meeting", *National Post*, 5 September 2001). Without Manley's concern with the main game of Canadian foreign policy – good relationships with the United States – Fry had greater room to practise her variant of statecraft. But Fry also had very different goals in terms of domestic policy and constituency building. Whereas Manley could put the central onus on what he and DFAIT felt was in the Canadian national interest, Fry's fragile political future (if there was to be one in the aftermath of a number of gaffes she committed) seemed to rest on how well she delivered on the anti-racism agenda.

At the societal level, the heated atmosphere of the Durban conference brought the divergent sensitivities within the NGO community to boiling point. Picking up the theme of social cohesion in the original Canadian document, the pro-Israel groups emphasised maintaining a strong degree of solidarity on the Middle East among Canadian groups. As one representative of the Canadian Jewish Congress argued: "If one part of the Canadian community is under attack, then every Canadian community is under attack" (Manuel Prutschi, quoted in Corinna Schuler, "Fry defends decision to stay at racism meeting", *National Post*, 5 September 2001). The anti-racist coalition, however, stressed diversity, anti-racism, and discrimination, together with social transformation. They saw any attempt to subordinate these principles to the Israel–Palestine confrontation as an outdated mode of power politics. The extent of this backlash comes out in the words of a delegate from the National Council of Haitian Origin: "One caucus wants to impose its view on all the rest of us. It's disgusting" (Keder Hyppolite, quoted in Corinna Schuler, "Fry defends decision to stay at racism meeting", *National Post*, 5 September 2001).

In this atmosphere, acrimony and accusations of bad faith and betrayal came to the fore instead of any sense of partnership. In the face of the provocative language sanctioned by the Durban proceedings, above all at the NGO Forum, the pro-Israel representatives were disinclined to give the conference any more legitimacy by staying to the end. By walking out, however, they accentuated not only their own minority status, as Anne Bayefsky said, "nobody walked out but us" (Bayefsky, quoted in Mark MacKinnon, "Pressure's on Canada to leave race forum", *Globe and Mail*, 5 September 2001), but the willingness of other NGOs to accept the divisive language on the Middle East as a quid pro quo for progress in other areas. Some groups took this route with little if any regret, echoing the sentiments of one trade union official that any "call on Canada to walk out disregards" the importance of this conference for black people and other minority groups (Hassan Yussef, executive vice-president of the CLC, quoted in Mark MacKinnon, "Pressure's on Canada to leave race forum", *Globe and Mail*, 5 September 2001). Others, however, sought to justify their actions with elaborate explanations. Gina Daya, the acting director of Save the Children Canada, argued that "the fundamental purpose [for] participation in the WCAR was to bring attention to the number of children who suffer discrimination and racism" ("Why we stayed in Durban", letter to the *National Post*, 8 September 2001). Alex Neve, the secretary-general of Amnesty International Canadian Section (English Speaking), added: "Giving up in despair because of objectionable language in one area would have meant forfeiting any opportunity to help plan for the future" ("Why we stayed in Durban", letter to the *National Post*, 8 September 2001). In either case, the reactions merely served to underscore how deep the wounds had become. As Kathleen Mahoney, the chair of the Montreal-based organisation Rights and Democracy, prophesied, the Durban experience "shattered a lot of alliances and potential alliances for many years to come" (Mahoney quoted in Mark MacKinnon, "Deep divisions remain as racism conference ends", *Globe and Mail*, 10 September 2001).

Tests of leadership

Grand expectations were reined in with respect to the Durban conference, as they had been with every other conference since the Rio UNCED. Instead of working toward a bold statement about Canada's record and reputation on multiculturalism and its initiatives on racial tolerance, Canada had to put its energy into damage control. It seemed that potential policy over-stretch and political embarrassment were far more likely outcomes from Durban than the delivery of any public good. Canada abandoned the search for causes or cures for racism and discrimination, both globally and nationally, and concentrated on preventive measures for ensuring that there would be as few surprises as possible in terms of the optics or the tangible promises made.

The tone for this defensive approach, set by Prime Minister Chrétien, was fully consistent with his attitude throughout the whole cycle of UN world conferences. After his non-appearance at the Copenhagen, Cairo, or Beijing conferences, there was no expectation that he would personally attend the Durban conference. This time, however, Chrétien picked up the sensitivity of the conference on his political radar. The promotion of the type of issues at the core of this conference was a crucial card he and his Liberal party could play to trump the Reform/Canadian Alliance/Conservative opposition in the battle for influence for ethnic votes. Whatever the risks of espousing the cause of diversity and racism, the political incentive of his government having a presence at Durban was unassailable.

Beyond this explicit form of electoral calculus, Chrétien had a number of diplomatic motives for being cautious about the cost of the option of Canada's non-participation. One of these factors has already been mentioned: Canada's reluctance to take an active role at any international forum. As well as containing an element of status seeking, this attitude also represented a non-partisan attachment in Canada to problem solving in the external realm. Indeed Chrétien highlighted this rationale well into the negotiations at Durban: "In principle, I prefer to be present because when you are not there you cannot help the situation" (quoted in Robert Fife, "Gathering: 'Not Useful': Chrétien", *National Post*, 7 September 2001; Allan Thompson, "Summit 'not very useful', Chrétien says", *Toronto Star*, 7 September 2001).

Another rationale came in Chrétien's basic instinct to differentiate Canada from the United States – especially when the world's superpower deviated from the rules of the multilateral game. By this logic the United States' decision to first send a low-level official delegation to Durban – and subsequently to withdraw altogether – opened up some attractive possibilities for Canada. From one angle, it raised the profile of like-minded coalitions working through established structures such as the WEOG, JUSCANZ or other ad hoc coalitions. From a completely different standpoint, it allowed the possibility that Canada might act as the eyes, ears – and even the voice – of the United States on specific issues.

Psychologically, the decision to be in and stay in at Durban was another case where Chrétien chose to do the opposite of what former prime minister Brian Mulroney advocated. Acting as the anti-Mulroney had helped Chrétien's political fortunes on matter of style since 1993. So Mulroney's public call for Canada to "abandon" Durban paradoxically strengthened Chrétien's determination to stay the course (quoted in Robert Fife, "Abandon 'anti-semitic' forum, Mulroney urges Canadians", *National Post*, 6 September 2001).

The contradiction in all of these machinations was that the motives for a continued presence at the conference were at odds with the instinct for safety first so strongly embedded in Canadian statecraft. "Being there" played well diplomatically but it raised the political risks. The Chrétien government had found itself on the defensive during the November 2000 general election with respect to its relationship with the Canadian Jewish Community over its support for UN Security Resolution 1322, which criticised Israel for using excessive force. Indeed, Chrétien felt the need to issue a letter to Canadian Jewish leaders, expressing regret that the vote had "added to their distress and frustration" and reminding them that this one action could not "define, or re-define the deep and long-standing friendship that exists between Canada and Israel" (CBC transcript, "Chrétien reaffirms ties to Israel", 7 November 2000: 13:43).

The danger was that the opposition would then exploit a rift over Durban in the same way as they had tried on the earlier UN resolution. Stockwell Day, the Alliance leader, had a rare moments of political success when he attacked the Liberals on the issue in a speech at a synagogue in Thornhill, Ontario, a Toronto area with a large Jewish population. This barb, in combination with Mulroney's blast with respect to the Liberals' refusal to leave Durban, revealed the potential for opposition parties to run with the issue in a manner detrimental to the Chrétien government: "This is unacceptable for Canada. We can't be tepid in our support on matters of such principle so I am dismayed that Canada has not brought back its delegation" ("Abandon 'anti-semitic' forum", *National Post*, 6 September 2001).

These risks were compounded by the decision to have Hedy Fry lead the Canadian delegation instead of John Manley. Manley had little experience – or interest – in participating in the Durban type of conference. His political background before his appointment as foreign minister had been almost exclusively in the economic/high-tech field. In this office he had quickly moved away from the Axworthy legacy of activist and free-wheeling internationalism. His bias was towards special forms of bilateralism, whether in the context of the Canada–US main game or in the confirmation of "Israel's right to exist within secure borders" as the "cornerstone" of Canada's Middle East policy (CBC transcript, "Manley defends Canada's support of UN Resolution", 27 October 2000; for more detail on the nature of this main game, see Cooper, 2002).

Yet despite these personal inclinations, Manley could have brought many attractive features to bear if he had remained at the head of the Canadian delegation. His position as foreign minister alone gave him considerable weight in the negotiations. Moreover, his sense of innate caution and personal discipline made him a reliable minister in the pursuit of a preventive approach at Durban. Even as he expressed his personal distaste for the unfortunate direction that the conference was taking, he did not give up hope that Canada could "make a positive contribution" and that "a renewed and forward-looking global commitment to eradicate racism" could be reached (CBC transcript, "Manley backs out of UN racism conference", 30 August 2001).

Fry's lead position compounded the risks of Canada's presence at Durban. In stark contrast to Manley's image as a safe pair of hands, Fry had a reputation as a loose cannon. The origin of this image was mainly her involvement in another controversy over racism. Standing up in the House of Commons in early 2001, she claimed that people were burning crosses on the lawns in Prince George, BC "as we speak". She later acknowledged that her claim could not be supported.

With this less than propitious structure in place, there was a need for another set of safe hands to keep order in and through the Canadian delegation at Durban. Paul Heinbecker, the Canadian ambassador to the UN, was parachuted into the assembled team. The quintessential

Canadian diplomatic manager, Heinbecker had been at the centre of action for all of the major events of Canadian foreign policy over the previous decade. From the Gulf War in the early 1990s, the 1995 Canadian–Spanish Turbot War, the intervention in Zaire/Central Africa in late 1996, and the 1999 Kosovo crisis, to the 2003 Canadian attempt to work out a compromise at the UN on Iraq, Heinbecker had handled each of these episodes with an impeccable eye to detail and concern with Canada's fundamental interests.

Differences inevitably emerged between the way Fry and Heinbecker interpreted the context of the conference and Canada's capacity for taking a leadership role, especially in regard to the thorny question of the Middle East. Fry was openly critical of the walkout by the United States and Israel, saying that their actions would "make the work undertaken in Durban that much more difficult" ("Canada hangs in at summit", *Toronto Star*, 4 September 2000). She was optimistic, however, that Canada had stepped into the vacuum and applied the sort of technical leadership that made a difference on this sensitive dossier. In showcasing this effective use of the room that had opened up, Fry summed up the last few days of the conference: Canada was "given the job around the table to remove pieces of the text on the Middle East that were specifically referring to Israel by name and that were very pejorative. We pulled those [references] out. We wanted to pull out more the ones that were sort of casting innuendo. We didn't get those removed so we made a statement of reservation" (quoted in Brian McKenna "Canada's voice heard, Fry Says", *Toronto Star*, 9 September 2001).

Heinbecker, in his own public statements, showed far greater sensitivity not only to the United States and Israel but to the Canadian Jewish community. Trying to dispel the notion that there had been any compromise in Canada's position, Heinbecker made a considerable effort to get it into the public record that Canada had "not sacrifice[d] its principles" (quoted in Pamela Constable, "Racism Meeting Reaches Accord", *Washington Post*, 9 September 2001). Nonetheless, as indicated by Fry's use of the words "pejorative" and "innuendo", these differences became more subtle as the conference progressed. This convergence came about because Fry's illness with laryngitis limited her participation in the conference proceedings and because Heinbecker became the de facto leader – and certainly the public voice – of the Canadian delegation. The most telling sign of this change came when the Durban document was declared adopted in the concluding plenary session. Rather than Fry registering Canada's displeasure, in her capacity as head of the Canadian delegation, it was Heinbecker who took the microphone: "Canada is still here today only because we wanted to have our voice decry the attempts to delegitimise the state of Israel, and to dishonour the history of the Jewish people. The Canadian delegation registers its strongest objections and disassociates itself from all text in this document directly [related] to the situation in the Middle East" (quoted in Mark MacKinnon, "Deep divisions remain as racism conference ends", *Globe and Mail*, 10 September 2001).

Tests of discipline

The primary test regarding discipline in relation to Durban was whether the conference confirmed a pattern of normative direction set by previous UN conferences. Was this conference instrumental in further locking the global structure into the dominant set of rules based on market fundamentalism? Or, by way of a renewed impetus towards a form of double movement, did the conference open up possibilities in the direction of a different kind of international order based on multilateral norms of equity and fairness?

As with the other UN conferences, it is relatively easy to minimise the connection between Durban and such economic-driven issues. After all, with the exception of the Copenhagen Social Summit (and to some extent the later Johannesburg Summit on Sustainable Development), the economic agenda was kept to the margins of the problem-solving agenda. Here it is pertinent to reiterate the complaints issued by Canada's National Action Committee (NAC) and like-minded elements of the women's movement about the lack of an alternative voice at Beijing speaking of the benefits of participation in and access to the dominant structures of the market, not to question the underlying assumptions of these structures or to consider alternative models (for a good analysis, see Chinkin, 2000).

Due to the preoccupation with the Middle East, this disconnect was exaggerated at the Durban conference. As mentioned, the willingness of a many societal activists to look the other way on language with respect to the Israel–Palestine conflict was simply an awkward device for signalling an impatience to get on with the wider agenda. To have allowed this issue to drag on beyond the time allocated to it represented an abdication of responsibility for advancing social change and an alternative global order.

Yet, notwithstanding these constraints, questions relating to the nature of economic discipline did surface at Durban. Representatives from a variety of state and societal delegations declared their concern with trends in global economic conditions. At the opening session of the NGO Forum, South Africa's President Mbeki explicitly linked racism and class struggle: "The rich rule throughout the world use racism as a means of justifying their oppression of the poor" (quoted in George W. Shepherd,

"A New World Agenda for the 21st Century: The World Conference on Racism and Xenophobia in Durban, South Africa", available from http://www.hri.ca/racism/analyses). Paragraph 25 of the final NGO document, in an analogous fashion, expressed its deep concern with "current forms of globalization and policies of international financial and trade institutions as well as the activities of transnational corporations" for their role in preventing the "full realization of economic, social and cultural rights of all people" in maintaining "the social exclusion of groups that are most marginalized", and in heightening "tension and manifestations of racism, racial discrimination, xenophobia and related intolerance" (http://www.racism.org.za/index.html).

The issue-specific test of how this question could be answered in operational terms was the issue of reparations for slavery. The demand for restitution for the exploitation of slavery, and particularly the Atlantic slave trade, was the major new issue raised at Durban. At first glance, the evidence points to a reaffirmation of economic liberal orthodoxy. Objections to this initiative were mobilised on a number of grounds: the length of time that had passed, the issue of locating benefactors, and the division of the claims between the counties that had participated in the slave trade.

Canada's response to this demand exemplified its preventive bias. As neither a formal colonial power nor a slave-owning state, Canada agreed to go along with a statement of "profound regret" for the slave trade. Indeed, its most significant burst of entrepreneurial diplomacy was directed towards this aim. Working with familiar partners such as Norway, Australia, New Zealand, and Japan, Canada moved to forge a compromise between the African countries and their NGO allies campaigning for reparations and the European countries that were primarily targeted for providing restitution. The bottom line for Canada, however, was to ensure that the parameters for this compensatory ingredient were strictly drawn. Consistent with the discipline required to run the global economic system, there could be no relaxation of the principle that this would be a symbolic not a material gesture. As Heinbecker made plain: "Under international law, there is no right to a remedy for historical acts that were not illegal at the time at which they occurred" (Heinbecker quoted in Mark MacKinnon, "Deep divisions remain as racism conference ends", *Globe and Mail*, 10 September 2001).

If this principle precluded direct links with respect to the establishment of a new order, some subtle indications surfaced that the proposed agreement had implications in terms of a wider quid pro quo. In the context of the Durban conference itself, even some critics of the event refer to an altered "moral tone" that allowed for "the adoption of several resolutions recognizing the need for greater assistance to Africa and other disadvantaged areas of the world through debt cancellation" (quoted in George W. Shepherd, "A New World Agenda for the 21st Century: The World Conference on Racism and Xenophobia in Durban, South Africa", available from http://www.hri.ca/racism/analyses)

Durban, therefore, had dual implications for rule making in the world economy. An immediate effect was to draw a line that the rich were not prepared to cross in considering economic redistribution. At the same time, nonetheless, it nudged some of these same actors to think more seriously about their recommendations for formulating not only a post-Durban but a post-Washington consensus. As the *Toronto Star* pointed out: "Looking to Africa itself, countries that profited from the slave trade should make some amends by offering far more generous aid through agencies like the World Bank or via the special fund. They should open their markets to Africa, encourage investment there and speed debt relief" ("A debt to Africa", *Toronto Star*, 7 September 2001; see also "Canada to make African aid a priority: Minna", *Toronto Star*, 7 September 2001).

It is not farfetched to see Durban, although still tentative in its application, as a catalyst for the initiatives that Canada eventually tried to place on the G-8 agenda at the 2002 Kananaskis Summit. In making these moves, the Chrétien government showed it was prepared to rethink some of the strictures of economic orthodoxy. Chrétien's concern for his legacy unquestionably played a significant role in this new position. However, in making "its first priority" that of "reducing poverty in Africa", Canada also made a genuine commitment "to have the G-8 and Africa agree on a new paradigm and find the real resources to make it work" (Kirton, 2002: 226).

What was missing from Durban was the involvement of business. Unlike at the World Social Summit at Copenhagen, or the entire Rio–Kyoto–Johannesburg process, the private sector chose to ignore the event in the hope that it – and its agenda of reparations – would simply go away. Disciplinary action was left to states. This no-show attitude was entirely consistent not only with market principles of non-interference with the climate for business investment but with calls for firms to be held accountable for past actions. Nonetheless, a laissez-faire approach along these lines seemed ineffective in keeping companies' obligations out of the spotlight. Moreover, this stance was at odds with the alternative public–private strategy built up through the Global Compact and partnerships between a cluster of major corporations, groups such as the International Chamber of Commerce, some NGOs (including Amnesty International), and the UN (see, for example, Ruggie, 2000). The nature of any strategy at the issue-specific level raises a number of distinctive problems. But, as seen through the experience of the Johannesburg

Summit, initiatives along these lines have the power to raise imagination and momentum as well as controversy (on some of the features, debates, and implications concerning bringing business into the UN system, see Vanessa Houlder and Alan Beattie, "Shades of green", *Financial Times*, 19 August 2002; Tesner and Kell, 2000; Utting, 2002; Zacher, 1999).

Tests of sovereignty

The way the tests of sovereignty played out at Durban magnified the tension between the aspects of governance that are in constant and voluntary evolution and the components that remain stable. The Canadian state was quite ready to bend its procedural control when it was defined in terms of autonomy. At the outset of the negotiating process, the guiding principles of Canada's participation were tolerance, diversity, and a measure of self-criticism. Unlike its attitude at most of the other UN conferences under review, the state did not focus primarily on what other countries should be doing inside their borders. Nor did the Canadian approach to problem solving appear to suffer from the extended inside/outside contradictions evident in several preceding conferences. Canada initially sought to act on the WCAR agenda unilaterally on the domestic front as well as collectively on the external front. As the Heritage Canada preparatory document framed this domestic–international interface: "While we work to contribute to a world that values all people equally we must take action at home as well as work with the international community to combat racism" (http://www.unhchr.ch/html/racism/02-documents-cnt.html).

When autonomy was defined in terms of territoriality and international legal status, however, the Canadian state was much less willing to accept any fundamental alteration in the meaning of sovereignty. As at the Vienna conference, this dichotomy between flexibility on autonomy and a firm line on territoriality stood out particularly when Indigenous matters were under discussion. In the preparations for Durban, the unique status of Aboriginal peoples in Canada – or First Nations – was given privileged attention. Canadian Heritage was careful to highlight the "specific challenges related to racism and intolerance" that this constituency faced. In considering solutions, emphasis was placed on the need for a "parallel consultations process established by Aboriginal peoples themselves" in order to "respond to their needs and respect their traditions, cultures, customs, and languages" (http://www.canadianheritage.gc.ca/wn-qdn/wcar-cmcr/wcar.htm).

Yet, despite these efforts to find a symmetry between their interests, Durban exacerbated rather than tempered the relations between Indigenous groups and the Canadian state. No internal dynamic of serious negotiations was launched through the Durban process, nor was there any new meeting of minds on policy direction or delivery apparatus. This rift was reflected in a public display of bad temper and discordant views even before the conference officially started. Before leaving for Durban, Matthew Coon Come, the newly elected grand chief of the Assembly of First Nations (AFN), expressed concern that Canada would "not tell the truth about racism, and even the ongoing use of state violence against indigenous peoples" ("Coon Come's contention", *Globe and Mail*, 28 August 2001).[70] At the NGO Forum, Coon Come pursued this theme further by comparing the Canadian "racist and colonial syndrome of dispossession and discrimination" with the experience of South Africa under the apartheid system (quoted in Corinna Schuler, "Canadian apartheid grabs local headlines", *National Post*, 31 August 2001; see also WCAR, daily reports from NGO Forum, Day 2, Wednesday, August 29, available from http://www.unhchr.ch/html/racism/02-documents-cnt.html). Leaders from the federal government replied that such language was unhelpful and would have the effect of freezing the AFN leader out of any future talks on an agenda of reform. Bob Nault, the Minister of Indian and Northern Affairs, asserted that unless there was an apology, Coon Come was "going to find it very difficult for people to do business with him" (quoted by Valerie Lawton, "Minister demands native leader apologize", *Toronto Star*, 1 September 2001). Prime Minister Chrétien added that "for Matthew Coon Come to be [at Durban] dumping on Canada" was "not very useful" ("Summit 'not very useful', Chrétien says", *Toronto Star*, 7 September 2001).

From the perspective of the Canadian state, these tactics of embarrassment indicated just how far Indigenous groups were prepared to go to "name and shame" Ottawa before an international audience. Rather than attempting to embrace a form of constructive engagement with the government on the basis of an anti-racism agenda, the AFN seemed to be trying to undermine Canada's reputation as a good international citizen. Fuelling this official backlash further was a frustration with what was seen as the Indigenous groups' tendency to bite the hand that fed them. Gestures of generosity by the federal government (including providing funds for the six-member delegation from the AFN) were not reciprocated by "good" diplomatic behaviour.

From the perspective of the Indigenous groups, the true test for sovereignty rested not just on the willingness of the Canadian state to give up some of its autonomy (in terms of releasing policy determinism in favour of a bargaining process and subsidiary processes) but on whether it was ready to embrace forms of segmented territoriality. As long as the state clung on to this fundamental expression of inequality of status, manifested above all by Ottawa's claim to territorial supremacy, the basic questions of sovereignty remained open and hotly contested.

By this test the Canadian state earned a failing grade at Durban. Having previously lost ground on the use of the term "Indigenous peoples", the federal government was now seen to be pushing for the inclusion in the Government Declaration of paragraph 27, which negated these gains, affirming that the term "Indigenous peoples" in the Declaration and Programme of Action "cannot be construed as having any implications as to rights under international law". Ted Moses, the former Cree ambassador to the UN and now the grand chief of the Grand Council of the Cree, complained that by this logic, the concepts at the heart of the conference's agenda did not apply to Indigenous groups (Ted Moses, "Anti-racist except for us", *Globe and Mail*, 29 August 2001).[71] Their rights would not be inherent within inalienable and universal principles but would be determined by state actors in the context of ongoing multilateral negotiations.

The continuing attempt to impose stricter parameters on the question of sovereignty by the Canadian state and "like-minded" countries promoted a vigorous response from the NGO community as well. Paragraph 142 of the NGO Forum explicitly called for a breaking of state-centric notions of territorial-based sovereignty: "Indigenous Peoples have the inherent right to possession of all their traditional and ancestral lands and territories" (http://www.racism.org.za/index.html). Furthermore, the resistance of states with respect to withdrawing paragraph 27 led to a decision to abandon the conference on the part of the Indigenous People's Caucus of the NGO Forum in general and the AFN in particular.

Tests of culture and civilisation

Whether one considers that the Durban conference was animated by a fault-line between the West and the Rest depends on one's estimation of the importance of cultural factors. Even leaving aside the trauma of the 11 September attack, which occurred immediately after the conference, a plausible case can be made that the cleavage motivating terrorism was an undercurrent of the conference. Certainly a concerted attempt was made before the conference to frame both of the major issues – the Palestine–Israel conflict and the demand for reparations for slavery – in terms of the legacy of Western colonialism and institutionalised racism, the need for recognition of the collective rights of the oppressed, and the sustained Western defence of the established order.

While it would be a mistake to dismiss the cultural dimension out of hand, a closer examination of the Durban conference reveals the flaws of this type of overarching explanation. As at the Cairo conference, Durban highlighted many of the myths and distortions associated with rigid and exclusive categorisations. Notwithstanding the image of the "West" as a cohesive civilisational entity, the division between the United States and its partners was a crucial variable in negotiation strategy. Consistent with its pattern of exceptionalism and the specific mentality of the administration of George W. Bush, the United States was quick to cut and run from the conference. The Europeans on the other hand – along with Canada and other like-minded countries – dug in and contested the particulars of the Declaration and Programme of Action.

Nor did the "non-West" display any heightened degree of ideational homogeneity or practical solidarity. Although the mobilisation campaign against Israel was led by the Islamic countries, differences in interest among them continued to be manifest. On the one hand, Iranian diplomats criticised the conference for not going far enough in condemning Israel's practices as "a clear manifestation of racism" and addressing "the causes of oppression against the Palestinian people" (Iranian delegate quoted in Pamela Constable, "Racism Meeting Reaches Accord", *Washington Post*, 9 September 2001). Egyptian diplomats, on the other hand, called for a balanced approach, with a statement that could be taken seriously as a map of action. In the words of a former Egyptian foreign minister: "What is the use of a document that will be tilted. It will be condemned and thrown away and not implemented at all?" (CP-AP, "Canada hangs in at summit", *Toronto Star*, 4 September 2001).

Downgrading the applicability of the cultural explanation even further was the convergence of points of view among "non-West" states and "Western" NGOs. This shift in circumstances was most apparent on the Middle East, where the NGO Forum went further than the Government Declaration in criticising Israel. One rationale for this outcome was the societal tradition of sharing identity with the struggles of the oppressed. But measures of opportunism and compensation were also present. As noted, some NGOs conceded or overlooked the language on the Palestine–Israel issue so as to move on to issues more central to their mandate. Other civil society actors may have jumped on the issue as a convenient tool by which they could downplay their own image problem as being too closely identified with "Western" values and interests.

The reparation issue gives another twist to this same theme. At one level, the issue could be seen as a state-centric conflict between representatives of countries that participated in the Atlantic slave trade and leaders of the West African territories from where the slaves were originally taken. Overlapping with this official negotiation process, though, was a society-driven campaign for restitution. Here it is of considerable import to note that, despite the presence of a transnational element, out in front of this effort were prominent members of the African-American community such as Jesse Jackson, Charles Ogletree, and Johnnie Cochrane (on the case for reparations, see Robinson, 2000). Using the compensation made to Holocaust victims as a precedent, activists in the Black Leadership Forum, along with an extended coalition of groups and individuals, pressed hard at Durban for financial redress for slavery not only through international channels but within the United States itself.

Blurring the lines of a civilisational divide still further were the divergent tactics employed by state and societal actors on the reparations issue. Imbued with the United States' legal culture, the African-American activists held to the view that this campaign was one stage of a lengthy process through multiple court proceedings. The majority of African leaders had a far more immediate and instrumental attitude, treating the issue as a means of applying pressure for getting the continent back on the international policy radar. President Olusegun Obasanjo of Nigeria, like the NGO activists, persisted in his condemnation of slavery as the "ultimate crime against humanity". Instead of pressing for the launching of individual or national claims as a means of restitution, however, he expressed willingness to accept an apology if that constituted a first step towards deepening the development commitment of rich countries to Africa (James Lamont, "Quest to win reparations for slavery finds forum", *Financial Times*, 31 August 2001).

Tests of difference

It may be farfetched to make a claim that women experienced any sense of ownership, either on an individual or a collective basis, of the Durban conference. It is more fruitful to speak about the capacity of women to make a difference in terms of the character of the WCAR. A number of women took on influential roles at Durban, most notably Mary Robinson in her capacity as secretary-general and Nkosazana Diamini-Zuma as president of the conference. In terms of their diplomatic style, both of these key figures were remarkable for the determined outlook and optimistic spirit they maintained throughout the difficult negotiations. Diamini-Zuma worked resolutely to broker an acceptable deal, nudging the parties along to the end. Amidst all the frustration and bickering, Robinson was still able to put a long-term ideational spin on the results: "This has been an exhausting nine days for us all, but I believe it has been worth it. The language will resonate around the world. That's an achievement of which we should all be proud" (Pamela Constable, "Racism Meeting Reaches Accord", *Washington Post*, 9 September 2001; Corinna Schuler, "Let's hope they don't try this again", *National Post*, 10 September 2001).

Nonetheless, increased access does not necessarily mean influence. To report that women participants at Durban were given lead positions is not to say that this status trumped the influence of male figures. UN Secretary-General Kofi Annan opened the conference before handing proceedings to conference Secretary-General Robinson. President Mbeki welcomed delegates before Foreign Minister Diamini-Zuma did so. Nor, it should be mentioned as a corollary, does this repositioning in the hierarchy mean effectiveness. From the realists' perspective, Robinson and Diamini-Zuma could be considered naïve for taking on responsibilities that were by their very nature onerous and susceptible to failure. From a populist neo-liberal perspective, both could be considered merely pawns in a larger game directed by illiberal states and their allies among NGOs.

Extending this argument in a very different (albeit still critical) direction, an exclusive concentration on the prominent roles of these individuals may underplay how anomalous their status actually was. From this standpoint, rather than showcasing the few women at the top of the multilateral system, it would be more appropriate to take into account the presence of prominent women throughout the negotiating process. As demonstrated by the presence of a number of highly placed individuals at the NGO Forum, a societal orientation also attracted some stargazing whether in acknowledging the role of women such as Irene Kahn within Amnesty International, or the reputation of such figures as Winnie Mandela and Angela Davis. Nonetheless, to more fully indicate what took place, the actions of the anonymous need to be acknowledged as much as the participation of the celebrated. George Shepherd, in an insightful monograph on the Durban conference, recounts an episode that highlights the need for a comprehensive outlook: "During one of [the] panels on globalisation, the proceedings were interrupted by a demonstration of hundreds of South African women who demanded to participate. When they were given the microphone they complained bitterly they had been made promises of food and board by the preparatory committee but that nothing had been forthcoming" (quoted in George W. Shepherd, "A New World Agenda for the 21st Century: The World Conference on Racism and Xenophobia in Durban, South Africa", available from http://www.hri.ca/racism/analyses).

Following the same format, the seemingly abundant integration of women into the national delegations needs to be reviewed with more circumspection. This caveat is certainly justified in any detailed examination of the Canadian case. Hedy Fry may have been given some room to mobilise important components of the state apparatus and a diverse range of societal actors in the run-up to Durban, but when the WCAR reached its sensitive moments, Fry's freedom of action was reined in and managed by handlers with a greater concern for interests than for identities. Paralleling the constraints imposed on Robinson and Diamini-Zuma at the international level, making and operating the rules of the game was well beyond Fry's reach. The potential openings for women at the start-up phase only camouflaged the rigid contours of the system, and distorted the extent to which some unorthodox or "erratic" actors could be controlled and normalised.

Alternatively, at the societal level, it is tempting to view the reach and presence of women as being governed by essentialist principles. Yet, despite the strength of the women's movement's inclusive psychology and its claims of transcendent notions of tolerance for diversity, the movement found itself being divided by the complexities of identity politics. Counter to its stereotype, this component of civil society was not immune from the shattering of alliances and partnerships within it. Instead, as highlighted by the rift in the Canadian delegation on both the Middle East issue and the reparation demands, women moved to become vociferous partisans. While the anxiety this provoked revealed the impact of this crisis of identity, these feelings could not hold back the move towards fracture not along gender lines but on divergences of political discourse and prescriptions for policy action. This dissension surfaced most explicitly on the question of whether Canada should follow the lead of the United States and Israel and exit the conference. Anne Bayefsky in no uncertain terms called for the Canadian delegation to depart: "We want Canada to leave now. There is no indication that the Palestinians and their Arab allies are prepared to compromise" (quoted in Corinna Schuler, "Fry defends decision to stay at racism meeting", *National Post*, 5 September 2001; see also Anne Bayefsky, "We must not stay any longer", *Globe and Mail*, 5 September 2001). Maria Omene of the Immigrant Women of Saskatchewan (along with others such as Margaret Parsons, the chair of the African Canadian Legal Clinic) pressed for the stay option: "These issues are very important to people of African descent" (Omene quoted in Mark MacKinnon, "Africans harden stand on reparations", *Globe and Mail*, 5 September 2001).

Rethinking the boundaries of global governance

When all is said and done, the fundamental value of Durban – as in the case of the other UN world conferences – has been its ability to stay on the front lines of global governance. Procedurally, the deep if still uneven penetration of these conferences by multiple actors, and especially NGOs, has become one of the defining characteristics of this area of engagement. Substantively, these events have positioned themselves at the head of the effort by international institutions to tackle the disparate problems associated with acceleration of globalisation through the 1990s and into the twenty-first century. In some domains, this positioning has carried the conferences forward into novel areas of problem solving involving innovative forms of re-regulation. In other areas, it has meant becoming a movable form of think-tank with a mandate to come up with workable ideas that will ease – if not rectify completely – the growing discrepancies between rich and poor in the global polity (for an insightful commentary of this process in the general contest, see Emmerij et al., 2001: 214; for a positive review of the conferences from a Canadian NGO perspective, see Foster and Anand, 1999).

In meeting the tests of value, the world conferences can be credited with helping to raise the level of engagement and the sustained quality of the UN's response to the world's ills. Agenda setting is certainly not sufficient in itself to confirm an appreciation of value. But the UN world conferences appear to be a necessary ingredient if many of the questions raised in this book – on diplomacy, partnership, leadership and the rest – are to be addressed. While it is easy for states (especially those without a secure pattern of multilateral behaviour) to deny or ignore the reality, the demands for international cooperation have risen. Although problem solving can and will still be exercised through intergovernmental channels, gaps will continue to exist if this is to be the exclusive formula.

NGOs are also left the choice of disengaging from these conferences. However, despite all the limitations of this route and the pull towards detachment, a pattern of engagement has not only been maintained but reinforced – albeit often through selective and uneven means. One result of this advance in the construct of multi-level agency and structure has been the appearance of a very different challenge – at least in states such as Canada – to the way foreign policy is made. As the experience of the UN world conferences keenly demonstrates, vertical patterns of policy formulation and consideration have been joined – and in many ways overtaken – by the logic of multiple and transnational networking.[72] State and societal actors alike have to be agile to keep up with the opportunity structures available to (or closed off from) them by way of ideas, information, tactical space, and institutional development.

With these types of change in train, the UN world conferences also operate on the front lines of the tensions between interest and identity. Despite the hopes and expectations of global civil society, national interests continue to matter, with state actors attempting to shape and win back manoeuvring room in the globalised context they must operate in. To be sure, states have to work to achieve these aims in the absence of many of their long-standing assets. These deficiencies include many of the architectural features and attendant capabilities linked to the classic Westphalian state. They encompass as well the sense of collective identity that states could traditionally count on. NGOs and civil society can work closely with state officials on a tactical basis but the threads of loyalty that can allow sustained cooperation have become thin and exposed (on this point, see Rosenau, 1999).

The NGOs' position on the front lines of global governance contains for its part a marked element of fragility or instability. Many NGOs have abundant skills in supplying knowledge and policy recommendations. They have gained enough legitimacy as well to be accepted components of the conference process, albeit still short of being equal partners. What confuses matters has been the mix vis-à-vis the NGOs' operating style within and between interests and a diverse and ever-changing pattern of identities. The interest dimension is enough to separate them from states; the identity dimension stretches the line much further. Not only do NGOs depart from a statist perspective on "Who is us?", but their allowance for tolerance of multiple identities makes for enormous contradictions within the NGO community. On some issues a tight bond of solidarity has developed among societal groups with respect to environmentalists, human rights, or population and women's activities. On other issues, this unity has become fragmented by the introduction of other categories of identity including racial characteristics, religion, and sexual preference.

This mix lends considerable richness to the putative imagery of global governance. In synchronisation with the trend found on the state dimension, it also opens the way to a heightened form of disaggregation; that is to say, a process by which the pattern of global governance – together with the provision of welfare benefits on a global scale – is divided into segments, each of which has its own distinctive shape and time-line. This dynamic makes the task of mediating among varied and often competing identities extremely difficult. While compromises on material issues can often be reached, this solution is far less likely to be operational on identity questions.

Any success in extending the front lines of global governance will, therefore, be an untidy process. The test of effectiveness will ultimately be successful by imparting a culture of inclusiveness in qualitative as well as quantitative terms. But working with ever larger numbers of different and often competing actors will entail inevitable collisions, in which technical problem solving will be subordinated to questions of status and accountability, and perceptions of justice. Global governance, especially under conditions where issues of poverty eradication and equalisation become the key policy sites (on this agenda see, for example, Grunberg and Khan, 2000; Thérien, 1999; World Bank, 2000) will inevitably become more not less politicised.

The multiple personalities that emerge from the complex set of images and roles taken on by Canada through the UN world conferences give ample testimony to Canada's significance as a case study. What stands out about Canada's performance is its multi-faceted, often contradictory nature. In some crucial ways, the expression of Canadian statecraft through the cycle of UN conferences is that of a fading – or at least a distracted – country (Appel Molot and Hillmer, 2002). Rio held out the prospect of a pattern of enthusiastic engagement for Canada in the life of the UN conferences – a robust approach containing the possibility for novel and ambitious modes of bureaucratic mobilisation and issue-specific leadership. What developed out of that experience over the next 10 years was very different. Not only was the Rio process itself compromised by a lack of delivery, but Rio proved to be the exception not the rule in inculcating a sense of optimism that the UN conferences could be used as a detonator as part of a big-bang strategy, blasting through to a new form of global governance in one grand moment.

The reasons for Canada's image of retreat and retrenchment are wrapped up with a number of themes highlighted in this book: the fragile relationship between state and societal actors; Prime Minister Chrétien's detachment from the conferences because of his personal style of caution and his unwillingness to go beyond a focused instrumental agenda in foreign policy; the weight of external pressures from the "disciplines of global capital" translated through deficit and debt reduction at home and a contraction of the parameters of foreign policy; the tensions between a willingness to bend on autonomy and the compulsion to hang tightly onto territorial control even at the cost to its reputation as a good international citizen on Indigenous issues; and risk aversion in refusing to get too heavily embroiled in normative questions concerning sensitive issues such as abortion.

This side of Canada's personality, however, is offset by a very different cluster of traits that came to the fore during the cycle of UN world conferences. Some of these characteristics – or built-in habits – feature the standard repertoire of Canadian diplomacy that goes back to the so-called "golden age" of Canadian statecraft through the post-1945 era. While it is easy to ridicule the use of these traits as an operational guide, their influence on the process, wording, and results of the entire range of negotiations should not be underestimated. To focus attention exclusively at the political level (or, for that matter, on the emotions and persistence of NGOs) neglects the talent displayed by Canadian state officials throughout this project. Despite diminishing resources, erratic and limited direction and mandates at the political level, a lack of cohesion in terms of priorities, high expectations from civil society, and exposure on a number of highly demanding and controversial issues, the Canadian diplomats on the ground soldiered on doing many small (and some quite big) things well. Indeed, as much as anything else, this book serves as a reminder of the industry and specialised skill set of Canada's foreign service.

Nor does the invitation to celebrate these older instincts signal that the Canadian outlook towards the UN world conferences was caught looking too long in the rear-view mirror. No less than with societal actors, the diversity and flexibility of state officials must be acknowledged. This pattern of responsiveness certainly appears in the reinvention of many of the politicians analysed in this work. The classic case is Brian Mulroney, the champion of the Canada–US Free Trade deal, becoming the standard-bearer of environmentalism at Rio. But other images making an appearance in this narrative point to the same conclusion. Lloyd Axworthy, for example, frustrated at the constraints imposed by working through the channels of the UN, worked to compress time and space into "just in time" initiatives on land mines and the International Criminal Court. Conscious of the need for a legacy, Chrétien cut himself free from his risk-aversion psychology and moved decisively at the Johannesburg World Summit on Sustainable Development to announce that his government would ratify the Kyoto agreement by the end of 2002. Transcending his image as the central deficit-fighter, Paul Martin has become a highly visible and sophisticated campaigner for global governance reform. Amidst his campaign to replace Chrétien as leader of the governing Liberal party, Martin accepted UN Secretary-General Annan's invitation to co-chair the Commission on the Private Sector and Development in order to move forward with a new social contract not only between developed and developing states but between NGOs and private corporations (David Olive, "Martin shows his true colours at U.N.", *Toronto Star*, 29 July 2003). Martin tied his high-profile participation on this commission to a personal commitment to "chart out a position of major leadership with ... Canada playing a leading role on the world stage" (Shawn McCarthy, "Martin proposing a major role for Canada on the world stage", *Globe and Mail*, 26 July 2003).

Bureaucratically, Canada demonstrated a tolerance for doing things differently that belies the notion that it was coasting on its past reputational attributes. From an inside/out perspective, the conferences confirmed the diffuse profile of Canada's official engagement at the conferences. With a tolerance for internal negotiation that distinguished it from many states, Canada can be portrayed as being in the forefront of the model sketched out above, concerning the disaggregated and horizontally ordered nature of governance. A range of other departments and agencies did the heavy lifting throughout the cycle of conferences, including Environment Canada, Status of Women, Immigration Canada, and Heritage Canada. By stepping back from a control function, DFAIT endeavoured to minimise its sense of over-stretch. The question that remained was how and when the foreign ministry could combine this approach with an exertion of its capabilities as a manager-coordinator, and – as demonstrated most dramatically at Durban – occasionally as crisis manager (on these questions, see Cooper, 2001).

From an outside/in perspective, Canada caught the wave of many of the techniques vital to the extension of global governance. Notwithstanding the controversy and fatigue attached to this configuration, Canada maintained its pattern of working with civil society. In doing so, it served as a model of how foreign policy should be restructured to facilitate competence and credibility and even how the "foreign" in international activity should be redefined. It is also a flexible strategy, allowing myriad approaches with a capacity for short-term coalitions and an allowance for difference among NGOs and individuals. One variation privileges different styles of new – or complex – multilateralism (on this theme, see Cooper, English and Thakur, 2002; O'Brien et al., 2000). Another puts the onus on state officials to come to terms with the push by civil society by producing and articulating ideas of their own.

The most compelling way to capture Canada's contribution to the UN world conferences, therefore, is through the imagery of flexibility, ambiguity, and improvisation. The residue of an older dominant worldview and ways of doing things remains in place, but in other ways the differences between Canadian statecraft and society-craft have become blurred and intertwined. Whatever the gaps between them, these two manifestations of diplomacy share common characteristics: persistence; a search for solutions that transcend the national state and span the older international/domestic divide; some understanding of hybrid and multiple identities; a concern about making multilateralism work across a wider terrain; and a consideration that – rightly or wrongly – international institutions matter. The normative gaze of what constitutes the demarcation of this project – accentuated by the tragedy of 11 September 2001 – will continue to be contested between them. But if there is any momentum left at all for further innovation, the manner by which Canadian diplomacy meets the test will send us an important signal about what things are happening – and how and where – on the front lines of global governance.

Notes

1. The extreme end of these criticisms can be located on a number of web sites. The waste of money/regulatory twin theme has been the mainstay of much of the press coverage of the conferences in the business-oriented media. A Canadian critic refers to the threat of "nanny globalism" (Lorne Gunter, "Whose world is it anyway?", *National Post*, 28 August 1999). For a good assessment of some of these arguments, see Fomerand (1999), especially p. 125.
2. Anglo-American realists have traditionally either ignored or ridiculed the conferences. A classic example of the first approach is Henry Kissinger's silence on the world conferences in *Diplomacy* (Kissinger, 1994), and in *Does America need a Foreign Policy?: Diplomacy for the 21st Century* (Kissinger, 2001). The stream of ridicule comes out in phrases such as "manifestos of meaningless" attributed to earlier world conferences (Puddington, 2001: 34).
3. For expansions of this theme, see Marshall (1999: 49), Langhorne (1998), and Talbott (1997: 69–83).
4. On the importance of multilateralism, see Keohane (1990: 731–764) and Ruggie (1992: 561–598).
5. For elaborations of the frontier analogy, see Rosenau (1997) and Van Rooy (1997: 93–114).
6. Although Donnelly expressed his fears about the imbalance within this agenda, he acknowledged that an important exception to this trend could be located in the attention paid to the connection between general civil and political rights and women's rights (Donnelly, 1981: 635). For a more positive reading, see Alston (1992).
7. Environmental specialists such as James McCormick concur that Stockholm stands as "the landmark event in the growth of international environmentalism" (McCormick, 1989: 88).
8. Canadian press commentary on Strong's appointment can be seen in John D. Harbron, "Maurice Strong: next stop the U.N.", *Toronto Telegraph*, 18 September 1970; "CIDA president to UN environment affairs post", *Globe and Mail*, 17 September

1970; and "Canadian to lead UN attack on pollution", *Toronto Star*, 16 September 1970.
9. For the clearest expression of the rejectionist character of the United States' UN-directed diplomacy, see Moynihan (1978).
10. The sympathetic response to the UN initiative is captured in the major document produced by the Friends of the Earth for the Stockholm conference: "The UN is the only body we have where all countries can and do talk to each other. Since we must somewhere make a start at getting everybody together, the UN is the best place we have, and it has already done what no other body has been able to do: get people to agree to talk about the earth. It is, of course, depressing that the sort of argument we have just looked at is the only way in which countries seem to be able to talk to each other about anything, but that is their fault, not the UN's, and so far nobody has found a short-cut" (Friends of the Earth, 1972).
11. For background on his career, see Humphrey (1984) and Hobbins (1994).
12. Macdonald continued to work closely with the Canadian delegation on an initiative to appoint a UN High Commissioner for Human Rights. Working closely with a number of middle and smaller countries, including the Netherlands, Sweden and Costa Rica, this campaign was rebuffed in 1971 (see, for example, Rae Corelli, "UN defectors stall Canada's fight for a rights czar", *Toronto Star*, 15 December 1971).
13. The Olympic Games of Pollution were also held with mock medals going to firms with "outstanding accomplishments in Pollution" (Adamson, 1990: 34).
14. Tussie and Riggirozzi add retrospectively that there was a "before and after Stockholm". The conference "laid down the foundation for widening the participation of civil society in global policy arenas" as well as redefining "relations among the NGOs themselves, which, at the same time, were asserting more encompassing demands" (Tussie and Riggirozzi, 2001: 171).
15. Although united in their opposition to the arms race and Vietnam, these individuals engaged in some of the bitterest arguments. The most vivid images emerged out of guerrilla endeavours such as the parade of a huge papier-mâché whale around Stockholm in support of a 10-year moratorium on whaling (Morphet, 1996).
16. This critique echoes a strong current running through US thinking about multilateral diplomacy. See also Moynihan's dismissal of diplomacy based on a "humanitarian program" in Moynihan (1979).
17. This choice between adaptation and decline when faced by thick globalisation is picked up in another work, in which Princen and a co-author suggest that the need for "an integrative, interdisciplinary, multilevel" approach is beyond the reach of traditional diplomacy and diplomats schooled in diplomatic protocol, classical European power politics, East/West superpower confrontation or trade negotiation" (Princen and Finger, 1994: 31).
18. One leading English scholar/activist is effusively complementary of this connection: "Canada's persistent support for women and for gender perspectives throughout the UN has been beneficial for all women" (Ashworth, 1999: 276).
19. The acting Executive Director of the FOE, Robert Horning, had expressed pessimism about UNCED and Canada's performance on specific issues, particularly on the standards for climate change, well before the conference (Liberal Roundtable, 1992).
20. Several representatives of NGOs have circulated memoranda to this effect. See, for example, comments made by Janine Ferretti, the executive director of Pollution Probe, on the need for more extensive dialogue based on a new "sense of partnership" (quoted in James Rusk, "Groups demand Rio action plan from government", *Globe and Mail*, 8 July 1992). Ferretti sent a memo to this effect (Ferretti, 1992). A similar trend took place in the human rights arena: with their experience through the Vienna process a 29-

member group of NGOs tried to formalise due to the perceived the need to "work more forcefully for the emergence and buildup of a strong, global human-rights movement" (Pierre Sané, Secretary General of Amnesty International, quoted in Linda Hossie, "Human-rights groups find they lack cohesion", *Globe and Mail*, 29 June 1993).

21. Subtitled "Co-opting the environment" this article constituted a sharp criticism of Janine Ferretti, who McDonald says was the "only environmentalist on the official Canadian delegation" at Rio before joining one of the NAFTA Sectoral Advisory Groups on International Trade (SAGITs) and the North American Commission on the Environment. Ferretti is quoted as arguing: "Anybody who knows anything about how to influence policy and how to get things changed recognises that they have to work within the system. Our view at Pollution Probe is it's not going to happen by standing on the sideline".
22. One of the best expressions of this can be seen in the comments of Anne Park, as head of the Canadian delegation to the 48th Session of the UN Commission on Human Rights (Park, 1992; see also Pal, 1994: 252–253).
23. On Amnesty International more generally, see Clark (2001) and Thakur (2001).
24. For more on the tensions between state and societal actors at Vienna, see Gaer (1995).
25. Stairs terms this the "quaint appellation that political scientists assign to factors of personality, competence, and character" (Stairs, 2001: 25).
26. As Donald J. Savoie records on these sort of tough questions, the machinery in the Chrétien government was designed to protect the "political credibility and capital of the Prime Minister" (Savoie, 1999: 269).
27. To Chrétien the key to political survival was avoiding or at least managing "small mistakes", not embracing big policy ideas (Savoie, 1999: 349).
28. David Malone, head of the International Peace Academy and DFAIT official, confirms that Canada's search for a "safer footing" on the international stage under the Chrétien government came about in part because "until Canada's finances were in order it would be seriously limited in its ability to act" (Malone, 2001: 568).
29. Mulroney nudged the United States to sign the document which, while "far from perfect is a big advance from what we have", quoted in Dennis Bueckert, "Mulroney prods Bush on treaty to protect species", *Montreal Gazette*, 12 June 1992.
30. As related in one journalistic account, Raymond Chrétien urged the Prime Minister to "Play and play fast" (David Pugliese, "Nobel Fever", *Saturday Night*, May 1997; see also Kirton, 1997).
31. On the "national unity" dimension, see Hugh Winsor, "Rescue mission a proud endeavour", *Globe and Mail*, 15 November 1996; and Terrance amend to Willls, "PM keeps one eye on Quebec when developing Zaire plan", *Montreal Gazette*, 19 November 1996. For a flavour of the positive reception the initiative received initially in Quebec, see Jocelyn Coulon, "Un grand moment pour la diplomatie canadienne", *Le Devoir*, 15 November 1996).
32. Chrétien, however, did not try to hide his sensitiveness to charges that Canada was playing the role of a laggard on social policy. When Chrétien accepted the Franklin Delano Roosevelt International Disability Award on behalf of Canada, he defended his record against charges from social activists that this award was undeserved: "Today I want to say to my partners – here in this room and beyond – that as Canada begins to move into a post-deficit era, as we make strategic investments that enhance opportunity for all, Canadians with disabilities will be included" (quoted in Shawn McCarthy, "Prime Minister defends Canada's record on disabled", *Globe and Mail*, 3 March 1998).
33. As Jeffrey Simpson relates, the dictum in official Ottawa during this time was "check it with Derek". This concentrated style of decision making "funneled all important infor-

mation through himself to the prime minister, brought coherence to PMO decisions and focused the PM's and the government's attention on the few huge issues that would decide its electoral fate" (Simpson, 1993: 59).
34. This breadth of bureaucratic participation comes out, for example, in the Report of the Seminar, Convened by the Canadian Department of External Trade and International Trade and the Department of the Environment, "From Stockholm to Rio 1972–1992", Willson House, Meech Lake, Quebec, 8–9 December 1991.
35. Described as a "caretaker" minister with no intuition for foreign affairs, McDougall had been margainalised by Mulroney in his efforts to use high-level foreign policy initiatives to rescue his reputation among Canadians. She was also sidelined by her aspirations to succeed Mulroney and her decision not to attend the Vienna conference because of the timing of the leadership convention (see, for example, Olivia Ward, "McDougall's U.N. debut awkward", *Toronto Star*, 26 September 1991; John Cruickshank, "Putting a foot in a minister's mouth", *Globe and Mail*, 23 August 1991; and Carol Goar, "Canada losing profile under McDougall", *Vancouver Sun*, 14 November 1992).
36. This point is not to discount the premium that Chrétien placed on loyalty from his ministers (Savoie, 1999: 97–98).
37. The core argument of this work is that a limited form of democracy has been promoted to substitute a consensual form of social control for coercion.
38. The "Friday Group" was an informal group composed of senior business executives, including the BCNI and the CPPA, which met periodically to try to come to terms with the challenges of sustainable development and the impact of environmental considerations on competition.
39. May's memo at the end of UNCED is relevant here. She noted: "I also worked extensively with Forestry Canada [officials] in keeping up with the touch and go negotiations on the Forest Agreed Statement of Principles. On this issue I collaborated with other concerned Canadian NGO[s] ... as with the international negotiating NGO group. The final text of the agreed statement of principles was probably not satisfactory to anyone. It resulted from an extremely acrimonious North/South debate. All concerns about forests as critical ecosystems were subsumed in a highly politicised atmosphere of discord. On this issue, Canadian NGOs had a sympathetic ear from government negotiators. We basically had goals much closer to each other's than to those of countries like Malaysia that so effectively blocked progress" (May, "Report on Participation", 30 July 1992, mimeo).
40. Among the representatives from NGOs invited to the National Forum were Mary Simon, Nancy Worsfold and Elizabeth May (DFAIT, 1994).
41. For details of the make-up of the Canadian delegation and the general organisational process see WSSD, Copenhagen, Denmark, A/Conf. 166.9, 6–12 March 1995, 19 April 1995; WSSD, 6 March 1995, A/Conf. 166/1, 23 February 1995; Preparatory Committee for the WSSD, Organizing Session, New York, 12–16 April 1993, A/Conf. 166/PC/INF.1, 20 May 1995.
42. The NGOs tracking the WSSD through the *Earth Negotiations Bulletin* were explicit in their view that the Summit was a missed opportunity, with no movement on bilateral debt relief, the Tobin tax, or the establishment of additional resources (International Institute for International Development, *Earth Negotiations Bulletin*: A Reporting Service for Environment and Development Negiotations, 12 March 1995; http:www.issd.ca/vol10/1044015e.html). For a full narrative of the negotiations see http://www.iisd.ca/linkages/vol10.
43. LIFT was one of nine Canadian antipoverty groups that presented submissions to the UN Committee on Economic, Social and Cultural Rights. (Margaret Philp, "Canada evasive in report on social issues", *Globe and Mail*, 12 November 1998).

44. For a road map on how the WSSD could "regain momentum" through a new international initiative, see Jolly (1997).
45. The National Action Committee on the Status of Women led the campaign for Canada to declare itself a refuge for women who had been victims of violence around the world (see Stephanie Innes, "Canada proposed as international refuge for abused women", *Globe and Mail*, 30 November 1992).
46. A similar argument was made by representatives of international NGOs. The director of Equality Now, a New York-based human international rights group, questioned: "If Nada's claim of persecution had been based on grounds of race, ethnic origin, or religion, would she have been granted refugee status by the Canadian Immigration and Refugee Board? It's not too late for the Canadian government to right this wrong and demonstrate its commitment to gender equality" (Jessica Neuwirth, "A Test of Canada's Gender Equality", *Christian Science Monitor*, 26 November 1992).
47. Judge Mawani participated on a panel devoted to the guidelines on gender-based persecution through the NGO Forum at the Vienna conference.
48. From Ottawa's perspective, the route forward for First Nations to obtain any new rights was through bilateral negotiation not through an international document.
49. The Chair of the UN's Working Group on Indigenous Populations told the conference that she "shared the pain" of natives after the word "peoples" was discarded (quoted in Rudy Platiel, "Ottawa out to sabotage native rights", *Globe and Mail*, 23 June 1993).
50. Several Indigenous representatives pointed the finger directly at Canadian culpability. As Konrad Sioui, the chief of the Bear Clan of the Huron-Wyandot said: "They've succeeded in convincing other nation-states of the world that if they use the world 'peoples' when they talk about us that it might break up their countries" (Smith, 1993b: 2).
51. In his major address to the conference Moses expressed indignation at the states that were using a strategy of evasiveness: "They have called us 'populations,' 'communities,' 'groups,' 'societies,' 'persons,' 'ethnic minorities' and 'people' in the singular, anything but what we are – PEOPLES" (statement by Ambassador Ted Moses on behalf of the Indigenous peoples of the North American Region to the World Conference on Human Rights, Vienna, 14–25 June 1993, available from http://www.gcc.ca/Political-Issues/internationalstatement_by_ted_moses_on_Vienna.htm)
52. This justification continued to be given. See, for example, the work of Denis Marantz, who served as departmental coordinator for international Aboriginal affairs at DFAIT. Marantz argues that "enough aboriginal groups subscribe to the concept of self-determination ... to justify government concern for the disruptive effects such claims can have" (Marantz, 1996: 26).
53. For an analysis that focuses on the transformation of "spiritual power" into an "abuse of power", see Neale (1998).
54. Significantly for future events pertaining to the Kyoto accord, however, Canada stood apart from the Like-Minded Countries Declaration on Climate Change.
55. Marchi's major speech at Cairo is worthwhile quoting at length to glean the nuance contained in it: "let me be clear; Canada does not promote abortion as a method of family planning; however, [the] hard truth is that thousands of women die annually from unsafe abortions. We must act now to address this serious public health concern. This is not, after all, a conference about abortion; it is about caring; it is about real, sustainable solutions for those in grave need" (Marchi, 1994).
56. Other groups that were represented on the Advisory Council were the Canadian Federation of Demographers, Network on International Rights, Canadian Ethnocultural Council, Canadian Public Health Association, Association Québeçoise des Organismes de Coopération Internationale, Conservation Council of Ontario, EED Foundation/FOE, Inuit Circumpolar Conference, Canadian Federation of University Women, and

Assembly of First Nations. A constellation of Canadian NGOs sought accreditation through the Cairo process, without moving onto the Canadian delegation. These groups included REAL Women of Canada (Richmond Hill), Centre Sahel at Laval University, International Institute of Concern for Public Health (Toronto), Citizens for Foreign Aid Reform (Etobicoke), Foundation for International Training (Don Mills), Alliance for Life (Winnipeg), Association Québeçoise des Organismes de Coopération Internationale (Montreal), Family Action (Vanier), Federation of Canadian Demographers (UWO), Children's Foundation of Canada (Ottawa), Sustainable Population Society (Edmonton), Centre d'Études arabes pour le développement (Montreal), and the Canadian Ethnocultural Council (Ottawa).

57. Worsfold's own status as a member of the official Canadian delegation was enhanced by her organisation of a special (and widely attended) meeting on migration issues between Marchi and international NGOs held at the parallel NGO forum.
58. At the 1975 conference, 1,300 delegates from 133 countries, with representatives from 113 NGOs had attended; 5,000 participants from 82 countries took part in the parallel NGO Tribune. By 1985 the figures had risen to 2,000 delegates from 157 states at the official Nairobi conference, and 13,500 representatives from 150 countries at the NGO Forum. This upswing continued in 1995. The official Beijing conference and the parallel NGO Forum in Huairou together attracted close to 50,000 people (two-thirds of these participants being women). Close to 5,000 delegates and 4,000 NGO representatives took part in the official conference. The NGO conference hosted some 30,000 attendees.
59. A quite different analysis came from Betty Friedan, who took the line that women could persevere despite the difficulties: "The Chinese government was very nervous, because the Forum is such an expression of democracy. I don't think they're anti-women. I just don't think they take women seriously (quoted in Rod Mickelburgh, "China steps up pressure on women's conference", *Globe and Mail*, 30 August 1995).
60. Both of these groups remained steadfast champions of freedom of expression throughout the conference (see, for example, Rod Mickelburgh, "Broadbent blasts police at women's conference", *Globe and Mail*, 9 September 1995).
61. Rebick commented that: "Reading the Globe and Mail or any other Western media, it would be easy to assume that the Chinese did not want this NGO Forum on their soil, but everything that I experienced in China suggested just the opposite" (Rebick, 1995: 28).
62. In attacking the Beijing Platform of Action, the group said the text was "a fraudulent document [that] impose[d] Western feminist cultural values worldwide" (Jane Gadd, "Canada's focus upsets right wing", *Globe and Mail*, 12 August 1995).
63. "Guidelines on Women Refugee Claimants Fearing Gender-related Persecutions" had become official policy in June 1994, with the announcement by Immigration Minister Marchi that Canada would be more sensitive to cases of sexual abuse. These guidelines expanded the Women in Crisis programme mentioned earlier.
64. This view was shaped in part by her positive appraisal of the Vienna conference, which she attended as a representative from NAC, quoted in CP, "Women's agenda bolstered in Vienna", *Globe and Mail*, 23 June 1993. Going into the Beijing conference she asserted: "We're building from conference to conference – pushing the UN into a more democratic process. What's exciting about Beijing is the chance for women all over the world to meet and consolidate politically" (quoted in Doris Anderson, "Women pry open U.N. conferences", *Toronto Star*, 21 November 1994). Acting as a mentor for the less experienced and legally astute, Day went out of her way all through the Beijing process to instil society-craft with the means to be most effective (Riddell-Dixon, 2001: 69; see also Jonathan Manthorpe, "Canadian lesbians held briefly by UN security guards", *Calgary Herald*, 9 September 1995). Nor, as her participation in the demon-

stration at the conference showcased, did it mean that other "outsider" avenues were discarded.
65. Indeed, there are some striking parallels between the Durban conference and the controversy in the mid-1970s about Canada's hosting of a UN-sponsored conference on crime prevention in Toronto. The decision by the Trudeau government to withdraw its hospitality came amidst fears that Canada would be caught between an intensive lobbying effort by Jewish groups, the Ontario government, and opposition parties and the presence of PLO observers at the meeting. The "battle ground" atmosphere was intensified by a 4 July 1975 bombing in Jerusalem that killed 13 people, and Israeli retaliation (see, for example, Michael Benedict, "PLO raid turned Ottawa against UN conference", *Toronto Star*, 26 July 1975; on the wider debate, see Taras and Goldberg, 1989).
66. Posner maintained a far more positive take on the results of the conference: "I think there is no ignoring the fact that a range of issues relating to race and discrimination have been put on the table, and that there is a recognition by many human rights groups that their situations are similar. I still hope that some sort of global movement will emerge from that" (quoted in Nicole Itano, "No unity at racism conference", *Christian Science Monitor*, 7 September 2001).
67. Zoeller worked closely with the Research Director of the WCR Project, Human Rights Documentation Centre, and the South Asia Human Rights Documentation Centre, prior to the conference (http://www.hri.ca/racism/Projects/intro.shtml).
68. Matas had served as the president of the Canadian Council for Refugees and as a member of the International Council of Voluntary Agencies. Bayefsky had served as an adviser to the Canadian delegation to the Vienna Conference on Human Rights.
69. This sense of universalism served as the glue for at least an "uneasy" consensus and "outline of priorities for action" by NGOs located in both the North and South at the 1993 conference (Boyle, 1995: 81).
70. This argument concerning an inside/outside double standard was reiterated by Professor Russel Barsh: "I think it is very much a part of Canadian culture to be offended by racism, but to be quite offended by actual complaints of racism" (quoted in Simon Tuck, "Natives suffer 'deadly reality', chief says", *Globe and Mail*, 27 August 2001).
71. For an interesting article on the way in which the "assumption of sovereignty" has "shaped the apprehension engagement of Indigenous peoples' concerns", see Shaw (2002).
72. This point is salient even if the argument from Ann Florini proves to be correct: "The heyday of UN mega-conferences is over, done in by budget constraints, general exhaustion, and not least, the feeling on the part of some governments that civil society's role in them was getting out of hand". As she adds: "The transnational networking made possible by the conferences has created or enforced non-governmental linkages involving all sorts of groups in a wide range of countries" (Florini, 2000: 226).

References

Abzug, B. and the UN Department of Public Information (1995) *Women: Looking Beyond 2000*, New York: UN.

Adamson, D. (1990) *Defending the World: The Politics and Diplomacy of the Environment*, London: I.B. Tauris, p. 34.

Adelman, H. and D. Cox (1994) "Overseas Refugee Policy", in H. Adelman, A. Borowski, M. Burstein and L. Foster, eds., *Immigration and Refugee Policy: Australia and Canada Compared*, vol. I, Toronto: University of Toronto Press, pp. 263, 271.

Adelman, H., A. Borowski, M. Burstein and L. Foster, eds. (1994) *Immigration and Refugee Policy: Australia and Canada Compared*, vol. II, Toronto: University of Toronto Press, p. 356.

Ajami, F. (1993) "The Summoning", *Foreign Affairs* 4(2): 2–9.

Alston, P., ed. (1992) *The United Nations and Human Rights*, Oxford: Clarendon.

Alter Chen, M. (1995) "Engendering World Conferences: The International Women's Movement and the United Nations", *Third World Quarterly* 16(3): 483.

Annan, K. (1998) "The Quiet Revolution", *Global Governance* 4(2): 123–138.

Ansell, C. K. and S. Weber (1999) "Organizing International Politics: Sovereignty and Open Systems", *International Political Science Review* 20(1): 73–94.

Appel Molot, M. (1994) "Testimony before the Special Joint Committee of the Senate and the House of Commons on Reviewing Canadian Foreign Policy", *Minutes of Proceedings and Evidence*, 14 June 1994, 39: 36.

Appel Molot, M. and N. Hillmer (2002) "The Diplomacy of Decline", in N. Hillmer and M. Appel Molot, eds., *A Fading Power. Canada Among Nations 2002*, Toronto: University of Oxford Press, pp. 1–33.

Arneil, B. (1999) *Politics and Feminism*, Oxford: Blackwell.
Ashworth, G. (1995) *Diplomacy of the Oppressed: New Directions in International Feminism*, London: Zed.
—— (1999) "The Silencing of Women", in T. Dunne and N. J. Wheeler, eds., *Human Rights in Global Politics*, Cambridge: Cambridge University Press, p. 276.
Aucoin, P. (1986) "Organizational Change in the Machinery of Canadian Government: From Rational Management to Brokerage Politics", *Canadian Journal of Political Science* 19(1): 1–27.
Australian Provisional Government Council (1990) "Towards Aboriginal Sovereignty", *Chain Reaction*, 16 July: 62.
Axworthy, L. (1995) "Testimony to House of Commons Standing Committee on Human Resources Development", *Minutes of Evidence and Proceedings*, 5 April 1995, 73: pp. 5, 9–10.
Ayres, J. M. (1997) "From National to Popular Sovereignty? The Evolving Globalization of Protest Activity in Canada", *International Journal of Canadian Studies* 16: 114.
Baines, E. K. (2002) "The Contradictions of Canadian Commitments to Refugee Women", in C. Turenne Sjolander, H. Smith and D. Stienstra, eds., *Gendered Discourses, Gendered Practices: Feminists (Re)Write Canadian Foreign Policy*, Don Mills, Ont.: Oxford University Press, pp. 155–171.
Bakker, I., ed. (1994a) *Rethinking Restructuring: Gender and Change in Canada*, London: Zed/North-South Institute.
—— (1994b) *The Strategic Silence: Gender and Economic Policy*, London: Zed.
Balloch, H. (1992) "Testimony to Subcommittee, Development and Human Rights", *Minutes of Evidence and Proceedings*, 8 June 1992, 24: 39–40.
Banting, K. (1996) "Social Policy", in G. B. Doern, L. A. Pal and B. Tomlin, eds., *Border Crossings: The Internationalization of Canadian Public Policy*, Toronto: Oxford University Press, p. 45.
Barkin, S. J. and B. Cronin (1994) "The State and Nation: Changing Norms of Sovereignty in International Relations", *International Organization* 48(1): 109.
Barlow, M. and B. Campbell (1995) *Straight Through the Heart: How the Liberals Abandoned the Just Society*, Toronto: HarperCollins, p. 8.
Barry Jones, R. J. (2000) *The World Turned Upside Down? Globalization and the Future of the State*, Manchester: Manchester University Press, p. 97.
Barsh, R. L. (1995) "The Aboriginal Issue in Canadian Foreign Policy, 1984–1994", *International Journal of Canadian Studies* 12: 107–134.
Bayefsky, A. F. (1990) *Gender, Equality and International Law*, Women and the Law Workshop Series, 1990/91, No. 1-90F, 12 October 1990, Ottawa: Faculty of Law, University of Ottawa.
—— (1994) "General Approaches to Domestic Application of Women's International Human Rights Law", in R. J. Cook, ed., *Human Rights of Women: National and International Perspectives*, Philadelphia: University of Pennsylvania Press, pp. 351–374.
Bazell, R. J. (1971) "Human Environment Conference: The Rush for Influence", *Science* 174(4007): 390–391.

Bernstein, J. (1992) *CPCU Report on Canadian Government and NGO Participation at United Nations Conference on Environment and Development (UNCED)*, 25 June 1992, Ottawa: Canadian Participatory Committee for UNCED.
Bernstein, J. and D. McGraw, eds. (1992) *Report of the Proceedings of "Countdown to Rio"*, 21–22 February 1992, Ottawa: CPCU.
Berridge, G. R. (1991) *Return to the UN: UN Diplomacy in Regional Conflicts*, London: Macmillan.
—— (1995) *Diplomacy: Theory and Practice*, London: Prentice Hall.
Biersteker, T. J. and C. Weber (1996) *State Sovereignty as Social Construct*, Cambridge: Cambridge University Press.
Black, C. (1994) "A Life in Progress", quoted in M. Bliss, *Right Honourable Men: The Descent of Canadian Politics from Macdonald to Mulroney*, Toronto: HarperCollins, 284n.
Boardman, R., ed. (1992) *Canadian Environmental Policy: Ecosystems, Politics, and Process*, Toronto: Oxford University Press.
Boulding, E. (1988) *Building a Global Civic Culture: Education for an Interdependent World*, New York: Teachers College Press, p. 136.
Bourassa, R. (1985) *Power from the North*, Scarborough, Ont.: Prentice Hall.
Boutros-Ghali, B. (1992) *An Agenda for Peace: Preventative Diplomacy, Peacemaking and Peace-keeping*, New York: UN.
Boychuk, R. (1992) "Descending from the Earth Summit", *Canadian Forum*, October 1992, p. 35.
Boyle, K. (1995) "Stock-taking on Human Rights: The World Conference on Human Rights, Vienna 1993", Special Issue on Human Rights and Politics, *Political Studies* XLIII: 81.
Broadhead, L.-A. (2001) "Canada as a Rogue State: Its Shameful Performance on Climate Change", *International Journal* LVI(3): 461–480.
Brooks, D. B. and L. Douglas (1975) "Population, Resources, Environment: the View from the UN", *Canadian Forum*, January: 6.
Bull, H. (1977) *The Anarchical Society*, London: Macmillan, p. 162.
—— (1983–1984) *Justice in International Relations: The Hagey Lecture*, Ont.: University of Waterloo, p. 14.
Bunch, C. and S. Fried (1996) "Beijing '95: Moving Women's Human Rights from Margin to Center", *Signs: Journal of Women in Culture and Society* 20: 7.
Bunch, C. and N. Reilly (1994) *Demanding Accountability: The Global Campaign and Vienna Tribunal for Women's Human Rights*, New Brunswick, NJ/New York: Rutgers University Center for Women's Global Leadership/UNIFEM.
Bunch, C., M. Dutt and S. Fried (1996) "Beijing '95: Global Referendum on the Human Rights of Women", *Canadian Women Studies* 16(3): 9.
Burley, A.-M. (1993) "Regulating the World: Multilateralism, International Law, and the Projection of the New Deal Regulatory State", in J. G. Ruggie, ed., *Multilateralism Matters: The Theory and Praxis of an Institutional Form*, New York: Columbia University Press, pp. 125–147.
Buzan, B. and R. Little (1999) "Beyond Westphalia?: Capitalism After the Fall", in M. Cox, K. Booth and T. Dunne, eds., *The Interregnum: Controversies in World Politics 1989–1999*, Cambridge: Cambridge University Press, p. 99.

Cairns, A. C. (1992) *Charter versus Federalism: The Dilemmas of Constitutional Reform*, Montreal: McGill-Queen's University Press, p. 31.
—— (2003) "Afterword: International Dimensions of the Citizen Issue for Indigenous Peoples/Nations", *Citizenship Studies* 7(4): 497–512.
Camilleri, J. A. (1995) "State, Civil Society, and Economy", in J. Camilleri, A. P. Jarvis and A. J. Paolin, eds., *Reflections on the State in Transition: Reimagining Political Space*, Boulder, Colo.: Lynne Rienner, p. 211.
Camilleri, J. and J. Falk (1992) *The End of Sovereignty?*, Aldershot: Edward Elgar.
Canada, House of Commons, Standing Committee on the Environment (1992) *Minutes of Proceedings and Evidence*, 7 May 1992, 74: 71.
Canada, House of Commons (1994) "A Model Forest Nation in the Making: Report of the Standing Committee on Natural Resources", Ottawa, June 1994, p. 46.
Canadian Institute of International Affairs (1974) in co-operation with The Family Planning Federation of Canada and the Inter-Church Project on Population, *Public Consultation on Population: A Report to the Government of Canada*, Toronto: Canadian Institute of International Affairs.
Canadian Secretariat WCAR (2000) "Canada's Consultations for the World Conference against Racism", draft discussion paper, Canadian Secretariat WCAR, Department of Canadian Heritage, Multiculturalism, Government of Canada, September 2000.
Canadian Women's Committee on Reproduction, Population and Development (1994) "A Canadian Women's Report on Canadian Policies and Practices in the Areas of Reproduction, Population and Development", August 1994, p. 21.
Capeling-Alakija, S. (1996) "Politics, Paradox, and the International Women's Movement", in A. Dworkin and S. Capeling-Alakija, eds., *The Walter Gordon Series in Public Policy, The Future of Feminism*, Massey College, University of Toronto, 2 May 1995: Toronto.
Caporaso, J. (1989) *The Elusive State: International and Comparative Perspectives*, Newbury Park, Calif.: Sage.
Carson, R. (1962) *Silent Spring*, Boston: Houghton Mifflin.
Cerny, P. G. (2000) "Structuring the Political Arena: Public Goods, States and Governance in a Globalizing World", in R. Palan, ed., *Global Political Economy: Contemporary Theories*, London: Routledge, p. 34.
Chant, D.A. (1972) "No Empty Ritual, Conference Went Beyond its Limited Goals", *International Perspectives* (September–October): 11–12.
Chatterjee, P. and M. Finger (1994) *The Earth Brokers: Power Politics and World Development*, London: Routledge, p. 112.
Chinkin, C. (2000) "Gender and International Society: Law and Policy", in R. Thakur and E. Newman, eds., *New Millennium, New Perspectives: The United Nations, Security, and Governance*, Tokyo: United Nations University Press, pp. 242–260.
Chrétien, J. (1991) "Pursuing a Vision: Canadian Foreign Policy and the New Internationalism", notes for a speech by the Hon. Jean Chrétien, Leader of the Liberal Party of Canada, George Ignatieff Theatre, Trinity College, Toronto, Ontario, 14 June 1991, p. 7.

CIDA (1987) *CIDA in the Population GAME*, Ottawa: CIDA.
—— (1989) *Population Research Review*, Ottawa: CIDA.
—— (1992) *Bangladesh Country Program*, Ottawa: CIDA.
—— (1993) "Population and Sustainable Development: CIDA's Draft Statement", July 1993, Ottawa: CIDA.
Clark, A. M. (1995) "Non-Governmental Organizations and Their Influence on International Society", *Journal of International Affairs* 48(2): 512–517.
—— (2001a) *Diplomacy of Conscience: Amnesty International and Changing Human Rights Norms*, Princeton: Princeton University Press.
Clark, I. (2001b) *The Post–Cold War Order: The Spoils of Peace*, Oxford: Oxford University Press.
Clark, A. M., E. J. Friedman and K. Hochstetler (1998) "The Sovereign Limits of Global Civil Society: A Comparison of NGO Participation in UN World Conferences on the Environment, Human Rights, and Women", *World Politics* 51(1): 26.
Clarkson, S. (1991) "Disjunctions: Free Trade and the Paradox of Canadian Development", in D. Drache and M. S. Gertler, eds., *The New Era of Global Competition: State Policy and Market Power*, Montreal and Kingston: McGill-Queen's Press, p. 116.
Claude Jr., I. L. (1984) *Swords into Ploughshares: The Problems and Prospects of International Organization*, New York: Random House, p. 66.
Commission on Global Governance (1995) *Our Global Neighborhood: The Commission on Global Governance*, New York: Oxford University Press, p. XVI.
Conca, K., M. Albert and G. D. Dabelko, eds. (1998) *Green Planet Blues: Environmental Politics from Stockholm to Kyoto*, Boulder, Colo.: Westview Press.
Constantinou, C. M. (1996) *On the Way to Diplomacy*, Borderlines, vol. 7, Minneapolis/London: University of Minnesota Press, p. 4.
Consultation between The United Nations and Non-Governmental Organizations (1949) *United Nations Studies* 3, New York: Interim Committee of the Non-Governmental Organizations for Consultative Status with the United Nations, Carnegie Endowment For International Peace.
Cook, R. J. (1994) *Human Rights of Women: National and International Perspectives*, Philadelphia: University of Pennsylvania Press.
—— (2001) "Effectiveness of the Beijing Conference in Fostering Compliance with International Law Regarding Women", in M. G. Schechter, ed., *The United Nations-sponsored World Conferences: Focus on Impact and Follow-up*, Tokyo: United Nations University Press, pp. 65–84.
Cooper, A. F. (1993) "Questions of Sovereignty: Canada and the Widening International Agenda", *Behind the Headlines* 50(3), Toronto: CIIA, pp. 1–16.
—— (1997a) *Canadian Foreign Policy: Old Habits and New Directions*, Scarborough, Ont.: Prentice Hall.
—— (1997b) *Niche Diplomacy: Middle Powers after the Cold War*, Basingstoke: Macmillan.
—— (2000) "Between Will and Capability: Canada and the Zaire/Great Lakes Initiative", in A. F. Cooper and G. Hayes, eds., *Worthwhile Initiatives? Canadian Mission-Oriented Diplomacy*, Toronto: Irwin Press, pp. 64–78.

—— (2001) "Vertical Limits: A Foreign Ministry of the Future", *Journal of Canadian Studies* 35(24): 111–129.

—— (2002) "La politique étrangère du Canada après le 11 septembre: Une analyse préliminaire", *Etudes internationales* XXXIII(4): 629–646.

Cooper, A. F. and J.-S. Fritz (1992) "Bringing the NGOs In: UNCED and the Evolution of Canada's International Environmental Policy", *International Journal* XLVII(4): 796–817.

Cooper, A. F. and B. Hocking (2000) "Diplomacy and the Re-calibration of State–Societal Relations", *Global Society* 14(3): 361–376.

Cooper, A. F. and L. Pal (1996) "Human Rights and Security Policy", in G. B. Doern, L. A. Pal and B. Tomlin, eds., *Border Crossings: The Internationalization of Canadian Public Policy*, Toronto: Oxford University Press, pp. 222–223.

Cooper, A. F., J. R. English and R. Thakur, eds. (2002) *Enhancing Global Governance: Toward a New Diplomacy?*, Tokyo: United Nations University Press.

Cooper, A. F., R. A. Higgott and K. R. Nossal (1993) *Relocating Middle Powers: Australia and Canada in a Changing World Order*, Vancouver, BC: UBC Press.

Cox, R. W. (1969) "The Executive Head: An Essay on Leadership in International Organization", *International Organization* XXIII(2): 205–230.

—— (1986) "Social Forces, States and World Order: Beyond International Relations Theory", in R. O. Keohane, ed., *Neorealism and its Critics*, New York: Columbia University Press.

—— (1991) "The Global Political Economy and Social Choice", in D. Drache and M. Gertler, eds., *The New Era of Global Competition: State Policy and Market Power*, Montreal: McGill-Queen's Press, pp 335–350.

—— (1992a) "Towards a Post-Hegemonic Conceptualization of World Order: Reflections on the Relevance of Ibn Khaldun", in E.-O. Cziempel and J. N. Rosenau, eds., *Governance without Government: Order and Change in World Politics*, Cambridge: Cambridge University Press, pp. 132–159.

—— (1992b) "Global Perestroika", in R. Miliband and L. Panitch, eds., *New World Order? The Socialist Register*, London: Merlin, pp. 26–43.

—— (1993) "Structural Issues of Global Governance: Implications for Europe", in S. Gill, ed., *Gramsci, Historical Materialism, and International Relations*, Cambridge: Cambridge University Press, p. 263.

—— (1994a) "Political Economy and World Order?" in R. Stubbs and G. R. D. Underhill, eds., *Political Economy and the Changing World Order*, Toronto: McClelland & Stewart, pp. 45–59.

—— (1994b) "Global Restructuring", in R. Stubbs and G. R. D. Underhill, eds., *Political Economy and the Changing World Order*, Toronto: McClelland & Stewart.

—— (1995) "Critical Political Economy", in B. Hettne, *International Political Economy: Understanding Global Disorder*, Halifax, NS: Fernwood, pp. 42–43.

—— (1997a) "Global Structural Change and Multilateralism" in S. Gill, ed., *Globalization, Democratization and Multilateralism*, New York: St. Martin's Press, p. 528.

—— (1997b) "An Alternative Approach to Multilateralism for the Twenty-First Century", *Global Governance* 3(1): 103–116.

────── (2000) "Political Economy and World Order: Problems of Power and Knowledge at the Turn of the Millennium", in R. Stubbs and G. R. D. Underhill, eds., *Political Economy and the Changing Global Order*, Don Mills, Ont.: Oxford University Press, p. 25.

Cox, R. W. and M G. Schechter (2002) *The Political Economy of a Plural World: Critical Reflections on Power, Morals and Civilization*, London: Routledge.

Crane, B. (1994) "International Population Institutions: Adaptation to a Changing World Order", in P. Haas, R. Keohane, and M. Levy, eds., *Institutions for the Earth: Sources of Effective International Environmental Protection*, Cambridge: MIT Press, pp. 351–396.

Crozier, M., S. Huntington and J. Watanuki (1973) *Crisis of Democracy: Report of the Governability of Democracies to the Trilateral Commission*, New York: New York University Press.

Day, S. (1996) "Women's Sexual Autonomy: Universality, Sexual Rights and Sexual Orientation", *Canadian Women Studies* 16(3): 53.

Deacon, B. (1999) "Social Policy in a Global Context", in A. Hurrell and N. Woods, eds., *Inequality, Globalization, and World Politics*, Oxford: Oxford University Press, pp. 211–247.

Deacon, B., M. Hulse and P. Stubbs (1997) *Global Social Policy: International Organizations and the Future of Welfare*, London: Sage.

Dean, J., ed. (1997) *Feminism and the New Democracy: Resiting the Political*, London: Sage, p. 2.

Department of External Affairs and International Trade (1991) *Foreign Policy Themes and Priorities, 1991–92 Update*, Ottawa: EAITC, December, p. 2.

Der Derian, J. (1987) *On Diplomacy: A Genealogy of Western Estrangement*, London: Basil Blackwell.

Detter de Lupis, I. (1989) "The Human Environment: Stockholm and its Follow Up", in P. Taylor and A. J. R. Groom, eds., *Global Issues in the United Nations' Framework*, Basingstoke: Macmillan, p. 212.

Dewar, E. (1995) *Cloak of Green*, Toronto: James Lorimer, chap. 23.

DFAIT (1994) "Working Groups", National Forum on Canada's International Relations, 21 and 22 March 1994, Ottawa: DFAIT, mimeo.

────── (1995) *Canada in the World: Government Statement*, Canada: DFAIT, pp. 40, 42.

Dias, C. J. (2001) "The United Nations World Conference on Human Rights: Evaluation, Monitoring, and Review", in M. G. Schechter, ed., *The United Nations-sponsored World Conferences: Focus on Impact and Follow-up*, Tokyo: United Nations University Press, pp. 29–62.

Dobell, P. C. (1985) *Canada in World Affairs XVII, 1971–1973*, Toronto: The Canadian Institute of International Affairs.

Doern, G. B. (1992) "Johnny-green-latelies: the Mulroney Environmental Record", in F. Abele, ed., *How Ottawa Spends: The Politics of Competitiveness 1992–93*, Ottawa: Carleton University Press, pp. 353–376.

────── (1993) *Green Diplomacy: How Environmental Policy Decisions are Made*, Toronto: C.D. Howe Institute, pp. 71–80, 90–91.

Doern, G. B. and J. Kirton (1996) "Foreign Policy", in G. B. Doern, L. A. Pal and B. Tomlin, eds., *Border Crossings: The Internationalization of Canadian Public Policy*, Toronto: Oxford University Press, p. 256.

Doern, G. B. and B. W. Tomlin (1991) *The Free Trade Story: Faith and Fear*, Toronto: Stoddart, p. 272.

Donnelly, J. (1981) "Recent Trends in UN Human Rights Activity: Description and Polemic", *International Organization* 35(4): 634–635.

——— (1989) *Universal Human Rights in Theory and Practice*, Ithaca: Cornell University Press, pp. 47, 51–54.

——— (1993) *International Human Rights*, Boulder, Colo.: Westview Press.

Donnelly, J. and R. E. Howard (1986) "Human Dignity, Human Rights, and Political Regimes", *American Political Science Review* 80(3): 801–817.

Dorsey, E. (1997) "The Global Women's Movement: Articulating a New Vision of Global Governance" in P. F. Diehl, ed., *The Politics of Global Governance: International Organizations in an Interdependent World*, Boulder, Colo.: Lynne Rienner, pp. 335–359.

Doty, R. L. (1996) *Imperial Encounters: The Problems in Representation in North-South Relations*, Minneapolis: University of Minnesota Press, p. 126.

Duffield, M. (1997) "NGO Relief in War Zones: Towards an Analysis of the New Aid Paradigm", *Third World Quarterly* 18(3): 527–542.

Dunne, T. (2000) "Colonial Encounters in International Relations: Reading Wright, Writing Australia", in S. O. Vandersluis, ed., *The State and Identity Construction in International Relations*, London: Millennium/Macmillan, pp. 109–128.

Eayrs, J. (1971) *Diplomacy and its Discontents*, Toronto: University of Toronto, p. 69.

Edwards, M. and D. Hulme, eds. (1996) *Beyond the Magic Bullet: NGO Performance and Accountability in the Post–Cold War World*, West Hartford, Conn.: Kumarian.

Emmerij, L., R. Jolly and T. G. Weiss (2001) *Ahead of the Curve? UN Ideas and Global Challenges*, Bloomington, Ind.: Indiana University Press.

Evans, T. (1997) "Democratization and Human Rights", in A. G. McGrew, ed., *The Transformation of Democracy?: Globalization and Territorial Democracy*, Milton Keynes: Open University Press, pp. 122–148.

——— (2001) *The Politics of Human Rights: A Global Perspective*, London: Pluto, p. 95.

Evans, P. B., H. K. Jacobson and R. D. Putnam, eds. (1993) *Double-Edged Diplomacy: International Bargaining and Domestic Politics*, Berkeley, Calif.: University of California Press.

Falk, R. A. (1994) "Democratizing, Internationalizing and Globalizing", in Y. Sakamoto, ed., *Global Transformation: Challenges to the State System*, Tokyo: United Nations University Press, p. 477.

——— (1995) *On Humane Governance: Toward a New Global Politics*, University Park, Penn.: Pennsylvania State Press.

——— (2000) "The Quest for Humane Governance in an Era of Globalization", in D. Kalb et al., eds., *The Ends of Globalization: Bringing Society Back*, Lanham, Md.: Rowan and Littlefield.

Falk, R. A., S. S. Kim and S. Mendlovitz, eds. (1991) *The United Nations and a Just World Order*, Boulder, Colo.: Westview.
Ferretti, J. (1992) "Report on UNCED", 23 June 1992, memo.
Finestone S. (1995) *Notes for an Address by the Hon. Sheila Finestone, Secretary of State (Status of Women and Multiculturalism), at the Fourth World Conference on Women, Beijing China, September 6, 1995*, Ottawa: Status of Women, 1995.
Finger, M. (1994) "NGOs and Transformation: Beyond Social Movement Theory", in T. Princen and M. Finger, eds., *Environmental NGOs in World Politics: Linking the Local and the Global*, London: Routledge, pp. 34–35.
Finkle, J. L. and B. B. Crane (1975) "The Politics of Bucharest: Population, Development and the New International Economic Order", *Population and Development Review* 1(3): 87–114.
Finnemore, M. and K. Sikkink (1998) "International Norm Dynamics and Political Change", *International Organization* 52(4): 887–917.
Fletcher, C., ed. (1994) *Aboriginal Self-Determination in Australia*, Canberra: Aboriginal Studies Press.
Florini, A. M. (2000) "Lessons Learned", in A. M. Florini, ed., *The Third Force: The Rise of Transnational Civil Society*, Washington, DC: Carnegie Endowment for International Peace, p. 226.
Fomerand, J. (1999) "UN Conferences; Media Events or Genuine Diplomacy?", in J. P. Muldoon Jr. et al., eds., *Multilateral Diplomacy and the United Nations Today*, Boulder, Colo.: Westview, p. 125.
Forsythe, D. P. (2000) *Human Rights in International Relations*, Cambridge, UK: Cambridge University Press, pp. 55–83.
Foster, J. W. and A. Anand, eds. (1999) *Whose World Is It Anyway: Civil Society, the United Nations and the Multilateral Future*, Ottawa: The United Nations Association in Canada.
Fowler, R. (1996) "Reflections: Ambassadors' Round Table", in F. Osler Hampson and M. Appel Molot, eds., *Big Enough to be Heard: Canada Among Nations*, Ottawa: Carleton University Press, p. 35.
Fréchette, L. (1996) "Reflections: Ambassadors 'Round Table'", in F. Osler Hampson and M. Appel Molot, eds., *Big Enough to be Heard: Canada Among Nations*, Ottawa: Carleton University Press.
Fredriksson, G. (1986) *Olof Palme*, Lund: Svenska Institutet, pp. 12–13.
Freeman, M. (1995) "Human Rights: Asia and the West", in J. T. H. Tang, ed., *Human Rights and International Relations in the Asia-Pacific Region*, London: Pinter, p. 15.
Freeman, G. P. (1998) "The Decline of Sovereignty? Politics and Immigration Restriction in Liberal States", in C. Joppke, ed., *Challenge to the Nation-State*, Oxford: Oxford University Press, pp. 86–108.
Friends of the Earth (1972) *The Stockholm Conference – Only One Earth: An Introduction to the Politics of Survival*, London: Earth Island/Angus and Robertson.
Fukuyama, F. (1992) *The End of History and the Last Man*, New York: Free Press.
——— (1993) "Capitalism and Democracy: The Missing Link", in L. J. Diamond

and M. Plattner, eds., *Capitalism, Socialism and Democracy Revisited*, Baltimore, Md.: Johns Hopkins University, pp. 94–104.

Gaddis, J. L. (1992) "The Cold War, The Long Peace, and the Future", in M. J. Hogan, ed., *The End of the Cold War: Its Meaning and Implications*, Cambridge: Cambridge University Press, p. 22.

Gaer, F. D. (1995) "Reality Check: Human Rights NGOs Confront Governments at the UN", *Third World Quarterly* 16(3): 389–404.

George, J. (1994) *Discourses of Global Politics: A Critical (Re)Introduction to International Relations*, Boulder, Colo.: Lynne Rienner, pp. 197–200.

Gill, S. (1995a) "Globalization, Market Civilization and Disciplinary Neo-liberalism", *Millennium* 24(3): 72, 412.

—— (1995b) "Theorizing the Interregnum: Double Movement and Global Politics in the 1990s", in B. Hettne, ed., *International Political Economy: Understanding Global Disorder*, Halifax, NS: Fernwood, p. 79.

—— (1997) "Global Structural Change and Multilateralism", in S. Gill, ed., *Globalization, Democratization and Multilateralism*, New York: St. Martin's Press.

Gillespie, P. (1991) "Development Prospects in Bangladesh: Critical Options for Canadian Aid", *Canadian Journal of Development Studies* XII(1): 192–193.

Goetz, A. M. (1991) "Feminism and the Claim to Know: Contradictions in Feminist Approaches to Women in Development", in R. Grant and K. Newland, eds., *Gender and International Relations*, Bloomington, Ind.: Indiana University Press, p. 145.

Gordenker, L. and T. Weiss (1997) "Devolving Responsibilities: A Framework for Analysing NGOs and Services", *Third World Quarterly* 18(3): 443–455.

Grayson, J., ed. (1995) *The World's Forests: International Initiatives Since Rio*, Oxford: Commonwealth Forestry Association.

Greenpeace International (1992) *Beyond UNCED*, Amsterdam: Greenpeace International.

Greenspon, E. and A. Wilson-Smith (1996) *Double Vision: The Inside Story of the Liberals in Power*, Toronto: Doubleday.

Griffiths, F., ed. (1987) *Politics of the Northwest Passage*, Montreal: McGill-Queen's University Press.

Grunberg, I. and S. Khan (2000) *Globalization: The United Nations Development Dialogue: Finance, Trade, Poverty, Peace-building*, Tokyo: United Nations University Press, pp. 129–196.

Gurtov, M. (1993) "Open Borders: A Global Humanist Approach to the Refugee Crisis", *World Development* 19(5): 485–496.

Hall, J. A. (1996) *International Orders*, Cambridge: Polity Press.

Halliday, B. (1992) "Testimony to the Sub-Committee on Development and Human Rights, Standing Committee on External Affairs and International Trade", *Minutes of Proceedings and Evidence*, 25 March 1992, 16: 21.

Halliday, F. (1994) *Rethinking International Relations*, Vancouver: UBC Press, pp. 228–235.

—— (1997) "A New World Myth", *New Statesman*, 4 April, pp. 42–43.

Hanson, E. O. (1987) *The Catholic Church in World Politics*, Princeton: Princeton University Press.
Harris, N. (1986) *The End of the Third World: Newly Industrializing Countries and the Decline of an Ideal*, Harmondsworth: Penguin.
Hartman, B. (1987) *Reproductive Rights and Wrongs: The Global Politics of Population Control and Contraceptive Choice*, New York: Harper and Row.
Held, D. (1991) *Democracy, the Nation-State and the Global System*, in *Political Theory Today*, Cambridge: Polity Press.
Held, D., A. McGrew, D. Goldblatt and J. Perraton (1999) *Global Transformations: Politics, Economics and Culture*, Cambridge: Polity Press, p. 85.
Herter, C. A. and J. E. Binder (1973) "The Role of the Secretariat in Multilateral Negotiation: The Case of Maurice Strong and the 1972 UN Conference on the Human Environment", Johns Hopkins University, Foreign Policy Institute, Case Studies Number 21.
Heschel, S. (1995) "Feminists Gain at Cairo Population Conference", *Dissent*, Winter: 15–18.
Hettne, B. (1995) "Introduction", in B. Hettne, ed., *International Political Economy: Understanding Global Disorder*, Halifax, NS: Fernwood, p. 24.
Higer, A. (1999) "International Women's Activism and the 1994 Cairo Conference", in M. Meyer and E. Prugl, eds., *Gender Politics in Global Governance*, Lanham, Md.: Rowman and Littlefield.
Higgott, R. (2001) "Economic Globalization and Global Governance: Towards a Post-Washington Consensus?" in V. Rittberger, ed., *Global Governance and the United Nations System*, Tokyo: United Nations University Press, pp. 137–138.
Higgott, R. and S. Reich (1997) "Intellectual Order for the Global Order: Understanding Non-State Actors and Authority in the Global System", paper presented at the Inaugural Conference Warwick University, Centre for the Study of Globalisation and Regionalisation, 31 October–1 November 1997, p. 3.
Higgott, R. A., G. R. D. Underhill and A. Bieler, eds. (1999) *Non-State Actors and Authority in the Global System*, London: Routledge.
Hildyard, N. (1995) "Foxes in Charge of the Chickens", in W. Sachs, ed., *Global Ecology: A New Arena of Political Conflict*, London: Zed Books.
Hirst, P. and G. Thompson (1996) *Globalization in Question: The International Economy and the Possibility of Governance*, Cambridge: Polity Press.
Hobbins, A. J., ed. (1994) *On the Edge of Greatness: The Diaries of John Humphrey*, Montreal: McGill-Queen's University Press.
Hocking, B. (1995) "Beyond 'Newness' and 'Decline': The Development of Catalytic Diplomacy", Discussion Papers in Diplomacy No. 10, Centre for the Study of Diplomacy, University of Leicester, October, 1995.
—— (1999a) "Foreign Ministries: Redefining the Gatekeeper Role", in *Foreign Ministries. Change and Adaptation*, London: Macmillan, pp. 1–15.
—— (1999b) "Catalytic Diplomacy: Beyond 'Newness' and 'Decline'", in J. Melissen, ed., *Innovation in Diplomatic Practice*, Basingstoke: Macmillan.
—— (2000) "Globalization, National Diplomatic Systems and Global Policy Networks", paper delivered to the International Political Science Association Congress, Quebec City, 1–5 August 2000.

Hoffmann, S. (1981) *Duties Beyond Borders: On the Limits and Possibilities of Ethical International Politics*, Syracuse, NY: Syracuse University Press.

—— (1990) "A New World and Its Troubles", *Foreign Affairs* 69: 115–122.

—— (1998) *World Disorders: Troubled Peace in the Post–Cold War Era*, Lanham, Md.: Rowan & Littlefield.

Holmes, J. W. (1970) *The Better Part of Valour: Essays on Canadian Diplomacy*, Toronto: McClelland and Stewart, p. vii.

Holsti, K. J. (1993) "International Relations at the End of the Millennium", *Review of International Studies* 19(4): 401–408.

—— (1999) "Scholarship in an Era of Anxiety: The Study of International Politics during the Cold War", in T. Dunne, M. Cox and K. Booth, eds., *The Eighty Year Crisis; International Relations, 1919–1999*, Cambridge: Cambridge University Press, p. 289.

Humphrey, J. (1984) *Human Rights and the United Nations: A Great Adventure*, Dobbs Ferry: Transnational Publishers.

Humphries, D. (1996) *Forest Politics: The Evolution of International Cooperation*, London: Earthscan, p. 160.

Hunter, L. (1992) NDP MP for Saamich-Gulf Islands, *House of Commons, Debates*, 7 May 1992, p. 10339.

Huntington, S. (1993) "The Clash of Civilizations?" *Foreign Affairs* 72(3): 22, 24, 29, 45.

—— (1996) *Clash of Civilizations and the Remaking of World Order*, New York: Simon & Schuster.

Ignatieff, M. (1993) *Blood and Belonging: Journeys into the New Nationalism*, Toronto: Penguin.

—— (2000) *The Rights Revolution*, Toronto: House of Anansi, pp. 82–84.

Immerfall, S. (1998) "Territory and Territoriality in the Globalizing Society: An Introduction", in S. Immerfall, ed., *Territoriality in the Globalizing Society: One Place or None?*, Berlin: Springer, p. 7.

Immigration and Refugee Board of Canada (1993) *Guidelines on Women Refugee Claimants Fearing Gender-Related Persecution*, March 9, Ottawa: Immigration and Refugee Board, 1993.

International Women's Health Coalition (1994) *Women's Voices 1994: Women's Declaration on Population Politics (In Preparation for the International Conference on Population and Development 1994)*, New York.

Jacobson, D. (1997) *Rights Across Borders: Immigration and the Decline of Citizenship*, Baltimore, Md.: Johns Hopkins University Press.

James, A. (1980) "Diplomacy and International Society", *International Relations* 6(6): 932.

—— (1993) "Diplomacy", *Review of International Studies* 19(1): 91–100.

Jervis, R. (1993) "International Primacy: Is the Game Worth the Candle?" *International Security* 17(4): 52–67.

Joffe, P. (1995) "Sovereign Injustice: Forcible Inclusion of the James Bay Cree Territory into a Sovereign Quebec", Nemaska: Grand Council of the Cree.

Johnson, S. (1995) *The Politics of Population: The International Conference on Population and Development: Cairo 1994*, London: Earthscan.

Jolly, R. (1997) "Human Development: The World after Copenhagen", *Global Governance* 32(2): 233–248.

Jurgensmeyer, M. (1994) *The New Cold War? Religious Nationalism Confronts the Secular State*, Berkeley, Calif.: University of California Press.

Kaufman, J. (1988) *Conference Diplomacy*, Dordrecht: Martinus Nijhoff/UNITAR, p. 100.

Kaul, I., I. Grunberg and M. A. Stern, eds. (1999) *Global Public Goods: International Cooperation in the 21st Century*, New York: Oxford University Press, p. 451.

Keating, T. (2002) *Canada and World Order: The Multilateralist Tradition in Canadian Foreign Policy*, Don Mills, Ont.: Oxford University Press.

Keck, M. and K. Sikkink (1998) *Activists across Borders: Advocacy Networks in International Politics*, Ithaca, NY: Cornell University Press.

Keeble, E. and H. A. Smith (1999) *(Re)Defining Traditions: Gender and Canadian Foreign Policy*, Halifax, NS: Fernwood.

Keohane, R. O. (1989) *International Institutions and State Power*, Boulder, Colo.: Westview.

——— (1990) "Multilateralism: An Agenda for Research", *International Journal* 45(4): 731–764.

——— (1993) "Sovereignty, Interdependence and International Institutions", in L. B. Miller and M. J. Smith, eds., *Ideas and Ideals: Essays on Politics in Honor of Stanley Hoffmann*, Boulder, Colo.: Westview, pp. 91–107.

——— (1995) "Hobbes's Dilemma and Institutional Change in World Politics: Sovereignty in International Society", in H.-H. Holm and G. Sorensen, eds., *Whose World Order?: Uneven Globalization and the End of the Cold War*, Boulder, Colo.: Westview Press.

Khagram, S., J. V. Riker and K. Sikkink, eds. (2002) *Restructuring World Politics: Transnational Social Movements, Networks, and Norms*, Minneapolis, MN: University of Minnesota Press.

Kirton, J. (1988) "Managing Global Conflict: Canada and International Summitry", in M. Appel Molot and B. Tomlin, eds., *Canada Among Nations, 1987: A World Of Conflict*, Toronto: James Lorimer, p. 33.

——— (1997) "Foreign Policy under The Liberals: Prime Ministerial Leadership in the Chrétien Government's Foreign Policy-Making Process", in F. Osler Hampson, M. Appel Molot and M. Rudner, eds., *Canada Among Nations 1997: Asia Pacific Face-off*, Ottawa: Carleton University Press, pp. 21–50.

——— (2002) "Canada as a Principal Summit Power: G-7/8 Concert Diplomacy from Halifax 1995 to Kananaskis 2002", in N. Hillmer and M. Appel Molot, eds., *A Fading Power. Canada Among Nations 2002*, Toronto: University of Oxford Press, p. 226.

Kissinger, H. (1994) *Diplomacy*, New York: Simon & Schuster.

——— (2001) *Does America need a Foreign Policy?: Diplomacy for the 21st Century*, New York: Simon & Schuster.

Knelman, F. H. (1972–1973) "Stockholm in Retrospective", *International Journal* 27: 28–49.

Knutsen, T. L. (1999) *The Rise and Fall of World Orders*, Manchester: Manchester University Press.

Kolk, A. (1996) *Forests in International Politics*, Utrecht: International Books.

Korbin, S. J. (1998) "The MAI and the Clash of Globalizations", *Foreign Policy* 112: 97–109.

Krasner, S. D. (1999) *Sovereignty: Organized Hypocrisy*, Princeton: Princeton University Press.

Kuptana, R. (1993) President, Inuit Tapirisat of Canada, "Speaking Notes for the North American Region Indigenous Nations U.N. Satellite Meeting", 7 April 1993, pp. 1, 4.

Langhorne, R. (1998) "Diplomacy Beyond the Primacy of the State", paper presented at the annual conference of the International Studies Association, Minneapolis, 20 March 1998.

Leclair, M. (1994) Chief Administrative Officer, Métis National Council, "Testimony before the Special Joint Committee of the Senate and the House of Commons on Reviewing Canadian Foreign Policy", *Minutes of Proceedings and Evidence*, 9 June 1994, 36: 32

Lennon, K. and M. Whitford (1994) "Introduction", in *Knowing the Difference*, Routledge: London, p. 12.

Liberal Party of Canada (1993) *Liberal Foreign Policy Handbook*, Ottawa: House of Commons, Office of the Leader of the Opposition.

Liberal Roundtable (1992), notes on "Liberal Roundtable" on UNCED, chaired by Lloyd Axworthy and Charles Caccia, East Block, Parliament Hill, Ottawa, 19 February 1992.

Lipschutz, R. D. (1992) "Reconstructing World Politics: The Emergence of Global Civil Society", *Millennium: Journal of International Studies* 2(3): 398–399.

Lyons, G. M. (1989) "In Search of Racial Equality: The Elimination of Racial Discrimination", in P. Taylor and A. J. R. Groom, eds., *Global Issues in the United Nations' Framework*, Basingstoke: Macmillan, pp. 89–90.

Macdonald, D. and H. Smith (1999–2000) "Promises Made, Promises Broken: Questioning Canada's Commitments in Climate Change", *International Journal* LV(1): 107–124.

Mahbubani, K. (1992) "The West versus the Rest", *National Interest* 28: 3–13.

Mahoney, K. (1992) "Human Rights and Canadian Foreign Policy", *International Journal* 47(3): 556, 573.

Mahoney, K. E. and P. Mahoney, eds. (1993) *Human Rights in the Twenty-First Century: A Global Challenge*, Dordrecht: M. Nijhoff.

Malone, D. (2001) "Foreign Policy Reviews", *International Journal* LVI(4): 568.

Mandelbaum, M. (1996) "Foreign Policy as Social Work", *Foreign Policy* 75(1): 16–32.

Marantz, D. (1996) "People or Peoples: Equality, Autonomy and Self-Determination: The Issues at Stake of the International Decade of the World's Indigenous People", Essays in Human Rights and Democratic Development, Paper #5, Montreal: International Centre for Human Rights and Democratic Development, p. 26.

Marchi, S. (1994) "Notes for an Address by The Honourable Sergio Marchi, Minister of Citizenship and Immigration", pp. 3–4.

Marsden, L. (1992) "Timing and Presence: Getting Women's Issues on the Trade Agenda", Working Paper Series: Gender, Science and Development Programme, International Federation of Institutes for Advanced Study, Toronto, July 1992.

Marshall, Sir Peter (1999) *Positive Diplomacy*, Houndmills, Hampshire: Macmillan, p. 49.

Mathews, J. T. (1997) "Power Shift", *Foreign Affairs* 76: 52–55.

Mawani, N. (1993) "The Factual and Legal Legitimacy of Addressing Gender Issues", *Refugee* 13(4): 7–10.

Mercredi, O. and M. E. Turpel (1993) *In the Rapids: Navigating the Future of First Nations*, Toronto: Viking.

May, E. (1990) *Paradise Won: The Struggle for South Moresby*, Toronto: McClelland & Stewart, pp. 178–179, 232.

—— (1992) "Report on Participation in the Earth Summit", to the CEN International Affairs Caucus, July 30, 1992, mimeo.

McBride, S. and J. Shields (1997) *Dismantling a Nation: The Transition to Corporate Rule in Canada*, 2nd ed., Halifax, NS: Fernwood.

McCormick, J. (1989) *The Global Environmental Movement*, London: Bellhaven.

McQuaig, L. (1998) *The Cult of Impotence: Selling the Myth of Powerlessness in the Global Economy*, Toronto: Viking.

Mingst, K. A. and C. Warkentin (1996) "What Difference Does Culture Make To Multilateral Negotiations?" *Global Governance* 2(2): 169–188.

Mittelman, J. H. (1995) "Rethinking the International Division of Labour in the Context of Globalization", *Third World Quarterly* 16(2): 273.

Mohanty, C. T. (1991) "Under Western Eyes: Feminist Scholarship and Colonial Discourse", in C. T. Mohanty, A. Russo and L. Torres, eds., *Third World Women and the Politics of Feminism*, Bloomington, Ind.: Indiana University Press, pp. 51–80.

Morgan, R. (1996) "The NGO Forum: Good News and Bad", *Women's Studies Quarterly* 1 and 2: 46, 47.

Morphet, S. (1996) "NGOs and the Environment", in P. Willetts, ed., *The Conscience of the World. The Influence of Non-Governmental Organisations in the UN System*, London: Hurst, pp. 98–146.

Morss, E. R. (1991) "The New Global Players: How They Compete and Collaborate", *World Development* 19(1): 44–57.

Moses, T. (1994) Cree Ambassador to the UN, "Testimony before the Special Joint Committee of the Senate and the House of Commons on Reviewing Canadian Foreign Policy", *Minutes of Proceedings and Evidence*, 9 June 36: 25.

Moynihan, D. (1978) *A Dangerous Place*, Boston: Little, Brown.

—— (1979) "The Politics of Human Rights", in W. Laqueur and B. Rubin, eds., *Human Rights Reader*, Philadelphia: Temple University Press, p. 33.

Mulay, S. (1994) "Women and New Contraceptive Technologies: A Critique from the Canadian Feminist Perspective", presentation on behalf of NAC, and in consultation with FQPN and WHI to the Independent Commission on Population and Quality of Life, Washington, DC, 30 March 1994.

Murphy, C. (2001) "What the Third World Wants: An Interpretation of the Development and Meaning of the New International Economic Organization", in P. Diehl, ed., *The Politics of Global Governance*, Boulder, Colo.: Lynne Rienner, pp. 261–276.

NAC (1995) "Structural Adjustment: Canada Style", *Action Now!* 5(3/4): 1.

National Action Committee (1994) Joint Press Release from the National Action Committee on the Status of Women and the Canadian Women's Committee on Reproduction, Population and Development, 30 August 1994, quoted in "Canadian Women Speak Out on Population", citing letter to André Ouellet, Minister of Foreign Affairs, by Shelagh Day vice-president of the NAC, mimeo.

Neale, P. R. (1998) "The Bodies of Christ as International Bodies: the Holy See, Wom(b)an and the Cairo Conference", *Review of International Studies* 24(1): 101–118.

Network on International Human Rights (1992) "Transforming the Model: Building Effective Relations between NGOs and Government on International Human Rights", Minutes of the Meeting of the Network on International Human Rights, 25–27 September 1992, University of Ottawa, Ottawa.

Neufeld, M. (1995) "Hegemony and Foreign Policy Analysis: The Case of Canada as Middle Power", *Studies in Political Economy* 49: 7–29.

Newman, E. "Security and Governance in the New Millennium: Observations and Synthesis", in R. Thakur and E. Newman, eds. (2000) *New Millennium, New Perspectives: The United Nations, Security, and Governance*, Tokyo: United Nations University Press, pp. 10–11.

New York Declaration on High Seas Overfishing (1992) Protecting the Commons, proposed by NGOs and Governments, 31 March 1992.

NGO-Newsletter (1994) reprinted in M. Nowak, ed., *The World Conference on Human Rights: Vienna, June 1993: The Contribution of NGOS: Reports and Documents*, Vienna: Manzsche-Verlags-und-Ludwig Boltzmann Institute of Human Rights, pp. 205–232.

Nicolson, H. (1939) *Diplomacy*, Oxford: Oxford University Press.

North-South Institute (1989) "The Wider World: Challenges for the Second Mulroney Mandate", *Review '88 Outlook '89*, Ottawa: North-South Institute.

Nossal, K. R. (1982) "Personal Diplomacy and National Behaviour: Trudeau's North–South Initiatives", *Dalhousie Review* 62: 278–291.

—— (1988) "Political Leadership and Foreign Policy: Trudeau and Mulroney", in L. A. Pal and D. Taras, eds., *Prime Ministers and Premiers: Political Leadership and Public Policy*, Scarborough, Ont.: Prentice-Hall.

—— (1994) *Rain Dancing: Sanctions in Canadian and Australian Foreign Policy*, Toronto: University of Toronto Press.

—— (1997) *The Politics of Canadian Foreign Policy*, 3rd ed., Scarborough, Ont.: Prentice-Hall, p. 122.

—— (1998–1999) "Pennypinching Diplomacy: The Decline of 'Good International Citizenship' in Canadian Foreign Policy", *International Journal* 54(1): 88–105.
Nossal, K. R. and R. Stubbs (1997) "Mahathir's Malaysia: An Emerging Middle Power", in A. F. Cooper, *Niche Diplomacy: Middle Powers after the Cold War*, Basingstoke: Macmillan, pp. 147–163.
O'Brien, R., A. M. Goetz, J. A. Scholte and M. Williams (2000) *Contesting Global Governance: Multilateral Economic Institutions and Global Social Movements*, Cambridge: Cambridge University Press.
Office of the Prime Minister (1991) "Notes for an Address by Prime Minister Brian Mulroney on the Occasion of the Centennial Anniversary Convocation, Stanford University, California, 29 September 1991".
—— (1992) "Notes for an Address by Prime Minister Brian Mulroney, Earth Summit, Rio de Janeiro, June 12, 1992", p. 1
O'Gorman, E. and V. Jabri (1999) "Locating Difference in Feminist International Relations", in V. Jabri and E. O'Gorman, eds., *Women, Culture, and International Relations*, Boulder, Colo.: Lynne Rienner, p. 10.
O'Hagen, J. (1995) "Civilisational Conflict? Looking for Cultural Enemies", *Third World Quarterly* 16(1): 19–38.
Ono, M. (2001) "From Consensus-building to Implementation: The Follow-up to the UN Global Conferences of the 1990s", in M. G. Schechter, ed., *The United Nations-sponsored World Conferences: Focus on Impact and Follow-up*, Tokyo: United Nations University Press, pp. 169–183.
Pal, L. A. (1988) "Hands at the Helm? Leadership and Public Policy", in L. A. Pal and D. Taras, eds., *Prime Ministers and Premiers: Political Leadership and Public Policy*, Scarborough, Ont.: Prentice-Hall.
—— (1994) "A World Of Difference: Human Rights in Canadian Foreign Policy", in R. M. Campbell and L. A. Pal, eds., *The Real Worlds of Canadian Politics: Cases in Process and Policy*, 3rd ed., Peterborough, Ont.: Broadview, pp. 211–272.
—— (1995) "Competing Paradigms in Policy Discourse: The Case of International Human Rights", *Policy Sciences* 28: 185–207.
Palan, R. (1999) "Global Governance and Social Closure", in M. Hewson and T. J. Sinclair, eds., *Approaches to Global Governance Theory*, Albany, NY: State University of New York, pp. 55–70.
Park, A. (1992) "Testimony before the House of Commons Sub-Committee on Development and Human Rights of the Standing Committee on External Affairs and International Trade", *Minutes of Proceedings and Evidence*, 25 March, 16: 5–24.
Pearce, J. (1993) "NGOs and Social Change: Agents or Facilitators?", *Development in Practice* 3(3): 223.
Peterson, V. S. (1992) "Security and Sovereign States", in *Gendered States: Feminist (Re)Visions of International Relations Theory*, Boulder, Colo.: Lynne Rienner, p. 32.
Peterson, V. S. and A. Runyan (1993) *Global Gender Issues*, Boulder, Colo.: Westview.

Pettman, J.J. (1996) *Worlding Women: A Feminist International Politics*, London: Routledge, p. 22.
Piscatori, J. (1984) "Islam in the International Order", in H. Bull and A. Watson, eds., *The Expansion of International Society*, Oxford: Clarendon Press, p. 313.
Potter, E. H. (1996) "Redesigning Canadian Diplomacy in an Age of Fiscal Austerity", in F. Osler Hampson and M. Appel Molot, eds., *Big Enough to Be Heard: Canada Among Nations 1996*, Ottawa: Carleton University Press, p. 47.
Prakash, A. and J. A. Hart, eds. (1999) *Globalization and Governance*, London: Routledge.
Pratt, C. (1983–1984) "Dominant Class Theory and Canadian Foreign Policy: The Case of the Counter-Consensus", *International Journal* 39(1): 99–135.
―――― (1998) "DFAIT's Takeover Bid of CIDA: The Institutional Future of the Canadian International Development Agency", *Canadian Foreign Policy* 5(2): 1–14.
Princen, T. (1994) "NGOs: Creating a Niche in Environmental Diplomacy", in T. Princen and M. Finger, eds., *Environmental NGOs in World Politics: Linking the Local and the Global*, London: Routledge, pp. 29–47.
Princen, T. and M. Finger (1994) *Environmental NGOs in World Politics: Linking the Local and the Global*, London: Routledge, p. 31.
Ptolemy, K. (1989) "First International Consultation on Refugee Women: Geneva (November 1988)", *Canadian Woman Studies* 10(1): 21–24.
Puddington, A. (2001) "The Wages of Durban", *Commentary* 112(4): 31, 34.
Putnam, R. D. (1988) "Diplomacy and Domestic Politics: The Logic of Two-Level Games", *International Organization* 42(3): 427–460.
Rabkin, J. A. (1998) *Why Sovereignty Matters*, Washington, DC: American Enterprise Institute.
Ramakrishna, K. (1992) "North-South Issues, the Common Heritage of Mankind and Global Environmental Change", in I. Rowlands and M. Greene, eds., *Global Environmental Change and International Relations*, Basingstoke: Macmillan, p. 195.
Raustiala, K. (1996) "States, NGOs, and International Environmental Institutions", *International Studies Quarterly* 41(4): 720.
Ravenhill, J. (1998) "Cycles of Middle Power Activism: Constraint and Choice in Australian and Canadian Foreign Policies", *Australian Journal of International Affairs* 52(3): 322.
REAL Women (1994a) "International Intrigue against the Family", *Reality* XIII(5).
―――― (1994b) "Canadian Government Pushing Feminism and Abortion in Third World Countries", *Reality* XIII(15): 7–9.
―――― (1994c) "Promotion of Feminism Abroad: Reality, REAL Women and The U.N. Population Conference in Cairo", *Reality* XIII(15): 1–5.
Rebick, J. (1995) "Beijing Diary", *Canadian Forum*, December: 27–36.
Red Book (1993) *Creating Opportunity: The Liberal Platform for Canada*, Ottawa: Liberal Party of Canada, 1993, p. 108.
Reich, R. B. (1991) *The Work of Nations: Preparing Ourselves for 21st Century Capitalism*, New York: Knopf.

Reid, T. (1997) Testimony to the Standing Senate Committee on Foreign Affairs, *Minutes and Proceedings*, 10 December 1997, p. 15.

Reinicke, W. H. (1998) *Global Public Policy: Governing Without Government?* Washington, DC: Brookings.

Review Committee on Overseas Representation (1969) *Report of the Review Committee on Overseas Representation 1968–69*, London: HMSO.

Reynolds, D. (1992) "Beyond Bipolarity in Space and Time", in M. J. Hogan, ed., *The End of the Cold War: Its Meaning and Implications*, Cambridge: Cambridge University Press, pp. 245–256.

Riddell-Dixon, E. (1997) "Individual Leadership and Structural Power", *Canadian Journal of Political Science* XXX(2), especially p. 267.

——— (2001) *Canada and the Beijing Conference on Women: Governmental Politics and NGO Participation*, Vancouver: UBC Press.

Rife, R. (1998) "Observing the Governments of the World at Work", in J. Auth, ed., *To Beijing and Beyond: Pittsburgh and The United Nations Fourth World Conference*, Pittsburgh, Pa.: University of Pittsburgh Press, p. 15.

Rioux, J.-F. and R. Hay (1997) "Canadian Foreign Policy: From Internationalism to Isolationism?" Norman Paterson School of International Affairs, Occasional Paper 16, Carleton University, Ottawa.

Risse-Kappen, T., ed. (1995) *Bringing Transnational Relations Back In: Non-State Actors, Domestic Structures and International Institutions*, Cambridge: Cambridge University Press.

Roberts, A. and B. Kingsbury (1994) *Presiding Over a Divided World: Changing UN Roles, 1945–1993*, Boulder, Colo.: Lynne Rienner, p. 24.

Robinson, W. I. (1996) *Promoting Polyarchy: Globalization, US Intervention and Hegemony*, Cambridge: Cambridge University Press.

Robinson, R. (2000) *The Debt: What America Owes to Blacks*, New York: Putnam.

Roche, D. (1992) "Testimony by Doug Roche to House of Commons Standing Committee on External Affairs and International Trade", *Minutes of Evidence and Proceedings*, 10 December 1992, 50: 15.

Rosecrance, R. (1996) "The Rise of the Virtual State", *Foreign Affairs* 75: 59–60.

Rosenau, J. N. (1990) *Turbulence in World Politics: A Theory of Change and Continuity*, Princeton: Princeton University Press.

——— (1995) "Sovereignty in a Turbulent World", in G. Lyons and M. Mastanduno, eds., *Beyond Westphalia?: State Sovereignty and International Intervention*, Baltimore, Md.: Johns Hopkins University Press, p. 193.

——— (1997) *Along the Domestic Foreign Frontier: Exploring Governance in a Turbulent World*, Cambridge: Cambridge University Press.

——— (1999) "States, Sovereignty, and Diplomacy in the Information Age", paper presented at the International Studies Association Conference, Virtual Diplomacy: A Revolution in Diplomatic Affairs, 18 February 1999, available from http://www.usip.org/oc/vd/vdr/jrosenauISA99.html.

Rowland, W. (1973) *The Plot To Save the World: The Life and Times of the Stockholm Conference and the Human Environment*, Toronto: Clarke, Irwin.

Ruggie, J. G. (1983) "Continuity and Change in the World Polity: Toward a Neorealist Synthesis", *World Politics* 35(2): 261–285.
——— (1992) "Multilateralism: Anatomy of an Institution", *International Organization* 46(3): 561–598.
——— (1993a) "Multilateralism: The Anatomy of an Institution", in J. G. Ruggie, ed., *Multilateralism Matters: The Theory and Praxis of an Institutional Form*, New York: Columbia University Press, p. 25.
——— (1993b) "Territoriality and Beyond: Problematizing Modernity in International Relations", *International Organization* 47(1): 152, 173–174.
——— (1996) *Winning the Peace: America and World Order in the New Era*, New York: Columbia University Press, p. 20.
——— (1999) "The New United Nations: Continuous Change and Reform", in *Behind the Headlines*, 56(1), Toronto: CIIA, p. 17.
——— (2000) "Globalization, the 'Global Compact' and Corporate Social Responsibility", *Transnational Associations* 6: 291–314.
Ryan, S. (2000) *The United Nations and International Politics*, New York: St. Martin's Press.
Sassen, S. (1996) *Losing Control? Sovereignty in an Age of Globalization*, New York: Columbia Press.
——— (1998) "Towards a Feminist Analysis of the Global Economy", in *Globalization and Its Discontents: Essays on the New Mobility of People and Money*, New York: New Press, p. 92.
Sauvé, The Hon. Jeanne (1974) "Global Population Problems", a statement by The Hon. Jeanne Sauvé, Minister of the Environment, to the World Population Conference, Bucharest, 20 August 1974, in *Statement and Speeches*, 75/21, Department of the Environment: Ottawa, p. 4.
Savoie, D. J. (1990) *The Politics of Public Spending in Canada*, Toronto: University of Toronto Press, pp. 190–191.
——— (1994) *Thatcher, Reagan, Mulroney: In Search of a New Bureaucracy*, Toronto: University of Toronto Press, p. 272.
——— (1999) *Governing from the Centre: The Concentration of Power in Canadian Politics*, Toronto: University of Toronto Press.
Schechter, M. G. (2001) "Conclusions", *The United Nations-sponsored World Conferences: Focus on Impact and Follow-up*, Tokyo: United Nations University Press, p. 221.
Scholte, J. A. (1997) "The Globalization of World Politics", in J. Bayliss and S. Smith, eds., *The Globalization of World Politics: An Introduction to International Relations*, Oxford: Oxford University Press, p. 21.
——— (2000) *Globalization: A Critical Introduction*, Basingstoke: Palgrave, pp. 15–16.
Seward, S. and K. McDade (1988) *Immigrant Women in Canada: A Policy Perspective*, Ottawa: Canadian Advisory Council on the Status of Women.
Shaw, M. (2000) *Theory of the Global State: Globality as Unfinished Revolution*, Cambridge: Cambridge University Press.
Shaw, K. (2002) "Indigeneity and the International", *Millennium* 31(1): 55–81.
Shenstone, M. (1992) *World Population Growth and Movements: Policy Implica-*

tions for Canada, Ottawa: EAITC Policy Planning and Coordination Bureau, No. 92/7, 1992.
―― (1997) *World Population Growth and Movement: Towards the 21st Century*, Ottawa: Canadian Centre for Foreign Policy Development.
Sikkink, K. (1993) "Human Rights, Principled Issue-Networks, and Sovereignty in Latin America", *International Organization* 47(3): 411–441.
Simmons, A. B. and K. Keohane (1992) "Canadian Immigration Policy: State Strategies and the Quest for Legitimacy", *Canadian Review of Sociology and Anthropology* 29(4): 421–452.
Simon, M. (1994) Member of the Board, Inuit Tapirisat, "Testimony before the Special Joint Committee of the Senate and the House of Commons on Reviewing Canadian Foreign Policy", *Minutes of Proceedings and Evidence*, 9 June 1994, 36: 30.
Simpson, J. (1993) *Faultlines: Struggling for a Canadian Vision*, Toronto: Harper-Collins, p. 59.
Slaughter, A.-M. (1997) "The Real New Order", *Foreign Affairs* 76(5): 183–197.
Slim, H. (1997) "To The Rescue: Radicals or Poodles?" *The World Today*, August/September, pp. 209–212
Smith, D.B. (1993a) "Natives Score Victory against Ottawa", *Windspeaker* 11(8): 1.
―― (1993b) "Missing 's' a Threat to Rights", *Windspeaker* 11(7): 1, 2.
Smith, M. (1999) "The European Union", in B. Hocking and S. McGuire, eds., *Trade Politics: International, Domestic and Regional Perspectives*, London: Routledge, p. 276.
Smith, H. A. (2000) "Niche Diplomacy and Mission-Oriented Diplomatic Behaviour: A Critical Assessment", in A. F. Cooper and G. Hayes, eds., *Worthwhile Initiatives? Canadian Mission-Oriented Diplomacy*, Toronto: Irwin Press, pp. 12–22.
―― (2001) "Shades of Grey in Canada's Greening during the Mulroney Era", in N. Michaud and K. R. Nossal, eds., *Diplomatic Departure: The Conservative Era in Canadian Foreign Policy, 1984–93*, Vancouver: UBC Press, pp. 71–83.
Smouts, M.-C. (1999) "United Nations Reform: A Strategy of Avoidance", in M. G. Schechter, ed., *Innovation in Multilateralism: Multilateralism and the UN System*, Tokyo: United Nations University Press, pp. 29, 40.
Sorensen, G. (1998) "International Relations Theory after the Cold War", in T. Dunne, M. Cox and K. Booth, eds., *The Eighty Years Crisis: International Relations 1919–1999*, Cambridge: Cambridge University Press, p. 99.
Spivak, G. (1996) "Woman as Theatre: United Nations Conference, Beijing, 1995", *Radical Philosophy* 75: 2–3.
Stairs, D. (1977–1978) "Public Opinion and External Affairs: Reflections on the Domestication of Canadian Foreign Policy", *International Journal* XXXIII(1): 144–145.
―― (1998) "The Policy Process and Dialogues with Demos: Liberal Pluralism with a Transnational Twist", in F. Osler Hampson and M. Appel Molot, eds., *Canada Among Nations 1998: Leadership and Dialogue*, Toronto: Oxford University Press, pp. 23–53.
―― (2001) "Architects or Engineers? The Conservatives and Foreign Policy",

in N. Michaud and K. R. Nossal, eds., *Diplomatic Departure: The Conservative Era in Canadian Foreign Policy, 1984–93*, Vancouver: UBC Press, p. 25.

Steans, J. (1998) *Gender and International Relations: an Introduction*, New Brunswick, NJ: Rutgers University Press.

Stefanick, L. and K. Wells (1998) "Staying the Course or Saving Face? Federal Environmental Policy Post-Rio", in L. A. Pal, ed., *How Ottawa Spends 1998–99, Balancing Act: The Post-Deficit Mandate*, Toronto: Oxford University Press, p. 252.

Steiner, H. J. (1991) *Diverse Partners: Non-Governmental Organizations in the Human Rights Movement*, Cambridge: Harvard Law School Human Rights Program and Human Rights Internet.

Stephenson, C. (1995) "Women's International Non-Governmental Organizations at the United Nations", in A. Winslow, ed., *Women, Politics, and the United Nations, Contributions in Women's Studies*, No. 151, Westport, Conn.: Greenwood, pp. 135–153.

Stienstra, D.(1994) *Women's Movements and International Organizations*, New York: St Martin's Press.

Stoett, P. J. (1996) "International Mechanisms for Addressing Migration", *Canadian Foreign Policy* 4(1): 111–138.

Stone, P. B. (1973) *Did We Save the Earth at Stockholm?*, London: Earth Island.

Stopford, J. and S. Strange (1991) *Rival States, Rival Firms; Competition for World Market Shares*, Cambridge: Cambridge University Press.

Strange, S. (1991) "The Name of the Game", in N. X. Rizopoulos, ed., *Sea Changes: American Foreign Policy in a World Transformed*, New York: Council on Foreign Relations.

—— (1992) "States, Firms and Diplomacy", *International Affairs* 68(1): 10.

—— (1996a) *The Retreat of the State: The Diffusion of Power in the Contemporary World Economy*, Cambridge: Cambridge University Press.

—— (1996b) "The Retreat of the State", in J. A. Hall, ed., *International Orders*, Cambridge: Polity Press.

Streek, W. (1996) "Public Power beyond the Nation State: The Case of the European Community", in R. Boyer and D. Drache, eds., *States Against Markets: The Limits of Globalization*, London: Routledge, pp. 299–315.

Strong, M. (2001) *Where on Earth Are We Going?*, Toronto: Vintage Canada.

Sylvester, C. (1994) "Empathetic Cooperation: A Feminist Model for IR", *Millennium* 23(2): 315–334.

Talbott, S. (1997) "Globalization and Diplomacy: A Practitioner's Perspective", *Foreign Policy* 108: 69–83.

Taras, D. and D. H. Goldberg, eds. (1989) *Domestic Battleground: Canada and the Arab-Israeli Conflict*, Kingston, Ont.: McGill-Queen's University Press.

Taylor, J. H. (2001) "The Conservatives and Foreign Policy-Making: A Foreign Service View", in N. Michaud and K. R. Nossal, eds., *Diplomatic Departure: The Conservative Era in Canadian Foreign Policy, 1984–93*, Vancouver: UBC Press, p. 217.

Terpstra, R. W. (1999) "Post–Cold War UN Diplomacy from Up-Close: Inside

Perspectives from An Outsider", in J. P. Muldoon, ed., *Multilateral Diplomacy and the United Nations Today*, Boulder, Colo.: Westview, p. 212.

Tesner, S. and G. Kell (2000) *The United Nations and Business: A Partnership Recovered*, New York: St. Martin's Press.

Thakur, R. (2001) "Human Rights: Amnesty International and the United Nations", in P. Diehl, ed., *The Politics of Global Governance: International Organizations in an Interdependent World*, Boulder, Colo.: Lynne Rienner, pp. 365–387.

Thérien, J.-P. (1999) "Beyond the North-South Divide: the Two Tales of World Poverty", *Third World Quarterly* 20: 723–742.

Thobani, S. (1995) "Beijing and Beyond", *Action Now!*, November (first of ten inserts on the 4th World Conference on Women).

Tuchman Mathews, J. (1989) "Redefining Security", *Foreign Affairs* 68: 162.

Tussie, D. and M. P. Riggirozzi (2001) "Pressing Ahead with New Procedures for Old Machinery: Global Governance and Civil Society", in V. Rittberger, ed., *Global Governance and the United Nations System*, Tokyo: United Nations University Press, p. 171.

ul Haq, M., I. Kaul, and I. Grunberg, eds. (1996) *The Tobin Tax: Coping with Financial Viability*, Oxford: Oxford University Press.

United Nations (1974) *UN World Population Conference, 1974*, New York: UN.

——— (1994) "Report of the International Conference on Population and Development", A/Conf.171/13.Rev.1.1994.

——— (1995b) *Population and Development: Programme of Action Adopted at the International Conference on Population and Development*, Cairo, 5–13 September 1994, vol. 1, New York: UN, 1995.

——— (1995a) *Declaration on Social Development and Programme of Action of the World Summit for Social Development*, New York: UN.

——— Briefing Papers (1997) *The World Conferences: Developing Priorities for the 21st Century*, New York: Department of Publications, United Nations.

——— Conference on the Human Environment (1972) "*Development and Environment*", report and working papers of a panel of experts convened by the Secretary-General of the UN Conference on the Human Environment, New York: UN.

——— Institute for Training and Research (1976) *A New International Economic Order: Selected Documents 1945–1975*, New York: UNITAR.

——— Press Release (1997) "Opening Address to the Fiftieth Annual Department of Public Information/Non-Governmental Organization (DPI/NGO) Conference", UN press release SG/M/6320, PI/1027, 10 September 1997.

Utting, P. (2002) *The Greening of Business in Developing Countries: Rhetoric, Reality, and Prospects*, London: Zed/UNRISD.

Vallier, I. (1972) "The Roman Catholic Church: A Transnational Actor", in R. O. Keohane and J. S. Nye Jr., eds., *Transnational Relations and World Politics*, Cambridge: Harvard University Press: 129–193.

Van Rooy, A. (1997) "The Frontiers of Influence: NGO Lobbying at the 1974 World Food Conference, The 1992 Earth Summit and Beyond", *World Development* 25(1): 93–114.

Vatikiotis, M. (1992) "Priming for Rio: Malaysia Set the Tone for Earth Summit Agenda", *Far Eastern Economic Review*, 14 May, p. 22.

Vickers, J., P. Rankin and C. Appelle (1993) *Politics As If Women Mattered: A Political Analysis of the National Action Committee on the Status of Women*, Toronto: University of Toronto Press, pp. 86, 88.

Vincent, R. J. (1983) "Change and International Relations", *Review of International Studies* 9(1): 63–70.

Walker, R. B. J. (1993) *Inside/Outside: International Relations as Political Theory*, Cambridge: Cambridge University Press.

Waltz, K. N. (1979) *Theory of International Politics*, New York: McGraw-Hill, p. 96.

Wapner, P. (1995) "Politics Beyond The State: Environmental Activism and World Civic Politics", *World Politics* 47(3): 311–340.

Watson, A. (1982) *Diplomacy: The Dialogue Between States*, London: Methuen Eyre.

WEDO (1996) *Beyond Promises: Governments in Motion One Year after the Beijing Women's Conference*, New York: WEDO.

Weiss, L. (1998) *The Myth of the Powerless State*, Ithaca: Cornell University Press.

Weiss, T. G., D. P. Forsythe and R. A. Coate (1994) *The United Nations and Changing World Politics*, Boulder, Colo.: Westview.

Welsh, D. A. (1991) "The New Multilateralism and Evolving Security System", in F. Osler Hampson and C. J. Maule, eds., *Canada Among Nations, 1992–93: A New World Order?*, Ottawa: Carleton University Press, p. 86.

Wendt, A. (1987) "The Agent Structure Problem in International Relations", *International Organization* 41(2): 335–370.

Whalley, J. (1988) " 'Comments' on Jeffrey J. Schott, Implications for the Uruguay Round", in J. J. Schott and M. G. Smith, eds., *The Canada-United States Free Trade Agreement: The Global Impact*, Washington, DC: Institute for International Economics, p. 176.

Wheeler, J., ed. (1999) *Human Rights in Global Politics*, Cambridge: Cambridge University Press, p. 276.

Whitaker, J. S. (1975) "Women of the World: Report from Mexico City", *Foreign Affairs* 54(1): 178.

Willetts, P. (1982) "Pressure Groups as Transnational Actors", in P. Willetts, ed., *Pressure Groups in the Global System: The Transnational Relations of Issue-Oriented Non-Governmental Organizations*, London: Frances Pinter.

Williams, A. (1998) *Failed Imagination? New World Orders of the Twentieth Century*, Manchester: Manchester University Press.

Winham, G. R. (1993) "The Impact of Social Change on International Diplomacy", paper delivered to the annual meeting of the Canadian Political Science Association, Ottawa, June 1993, pp. 1–40.

Wirick, G. (1993) "Canada, Peacekeeping and the United Nations", in F. Osler Hampson and C. Maule, eds., *Canada Among Nations 1992–93: A New World Order?*, Ottawa: Carleton University Press, p. 103

Wiseberg, L. S. (1995) "The Vienna World Conference on Human Rights", in E.

Fawcett and H. Newcombe, eds., *United Nations Reform: Looking Ahead After Fifty Years*, Toronto: Dundurn, p. 177.
World Bank (2000) *World Development Report 2000/2001: Attacking Poverty*, New York: Oxford University Press
World Commission on Environment and Development (1987) (Brundtland Commission) *The Common Future*, Oxford: Oxford University Press.
Young, I. M. (1990) *Justice and the Politics of Difference*, Princeton: Princeton University Press, p. 161.
Young, M. (1991) Library of Parliament, "Refugee Protection: The International Context", BP-280E, Ottawa: Government of Canada.
Young, O. R. (1999) *Governance in World Affairs*, Ithaca, NY: Cornell University Press, pp. 41–49.
Zacher, M. W. (1999) *The United Nations and Global Commerce*, New York: United Nations.
Zalewski, M. and J. Parpart, eds. (1991) *The "Man" Question in International Relations*, Boulder, Colo.: Westview.
Zartman, W. I. and M. Berman (1982) *The Practical Negotiator*, New Haven: Yale University Press, p. 226.

Index

Aboriginal: activists, 144; affairs, 258n.; peoples, 242; rights, 123, 126, Assembly of First Nations (AFN) 139, 243, 244
Abzug, Bella, 158, 188, 189
Africa: African-American, 246; and the Cairo conference, 174; and Canada, 240; Central, 238; markets, 241; priority for, 117; West, 245
Ajami, Fouad, 163
Akhter, Farida, 164
Albright, Madeleine, 193
Amnesty International: and Canada, 210; reputation of, 55; role of women in, 247; and slavery, 230; secretary-general of, 256n.; and UN conferences, 226; and the Vienna conference, 66; and women's rights, 200
Anawak, Caroline, 205
Anderson, Doris, 17
Anglican Church, 176
Annan, Kofi, 6, 44, 229, 247, 252
Apsey, Michael, 62.
Arafat, Yasser, 224–225
Archibald, Ruth, 170, 180, 202, 209, 212
Argentina: and like-minded countries, 166, 168; and the Vatican, 161
Ashipala, Selma, 193
Asia, 19, 24–25, 86–87, 127, 162–164, 260n.

Asia Pacific Economic Cooperation (APEC), 86–87, 127
Asian Women's Human Rights Council, 164
Association of South-East Asian Nations (ASEAN), 108
Astrom, Sverker, 29
Australia, 218, 240; and Aboriginal activists, 144; and the Cairo conference, 166; and Canada, 103, 159, 210, 211, 215; and Denmark, 114; and family reunification, 159; and forestry issues, 104; and New Zealand, 47, 134, 147, 152; Prime Minister of, 73; and the UN, 159; and the Vienna conference, 136, 166; and the Western Group, 143
Austria, 143, 147, 189–190, 193
Axworthy, Lloyd, 110, 111, 118–119, 121, 237, 252
Axworthy, Tom, 32
Ayres, Jeffrey, 130

Banting, Keith, 118
Barlow, Maude, 109
Barron, David, 62
Bauer, Jan, 47
Bayefsky, Anne, 55, 232, 234, 248
Beck, Pat, 205
Bélanger-Rochon, Denyse, 37

286

INDEX 287

Bell, John, 57
Beijing, city of, 199
Beijing Fourth World Conference on
  Women (1994): break from accepted
  practices, 184; and Canada, 200–201, 207,
  210–212, 214–216, 219, 221; and the
  Copenhagen Summit, 81, 87; and
  diplomatic process, 185–186; document,
  212; dynamics of, 197; goals of, 198;
  groups at, 198; and human rights, 186; and
  Gertrude Mongella, 28; and meaning of
  gender, 196; and NGOs, 188; outcome of,
  201, 208; Platform of Action, 192, 211,
  229, 259n.; process, 193, 202, 203;
  redefinition of, 217; role of men at, 199;
  run-up to, 195; and solidarity, 187; and
  the women's movement, 192
Beijing Platform of Action, 178, 187, 211,
  215, 218, 259n.
Bergeron-de Villiers, Louise, 202
Bhutto, Benazir, 163, 181, 193
Biegman, Nicolas, 168, 198
Bill of Reproductive Rights, 184
bipolarity: and the Cold War, 17, 28;
  collapse of, 14, 28; confines of, 25; dictates
  of, 8; and East-West rivalry, 1; end of, 20,
  153; system of, 42; and the Vienna
  conference, 23
Black, Conrad, 78
Black Leadership Forum, 246
Blondin-Andrew, Ethel, 201
B'nai Brith Canada, 232
Bosnia: declaration on, 24; non-interference
  in, 24; president of, 224; and violence
  against women, 48
Bouchard, Lucien, 89, 97
Boutros-Ghali, Boutros, 127
Bretton Woods (Conference), 101, 113–114,
  117, 167
Brewer, Allison, 215–216
Broadbent, Ed, 64, 133, 196, 201, 210
Brody, Reed, 67
Brown, Rosemary, 47
Brundtland, Gro Harlem, 73, 158, 193
Bucharest Conference on Population
  (1974): and Asian states, 163; and
  Canada, 29–31, 36; document, 18, 19;
  opposition to, 182; process, 49; and UN
  world conferences, 72; and the West, 16
Buck, Kerry, 202
Buckley, James, 157

Bujold, Marius, 119
Bull, Hedley, 42, 153
Bunch, Charlotte, 66, 158, 191
Burley, Anne-Marie, 95
Burney, Derek, 88
Bush, George Sr., 81, 84–85, 102, 157, 176
Bush, George W., 245, 256n.
Business Council on National Issues
  (Canada), 105, 115, 257 n.
Buxton, G.V., 58, 89

Cable News Network (CNN), 64, 87
Cairns, Alan, x, 52
Cairo International Conference on
  Population and Development (1994):
  agenda of, 81, 160; approach to, 93; and
  Canada, 168, 172–174, 212; and
  diplomacy, 156, 166; discord at, 155; and
  family reunification, 171; and Indigenous
  issues, 159; lead-up to, 161, 163; and
  morality, 158; and multilateralism, 80;
  negotiations at, 165, 170, 195; and the
  NAC, 178, 204; and NGOs, 175; outcome
  of, 179, 181; process, 157, 162, 165, 169,
  177, 181, 198, 259n.; standards of, 87; and
  society-craft, 183; theme of, 136; and the
  Vatican, 160, 161, 211; and women, 180,
  185
Camilleri, Joseph, 131
Campbell, Bruce, 109
Campeau, Arthur, 89
Canada: and Aboriginal rights, 126;
  behaviour of, 74, 92, 149; and the
  Bucharest Conference, 29–30; and the
  Beijing Conference, 208, 210–211,
  213–215; and the Cairo Conference,
  167–170, 176; and China, 209, 210; and
  the Convention on biological diversity,
  84; and diplomacy, 70, 90, 114, 207; and
  the Durban Conference, 231, 235, 237,
  241–242, 260n.; and the EC/EU, 136,
  171–172; and the environmental
  movement, 50, 84; foreign policy, 88; and
  global change, 7, 38, 51; and the Global
  Forestry Convention, 104; and global
  governance, 10; image of, 123, 135;
  identity of, 9; and Indigenous peoples'
  rights, 137–139, 143–144; and international
  agenda, 29; and international citizenship,
  125, 129–30; and international politics, 12;
  and international affairs, 33, 77; and

Canada: and Aboriginal rights (cont.)
isolationism, 76; and like-minded
countries, 47, 84, 97, 159, 166, 245, 258n.;
and the Mexico Conference, 37; as middle
power, x, 79; and the Nairobi Conference,
46; National Forum on Canada's
International Relations (Ottawa, 1994),
111; and NGOs, 46, 48–50, 52, 62, 92, 112,
116, 117; objectives of, 75; and ODA, 112;
and the OECD/G7, 67, 114; performance
at UN conferences, 71, 93, 249, 251–253;
and population control funding, 173; and
the Prep Com, 46; priorities of, 90; and
quiet diplomacy, 32; and refugee claims,
126, 132, 133; reputation of, 59, 60, 83,
103, 120, 147; role of, ix, 88, 96, 219, 236,
256n.; and sovereignty, 80, 123, 129, 149;
and the Stockholm Conference, 31,
territorial integrity of, 148; and the
United Nations, 8, 133, 150; and the
United States, 12, 57, 82, 85,118; and the
Vatican, 182; and the Vienna Conference,
148; and women's groups, 132, 133
Canada-Australia-New Zealand group, 47,
171, 210, 215
Canadian Council for International
Cooperation, 36
Canada, Department of the Environment,
57–58, 257n.; Environment Canada, 58,
70, 89, 252
Canada, Department of External Affairs
(prior to 1989); External Affairs and
International Trade (between 1989 and
1993) 55, 57
Canada, Department of Foreign Affairs and
International Trade (after 1993): and
Aboriginal Affairs, 258n.; and CIDA,
111–113, 173; and debt of developing
countries, 114; and the Durban
conference, 253, 252; and Lloyd
Axworthy, 119; and the international
system, 69; and the Mexico conference,
36; and the Vienna conference, 55, 59;
and the women's movement, 201; women
within, 202, 219
Canada, Department of Indian Affairs and
Northern Development, 55
Canada, Department of Justice, 59, 70, 138
Canada, House of Commons Standing
Committee of External Affairs and
International Trade, 90

Canada, Secretary of State for External
Affairs: advisor to, 89; Barbara
McDougall, 57, 64; J.H. Taylor, 82
Canada, Secretary of State for Latin
America, 174
Canada, Secretary of State for the Status of
Women, 201, 207
Canada-US Free Trade Agreement, 74, 79,
82, 88, 129, 130
Canadian Advisory Council on the Status of
Women, 37
Canadian Arctic Resources Committee, 58
Canadian Beijing Facilitation Committee,
203, 205, 220
Canadian Broadcasting Corporation:
Newsworld, 87; Quirks and Quarks, 174;
Radio, 162
Canadian Charter of Rights and Freedoms,
51
Canadian Council for Community Living,
117
Canadian Council for Refugees, 134
Canadian Environmental Law Association,
62
Canadian Environmental Network, 47, 50,
58
Canadian Federation of Business and
Professional Women Clubs, 206
Canadian Institute of International Affairs,
35, 49
Canadian International Development
Agency: autonomy of, 60; and
Bangladesh, 173; and the Beijing
Declaration, 209; contribution to
UNCED, 92; and DFAIT, 111–113, 173;
and external affairs, 89; and the foreign
ministry, 60–61, 70; and INGOs, 117; and
the NAC, 204; and the PPF, 175–176; and
the Vienna conference, 59
Canadian Jewish Congress, 234
Canadian Labour Congress, 116, 205
Canadian Nature Federation, 58
Canadian Network on International Human
Rights, 56
Canadian Parks and Wilderness Society, 58
Canadian Participatory Committee for
UNCED 45–47, 58, 61–63, 105–106
Canadian Population Task Force, 36–37
Canadian Pulp and Paper Association, 62,
105–106, 257 n.
Canadian Race Relations Federation, 233

INDEX 289

Canadian Women's Committee on Reproduction, Population and Development, 178
Canadian women's movement, 202–204, 206
Canadian Youth Working Group on the Environment and Development, 62
CARE Canada, 36
Carnegie Endowment for International Peace, 161
Carson, Rachel, 8, 18
Carter, Jimmy, 64
Castro, Fidel, 224–225
Catholic Church, 36, 159, 161, 172, 176, 214
Catley-Carlson, Margaret, 173
Centre for Aboriginal Education, 205
Centre for Women's Global Leadership at Rutgers University, 66, 158, 200, 229
Chamber of Commerce (Canadian), 116
Chamber of Commerce (International), 115–116, 241
Chant, Donald, 34
Charest, Jean, 53, 58–59, 89–90
Charlottetown, 36; Accord, 97; process, 138, referendum, 51.
Chatterjee, Pratap, 101.
Children's Summit, *See also*, New York World Summit for World Children.
Chrétien, Aline, 87.
Chrétien, Jean: approach of, 77, 235; and Canada-US relations, 86, 236; and Canadian leadership, 71, 90–91; and diplomacy, 80, 103, 114; and the Durban conference, 236–237; and foreign policy, 76; and the G-8, 241; and Kyoto, 74, 82; legacy of, 252; and liberal internationalism, 71, 76; and multilateralism, 71, 80; and NAFTA, 110; and NGOs, 72, 119, 121; performance of, 85, 109; role of, 93; and UN world conferences, 72–75, 81, 88, 91; and the Zaire/Great Lakes initiative, 87
Chrétien, Raymond, 87
Christopher, Warren, 157
citizenship, 138, 144, 149; cosmopolitan, 3; environmental, 84; international, 30, 76, 98, 125, 129, 143, 222; national, 132
Claude, Inis, 5
Claxton, Jackie, 202
Clinton, Bill, 85, 157, 176, 207, 209
Coalition building, 8, 46, 123, 142, 147, 168, 188, 210, 220– 221

Cochrane, Johnnie, 246
Cold War: and Apartheid, 24; bi-polarity, 17, 42; and the Durban Conference, 3, 102, 114; conflict, 28; discipline of, 13; dominant assumptions of, 14; and economic and social issues, 53; ideological divide, 153; end of, 10, 15, 22, 25, 27, 38–39, 45, 79, 96. *See also*, post-Cold War
Commission on Global Governance, 4
Commission on Private Sector and Development, 252
Congress of Black Women, 206, 221
Conservation Council of Ontario, 179
Cook, Rebecca, 55, 205
Coon Come, Matthew, 243
Copenhagen, city of: airport, 116
Copenhagen World Summit for Social Development / Social Summit (1995), ix, 5, 258n.; and Canada, 93, 172, 207; differences from Beijing, Cairo, and Rio, 217; and Jean Chrétien, 73, 80, 87–88, 110, 235; model, 229; and NGOs, 118; role of, 95, 115; and UN world conferences, 239; vision of development, 81; and women, 187, 203
Côté-Harper, Gisèle, 205
Cotler, Irwin, 232
Council of Canadians With Disabilities, 116–117
Council of Forest Industries, 62, 105–106
Cox, Robert, 99–103, 110, 115, 160, 204
Coyne, Andrew, 109
Cree: ambassador to the UN, 244; Grand Council (Quebec), 140; of Quebec, 139, 141, 142; of Northern Quebec, 145
Crosbie, John, 89, 166
Cuba, 17, 141
Cultural Survival Canada, 62
Czechoslovakia, 17, 45, 67

Daes, Erica-Irene, 142, 146
Davis, Angela, 247
Davis, Jack, 31, 57, 247
Day, Shelagh, 66, 216–217, 220
Day, Stockwell, 236
Daya, Gina, 234
Deacon, Bob, 95
de Hoog, Adrian, 57
Denmark, 114, 143, 147
Department of Indian Affairs and Northern Development, 59

development: democratic, 64, 201–202; and environment 5, 44, 50, 62, 73, 83, 101, 227; and population, ix, 5, 80–81, 87, 155, 165; social, 5, 27, 73, 80–81, 87, 95, 109–110; sustainable, 91, 224, 226, 229, 239, 252; and trade, 22; and women, 60, 65, 158
Development and Peace, 5
Diamini-Zuma, Nkosazana, 230, 246–248
Dion, Adèle, 202
Dillon, John, 115
diplomacy: intergovernmental, 6; new, 5–7, 40; guerrilla, 62; orthodox, 6; quiet, 29, 32, 169; secretive, 6; traditional, 6, 40, 95
Doern, Bruce, 78
Dominican Republic, 168
Donnelly, Jack, 20, 37, 157, 159, 254n.
Drozd, Natallya, 193
Dubos, René, 18, 33
Dunlop, Joan, 161
Durban World Conference on Racism (2001): and Aboriginal Peoples, 242; and anti-Israel bias, 232; and Canada, 237, 241, 244; critics of, 224, 226, 240; Declaration, 230, 238; and DFAIT, 233; and diplomacy, 228; and global governance, 224, 226; and Liberals, 237; and NGOs, 234, 248; process, 243; and September 11, 2001, 3, 225; and slavery, 240, 246; and sovereignty, 242; and state-social partnerships, 231; and UN world conferences, 223, 225, 235, 239, 260n.; and the United States, 227, 236; women at, 247
Earth Charter, 46–47
Economic Commission for Latin America and the Caribbean 52
Ecumenical Coalition for Economic Justice, 205
Environment Canada, 58, 70, 89
European Union: and Canada, 172, 215; and the Cairo Conference, 171; members of, 127; membership, 211; and Prep Com(s), 114, 171; and the United States, 132

Fairweather, Gordon, 133
Falk, Richard, 4, 15
Fall, Ibrahima, 27, 52
Fédération des Femmes du Québec, 37, 204
Federal Republic of Germany, 16
femocrat(s), 37, 60, 180, 202–203, 219
Ferderber, Rhonda, 202

Ferretti, Janine 47
Finestone, Sheila, 201, 204–205, 207–210, 212–213, 217
Finger, Matthias, 51, 101
Forest Stewardship Council, 107–108
Forestry Canada, 105, 257n.
Forward-looking Strategies for the Advancement of Women to the Year 2000, 211
Foster, John, 117
Fowler, Robert, 80
Fréchette, Louise, 81, 100
Friedan, Betty, 35
Freudenschuss-Reichl, Irene, 193
Friends of the Earth, 33–34, 62, 108, 255 n, 258 n.
Fry, Hedy, 232–234, 237–238, 247–248
Fukuyama, Francis, 14, 20, 38

Gaddis, John Lewis, 13
Gandhi, Indira, 22, 27, 45
German Democratic Republic, 16
Geneva Convention, 21, 48, 135
Gill, Stephen, 96, 99, 101–103, 110
Giscard d'Estaing, Olivier, 115
Glendon, Mary Ann, 193, 199
Global Compact, 241
Global Forestry Convention, 103–104, 107
Global Forum, 45, 62
global governance: agenda of, 110; 227; change in, 185; Commission on, 4; demands of, 75; direction of, 6, 10; and diplomacy, 9; and diplomatic method, 26; face of, 102, 120; multilateral, 32, 43, 104; pattern of, 250; perspective of, 123; pursuit of, 8; revolution in, 3; structure of 4, 10, 11; tests of, 3, 4, 39, 224; system, 38; and the UN, 7; and women's issues, 186. *See also*, governance
Global Tribunal, 64, 200
Gold, Sylvia, 37
Goods and Services Tax, 80, 109
Gore, Al, 157, 229
governance: agenda of, 61, 74; democratic, x; and diplomacy, 1, 5, 84; face of, 109; humane, 4; internal, 117; international, 25, 103, 106, 127; nature of, 252; pattern of, 88; practices of, 132; shaping of, 95; shift in, 56; system of, 98, 100; tone of, 87; understanding of, 5; world, 155. *See also*, global governance

government, 30, 36, 43, 70; agenda of, 87, 90, 176, 232; and business, 62–63, 106, 109, 116; apex of, 10; apparatus of, 96; authority of, 97; Baghdad, 127; Canadian, 30, 35, 48–49, 53, 62, 108, 111, 117, 120–121, 137–138, 144–148, 150, 174, 204–206, 210–211, 218, 243, 244; Canadian, declaration of, 244; Canadian, and foreign policy, 76; change of, 38; China (PRC), 37, 196, 206, 209, 210; Chrétien, 73, 74, 77, 80, 82, 86, 88, 91, 92, 103, 109–111, 114, 121, 204, 206, 235–237, 241, 252; conduct of, 51; Conservative, 109; control by, 36; global, 3; heads of, 45, 73, 82; interaction with NGOs, 35–36, 41, 46, 54, 59, 61–62, 79, 112, 130, 222, 245; interface with, 63; leaders, 70, 162; Liberal, 111–112, 203, 204–205, 208, 216, 217; machinery of, 69; Mulroney, 64, 73–74, 78–79, 104–105, 121, 128–129, 133, 139, 148, 166, 204; national, 71; and NAC, 215, policies, 99, 171, 185; Quebec, 140–141; role of, 63; self, 141; of states, 99; and trade unions, 99; world, 2, 4; and women's groups, 124, 221; and women's rights, 65, 164
Grameen Bank, 200
Grant, James, 27
Great Whale Project, 140
Greenpeace, 34, 55, 63–64, 66, 106–108, 129
Greenspon, Edward, 111
Greenwood, Norma, 164
Greer, Germaine, 35
Grey, Josephine, 117, 120
Gross national product, 92
Group of 7 Industrialised Countries 84, 86–87, 111, 114, 119, 152, 218
Group of 77 Developing Countries, 23
Gulf War, 23, 238

Hawke, Bob, 81
Hay, John, 85
Hayes, Sharon, 217
Held, David, 100
Heinbecker, Paul, 237–238, 240
Heritage Canada, 70, 232–233, 242, 252; Aboriginal Programs Branch, 232
Hettne, Bjorn, 102
Higgott, Richard, 120
Hirst, Paul, 100, 105
Hocking, Brian X, 11, 41, 47, 69, 107

Holy See: *See*, Vatican
Homemaker Magazine, 205
Hosek, Chaviva, 37
Human Resources and Development Canada, 70, 118, 119, 202
human rights: abuses, 54; activists, 53, 64, 66, 232; agenda, 48, 126, 153, 164; and CIDA, 60; and Canada, 59, 214; and Ibrahima Fall, 27, 52; and Indigenous peoples, 144; internationalization of, 20; movement, 66, 256n.; new regime for, 20; and NGOs, 51, 56, 61, 67, 226, 232, 250; organizations, 66, 260; policies, 126; and the post-Cold War era, 38; and refugee groups, 179; and sovereignty, 129; system, 142, 255n.; treaties, 142; UN Commission on, 141, 143; and UN Conferences, 14; and the Vienna Conference, 24; and the West, 24; women's, 60, 63–64, 177, 186
Human Rights Centre, University of Ottawa, 47
Human Rights Group, 67
Humphrey, John, 33
Huntington, Samuel, 10, 153–154, 156, 161–163, 181–182
Hurtado, Miguel de la Madrid, 22, 141
Hynes, Ross, 201, 209

Immigration and Refugee Board 133–134, 136
India, 22, 27, 45, 59, 70, 243
Indigenous: affairs, 143; challenge, 124, 126, 146; community, 126; diplomacy, 141; and ethnic groups, 121; issues, x, 159, 242, 251; independence, 146; groups, 124, 137–138, 140, 145–148, 150, 243; minorities, 141; organizations, 62, 145; peoples, 137, 142–143, 153; peoples, concerns of, 260n.; peoples, treatment of, 144; peoples, representatives, 137, 143, 148–149, 258n.; rights of, 46, 123, 126, 137, 139, 143; self-determination, 138; sovereignty, 150–151, 244; year, campaign for, 142
internationalism: constructive, 74; free wheeling, 237; liberal, 71–72; new, 129; Pearsonian, 76
International Centre for Human Rights and Democratic Development, 64, 201, 205, 210
International Criminal Court, 118, 252; for Women, 48

International Institute for International Development, 165–167, 171–172, 181, 195, 208, 211–212, 214
International Joint Commission, 57.
International Labour Organization, 115, 142–143
International NGOs, 112
International Organizations Bureau, 59–60
International Planned Parenthood Federation 30, 164, 175
International Service for Human Rights, 230
International Year of Indigenous Peoples (1992), 138
Inuit Circumpolar Conference, 62, 258n.
Iran: and the Beijing conference, 214; and Canada, 167; and the Cairo conference/ICPD, 162; and diplomacy, 182–183, 199, 245; and other Islamic countries, 156; and the Nairobi conference, 21; objections of, 168
Iraq, 127, 238
Islam(ic): and anti-islamophobia, 231; and the Cairo conference, 181–182; and family, 155; states/countries, 24, 156, 212, 245; and the West, 155, 163, 181; world, 161, 163; and the Vatican/Holy See, 174, 212
Israel; and Apartheid, 231; and the Durban Conference, 232, 234, 236–239, 244, 245, 248; relations with Palestine, 17–18, 24, 223, 226, 231; and the Beijing Conference, 192, 225

Jackson, Jesse, 246
Japan: and the Beijing conference, 210; and Canada, 240; Egypt's ambassador to, 197; and women, 168
Johannesburg Conference on Sustainable Development (2002), 224, 226; agenda of, 239; and Canada, 228; and Elizabeth May, 229; experience of, 242; and global disparities, 226; and Kyoto, 91, 252; process, 224, 241
Johannesburg World Summit on Sustainable Development, (2002): See also, Johannesburg Conference on Sustainable Development
Johnson, Bonnie, 176
Jones, Barry, 98
JUSCANZ Informal group made up of Japan, the United States, Canada, Australia, and New Zealand and a number of other states including the Netherlands and Norway, 210–211, 215, 236

Kahn, Irene, 247
Kananaskis Summit (2002), 241
Keating, Paul, 73
Keck, Margaret, 233
Keeble, Edna, 219
Keohane, Robert, 100
Kitani, Ismat, 193
Krasner, Stephen, 150
Kuptana, Rosemary, 144, 148–149
Kurds, 127
Kyoto: Accord, 258n.; agreement, 92, 252; city of, 74; conference, 73–74, 82, 91, 228, 241

Landolt, Gwen, 220
Landry, Monique, 89
l'Association des collaboratrices et partenaires en affaires, 221
Latin America, 20, 25, 52, 87, 147, 174
Law of the Sea, 57
Law Society of Upper Canada, 133
Leclair, Marc, 148
Lewis, Stephen, 73, 147, 174, 201
Liberal Foreign Policy Platform, 76
Licuanan, Patricia, 193, 198
Low Income Families Together,117, 120, 257 n.
L'R des centres des femmes du Québec, 206
Lubicon, 139, 141, 146

Macdonald, Ronald St. John, 33
MacMillan Bloedel, 106
MacRae, Rev. Robert B., 30
Mahoney, Kathleen, 55, 235
Malaysia: Mahathir Mohamad, 25, 107; and the Vienna Conference, 148
Malta, 161, 168.
Mandela, Nelson, 73
Mandela, Winnie, 247
Manley, John, 233–234, 237
Marchi, Sergio, 170, 172
Margolis, Eric, 134
Marsden, Lorna, 31–32, 174–175
Martin, Paul Jr., 110–112, 118, 208, 252
Martinez., Miguel Alfonso, 141, 143
Masdit, Supatra, 193, 196–197

Matas, David, 232
Match International, 36
Mathews, Jessica, 54, 131, 161
Mawani, Nurjehan, 134
May, Elizabeth, 47, 58, 73, 229, 257n.
Mbeki, Govan, 230
Mbeki, Thabo, 230, 239, 247
McBride, Stephen, 109
McDougall, Barbara, 64, 90, 129, 257n.
McGill University, 178
McNaughton, Alan, 31
Meech Lake, 51, 97, 257n.
Menchu, Rigoberta, 146
Mercredi, Ovide, 139
Métis National Council, 148; of women, 206
Mexico, 103, 130, 165, 193
Mexico City Conference on Population (1984): and abortion, 157; agreements at, 18; blueprint for action, 16; and Canada, 31, 36, 174; document, 182; and the Middle East, 21; and NGOs, 36; process, 176, protocol at, 37; and women, 180; and the World Population Plan of Action, 19
Mexico City Conference on Women (1975), 72
Michael, Lorraine, 205
middle power, x, 7, 13, 26, 28–29, 79, 104, 210, 230
Mi'kmaq, 140–141
Mingst, Karen, 154
Mittelman, James, 23
Mitterrand, Franois, 114
Mock, Alois, 147
Mohawks, 139
Mongella, Gertude, 28, 193, 195–198, 210
Morgan, Robin, 196
Moses, Ted, 140, 143–144, 244
Mulroney, Brian: and climate change, 74; and GATT/trade, 77, 88, 204, 252; and Commonwealth, 77, 82; and the Global Forestry Convention,103–109, 121; South Africa, 77, 82; and multilateralism, 71–74, 79, 128–129, 133, 139; NGOs 62, 64, 79, 111, 206; and the Rio Conference (1992), 71, 74, 82–85, 89, 148, 166, 256n; and social issues, style/approach, 75, 77–78, 80–81, 85, 90–93, 128, 174, 236–237, 257n.
multilateral: activism, 83; agenda, 12; agreements, 103; aid, 117; bias, 7; diplomacy, 69, 82, 96, 97, 98, 154, 168; forums, 70; and global governance, 32,43, 100, 104; leadership, xi; liberalism, 20; negotiations, 110, 155, 224; relations, 6; summits, 85, 86
multilateralism: bottom-up, 3; Canadian, 104, 136; constructive, 80, 93; and diplomacy, 3; orthodox, 96; and the post-war settlement, 10, 94; residue of, x; and the UN, 8, 76, 79– 80; and UN Conferences, 72, 102, 153
multilateralist: diplomatic identity, 28; new, 102, 110; and the United States, 28, 97, 157, 255n.

Nada, 132
Nairobi Conference on Women and Development (1985): agreements at, 19; and Arab countries, 21; and Canada, 32, 201, 219; delegates at, 259; and global sisterhood, 220; and NGOs, 37, 50; proceedings, 17; process, 187; strategies at, 38; and the United States, 18; and women's rights, 60
National Action Committee on the Status of Women: Canada, 66; and the Canadian women's movement, 203; and refugee status, 132; and victims of violence, 258n.
National Association of Women and the Law, 206
National Council of Haitian Origin, 234
National Council of Jewish Women, 176
National Council of Women of Canada, 205, 221
National Democratic Party (West Germany), 19
National Farmers' Union, 36
National Forum on Canada's International Relations, 111, 129
National Organization of Immigrant and Visible Minority Women, 221
National Task Force on the Environment and the Economy, 50
Native Council of Canada, 62, 145
Nault, Bob, 243
Navarro-Valls, Joaquin, 161, 191
nazi; banning of, 19
neo-liberal: economics, 103; line of argument, 2; market, 10, 95; perspective, 247; persuasion, 225; view, 3
Netherlands, 104, 107, 143, 166–167, 255n.
Neve, Alex, 235
New Democratic Party, 201

294   INDEX

New International Economic Order, 22–23, 27, 108, 226
New York Declaration on High Seas Fishing, 47
New York World Summit for World Children, (1990), 27, 73, 79, 82
New Zealand, 47, 134, 147, 152, 159, 166, 240
Ng, Winnie, 206
Nicolson, Harold, 6, 171
Niemann, Lindsay, 37, 60
non-governmental organizations: activist, 164; autonomy of, 116; and the Beijing conference, 202, 208, 218, 229; and business, 121; and Canada, 33, 50, 119; and the Cairo conference, 175; Canadian, 48–49, 51, 112, 175, 257n, 259n.; and the Canadian Environmental Network, 47; and CIDA, 61, 113, 117; constraints on, 35; and the CPCU, 106; and civil society, 35, 41, 52, 56, 79, 102, 137, 159, 228, 250; and diplomacy, 26, 42, 49, 68, 88; and Environment Canada, 58; environmental, 107; and human rights, 51, 226; international, 112, 258n.; and international citizenship, 222; and international social agenda, 32; and international development, 117–118; and the international system, 55, 145; interests of, 43, 105; legitimate, 225; and the New York Delegation on High Seas Overfishing, 47; older, 232; partnerships with, x, 10; problem-oriented, 187, relations to government, 42; and the Rio Conference, 46, 48, 59, 63, 84, 107, 255n.; and the San Francisco conference, 32; and the state, 39, 50, 52, 130; and the Stockholm conference, 34, 36; transnational, 152, 225; and UN world conferences, 42, 45, 67, 160, 226, 248, 249; and the Vatican, 162; and the Vienna conference, 52; Western, 165, 245
North American Free Trade Agreement, 63, 74, 80, 110, 118, 127, 129, 286n.
North Atlantic Treaty Organization, 86, 104, 143, 152
North-South divide, 80
Norway: and abortion, 169; and Canada, 210, 240; and coastal countries, 166; as a liberal country, 163; and the Durban and Mexico Prep Coms, 230; and like-minded countries, 143, 147; and Pakistan, 182; prime minister of, 73, 181
Norwegian Institute of Human Rights, 50
Nossal, Kim, X, 75, 82, 85, 88

Obasanjo, Olusegun, 246
Official Development Assistance, 56, 92, 111–113, 177
Ogletree, Charles, 246
Omene, Maria, 248
O'Neil, Maureen, 37, 60
Organisation for Economic Co-operation and Development, 111, 114–115
Organization on Security and Cooperation in Europe, 87
Ouellet, André, 76, 203
Oxfam, 36, 117

Pal, Leslie, X, 56, 75
Palme, Olof, 22, 29, 45
Park, Anne, 55, 59, 90, 166
Parsons, Margaret, 248
Pearson, Lester, 72, 90–91; Chair in International Relations (Oxford), 76; Pearsonian internationalism, 76; Pearsonian model, 76; Pearsonism, 129
Pellicer, Olga, 193.
People's Republic of China (PRC), 16–17; and the Beijing Conference, 192, 195; and Canada, 209, 210; and the Cairo Conference, 163, 164; and the Mexico Conference, 37; national policies, 22; one child policy, 177, 209; and the United Nations, 196; and the Vienna Conference, 143, 148
Pépin, Lucie, 205
Peterson, V. Spike, 187
Piscatori, James, 162
Plan for Gender Equality, 204
Planned Parenthood Federation (Canada): 36, 175–176
Planned Parenthood Federation (International): 30, 112, 164, 176, 200
Pollution Probe, 62, 255n., 256n.
Posner, Michael, 227, 260n.
post-Cold War: agenda, 20; challenges of, 130; conditions of, 43; era, 1, 3, 6, 8, 23, 26, 28, 38, 40; and global change, 7; multilateralism, 10; order, 185; politics, 155; and sovereignty, 126, 128, 131; system, 74; and UN Conferences, 12, 14;

and the United States, 97; values of, 7; and women's issues, 192. See also, Cold War
Potter, Evan, x, 80
Powell, Colin, 224
Pratt, Cranford, 50, 113
press corps, Canadian, 37
Prime Minister's Office, 71, 84, 88–90, 257n.
Princen, Thomas, 40, 43, 255n.
Privy Council Office 71, 88, 90
Probe International, 47
Public Service Alliance of Canada, 206
Puddington, Arch, 225

Ravenhill, John, 72
Rawlings, Jerry, 197
Rawlings, Nana, 197
Raymond, Valerie, 202
Reagan, Maureen, 18
Reagan, Ronald, 16, 19, 31–32, 77, 81, 157, 176
REAL Women, 180–181, 215, 217 220, 222
realist school (Anglo-American), 3
Red Book, 76, 109, 111
Regazolli, Zelmira, 193
Regehr, Sheila, 202, 209
Reich, Simon, 120
Reid, Tim, 116
Republic of Ireland, 258
Réseau nationale d'action éducation femmes, 221
Rhodesia, 21
Riche, Nancy, 205, 207
Riddell-Dixon, Elizabeth, 26, 202–203, 207
Rio de Janeiro Conference on Environment and Development (1992): agenda of, 62, 84, 105; and Canada, 73, 83, 103, 166, 255n.; challenge of, 61; and CIDA, 92; and the CPCU, 46, 105; and environmental issues, 44; and the foreign ministry, 58; and Forestry Canada, 257n.; forestry convention, 105; and international activity, 44; and Jean Chrétien, 73; and Kyoto, 73; and Malaysia, 25; and Maurice Strong, 227; and NGOs, 50; Prep Com for, 45, 104; Task Force, 89; and trans-national corporations, 102; and the Vienna conference, 56
Rivington, Diana, 209

Robinson, Mary, 230, 246–248
Robinson, William, 96
Roche, Doug, 92
Rodham Clinton, Hillary, 193, 197, 209
Roman Catholic Church, 158–159, 176
Rosenau, James, 131
Roulston, Thomas, 36
Ruggie, John, 21, 94, 102, 228
Runyan, Anne Sisson, 187

Sadik, Nafis, 27, 163
Sané, Pierre, 66, 200
Santiago Conference on Trade and Development (1972), 22
Santiago, Irene, 193, 196
Sassen, Saskia, 100, 132
Saudi Arabia, 133
Sauvé, Jeanne, 31
Savoie, Donald, X, 78
Schengen and Dublin Agreements, 136
Scholte, Jan Aart, 41
Science Magazine, 35
Senegal, 27, 193
September 11th 2001, 2, 4, 224–225, 244, 253
Shahani, Leticia, 197
Sharp, Mitchell, 30
Shaw, Martin, 28, 44
Shields, John, 109
Shepherd, George, 247
Sikkink, Kathryn, 127, 229, 233
Simms, Glenda, 205
Simon, Mary, 144–145
Small, Michael, 57, 89
Smith, Dan, 145, 146
Smith, Heather, X, 74, 219
Smouts, Marie-Claude, 14, 239
society-craft: accommodation with, 63; and the Beijing conference, 259n.; and Canada, 179, 183; Canadian, 201, 221, 253; conviction of, 159; diversity in, 69; form(s) of, 64, 194–195, 216, 229; and the NAC, 204; and NGOs, 231; process of, 231; and the state, ix; and state-craft, 41–45, 49, 51–55, 61–63, 67–68, 189, 200, 217, 221; terms of, 187; and UN conferences, 174–175, 227; and the Vienna conference, 47, 66; and women's groups, 185
Somavia, Juan, 27
Sorensen, Georg, 95

South Africa: and Apartheid, 19, 21, 24, 192, 243; and Canada, 133, 232, 243; and Canada and the EU, 215; Commonwealth of, 77; and the Copenhagen Summit, 73; and the Durban conference, 223, 239–240, 241, 247; and leadership, 230; prime minister of, 73; Republic of, 133; and women, 247

sovereignty: applications of, 125; area of, x; assumptions of, 260n.; autonomy and, 18; Canada and, 80, 123, 244; concept of, 127–128, 149; connotations of, 122; debate about, 10, 122, 126, 128; demise of, 39, 131; and Indigenous groups, 124, 145, 151; limits of, 135; loss of, 79; meaning of, 242; Quebec and, 97, 141, 144; state, 127–128, 130, 150, 185; territorial aspects of, 125–126, 130, 244; tests of, 123, 124, 137, 242–243; Westphalian model of, 149

Soviet Union, and the Bucharest Conference, 16, 17; and Canada 13; and the Teheran Conference, 19; and the United States, 20

Spanish Turbot War, 238

Special Joint Committee Reviewing Canadian Foreign Policy, 111

Spivak, Gayatri, 191

Stairs, Denis, 42–43, 51–52, 58, 63, 256n.

statecraft: the Beijing conference, 210, 219; and the Cairo conference, 159; Canadian, 72, 81, 23, 141, 171, 172, 201, 206–208, 212–214, 216–220, 236, 251, 253; character of, 67; contours of, 71; creative, 199; culture of, 231; and diplomacy, 40; and Hedy Fry, 234; and leadership, 72; mode of, 11; older forms of, 227; orthodox, 34, 42, 67; and personal political considerations, 71; recalcitrant, 141; and society-craft, 41–45, 49, 51–55, 61–63, 67–68, 189, 200, 217, 221, 229, 253; and sovereignty, 179; tests of, 183; traditional, 185; use of, 32; and women's movement, 187

Status of Women Canada, 37, 59–60, 202, 204, 209

Steinem, Gloria, 190

Strange, Susan, 56, 98

Strong, Maurice: and diplomacy, 27, 33, 35; reputation of, 52; as secretary-general of the Stockholm and Rio conferences, 26, 31, 45, 254n.; and the Rio conference, 52, 227, 271n.; as secretary-general of UNEP, 26

Stockholm Conference on the Human Environment (1972): aftermath of, 33; breakthrough of, 17; and Canada, 30–31, 34, 57; and the Eastern bloc, 16–17; and Indira Gandhi, 22; and international environmental policy, 44; and Maurice Strong, 26–27; and NGOs, 45; official component of, 33; process, 34; and the role of the state, 72; secretariat, 30; supporting conditions of, 18; and Sweden, 29; and the United States, 15; unofficial component of, 35

Stout, Madeleine Dion, 205

Summit of the Americas (Miami, 1994), 86

Sûreté du Québec, 140

Sweden: and Canada, 104, 167; as middle power, 29; and the Vienna Conference, 166

Tallaway, Mervat, 193, 197

Taylor, J.H., 82

Team Canada, 87, 110

Teheran Conference on Human Rights (1968): Canadian representation at, 33; and NGOs, 33; resolution condemning apartheid, 19; and the role of the UN, 20; and UN world conferences, 15.

Thakur, Ramesh, xi, 228, 253

Thobani, Sunera, 186, 205–206, 208, 211

Thompson, Grahame, 100, 105

Tobin, Brian, 114, 117, 119, 257n.

Tomlin, Brian, 78

Torrey Canyon, 18

Trinity College (University of Toronto), 76–77

triumphalism, 2

Trudeau, Pierre Elliott: 32–33, 72, 74, 260n., 276n.

Unilateral Declaration of Independence (Rhodesia), 21

United Church, 176

United Kingdom, 16

United Nations: 62; Canadian Ambassador to, 87; Canadian commitment to, 96; and the Durban Conference, 233; and Indigenous issues, 143; mission of, 119; and multilateralism, 8; and NGOs, 32, 44; principles of, 133; Report of the World

Commission on the Environment, 50, 58; Secretary General, 87; structural design of, 159; system, 167; and the United States, 28; and World Conferences, 1, 12
United Nations Association, 62
United Nations Centre for Human Rights (Geneva), 55, 166
United Nations Commission on Human Rights, 51
United Nations Commission on the Status of Women, 193
United Nations Development Fund for Women, 65
United Nations Development Programme, 30, 113–114
United Nations Division for the Advancement of Women, 193
United Nations Economic Commission for Europe, 15
United Nations Economic, Social and Cultural Organization, 16
United Nations Economic and Social Council, 32, 53, 119, 140
United Nations Environment Program, 26, 30
United Nations Fund for Population Activities, 28, 30, 164
United Nations High Commissioner for Refugees, 133–135
United Nations International Children's Emergency Fund, 27
United Nations Security Council, 7, 28, 127
United Nations Sub-Commission of the Prevention of Discrimination of Minorities, 137
United Nations Working Group on Indigenous Populations, 137, 140, 142
United States, 7–9, 16, 28, 85, 153, 157, 208, 224–227, 234, 236, 238, 245, 246, 248; Agency for International Development, 207; agenda of, 18; and Canada, 57; and Canada, the UC/EU, and Australia, 136; and CANZ, 210; and environmental issues, 84; and Europe, 64; and Free Trade, 79; Lawyers Committee for Human Rights, 227; and Mexico, 130; and the EU, 2, 3; and human rights, 157; and Iran, 183; and Norway and Finland, 170; and Paul Heinbecker, 238; position of, 12; and the Third World, 190; and the UN, 97, 157–158; and the USSR, 20, 32; and Vietnam, 29
Universal Declaration of Human Rights, 20, 230
University of Chittagong, 200
University of Ottawa Human Rights Centre, 47

Valcourt, Bernard, 133
Vatican; and the Cairo Conference, 159–162, 165, 169–171, 174, 182–183, 211; opposition by, 19; and the Roman Catholic Church, 176
Vienna Conference on Human Rights (1993): and Aboriginal or Indigenous rights, 123; actors at, 256n.; agenda of, 24; appraisal of, 259n.; and Canada, 133, 135–137, 144–145, 150, 166, 257n., 260n.; and CIDA, 61; constraints at, 92; crucial phase of, 146; differences from Rio, 217; gains at, 195; guidelines of, 16; and Indigenous groups, 124, 126, 142; and liberal values, 23; and Malaysia, 25; and NGOs, 48, 52, 61, 139, 166, 255n., 258n.; negotiations at, 55, 65; obstacles at, 53; process, 59, 65; reviews of, 66; and society-craft, 47, 67; and the United States, 157; and women's groups, 66, 185
von Nostitz, Manfred, 59

Walker, R.B.J., 159
Wall Street Journal, 111
Ward, Barbara, 18, 33
Wareing, Mark, 47
Warkentin, Craig, 154–155
Warzazi, Halima, 141–142Wells, Kathleen, 74
Western European and Others Group, 55, 59, 65, 159, 166, 236
Westphalia(n): international system, 6, 41; liars, 128; model, 149; state, 249; state-centred world, x; structure, 132; world, 11
Whalley, John, 79
Wilson-Smith, Anthony, 110–111
Winham, Gil, 9
Women's Environment and Development Organization, 188
Women and Environmental Education and Development, 62
Women's Environment and Development Organization, 158, 188–189, 228

women's rights, 11, 66, 166, 184, 217; advancement of, 166, 211, 219, 228; and Beijing Conference, 186, 196, 200, 212, 218; and Canada, 50, 60; issues at Vienna, 53, 64; and reproductive and sexual health, 177; and women's movement, 65
Women at Risk, 134
World Population Plan of Action, 19, 130
World Wildlife Federation, 55, 107
World Wildlife Fund, 33, 58
Worsfold, Nancy, 179

Yalden, Max, 147
Yemen, 156
YMCA, 36
Yunus, Muhammad, 200

Zionism, 17, 19, 21, 231
Zoller, Adrien-Claude, 230

Catalogue Request

Name: _____

Address: _____

Tel: _____

Fax: _____

E-mail: _____

To receive a catalogue of UNU Press publications kindly photocopy this form and send or fax it back to us with your details. You can also e-mail us this information. Please put "Mailing List" in the subject line.

**United Nations
University Press**

53-70, Jingumae 5-chome
Shibuya-ku, Tokyo 150-8925, Japan
Tel: +81-3-3499-2811   Fax: +81-3-3406-7345
E-mail: sales@hq.unu.edu   http://www.unu.edu